Rome and a Villa

Foreword by William Weaver

ELEANOR CLARK

Rome and a Villa

Drawings by Eugene Berman

STEERFORTH ITALIA

AN IMPRINT OF STEERFORTH PRESS · SOUTH ROYALTON, VERMONT

A Steerforth Italia edition
published 2000 by Steerforth Press,
by arrangement with HarperCollins Publishers, Inc.

Sections of this book have appeared in the following magazines:
*The Kenyon Review, Partisan Review, The Reporter, Commentary,
The Sewanne Review, The New York Review of Books, Vogue.*

Library of Congress Cataloging-in-Publication Data

Clark, Eleanor, 1913–1996
Rome and a villa : memoir / Eleanor Clark ;
[foreword by William Weaver ; drawings by Eugene Berman].
p.   cm.
Originally published: Garden City, N.Y. : Doubleday, 1952;
expanded ed. published 1974.
Includes index.
ISBN 1-883642-51-5 (alk. paper)
1. Rome (Italy) — Description and travel. 2. Rome (Italy) — Social life and
customs. 3. Clark, Eleanor, 1913 — 1996 — Homes and haunts —
Italy — Rome. I. Title.

DG806.2.C58 2000
945'.632 — dc21
00-025611

Manufactured in the United States of America

FIRST PRINTING

To Isabel and Laurance Roberts

*My aunt Julia was descended, on the maternal
side from a race of kings, and by her father
from the immortal gods.*
JULIUS CAESAR

Che gran dono de Dio ch'è la bellezza!
G. G. BELLI

CONTENTS

FOREWORD

$\mathcal{I}$ FIRST MET ELEANOR CLARK — in Rome, of course — sometime in the rushing, eventful autumn of 1947. The postwar Italian capital was bursting with life and with new arrivals, and yet it remained a small city, where it was easy to meet people and to make friends. Eleanor, born in 1913, was ten years my senior, but despite the difference in age and also in background (she was a New Englander, a Yankee; and I a Virginian), we shared a love of our adopted city, and we spent a good deal of time together, walking and conversing. Back in my Virginia cabin, her elusive, quirkish first novel, *The Bitter Box*, was among my favorite books; I had read her stories in the *New Yorker* and her articles in the *Partisan Review*. I knew that she had gone to Vassar in the now-legendary days of Elizabeth Bishop and Mary McCarthy; later, I learned of her post-college adventures in Mexico, in the circle of Leon Trotsky, when she lived in the house of Diego Rivera and Frida Kahlo. But when we met, mostly I was impressed by her fluent Italian and her profound curiosity, her warm insight into Italian life. Years after *Rome and a Villa* had established itself as a quiet classic, Eleanor, applying the same keen powers of observation, the same relentless, enthusiastic spirit of research, the same personal style to an entirely different subject — a popular mollusk — and, reducing her focus from a vast and various civilization to a small, specialized community, wrote another unexpected masterpiece, *The Oysters of Locmariaquer.*

Cultural Rome in the late 1940s had several nerve centers, and one of the most electric was the American Academy, a deceptively bland, academic-looking building on the Janiculum Hill, where the first peace-time batch of fellows was settling in: composers, artists, scholars, all armed with the prestigious Prix de Rome, which — in addition to a stipend — offered food and lodging at the Academy.

As a humble non-fellow, living in what I had convinced myself was colorful poverty and independence downtown, in the center of the city, I tried to feel scorn for the lucky prizewinners so comfortably installed and coddled in their American ivory tower. But, looking back, I suspect what I felt was not noble scorn but naked envy. Not so much of their housing, and surely not of their food (my cheap *trattorie* nourished me much more imaginatively), but of the company, the exciting intellectual give-and-take. Thanks to the directors of the Academy, the soft-spoken scholar Laurance Roberts, connoisseur of Japanese art, and his wife, the elegant and hospitable Isabel, the director's residence, the newly restored Villa Aurelia, was alive with stimulating concerts, talks, dinners, receptions. Distinguished American guests — Leonard Bernstein, Malcolm Cowley, Samuel Barber — came for short stays in the adjacent Villino. And Roman artists were ready, indeed eager, to scale the hill and mix with their American colleagues. The admired composer Goffredo Petrassi was a frequent guest, and the cultivated, convivial painter Renato Guttuso, though he was an outspoken Communist, frowned on by the U.S. embassy, was welcomed at the Villa Aurelia with open arms.

Rome and a Villa is dedicated to Laurance and Isabel, deservedly, for a good deal of the book was written within the protected confines of the Academy, where Eleanor Clark spent much of that winter and spring. It was there that I met her, and it was from there that she set out on her Roman walks.

Rome in those days was a walker's paradise, as it had been in previous centuries. It is no accident that the two most influential, acknowledged ancestors of Eleanor's book were entitled *Prome-nades dans Rome* (Stendhal) and *Walks in Rome* (Augustus Hare). In the late 1940s few Romans had cars, and, from the American Express office in Piazza di Spagna, you could walk — as I did daily — up the middle of the Via del Babuino, reading your mail, with no fear of being run over. But then, one morning the following spring, I witnessed what I later realized was a significant and dire event. I was visiting a friend of mine, a functionary of the Italian Radio, and I happened to look out of his window on the usually empty Via delle Botteghe Oscure below. At a certain point, a convoy of little cars — brightly colored miniatures, suggesting Dodgems or Tinker Toys — appeared at the western end of the street and slowly advanced, three abreast, in the direction of Piazza Venezia. This bright, speckled tide gradually filled the whole street.

Bewildered, but without any foreboding, I pointed out the cars to my friend and asked him what this demonstration meant. "Oh yes," he replied absently, "I read about it in the papers. The Fiat is launching a cheap new car, the 600."

Little did he — or I — know that we were seeing a historic, fateful event, an early symptom of the destructive motorization of the lazy, pedestrian Rome we both loved. Within months, it seemed, Via delle Botteghe Oscure and all the other streets of central Rome were jammed with little Fiats. The harmonious circle of Piazza del Popolo was transformed into a parking lot, as were most of the other open, decorative spaces of the city. Walkers were soon to become a despised minority, honked and shouted at, humiliated.

But in the meanwhile, before the onslaught of Roman traffic, Eleanor and I were able to take some serene walks together. Our talk ranged widely, from New York gossip to nineteenth-century Italian poetry (I was then studying Leopardi). Sometimes we made our way to a prearranged site, a church, a fountain at which Eleanor wanted to take another look. But she was never a cicerone, any more than her book is a formal guide. I don't recall her making notes, or even carrying a notebook. What I do remember — and it is hard to convey in words — is the sharpening of the senses that our walks inspired in me: I seemed to be more alert, as if her own keenness were somehow, subliminally, being transmitted to me. In the words of another dear friend and great walking companion, John Pope-Hennessy, I was learning how to look.

At this time Eleanor was in her early thirties. For me there was something awesome about her, in her striking good looks and her unflaunted but unequaled intelligence. Though I looked up to her, she did not talk down to me, and if she expressed an idea, it was with a kind of tentative tone, as if she were voicing something that surely had also occurred to me or was proposing a subject for reciprocal discussion, perhaps revision. In other words, she was ideal company. Some readers of *Rome and a Villa* have complained that the tone is authoritarian, categorical. I read the book differently. It is not a book you have to agree with; at times, it is even a book you seem invited to argue with, to match your impressions against the author's. A good part of the pleasure you will derive from *Rome and a Villa* lies in the fact that you can freely talk back to it.

When the first edition appeared in America, a German friend of mine — a brilliant but severe refugee professor — read it almost with anger. "Unbridled sensibility," he said in a tone of outrage. Devoted academic that he was, he wanted the book to present a greater order, to have a beginning, middle, and end, to venture premises and draw conclusions. Perhaps my friend was right: Eleanor's sensibility is always let off the leash, and it can go and sniff out corners, dig up bones, snap at a detail and worry it into greater sense. Eleanor provokes. The very first sentence, which one critic has called "unprepossessing," is a provocation: "The first thing about the Campidoglio, aside from what it is, is the stairs."

Any teacher of a creative writing workshop, confronted by this sentence, with that unorthodox repetition of "is," like a verbal hiccup, would reach for the red pencil. But that apparently ungainly echo is a timely warning: if you enter this book, you do so on the author's terms, and when she wants to repeat a word, or use a slang term, or a technical one, she will do so. And if she wants to make doubly sure that you look at those two contrasting flights of stairs to the top of the Capitoline hill, the heart of ancient Rome, then she will secure your attention with what could seem a stylistic misstep, much as an accomplished soprano may take a high note just a shade flat, to slide then into perfect pitch with greater, more triumphant effect.

In our unreflecting way, most of us, when we look at a flight of stairs, think of those stairs simply as a way to move from one level to another; we ignore their appearance, their significance, as we would ignore an elevator. In the Rome of Eleanor Clark, the great monument does not necessarily dominate a given space; she may glance at it obliquely, while her gaze focuses on the usually overlooked, modest building next to it. And while she is looking at the building — *reading* the building would perhaps be a more accurate description — she is also keen to the smells and sounds and dramas around her. If monuments are Rome's nouns, hoarse street cries and pungent aromas are its verbs. Eleanor Clark gives us Rome with its syntax complete.

"It is like music," she says — and she is talking about Hadrian's Villa — "so much that you seem sometimes to be hearing the buildings more than seeing them, as though at some level of the brain the eyes and ears functioned interchangeably."

If Rome is music, it is not Mozart or Bach: it is more unexpected, irregular, not quite so harmonious (Janacek? Bartok?). In her book Eleanor constantly refers to the unexpected, the accidental. In Rome, you come upon things. You find yourself — as if suddenly waking — in this place or that. Often, of course, these accidents are carefully contrived, and it is the old resident's favorite trick to take a newcomer to, for example, the Trevi fountain, through narrow, winding alleys arriving at that controlled white explosion of sculpture and water, alluringly audible well before you see it. In Eleanor's time (and mine) the oldest residents remembered when St. Peter's was reached in a similar fashion, before the lamentable, pompous Via della Conciliazione, with its stubby, lamp-base obelisks, replaced the tortuous streets of the Borgo.

It is possible that she came upon her own book as if by accident. The chapters were written and published, many of them, separately; then, somehow, they came together to make a volume. Lucky residents of the Academy that year were able to hear some pages read aloud by the author, in the preparatory phase.

The way the book was written — as separate articles, journal pages, reflective essays — again has led some critical readers to call it unorganized, a patchwork. But, indeed, as in one of my mother's artful quilts, the patches — their colorful patterns contrasting or echoing or blending — create a composition, a unity, a grand picture. And the long, central essay on Hadrian's Villa contrasts and somehow plays against the equally penetrating study of the Sicilian bandit Salvatore Giuliano. The emblematic ancient emperor, who has left an enduring monument to his own taste, is the unlikely but provoking companion to a newspaper-headline figure, who for weeks and months filled the pages of the Italian press — the tackier the paper, the more blaring the coverage. The adventures of Giuliano were followed in Rome (and by me, avid reader of the lowest Italian publications, including a lurid weekly called *Crimen*) with the intensity later devoted in the United States to O. J. Simpson. Now only Francesco Rosi's great, if neglected, film *Salvatore Giuliano* remains a lasting testimony to the dubious Sicilian hero.

Rome and a Villa is about history, of course. Not only Hadrian, but also other emperors and popes stride through it; and the unique nineteenth-century Roman dialect poet Gioacchino Belli concludes the book, with an injection of characteristic Roman irony. But *Rome and a Villa* is also history itself. Perhaps even the author did not realize how aptly she was capturing the essence of the city at midcentury: her thumbnail sketch of Signor T., in the chapter "Roman Journal I," spotlights a characteristic figure of fifty years ago, an unreconstructed Fascist who has survived the regime to live on into the shaky democracy of the first years of peace. To be sure, there are plenty of Fascists around in today's Rome, but they are born again, newly constructed, from a romantic nostalgia, rather like those unhappy youths in our own Deep South with their Confederate flags and their updated racism.

In Piazza Vittorio now, despite Rome's booming supermarkets, there are still the stands selling fruits and vegetables and cheap yard goods, and there are still the cats. The famous Carolina whom Eleanor affectionately describes, the comedienne-beggar, who won our hearts and made us open our pockets with her invented headlines, has long vanished from the Piazza Navona area (and begging itself has undergone some changes, even passing through a "chic" period, when rebellious students from well-off families considered it socially and politically correct to ask disoriented tourists for money).

I am not sure that Eleanor ever met Pier Paolo Pasolini; I think not. But the Rome she gives us is contemporary with the Rome of Pasolini's first novels and films. The dialect spoken by Pasolini's *ragazzi* was different from the *romanesco* of Belli, the language of Pasolini's characters includes strains of the language spoken by the boys' Sicilian or Calabrian or Apulian parents, entwined with the traditional Roman of the Trastevere quarter. Only a trained philologist could trace and decipher the development of today's Roman, but the Romans of Eleanor Clark's time would surely understand and communicate with the young men of today, lounging at the same bars, but now grasping cellular phones and sitting astride expensive motorcycles.

As I said, Eleanor did not like *Rome and a Villa* to be called a "travel" book, still less a guidebook. If it has to be given a label, personally I would prefer the old term *vademecum*, a book that goes with you, that informs but does not coerce. To be sure, if you are in Rome today, this book will prove excellent company. In the Italian language, the verb "to live" — *vivere* — is transitive, it can take a direct object. In Italian I could say Eleanor Clark lived Rome. And, whether you read *Rome and a Villa* in the comfort of your New England or Midwestern or Southern living room, or whether you read it at the Bar Gianicolo (expanded since the author's time, but still there), the experience will help you live Rome. And perhaps the city will also become transitive: Rome will live you.

William Weaver
Annandale-on-Hudson

PREFACE

to the 1992 edition

W HAT IS ROME? What is Rome to me? What *was* Rome to me? How did I, how could anybody, have the nerve to take on this subject? Well, luckily, life, death, anything in history do of course get taken on — and if we consider in our later years how we ever had the nerve in any particular instance, that needn't be of any consequence.

For the 1975 mini Holy Year, one of two each century known as quarter-century jubilees, I was able to bring out a slightly expanded edition of this book. The question looming over our thoughts of Rome in this edition is really a simple fact of calendar accident. This question is, of course, the approach of the year 2000 and its dramatic significance for the city.

Very likely the end of the second Christian millennium will have nothing of the terror the world of the Middle Ages felt at the close of the first. Not to be overlooked is that our own age has had its share of terrors comparable in scope, some now happily in abeyance. Bombarded as we are by a manufactured sense of crisis over all events large and small, all risk assuming triviality, including the transition to a new millennium. But whether or not this will prove to be true, and with or without sudden incursions from outer space or equally surprising developments within our own species, the chances are that most of Rome as we know it will still be there through the end of the century. Who knows? Or even through several others beyond that. The city's fabulous powers of retaining its past might go on surviving longer than we now dare to guess.

An autobiographical note: At age sixteen, waiting for Vassar College to consider me old enough to be a freshman, I had spent a head-over-heels year in Rome. When I returned there on a Guggenheim after World War II, in 1947, my project was to write a novel. It lasted there at most two weeks. I found I still retained the passion and the language, along with an intimacy with the city. This took over; good-bye novel. In an unborn stage, it may have drifted down the Tiber and into the Mediterranean; if so, it would perhaps have been in splendid company from the pen of Keats among so many others.

RETURN TO ROME

Preface to the 1974 edition

*T*HERE MAY BE BOOKS BESIDES *The Farmers' Almanac* that can profit from tinkering by their authors in later years. It has been tried often enough, even in novels and poetry, for which a wise general rule would seem to be that if the work had any inner logic and cohesion to begin with, they are unrecoverable; if it didn't, it is not worth fooling with. Aside from these introductory remarks, *Rome and a Villa* has one new chapter in this edition, "Beside the Pyramid," on the lovely foreign cemetery where Keats and Shelley are buried, but except for a few words and corrections the book has not been revised. It has been called a "personal" book, and no doubt it is; if it were not there would be no reason for it, but if it were only that it would be full of lies. Leaving out historians, who don't deal in any total truth either but are in a different kettle of fish from the one called letters — with or without the *belles* in front — the person never lived whose apprehension was up to more than bits and moments of Rome, from Goethe and Stendhal on down: a notion or emotion here and there, a fact, a flavor, a scene or story, a generalization, within overall limitations of personal and period taste. The rest has to be just signposts, reports of objects or happenings past and present, which may send people of different nature off on their own if they care enough. If it should work that way, fine, but hardly the point in this case; the book was not written as social service. Nor could it be brought up to date like a guidebook. For that it would have to be torn limb from limb and left dead on the table, which of course is only to speak of kind, not quality.

Still, in the signpost category there are some items that have to be mentioned, as they have become untrue or misleading since the book appeared in 1952. It had been written between 1948 and 1951 and nobody likes to tot up their life in quarter-centuries, but there it is: another Holy Year has come around, believe it or not, making the description here of the one of 1950 a useful piece of history, instead of the current event it then was. Of almost ancient history, so much has happened to the Church and to various public and private attitudes in the interval. The specific list of such matters, to be touched on as they come up, ranges from the altogether factual, such as the contents of the Lateran Museum having been moved to a handsome new wing of the Vatican Museums, so that the marvelous mosaic athletes are now seen on a floor where they belong, to a question of political atmosphere, especially with regard to the long years of fascism in Italy. Of course the architectural scars from that period remain and probably will for at least another century, so the passages about them seem dated in tone, not substance. Around 1950 Mussolini's regime and downfall, like the damage from World War II, were part of a raw and recent history that today is still far from forgotten by older people but figures very little if at all for the young. For anybody, including foreign visitors, there are plenty of fresher troubles to get excited about and many square miles of more recent buildings to deplore, though on the periphery, not the center of the city where the fascist bombast struck. To avoid beating a dead horse, a few sentences on the subject have been toned down for this edition. The rest seem valid "for the record" — a phrase it is odd sometimes to hear from thoroughly nonfascist Romans about the buildings themselves, inscriptions, statues and all. It's part of our history, keep it, is the idea; not that it would be financially possible not to, so the remark is really one of those wisely cynical shrugs of the shoulder Rome was always known for, dispensing with a lot of verbiage about the uses of the past, any past. Of course from the neofascists of the MSI (Movimento Sociale Italiano), stronger in southern Italy than from Rome north, that particular record gets better than tolerance.

The big, generic changes in Rome over the past twenty-five years are those shared with all the technological world, only cities and countries have their own ways of adjusting or failing to; and there are special circumstances. Venice empties; Rome bulges. The key words for the differences since 1950 are automobile, air travel, TV, overpopulation, pollution, and runaway capitalism; throw in some thirty-six governments since World War II, and a burst of national prosperity from the early '50s for some twenty years, putting many millions of native-owned cars on the streets and roads around, and you have a degree of speed, noise, chicanery, and confusion that can make one nostalgic for an old-time sack or barbarian invasion. This is a sack from within. From without too, of course. Tourist buses stream in endlessly over or under the Alps, elephants unopposed; outlying churches of great age shudder under air traffic bringing and taking mainly tourists all day every day. These transients, legitimately or not, to be served or preyed upon, are the big industry; Rome, with its furious rise of population from the poor south, still has no other except government and, most scandalously in late years, building. To house all those people of whom one in ten may have a useful job. Most must scrounge or die. There is a proliferation of middlemen and purse snatchers; the beggars, about the same in numbers, are now almost all women with doped children. Years ago such children were often awake. Drugs are of course easier to get than ever before, and that a number of young Americans have been involved in the trade there is by now an old story, but stories get old very fast these days; that was far from a common sight or topic in 1950. Another trade sometimes with links to that one, making and selling knickknacks and lousy art and junk jewelry, has changed the character of Piazza

Navona and the Spanish Steps except in the very middle of the night, and of Trastevere at all hours. Not that these young foreigners, of dropout cut, nothing like the indigenous street vendors, are all as bad by any means as most of their wares; of course not; they couldn't be, and the only public nuisance most of them seem to commit is to make it all look rather monotonous and dreary — one mood that never used to belong in Rome.

The actual, not psychological, air is murky too, from car exhaust; on many days you can't see Monte Cavo from the Janiculum. The buildings in the center are pitifully dirty from the same cause, most of the public parks unkempt from a different one; and as elsewhere in the world, crime, no longer mainly of passion, and mental illness are way up. Bank robberies and suicides have become common events, not to mention the new kinds of political violence, bombings and kidnappings, around the country, on which the Giuliano story has some bearing but TV has more. An overcrowded bus in Rome is still more fun than in most places but not often the party it used to be; part of the populace has become too genteel for that, from affluence, and many people are on edge, even though the native has some mysterious genius in getting alive on foot across a street and can even carry on a conversation in the process. True, they quite often get hit, adults and children, but they know the language, based on the screaming brake, and at the wheels of their own cars will be as speed crazy as the rest; apparently arrests for speeding are unthinkable, in the city or out, on thoroughfares or the narrowest streets of vecchia Roma. For a great many of these drivers a good bicycle would have been a luxury in 1950. Galloping inflation makes for nerve strain too; every purchase is a load of worry, even more than in most other countries. Oddly enough, the almost daily political parades and demonstrations, PCI (communist) or MSI, are at about the same pitch as in 1948, only far more effective in creating traffic jams.

Can Rome stand it, withstand it? survive in any recognizable way such a combination of forces? — of which rapacity by industrialists and government tolerance when not encouragement of same are far from the least.

Absurd questions. Look at what it has withstood before, over what length of time. Yes, but it was always changing, after each push and crisis a different Rome emerged, often with little respect for any previous one. It was the idea of Rome that survived everything, so the ticklish point right now must be the place and power of the idea. Of the idea of Rome in particular; of ideas in general. What is an idea anyway? The word gets to feel very fragile when you go poking at it, with all the racket in your ears and when you know you can be someplace else in no time if you have the plane fare or can somehow get it.

First empire, then Church held the particular idea together for its considerable number of centuries, and although the latter can still put on a splendid show and will probably do so for at least a few more Holy Years and twenty-five times that many Easters, it is scarcely the spiritual force or world drawing card it was as late as 1950. Yet the pull of Rome persists, though weakened, for those who live there — Romans rich or poor, immigrants from elsewhere in Italy, the various large foreign colonies — and even for a rare spirit now and then among the tourists, who are most conspicuously from Germany and Japan this year. Leaving out grounds of special interest, religious, scholarly, commercial, there can be only three causes: people, Time, and what the Romantic poets called Beauty. They were referring to something very different from what we see now, but never mind, the word still applies, at enough spots and moments to make one forget the weariness, the fever and the fret. And even forget that nearly everything one cares about is in a fairly small area, bounded more or less by the Aurelian walls, set no longer in romantic, if on one side malarial, countryside, but in a howling wilderness of new apartment complexes, dotted here and there with oases for the very rich.

That wilderness, of instant slums, pushing out farther every day like some malign vegetation disguised in steel and stucco, would have broken Saint Jerome's spirit in a night. Instant fortunes have been and are being made on them, of which the Vatican has reportedly raked in a good share, and they have made the word *abusivo* — illegal, against building regulations — one of the commonest in the language, and *edilizia*, for the building industry, about the dirtiest. The section called Magliana, all fields until the mid-'60s, has been much written about, for one thing because among other abuses the buildings, housing upward of forty thousand people, are below the level of the Tiber and subject to floods, also because the Communist Party has been particularly active in protests there, but it seems to be no worse than others in matters of water, electricity, sewage, and shoddy engineering.

The chapter on fountains in *Rome and a Villa* applies in no way to this huge new Rome, whose inhabitants are largely not born Romans, but that is not the main reason. There are no fountains; no piazzas; few or no trees; minimal spaces between buildings; no benches for the old, playgrounds for the young. In fairness to the builders or perhaps the municipal authorities, it seems that on one open strip in Magliana not used for the necessary open-air market an effort was made to do some planting, which was soon wrecked by some of the *cattivi* among the tenants themselves. How lucky if that were the worst; houses built in contempt for human life have got to be crime breeders, working in favor of the bad ones who are always with us but in vecchia Roma have never quite ruled the roost. Certain charms still operate there against evil, and are part of what this book is about. There, the rosy, cheerful bluster is much as it was; probably few of "the people" — however defined — could recite a sonnet or even a line by Belli nowadays, but over and over you can be amazed, far more than a quarter-century ago because of the new kinds of dread in the world, by the pleasantness of children's group games in a piazza at nightfall, and the tonic to the heart of those bells, that laughter.

That will be in a place closed to traffic or not conducive to much in the evening. The traffic prohibitions, such as they are, seem designed more as a boon to well-off shoppers, tourist or other, than for the well-being of the people. There are a few such streets, of fancy little shops, near the Piazza di Spagna, and very charming they are with their potted shrubberies, one even with what looks like several blocks' worth of red carpet though it must really be plastic or something. One wishes the public gardens came in for as much consideration.

There have been some more serious measures of protection. When you think of the billboards that disfigure all the main highways of Italy you wouldn't suppose there was any restraint on commercialism in the country at all, but there is some. The *edilizia* people, the developers, are for instance not putting up housing projects across the Forum and Palatine as they no doubt would if permitted. The ruins after all are essential to the idea of Rome, and that is even bigger business. Such places are not only preserved but elaborated; as at Hadrian's Villa, excavations continue, little signs all over tell you roughly what's what: Triclinium, House of Livia, etc. The Rome subway, crazy project born of desperation, that is, near-total congestion, has two spurs running; work on the rest, with attendant mess in Piazza Barberini and Piazza Esedra — both with dry fountains, the water pipes having been cut — is one of the big jokes around town, in the vein of Belli's description of eternity: "che dura sempre e nun finisce mai." The trouble is respect for ruins. When a new one is struck, which is all the time, they say the foremen try to hide it or get rid of it quickly, before the archaeological authorities can be told, but there are leaks, and again and again the subway defers to History. It is a battle between present and past, and what the nature of either is at this juncture the dry Triton and dolphin may know as well as anyone.

Twenty-five years ago TV was brand-new, air travel almost nil compared to now; the age of total exposure was just beginning; space exploration, with its deep surgery for better or worse on the mind, had not begun. This has been the fastest piece of time in human time, in fact you might say it's been quite a tiring century altogether, and over and over in Rome whose beneficence is above all of time you wonder: What are they seeing? What am I seeing, really?

Consider the above-mentioned Triton, by Bernini, and Michelangelo's Moses. When this book was written Piazza Barberini was about as ugly with billboards, the most vulgar hotel edifice in town and other money-motivated blight as it is now, yet it was still possible to think the Triton had a place and function there. It was a fragment of the long grace of memory, a small point of rest in the turmoil, for the soul's health. No longer. The insult and brutality of its surroundings have killed it at last; perhaps just that many more cars, that much more dirt and noise; and perhaps the billboards, mostly movie ads, have really gotten twice as big — they must have, there couldn't be any others that big in the world. There is a degree of mistreatment that art, like human flesh and spirit, can't bear, and the degree has been passed here. The Triton, the whole fountain, should be moved at once to a decent place, but will not be because an important street and bus stop are named for it.

Moses is half dead too, from a different process. You used to approach it in quietness and it came on like thunder. For one thing, S. Pietro in Vincoli is curiously hard to find and get to. Now from the buses outside you'd think it was a ball game. The church steps and portico are so thick with vendors, of all the usual plus little Moseses, you can hardly get through, and at the railing in front of the cause of all this the crowds are four or five deep all year round, more at Easter, in a cacophony of guides. A nice game is letting your mind fool around with the various languages, it makes a kind of scrabble, and you can't do it anymore in the Sistine Chapel, new regulation, the acoustics are so terrible nobody was seeing the ceiling. If anybody is seeing Moses it's a miracle. The whole uproar is for that one marble figure. Sometimes the guides go on a bit about the crypt, waiting for space at the railing or to give an impression of money's worth to their weary charges, but the associations of the place are not visible, at least fifty churches in Rome are more beautiful or interesting. Yet it is on all the tours, five-day, three-day, maybe even one-day. The effect is of red ants on a martyr. You remember that Moses as "mighty" and very large, and can hardly believe it's the same one, it looks so small and impotent.

Why do they go? Because it's on the itineraries mostly, along with all Rome; Bali last year, Africa next, and the percentage is anybody's guess as to how many would truly get more out of Disneyland. But volition does enter the picture, in odd ways. When Michelangelo's Pietà was shown in New York the crowds were record-breaking. In Easter week 1974, when it had been restored after the lunatic's attack and was back in its chapel behind a thick protective pane of glass, and when Saint Peter's like the rest of the city was mobbed, hardly anyone was lingering there; it was one of the quieter spots in Rome. Too much rival spectacle in the same building? Mystery of, as they say, the media?

Snobbery comes easy — *they* are getting nothing out of it, and *they* are spoiling it for the rest of us, as Wordsworth said about the first railroad to the Lake Country — and so does pious sociology: education, birth control, etc. Obviously once in a while in the shuffling multitudes there is going to be a soul saved, a mind stretched, while others that were alert before move toward despair. Computers are cracking up everywhere under these equations. Anyhow, "free" countries can't and shouldn't start prohibiting travel, and are not soon going to cut down population much, or improve education, or cure the restlessness and obscure longings for something else that drive the modern human animal forth to wander no matter how uncomfortably, no matter where. As long as the money and the oil hold out, this is it. So here the point is just what remains of the experience of Rome under these new conditions.

You get used to it — at a price, but still; you accommodate; you learn new psychological tricks. For the more intelligent of the very young, especially if they have had four or more years of Latin and a proper amount of other literature and of ancient and European history, in other words some education, no problem; they were raised in racket and never knew the place before; it is all wonderful. In fact they bring something wonderful to it, seeing, discovering, learning, enjoying so much, you can half believe the city is eternal after all and may never have had a chance before to be so great a school, or as Goethe called it, place in which to be reborn. Older foreigners, settled there or returning for a while, are apt to be saddened when not disgusted, at least a few times a week, as many Romans are too. Nevertheless, *Rome and a Villa* remains in substance whatever it was originally; nothing has been literally taken away from the city, as by Napoleon for one, or smashed, as so many times. There is only, around all that the book deals with, a new degree of difficulty, for the mind and for the legs. Locomotion, simply getting around, is a problem, and getting into museums is another, though less so at the Vatican. The others are understaffed and open only for absurdly short hours, because of city and state negligence, corruption, and financial straits. However, if you can hang around long enough you do get in, and there is all the rest, outdoors, in churches. The matter of getting in mentally, being in condition to see, takes a little extra patience and effort too. You fight now, or almost sneakily plot, for the moments of quietness, of any real rapport with anything; that is one of the tricks.

It works, often enough, with time might become habitual, and after all it isn't always necessary; Rome is strained, but not damned or utterly bereft by a long shot. You come on sudden, brief, mystifying quiet on a back street, where vines can breathe, on a profile you never noticed before or had forgotten, of one umbrella pine and two little double-decker bell towers seen across the Forum; on courtyards all a tumble of greenery and haphazard patchwork of steps, doorways, everything, hiding off the Via Margutta — mainly artists' quarters as before, and yes, "picturesque," as if we could afford to despise that; even on a public park kept by some special interest remarkably beautiful, as against the general neglect. One of those is the Villa Celimontana, apparently because the Italian Geographic Society has its headquarters there and does something about it. Lovely surprise: place of trees as fine as in any eighteenth-century engraving, and birds actually singing, even long views here and there through to a skyline strangely undisfigured; as strangely, a place cut off from noise, yet open to everybody and well frequented with no sign of any damage done or a will to do any. Aside from nightingales, a special case, songbirds never used to seem all that thrilling in the city, in the days when you could hear the fountains and hear yourself think, and perhaps there weren't that many before, more than in most Italian countryside, where they were shot or trapped for food. The disappearance of so much open land nearby may have driven them into the green spaces left in the city, where they are safe and can multiply. One of the sweeter ironies of the contemporary scene. A big factor for pleasure on the Palatine too, where again you are surprised to find the long view, over the Tiber and the Janiculum, not yet ruined by giant boxes, the Hotel Hilton on Monte Mario being out of sight.

The Palatine, by the way, gets poor pickings in this book, not through oversight. The necessary curiosity and impulse were used up, by Hadrian's Villa. Now, of the two, it seems to hold up better, as a way into the empire or into yourself as you prefer. It can't be that it scares people away, through a reputation as a paradise for eggheads, since the Roman Forum doesn't; that is always crawling with sightseers. Either there are really fewer up the hill, or it is just that you go not expecting much in the way of current tranquillity, in which to contemplate a history lacking in any, and so are almost neurotically grateful for what you find. It is Rome at one of its many bests, in both shady walks and sun-struck palace skeletons, and it is striking how often Italians strolling there will be saying. "Bello! Bello!" — a pleasant thing to hear, and they are right.

The word would be in order still even for Piazza del Popolo and Trinità dei Monti, in spite of their hell-bent traffic, but there is apt to be letdown around the corner. You have to brace yourself. The Oppio park, Nero's Golden House notwithstanding, is dreary with weeds, rubbish, and disrepair, and people's faces reflect the fact. Via Veneto, American Embassy notwithstanding, has stopped trying to look anything but tacky. The many acres of princely villa grounds within the city limits remain locked, unavailable to a public that more and more desperately needs them, or else become objects of cynical and exorbitant profiteering, as in current proceedings between the Torlonia family and the municipality over the Villa Albani: the big one out the Via Nomentana, not the smaller estate by the same name, where the fine Winckelmann collection is still visible only by special permit and the pavilion and grounds continue to serve when at all for private patrician amusements. Those land transactions, like others in different domains, get the connivance or better of a series of governments that, at least according to general gossip, make De Gasperi's of the postwar years look like a model of public service and probity; and in fact he was not bad, just hung up on the Vatican. Failure to take flood control measures that would have spared the devastation of Florence and Venice in 1966 seems to have been a fault shared by several generations.

As for Hadrian's Villa, perhaps the section that gives this book half its title would not have been written if the villa had been then as it is now, but that is not certain. Weather permitting, especially on Sundays and holidays when admission is free, the place is more than anything a public park, with the imperial layout an extra touch in the scenery; naturally, with such a press of people needing green leaves and breathing-space and having the means to get to them. Plus tourists as elsewhere, the crowd grown to a horde. If Moses weakens, can Hadrian be far behind? Some specific changes date back to the mid-'50s. The entrance had then already been changed from the one described here, on foot up Count Feder's fine cypress alley, to bring the cars and buses smack into the heart of the matter, alongside the great wall, the Pecile, that used to strike you so powerfully after the slow ramble working up to it, and hardly a stone's throw from the more intimate heart of the matter, called before the Maritime Theatre, now Island Nymphacum. The Valley of Canopus had, and has, lost its curious metaphysical suggestions to an elegance almost as bizarre, with a lake and swans and now a small museum housing statues dug up there in recent years. That last item, the museum, is more gain than loss, the loss being only the general one, of the sense of privacy, being alone with your thoughts, which was going anyway.

The skyline toward Tivoli, crucial to the sense of the villa, is so far marred by only one huge hideous square building. Toward Rome, the dome of Saint Peter's and what used to be called 42, now part of EUR (Esposizione Universale Roma), are no longer visible; the air is too dirty. On a sunny Sunday afternoon the whole shrunken place is like a country environ of any big city, only with a sprinkling of serious students and extra decibels from transistors, all turned full blast to the pro soccer games. A group of young men, cattivi or just pent up and stupid, throw stones from a cliff over a path alongside Canopus and a couple of middle-aged Italian ladies yell in fear and outrage, wanting to pass, but things are mostly peaceable. Another, steadier blare of appalling volume comes from a country fair set up just outside the grounds. At last visit the whole Academy section was closed off, perhaps for excavations though there could be none that extensive; Hadrian's little island was barred too, for desultory digging, evidently by some foreign group.

It was silly to be upset in the beginning; you get used to it; you just have to refocus.

Sheep are still grazing up there toward the Academy, and twenty-five years are nothing to the same old olive grove. Off-season, at off-hours, the old spell does operate, if you give it a chance. The trick here is to stop thinking, with regard to the future, but the past shrivels when that does, *for how long?* The villa is beautiful, it even begins to look big again, though of course not as it did to Piranesi; and it has been through worse, well, maybe worse, so many times before.

You find new favorites, new antipathies. It would be sick to have no change of taste in a lifetime, if the times were more static; as it is there is probably an abnormal factor of change in what one likes and dislikes, craves or rejects in art as in other things. Baroque architecture seems to suffer unduly at the moment; the wear and tear, the physical darkening from grime seem harder on it than on other styles; perhaps its curves and curlicues, its particular grace and fling of fantasy require less threatening surroundings. By the same token, the fourth through ninth centuries are more and greater than they looked before. The mosaics of those "dark" centuries are pouring with light these days and are, one is tempted to say "suddenly," all over the place.

Some are eyes in a jungle, easy to miss, in Renaissance or baroque settings although usually on their pristine sites, but many are in the churches least transformed and the same quirk of vision, if it is that, applies to the architecture. People commonly did go the long way around to bar medieval forms in Rome, no matter how receptive they might be to them somewhere else; the flamboyant, using the word untechnically, was so much the main modern show there, it tended to make plainer geometry look dull. By and large that wonderful other Rome — with few exceptions, of church interiors only, and only those not basically renovated after the twelfth or thirteenth centuries — was for the older and wiser, returning traveler or long-time inhabitant. That could be the whole story here. Or it could be that current malaise tips the scales that way, toward the structurally serene, the lack of hyperbole.

A good many such interiors were ruined in the nineteenth century, notable under Pius IX, if they hadn't been before, for example, S. Cecilia in Trastevere, where however the great display of earliest Christian times underneath has been much more fully exposed in recent years, and where the Cavallini frescoes can now be seen by the public two mornings a week for one hour. One of the finest early churches extant is not mentioned in the book because it was locked at the time, for work that turns out to be well worth waiting for. That is S. Costanza, named for the sister of Saint Agnes whose church is in the same compound — off the main tourist map and altogether one of the pleasantest spots in the city. A set of boccie courts, roofed but open-air, nestles under sister Agnes's wing; the saint's powers haven't extended to permitting any women to play, but then like all lady saints of her era she was of high birth and boccie, more than some other national versions of bowling, is a plebeian game. The men sound cheerful and so do the boys in an adjacent playground, part of some Catholic institution; vegetation thick and informal, with many blossoms. S. Costanza, small and circular, originally a mausoleum, made into church in thirteenth century, stripped in the 1960s of latter-day ac-

cretions and thus turned back into one of the most exquisite buildings in Rome. Usually empty. Fourth-century wall mosaics unique
among surviving paleo-Christian works in that medium, for their
pagan birds, flowers, vineyard scenes, and general gaiety, and for
their white ground. — Another that may or may not have been
locked but anyway got overlooked is S. Maria in Dominica, by the
entrance to the Celimontana garden and the little boat fountain
of uncertain provenance called the Navicella. Involving, like so
many architectural treasures, the name of Pope Pasquale I (early
to middle ninth century). Like S. Agnese, three naves divided by
ancient columns, in marvelous harmony of weight, line, proportion. Some Renaissance touches, portico, ceiling, rather good
than bad. S. Clemente and S. Lorenzo Fuori le Mura are more or
less as they were, the first with more digging done in its fascinating
subsoil, the latter with its superb job of post–World War II restoration more complete. The difference is in what one brings to them.

S. Stefano Rotondo, under restoration when *Rome and a Villa*
was written, still is: a process like the subway "che nun finisce
mai." Another remarkable circular structure, much larger than S.
Costanza, said to be probably fifth century, one of the oldest
churches in Italy; with twelfth-century addition of arched cross-
support held up by ancient columns of staggering girth and
height, to keep the old wooden roof from falling in, with result
more interesting than beautiful though it is hard to tell at present.
Originally ringed by a double portico, and one keeps mentally re-
creating, with the help of a plaster model out toward the nuns'
quarters, the now missing outer ring; at least for the first seven
hundred years, the whole complex must have been stunning.
Seventh-century mosaic with Christ as head in medallion over the
cross rather than crucified. Nice contrast to frescoes, of around
1600, of saints' martyrdoms all around the main walls.

That series, by several painters, is gruesomely of the Counter-
Reformation genre in Rome, set off by promulgation of decrees of
the Council of Trent, 1564. Antipathy for that unchanged in
twenty-five years. Caravaggio alone, among painters of religious
subjects in seventeenth-century Rome, survived proximity to the

Curia, yet sculpture and architecture could go into so grand a flourish of invention at the same time. Never mind the prattle about subject not mattering and its being fine painting just the same; it does matter, when it overpowers other perception, and *it* in this case, whatever you call it as painting, is not good art, since to react to it as such a viewer would have to surgically tie off a good half of his nature, evidently not an uncommon practice among some critics. Physical torture on the stage defeats its purpose in the same way but not so many people call it good theater just the same.

Another antipathy, increased by time: to S. Paolo Fuori le Mura, another place of course on all the tours. It is spoken of here as the coldest of the big basilicas, "pure in form and awesome in scale." True, but it is also objectionable, in a very big way, though with a lovely cloister if one could see it for the mobs, and some fine objects and enormous history, the latter to be taken mostly on faith. Other faith, of the kind a church is supposed to be about, must be at a premium in this one. A great deal of the old structure could have been saved after the fire in 1823 but was not, including many Cavallini frescoes. Leo XII, appealing to the faithful of the world for funds, entrusted the rebuilding to a group of architects headed by a dolt named Poletti. Oh Pasquale I, you should have been pope then. The funds must have come in handsomely. Expense is what one is mainly conscious of, along with the spectacle of the Church flaunting its temporal power and aiming to do so on a scale never known before. The pompous quadriportico at the entrance, of more unmitigated vulgarity, was added at the turn of the century; the interior would at least make a good ballroom and probably gives a good image of the more pretentious basilicas of the late empire. On the other hand, it would be beyond human powers if some of these impressions were not heightened, and implanted beforehand, by the new dismal surroundings of the past decade. Magliana is near across the Tiber, and what open spaces remain in the sprawl of much closer developments are left to weeds and dumps and, where out of sight of tourists, a small colony or two of the city's many shack dwellers.

It is something of an aesthetic as well as religious mystery that the reconstructed Saint Paul's should so fail in both ways, while Saint Peter's, to the casual eye not too unlike it in grandeur, scale, and intent, remains as truly grand as ever. This emends, with apology, one sentence in the book.

The Pozzo ceiling in S. Ignazio looks somehow sillier than it used to, as though it had slid over imperceptibly into camp, and his even fancier trompe-l'oeil stunt, the fake cupola in the same church, obviously a masterwork of its kind, is of the same kind.

One of the finest easel paintings in Rome, not mentioned in the text, is a very small one by Fra Angelico in the Vatican Museums, of Saint Francis receiving the stigmata. Of course it would have more rivals elsewhere. The new wing of the same museums, replacing the Lateran in that function, is a bit overtricky inside with its profusion of levels and kinds of space and sources of light, but nevertheless is the most satisfying large modern work of architecture in the city. One comes to miss good, or any, modern sculpture outdoors around town, though there are still Mirko's fine gates out at the Ardeatine Caves, and the great door by Manzù has finally been hung at Saint Peter's. Altogether the atmosphere for the functioning artist has become far from stimulating in Rome, although some good to very good ones still live there. The general sense of creative excitement that flared up in the early postwar years has gone down if not out, in reverse proportion to the volume of hubbub and trash. The movie world seems to have gone on prospering, as long as the nation did.

Carlo was born in Rome and the fact weighs extremely with him, though neither his mother, Assunta, nor his handsome, choleric father, Giuseppe, came from there. However, that was where they had the misfortune to meet and marry. Carlo was born in 1937, his brother two years earlier. Assunta, an accomplished dressmaker whose clientele never got beyond the poor, also did housework and made herself generally indispensable to a little spinster lady of means and romantic temperament, who in 1938 bought and moved to an enormous ruined fortress up the coast, over the sea, and above a pretty harbor and fishing village on the other side; she did this for complicated reasons involving long unrequited love for a rake of a monsignore, to whom she had lent large sums of money and who had lived for a while and recently died there.

Giuseppe was called to the army in 1939 and after five years in Albania became a prisoner of war. Assunta and her children went to live with the spinster lady, in the dingiest quarters in the fortress but out of the wind and with a sunny old orchard in back, and there the boys grew up. Assunta didn't have to cook for their benefactor because she was too miserly to eat much, but she did everything else for her and cooked for the various armed forces that came and lodged there, Italian, German, American, finding them equally mannerly on the whole. Only the withered little proprietress, of the engaging girlish laughter and eyes sharp as a bird's, became confused by such a succession of uniforms and would say in later years, "That Hitler, Shitler, what was his name?" A downed American pilot was torn to pieces one day in the street in nearby Orbetello, and the remains of an Italian airman were found much later wedged in the rocks below the fortress, forty feet down under the beautiful blue water. The bombings were always at night and most of the villagers returned by day to their homes if anything was left of them; not much was, of the whole village, at the end, but the fortress alongside was not even hit. Assunta with the children took refuge in a farm a two hours' walk away over donkey paths. The signorina stayed alone among the bombs "to watch over her investment" and trusted, wisely it turned out, in the protection of Saint Rita, for whom at the monsignore's instigation she had spent hundreds of hours embroidering bees and roses on ecclesiastical vestments. Later she spent other hundreds of hours on foot or in buses on the dusty roads, in an effort to collect from various authorities for war damage, and it was true that the fortress had undergone a lot of it, in previous centuries.

Eventually Giuseppe rejoined the family circle, charming and prone to rage as always, never holding a job for long. Many families of *sfollati*, bombed-out people, lived in squalor around the fortress too for a number of years, but gradually the village was reconstructed and they trickled back down, to the great relief of the owner and the family that was as good as her own, though that was not really acknowledged; she addressed them all in second person, by their first names, and was addressed in the third, as Signorina. In fantasy she had a swarm of friends who might come by for a visit any time, but in fact those four were all her human relations and one of them, Giuseppe, gave her a hard time.

They all crossed themselves passing a cemetery but not even the signorina with her bees and roses was a churchgoer in that period. The boys were raised among fights and festas in about equal proportions, a general talent for laughter and celebration alternating with wild angers, mainly from Giuseppe, at his failure in life, often from Assunta, at the abuse she took from him. She kept a severe, moralistic eye on the boys and baked excellent cakes for saints' days and such, in a little contraption of an oven over the charcoal. The water was carried from a cistern and from way down in the village for drinking. Carlo and his brother, yearning for bicycles, swam a great deal in the summer, with no style and terrific vigor, and the soles of their feet were tough as hooves from running barefoot over the razor-sharp lava rocks. Carlo, the one with a theatrical comic streak, thought it very funny to carry octopuses stuck around his arms, of course not the very big ones.

Both became car crazy and left school at fifteen, the brother to be an apprentice mechanic; Carlo went into bodywork. The old lady died and left everything to her favorite nephew, who had been near her only once in twenty years and then tried to have her committed as a lunatic, which she was not. Blood was thicker than water, and besides, Giuseppe had made those terrible scenes; not that he didn't get just as excited if he found a viper in the old walls, or even a harmless but hissing five-foot snake that he would imagine to be just as deadly. The fortress was sold, its *portone* by the drawbridge and current garbage dump locked. The family found a tiny apartment in Orbetello, with no bathroom, but by then everybody had bottled gas to cook with and Giuseppe drove a truck long enough so that they got a refrigerator. The village they had left became suddenly fashionable and full of expensive cars. The boys did pretty well and both married beautiful girls, one from another fishing village and the other, Carlo's bride, from a farm inland where her parents were *mezzadri*, sharecroppers. The brother was of more placid temperament and liked small-town life, but Carlo was aching all the time for Rome and found a job there in his trade, called *carrozzeria*, from the word for horse-drawn carriages. He and his wife lived a few years in a poor part of Monteverde on a slope of the Janiculum, and in 1966, when their little boy was two years old and the building they were waiting for was finished, moved to Magliana.

It was a dream. The apartment, five flights up with a balcony overlooking a roaring market in the mornings, a dead space the rest of the time, had two bedrooms, a nice living-dining room like in an American movie, a tiny kitchen, and a real modern bathroom. Only one faucet worked and the toilet overflowed and nobody could tell them where they were supposed to take the garbage but *pazienza*, it was all so new, things would be fixed. They bought an expensive bedroom suite and sideboard and sofa to go with their new style, the pretty wife Claudia working late nights as a dressmaker to help pay for things and Carlo, with an ulcer by then, all the overtime he could get. That would make often ten or more hours' work a day six days a week and a half day Sunday. The TV and five-year-old Fiat they already had. After the second baby, a girl, Claudia began getting sick too, with dizzy spells, and her mother-in-law, Assunta, persuaded her to give up the outside jobs. "So you'll eat less," she said. "You'll stop having meat. What does it matter? Better eat less than kill yourself, and you have the bambini to think of."

Claudia was gentle and lovely and able to wait through her husband's dark, silent moods; Assunta had warned her he had something of his father's high-strung makeup, without the violence or unsteadiness. It was a happy marriage, far luckier than the brother's, that wife turning out touchous and managerial, anyone would have guessed long back that the older boy was the one destined for cheerful family life, and perhaps it is that in a way, since he adapts placidly enough to being pushed around, as Carlo never would.

The water tasted bad but the faucets were fixed, every now and then. When Paolo was six the only state school for him was so far away and brutal from overcrowding, they took on the terrible expense of sending him to a private one. It was a fraud, cooked up to make money out of the Magliana people in their educational plight; the parents discovered late in the year that he couldn't read at all and nobody had tried to teach him anything, so from then on he went to the public school, where he has never caught up. At eight, going for the bread, he was hit by a car while his mother watched from the balcony, was in the hospital for some days with a bad head injury, and has had blurry eyesight ever since; the oculist says his eyes are just tired, he should rest them more. Since there is no safe place to play outside and school hours are short, morning and afternoon shifts alternating every month, he is home in front of the TV most of the time. Now at ten he eats very little, is pale and no bigger than his six-year-old sister but full of vivacious chatter; knows all the soccer team scores and next to no arithmetic; can do excellent mimicries of the crazy tenant next door, the communist leader downstairs, and other neighbors. It is the comedian's gift his father had as a boy and rarely has the energy for anymore. The ulcer is worse, Carlo is losing his teeth too, one toothache after another, and there is some other trouble, from breathing around car paint for twenty-two years. In his opinion, his son's difficulty in school is from hearing and speaking, outside the home, nothing but Romanaccio, a language with no resemblance to what he sees on a page. It doesn't occur to them not to speak of the boy's poor performance in front of him, and they do, continually, not in any accusation, just as if it were a fact of nature or the neighborhood, while he waits to get his oar in on some more interesting topic.

Over the Easter weekend, 1974, it was estimated that a million cars left Rome, returning Monday night. Theirs was one of them.

Normally, Sunday afternoon is the only time in the week when Carlo can drive the children to the park at the EUR, quite a long way across the Tiber; Magliana has no grass or trees nearer and they came back screaming with fatigue when Claudia tried taking them in the packed bus, between the ride and the wait for it nearly an hour each way. They are all tired anyway, because the dirt area under their balcony turns out not to be a dead space after all, late at night. Brawling, obscenity, rampaging motorcycles, when not political outbursts, keep them awake most nights. But whenever possible they drive out to visit the two sets of grandparents, crowding in like sardines at Assunta's and Giuseppe's place but that's all right, they always did and can get to beaches and fields and the soft-lit lagoons that provide eels for the Rome markets, and from Claudia's parents' farm, not really theirs but their home anyway, they bring back chickens and pigeons her father raises and very good wine and grappa he has made, the latter illegally, and fruits and vegetables and some good air in their lungs.

Assunta comes to visit them in Rome too several times a year, sleeping on a cot in the children's room, bringing an infusion of tough wisdom and high spirits and laughter and warnings against getting entangled with the neighbors. She has been standoffish herself always, finding nothing but trouble in getting close to people outside the family, and in Magliana, between communist bullying and every kind of chicanery from high and low, the threat is more overt. Carlo pays forty-five thousand lire a month rent; some others for the same space pay twenty-five thousand and some pay nothing, by some mystery of skulduggery or as a result of takeovers by force. There have been quite a few of those, and evictions in Italy are cumbersome, even without the floods and other sources of complaint in Magliana, such as death and some bad accidents attributed to the quality of the buildings. Carlo and Claudia didn't know the families in those cases, you don't really get to know anybody still less make friends, with no place to sit and sew and gossip and watch children play, and anyway Assunta is right, the atmosphere is bad. Always some new rumor, of this one and that one going to jail or hitting the jackpot with a new kind of swindle or friend in the government. As for the communists, Carlo had his bellyful of their tactics in 1948, when he was eleven years old, in the country, and got another bellyful of threats and lies from the organizer downstairs. "I've learned," he says, "that to get anywhere you have to be *cattivo, ma non sò se ci riesco*, I don't know if I can make it."

Another expense this year but a festive one is for Paolo's First Communion. It has to be done right, Assunta who still never goes to church would be the last to think otherwise. What you pay the priest is the least of it. There are picture cards with the boy's name and the announcement printed on them, and the little gift bundles of white candies in white tulle with a plastic bouquet on top, and the pewter statuette of a boy holding a lamb, to be given to all the relatives even quite remote and the godparents and the few other invitees there may be, and then after the ceremony in Rome they will rush off to a big banquet of the combined families at Assunta's place, where the problem will be to keep Giuseppe sober. But he has quieted down some in late years and may behave. Everybody is proud and pleased, but still the worries go on, a little worse every day. The little girl is a beauty like her mother; they dread bringing the children up in Magliana any longer. It is too *brutto*, too ugly and unhealthy in every way. They never see any part of old Rome; there isn't time. They want to move away, not to one of the other projects just like that one, and see no chance of it at all. If there were a decent empty apartment you'd have to pay a year's wages under the table before you could talk about it.

But when you ask Carlo why they don't go back to the region he grew up in, where there would be plenty of car work and the sea and country around and people not so corrupted by Roman ways, a glitter of excitement comes into his eyes and his voice goes hard; as a child when pushed too far he would turn adamant like that, but now he speaks with a kind of love that is like addiction, not in anger. "I'd go crazy there, I'm not like my brother. Mi piace Roma. I was born in Rome" — how noble he makes it sound, the old *civis romanus sum* — "and that's the way it is."

It is the holy side of Holy Year, 1975, that is going to make it, in some vital respects, very unlike 1950 or any previous quarter-century observance, though no doubt a duplicate of the previous one on the surface. The old raison d'être of the jubilee, the earning of indulgences, has now gone from shadowy to nil. The dogma of the Assumption of the Virgin, the canonization of little Maria Goretti, seem not 25 but 250 years in the past. As one intellectual Italian monsignore puts it, 1950 was the last Holy Year of the Counter-Reformation, Pope John and Vatican Council II have utterly changed the nature of the event. Indeed many high-along with low-ranking members of the clergy, though probably fewer in the United States than proportionately in other countries, feel the tradition itself is outlived and should be dropped. Certainly the notion of anybody's coming to true repentance from the trip under present-day conditions seems far-fetched, though there is always such a fringe. Mostly, any spiritual benefits will have depended on special programs and efforts by parish priests all over the Catholic world, weeks or months in advance, and so must partake of every shading and degree, split and faction, defense and attack making up the present crisis in the Church.

That crisis, of which arguments over celibacy, birth control, and papal infallibility, questions of monastic and clerical dress, nuns and priests getting married, the serious drop in numbers of candidates for the priesthood notably in France and Italy, are only among the better-known symptoms, is consideration number one. It shades over into number two: conflict at the upper echelons of the Vatican itself over its post-Council role, as power structure in the old sense, or as guide and stimulus to individual conscience, with ecumenism a crosscurrent on its own. The old guard in the Curia has a double antagonist and must be hard put to decide which part is more dangerous. There is loss of faith, in the ranks as out, but there are also defenders of faith, speaking a new kind of language, advocating new methods, and more than that, new concerns, whether or not tinged with Marxism or what passes for such. This has all been general knowledge for years, although as the writings of the late Cardinal Daniélou among others show, the issues are a great deal more complicated than they seem; general knowledge can be nine parts general error. Still, certain emphases would be hard to mistake, for example, harsh views of Vatican money practices, as in connection with the Italian building boom, and of its failure to denounce certain political atrocities. The whole idea of expediency is under attack as old hat, pertaining to the era of the Papal States and now working against the needs both of humanity and of the Church itself. Such ideas were not seditious during the brief years of Papa Giovanni's vicarage, 1958–63, and some, by no means all, who hold them were his devotees and are accordingly critical of both Paul VI and Pius XII. They want spiritual acts, not words, and tell about a Vatican postage stamp issued a little before Pius XII's death, with a picture of a light on in the pope's bedroom window over Saint Peter's square, and a legend to the effect that the room's occupant never stopped watching over his flock. The first night Pope John slept in the room he said, "When you sleep you sleep with the light off," and had the shutters pulled down.

Consideration number three is what the experience will add up to for the TV-nurtured, spectacle-surfeited mind of the world. This is a subdivision of the earlier question, of what Rome in particular and travel in general have become to the traveler, and has bearing on the speculation about Holy Year being perhaps outmoded. When the same scenes or at least their highlights can be watched from home, there may still be reasons for flying to the spot, but scarcely the same ones there were in 1950, already a far cry from walking to it. As for the craving, evidently on the increase in the world, for mass togetherness, at rock festivals, guru gatherings, Protestant-sect revivals or whatever, Rome will of course offer some satisfaction, of what kind and whether it should be counted in the category of virtue is debatable.

The Holy Week and Easter ceremonies, 1974, were the last big push by the Church in Rome before the year opening on Christmas Eve, and a good preview of a phenomenon as novel as it is ancient — the first Holy Year not only since Vatican II but since general worldwide television.

The pope was in poor health and had to back out of a few functions but he went through with the most significant, that is, the biggest, the most spectacular; the key points in the story of Christ's agony and resurrection as recorded in the New Testament naturally took on that preeminence in the course of centuries. On Maundy Thursday afternoon, dressed in fairly simple white evangelical garb, he was not carried into S. Giovanni in Laterano but entered it by a side door on foot, rapidly, in fact scuttled in, whether in humility or as a security measure, and proceeded to intone part of the mass in a somewhat wavering voice and to wash the feet of twelve boys clothed in white robes. One was aware that the feet had undoubtedly been well washed beforehand, and that shouldn't matter; the symbolic act can be more powerful than any realism, so it must have been something in the atmosphere that made the reenactment, of Jesus' humbling himself before the poor on that last tragic day, a lot less effective than it is in the book. That the twelve boys were poor seemed to be agreed or assumed; the press had different accounts of what else they were, orphans, retarded, or polio cases, the last version absurd since they all walked in. In spite of torrential rain the basilica was more or less jammed; at least up front by the cordon where the pope passed coming and going there seemed a fair chance of being crushed to death, chiefly by Germans; actually many special buses had come in from outlying towns and there were probably as many Italians as foreigners there.

On Good Friday the pope presided again, at the ritual of the Stations of the Cross, outside the Colosseum; as for all his appearances, the fact was announced in flyers pasted on walls everywhere. For anything else, publicity was lacking; it was hard or impossible to find out where certain services would be held, or where, for instance, there might be good music in a church, in case one should want to contemplate the meaning of the week in that way. One small newspaper notice stated that Pergolesi's *Stabat Mater* would be sung at S. Marcello on the Corso Good Friday afternoon, but it was a mistake, there was no choir or organ, only a sprinkling of old people in the church, who squeaked out something else about Mary in her grief; evidently Pergolesi was not sung live anywhere in Rome that week, nor were any of Stravinsky's religious works, ecumenism notwithstanding. A university chorus gave a good Palestrina concert one day, in the auditorium of a handsome new Catholic school, lent to the chorus for its year's series because the university was too riddled with conflict to have it there; that was the Church's only connection with the event. But one side chapel in every church in the city was very beautiful with flowers and candles that Friday, and the few quiet separate people, what are known as individuals, kneeling before them at any given time lent an air of devotion, even worship; enlightened or benighted according to the eye of the onlooker but to themselves for a while less foolish in the face of death.

There must have been some of that, against all odds, at the Colosseum — on the face of it a strange conjunction with the Stations of the Cross; it was co-opted for the purpose some generations back, as an antidote to the bawdy ones it served at the time; and on the reasoning that some of the martyrs to mobs and lions there must have been Christians. They still are, with slight substitutions for wild animals and overt blood lust. A few in the crowd clearly wished to be dipped once again in the comprehension of suffering that is basic to Christianity, in contrast to some Eastern religions, and which after all is not a bad thing, however you come by it; not that the drama of that evening doesn't go far beyond questions of fortitude and sympathy. At this run-through, the community in time accreted by it played second fiddle to that same attribute in the setting, and stupendous that was in the white superlighting — on the Colosseum to one side, the huge columns of the Temple of Venus and Rome on top of the steep rise to the other. The staging was marvelous, the voices over loudspeakers well amplified and respectful. "Jesus falls the first time . . . Jésus tombe pour la première fois . . . Gesù . . ." It was done in six languages. The papers reported the next day that the pope himself had carried the cross for the last four stations but by most of the vast public that could not be seen. In fact it was a surprise to learn that the whole performance had taken place up by the temple where most of the cameras and sound apparatus were set up; one had supposed it was going on at the main ground level. People talked, shifted around, shoved others who were trying to say their beads; three square-looking American teenagers, nothing like hippie types, giggled and chattered all through, under the smiling approbation of their well-heeled parents, who looked overjoyed that the kids weren't sulking for once. The lights dimmed; it was over; Christ was crucified. A good many of the people drifting away looked as probably most did when the best lion failed to eat anybody. It was too late for another show that night.

On walls all around the city, the rest of the country too, there was meanwhile a large poster ad for a make of blue jeans called Jesus Jeans, showing a girl's sexy rear from waist to knees, the lower half bulging lusciously below a tight pair of jeans briefs, as brief as they could be and still go under the crotch. The caption is close enough to Christ's exhortation, whether in our Bible or the Vulgate, to be taken for it: "Chi mi ama mi segua. He who loves me, let him follow me." The model was a twenty-three-year-old American named Donna Jordan. Big protests, among others from the small Italian Women's Lib group who said the ad exploited women, but the company's sales had quadrupled; the president explained the name was chosen because of the popularity of the Jesus freak movement. This brings up a prudery note, or rather two. Since this book was written the double Dr. Strom ads noted in the "Fountains" chapter, regarding venereal disease, have all been taken down, as have all the urinals where they mainly appeared; there is now only one Dr. Strom, who advertises only on the back of the telephone book, as treating varicose veins, and there is more urine on walls.

Good Friday note. On that evening died a spendthrift wastrel and alcoholic, aged thirty-seven, named Marzio Ciano, grandson of Mussolini. Reported to have thought the Duce was right to have his son-in-law and Foreign Minister Galeazzo Ciano, this man's father, executed, shortly before getting bumped off and strung up himself by the partisans in the north, at the end of World War II. A high-life version of the skid-row ending, and seedy footnote to a seedier chunk of history.

The church of S. Prassede, another blessing from that hero of the history or architecture Pope Pasquale I — in 822, on much older foundations, somewhat impurified by subsequent jobs — was three-quarters empty on Holy Saturday night, one of its few occasions of functioning splendor in the year. Only a few intellectuals strayed in before the service to admire the beautifully illuminated mosaics of the S. Zeno chapel, also Pasquale's project and called the most important Byzantine monument in Rome. The candle-lighting ceremony out in the courtyard, the return to the darkened church, the smile of the busy old woman providing everyone with a candle and making sure each was properly lit, seemed to promise the only truly moving event of the week. It failed. Nuns from the adjoining convent made up half the sparse congregation, and except among them there cannot have been anyone under fifty. After the fine beginning, and excitement of the mosaics before that, a dead weight fell; it seemed the clergy in charge, perhaps up through layer after layer of hierarchy, were suffering from something like stomachache, knowing they had lost their grip. The absence of anyone young somehow grew by the minute, into a positive force of deadlines. The priest droned on and on, in Italian not Latin, that daring concession to the times, about the crossing of the Red Sea. The relevance, which is there, didn't come across, and the record was stuck; there seemed to be no way of shaking off the Egyptians "e i loro cavalli e i loro cavalieri." A dozen of nuns, of no vocal accomplishment, moved into a huddle and served as choir when the time came, more pathetic for the triumph of art, along with that of Christ, on the mosaic arch over their heads, that too of the ninth century. Not that parochial efforts aren't often the most affecting, when they are the best that can be done, but for the Church in Rome with its vast treasure and other resources to permit such a poorhouse performance in one of its most venerable churches, indeed the most, was peculiar. It seemed that Christ would not bother to rise from the tomb among such doldrums. It was reported that the service at Saint Peter's the same evening was about as spiritless.

Easter dawned nevertheless, the rain held off through the morning, hundreds of buses had their route numbers changed to the ones for Saint Peter's, where as the rest of the world observed on TV the service was held outside, with altar, choir, and notables on the top landing, and the crowd instead of watching from home got itself watched milling about, when not applauding or crossing itself, though there was not much of that, in the square. The same six languages, in alternation this time so as not to try people's patience or run over the airwave schedule, were used for the Scripture readings, but at the end of his short homily from the upstairs balcony the pope said "Happy Easter" in about twenty, including Vietnamese. That was touching; it is nice to feel friendly with humankind far away when not all samples close by are at their best. One from this country, foul-smelling and filthy in mane and beard, was slumped on the cobblestones against a fountain basin, stoned, back to the altar and fly open, and there were others not far from that state. On such as these, Jesus looked with love and charity, so we are told. There were none of the old cries of "Viva il Papa!" perhaps partly because too many there were foreigners and the million cars had left Rome. Nobody seemed overcome with enthusiasm, or particularly let down either. It had been something to do, someplace to go; Easter would be just another Sunday otherwise.

As Holy Year would be just another year. A key difference in that is bound to be in the age level of those present, once participants, now with few exceptions merely spectators. Thousands of foreign students were in Rome for their Easter vacations and went to the big shows; there is no sign that the doings throughout 1975 will draw many but the middle-aged and up, from anywhere in the world.

Padre Pio, of whose reputed stigmata and popularity as faith healer the Church was so leery in 1950, had long since died, but his name was more in evidence than ever in his lifetime. It was in large type on posters everywhere, not as big as for the offending blue jeans but far more numerous, announcing a documentary movie about him. Another movie was bringing good business to several theaters at once, inspiring a lone cry of dissent two feet high in white paint on a wall, like a political slogan: CRISTO SÌ, SUPERSTAR NO!

PART I

THE CAMPIDOGLIO

$\mathcal{T}$HE FIRST THING ABOUT THE Campidoglio, aside from what it is, is the stairs.

Long flights of stairs are always beautiful, and here there are two, side by side, diverging by an odd little angle and with a narrow third one, covered by an arbor and absurdly steep, going up between them with an air of being useful and significant, as if there were no other way of getting up the hill. It is the air of almost everything in Rome. The left-hand stairs have 124 steps and are not quite in line with the facade at the top, the bare brown one, stuck on like a middle-western storefront, of the church of Santa Maria in Aracoeli. This is the highest point, the *arx*, where Juno sat, facing the other way however, and the stairs have a good holy look of an impossible proposition, though in fact there is an easy way into the church in back. The others, more lenient and not spiritual at all, bring you to the Campidoglio.

It is the center, the starting point — a very real center in various ways, and you can get your bearings from there, as you would climb the tallest tree to look over a thick dangerous landscape. Michelangelo made what is there now, the architecture that is; the Forum, that lovely lake of time, lies over in back; the Corso, another sort of business altogether, strikes away from the city's great white latter-day vanity, the Victor Emmanuel Monument, which you are in the lee of. It all, speaking of time too, arranges itself most tidily from here.

People used to come jogging down from the north by the post, firm in their travel aches and classical education, and at a certain turn the horses pulled up and the postilion cried "Ecco Roma!" and everyone tumbled out to see. They were following Hannibal's route more or less, and there at last it would be, oh, at last! — the Dome anyway and a few other long-known shapes over the terrifying teacup panorama. Happy people, having the whole depth and wonder of a destination borne in on them so for a moment.

Or the ones of long before, say in the sixth century, when the place was supposed to be a shambles and certainly its memory and half its population were gone, and even so they fell down and adored it, perhaps even literally, not having known among other things that a city could be so beautiful. Or the other kind, later, reformers, flagellants, big angry Luther running away like mad, trying to shake the evil dust from their feet and the laughter and murder and riches from their more delicate minds: wicked, wicked Rome, how it had betrayed them; but the dust would never be shaken till they died.

Or consider Dickens, Dr. Arnold, the English ladies Augustus Hare tells you about bargaining for lace at a certain corner of the ghetto; dark Hawthorne breathing in crime along the dark palace walls; and the English, French, German, American painters all trooping out boyishly in carriages for their annual picnic and mock pageant across the campagna. How knowing it all was, the thrill, the attachment, the indignation, the Protestant malaise. Here Caesar fell, they said to themselves, holding his toga close for modesty; here splashed the blood of the martyrs, and the captive kings walked beneath the yoke; here or there the sunset is most peculiarly Roman — they knew what they were talking about; and

Stendhal could be content for days to keep coming on still another canvas by "le divin Guercin." It is delightful to think of them all.

Now the tourist or student or wandering intellectual, the poor seeker after something or other, comes in like a wisp of fog in a fog bank, with his angst and his foggy modern eye, and there are not many words that can help him even a little to find his identity and his way; history, surrealism, faith. The *angst* is going to get a lot worse; the eye, if he stays long enough, will be pried open week by week as if every lash had been glued down; and meanwhile there are the mess and the blazing sun, the incongruities, the too-muchness of everything. The historian Taine said that really to profit from Rome you would have to be always in a gay mood, "or at least a healthy one"; he would not have thought of using the words nowadays.

Ecco Roma indeed . . . But still, in a way, there it is. Something, after all, is being presented to the glazed eyeball and paralyzed sense of the worrying traveler, who came most often not looking for Rome at all but for love; whose distress about national responsibilities is painfully mixed up with anxiety over his baggage.

He sees a city of bells and hills and walls (walls for defense, Servian, Aurelian, and Vatican, it was not often an open city; and heavy bars across the lower windows of the house walls, against all manner of crime); of many trees nordic and tropical together, pine, ilex, and palm, and water and a disturbing depth of shadows; of acres of ruins, some handsome, some shabby lumps and dumps of useless masonry, sprinkled through acres of howling modernity — an impossible compounding of time, in which no century has respect for any other and all hit you in a jumble at every turn; of roaring motors and other dreadful noises, where some roaring festa with fireworks is always going on; whose churches are junk shops of idolatrous bric-a-brac; which calls on your awe and is absolutely lacking in any itself; where spaces open out or close up before you suddenly as in dreams, and a tormenting dreamlike sexual gaiety seems to rise you cannot tell how from the streets; a place of no grandeur whatever of any kind you expected, ravaged by fascist vulgarities; in which the president's, until 1945 the royal,

palace looks from the outside like an old tobacco barn, and everything you came to revere turns up in a setting as of some huge
practical joke; a place beautiful at certain points, at certain moments, but closed to you, repellent, where you are always being reminded of something, you cannot tell what, but it is like the fear of
falling down a deep well.

It is too much. It is a place, beneath all its obvious racket, of
whispers and secrets, so various and insidious that to be open to
them can be the beginning of madness, and in fact it does induce
several kinds of aberration in foreigners. One you can detect behind those chilling phrases "It's not in my field," "It's not in my period," which are heard here more than in any other city. In every
academy and rooming house there are one or two of these tragic
wrecks, alcoholics of the single object; the numismatist, the fonto-
maniac, the expert on neoclassic doorknobs, the Mithraphile, the
lifelong annotator of a medieval manuscript, or of the single
Roman painting by an obscure English Romantic, the man who
tried to know the name of everything in the Forum; they are
drawn, fatally, from all over the world, or turned into this after
they came, and many would rather die than be dislodged. But they
are no worse off than most of the foreign visitors these days.

They swirl in herds through the Vatican Museums, around the
Colosseum — you would not think, as Dante said, that there
could be so many; or sit in bars for two weeks "getting the feel of
the place"; or drag about in a dim melancholy of expectation and
loneliness, often complicated by Roman stomach trouble; or take
up with the variety of little sad fifth-rate adventurers always available along the Via Veneto, especially for homosexuals, because
the city has become as much a world magnet in that respect as for
Catholic converts or illuminated manuscript worms.

There are painters again now too, lots of them, mostly Americans, and writers. For a whole generation, practically speaking
from 1914 to 1945, Rome ceased to exist for them; some foreign
scholars could stand the fascist dictatorship, or profit from it, but
for artists it was not inviting, nor a good idea; there was the case of
Ezra Pound, one of the most interesting examples of mental risk

in our century. Then suddenly the gates were open again and they came flocking back in with love and gratitude and pent-up need of this above all cities, and it was all brand-new, as if it had never been heard of before, but it is not like a hundred years ago nor even like the beginning of this century. There is no international picnic, and not much painting or writing either, at least for the first two or three years.

Rome, being one continuity, requires wholeness, and instills it; we bring to it in ideas disgust, in feelings failure, in art something like a splintered windshield; so we are both enthralled and for a long time in nearly mortal conflict with it.

They also call it Hollywood on the Tiber; fake ruins get thrown up around the real ones; there are tremendous cocktail parties.

The city has its own language in time, its own vocabulary for the eye, for which nothing else was any preparation; no other place was so difficult, performed under the slow action of your eyes such transmutations. So the ordinary traveler runs off in relief to Florence, to the single statement, the single moment of time, the charming unity of somewhat prisonlike architecture, and is aware later of having retained from his whizz tour of Rome some stirring around the heart; those images, huge, often grotesque, were what he had been looking for, only it would have taken so long. . . . Those who stay in Rome, where nothing is single or simple and the aesthetic experience is always subordinate to something else, unless they are too handicapped to start with, begin to change: an awful spectacle, which can go on for years, as though some queer yeast were working on an elephant.

On the plastic side it is fairly easy — a slow progression of taste, whatever one started with, usually leading up to a stage of having no taste at all. If anyone tells you he likes the Palace of Justice, up the Tiber from the Castel Sant'Angelo, you know he has just arrived in town and is naturally benighted, or is the opposite and has been there three years. But that is only part of it.

The rest is an expansion in time, such as you experience also in the petrified forests of America, only here it is more intimate and so more dangerous, like a slow journeying downward through water. There is a peculiar power in stones; you know it even from a little stone picked up on the seashore, with the ancient imprint of a starfish on it. It may happen to you to sit by a Roman fountain and find the starfish Nero crawling on your skin; it goes under, spreads in your veins, and begins to breathe with your breath; and that is only one of them. There will be strange distensions of your moral sense, your opinions on everything become unreliable. Rome is everybody's memory, as it was a hundred or a thousand years ago; the thing is to find a way into it.

You could start anywhere, it really doesn't matter, you will see so little anyway:

In the air, from which you get no idea of any "seven hills" (the number in any case has been juggled considerably: one hill consists entirely of ancient potsherds, another was carted away to make room for an emperor's forum, three of the original seven are now humped together as one) but you do see a few ups and downs, and the mountains high all around, beautifully streaked with snow in winter, of which you will always be conscious later as of the sea and its ship sounds around Manhattan; you see them from any rise, and along the Tiber, and down at the end of many long streets, as if it were a backdrop in a photographer's booth. They give the city a transitory look, these mountains; it seems that it could have grown up anywhere among them, or could be moved quite easily, but that is counteracted a little by the broken lines of the old aqueducts, not romantic at all from up there, coming in across the flat country; coming much farther than you would ever think from below, to blend with sections of the brick Aurelian wall right in the busiest tangle of the city. They are of course distinctly Roman, so are the eccentric color and course of the Tiber, and the fury of the little figures you see twitching about on the football (soccer) fields, but nothing is nearly as lovely or permanent-looking in this view as the railroad tracks: a cool graph of somewhat insane lines with their ends, in a sudden reversion to control, all coming sidelong together like a boxful of pencils.

You have a sense of being yourself in control of the situation from the air. Nothing looks very old; or rather great time with all its human reference becomes an abstraction and you can grasp it without much trouble, as an aviator could destroy the place without much sorrow; which only makes it more crushing when the enormity of the specific begins breaking over you, down below.

Or you could come in on those tracks, no clean geometry but whether in the compartment or the anarchically packed aisle a sausage machine of communications among strangers, of egos, curiosities, irritations, longings, and belongings caught in the moment of displacement, at the end of which the returning Roman, bête noire of your trip, salutes you with true princely graciousness just as in the days of the post chaise, becomes for a second your host, before removing himself from the little steaming wreckage, just then, of your life; and throw yourself the next morning on the big schoolbook things, Colosseum, Moses, Saint Peter's, etc.

Or in your impossible state take in the full impossibleness of Rome right there, moving from what has become, after long dissension, a very handsome modern railroad station, to Piazza Esedra: a place of late-nineteenth-century arcades (the Turin phase of the city) centering in that "horrible" fin-de-siècle fountain, set between the sprawling old hulk of the Baths of Diocletian and the commercial riot and rubbish of the Via Nazionale. In summer an all-girls' orchestra plays with demon exuberance at the swollen piazza café — there is this pushing out and out, a jungle florescence, all over the city in warm weather, everything has too much energy for its space; and at night, oblivious of the hell of neon that bursts forth along the Via Nazionale, the sexy and equally energetic fountain, with its naked cancan ladies and marine monsters, is lit up as if it were the most sacred pride of the city.

Or be genteel, jump off into one of those pleasant old watercolors of Rome, as in the little piazza called the Mouth of Truth after the big marble face of the sun in the church portico, whose mouth was supposed to snap shut if you put your hand in it and told a lie, but which was perhaps an ancient sewer lid; both could be true, and it is nice to think of such massive pieces of sculpture having that double function here and there in the streets. Everybody likes this spot; it is so comforting, so charmingly pure and right. The two little ancient postcard temples, the round and the rectangular, are as fine as in the pictures, the fountain gives a pensive air, and the church of Santa Maria in Cosmedin, also little, is of the "right" centuries: fourth to twelfth, nothing fancy or voluptuous. The modern or Bauhaus eye and the cozy sense are jointly satisfied; Rome is possible.

Yet after all it is not so tame; something, you see as you look back, has gotten jiggled in the old watercolor, as if you had looked at it through moving water; something is wrong. The little temples are angry. Up the sterile sun-cruel avenue the fascists made here, past their office buildings like houses for geneticide, the bits and columns of three other temples, holding in their Cerberus bite the tiny and otherwise nondescript church of San Nicola in Carcere, are something more than picturesque. You have to be careful, time can snap shut on your hand; against a wall, beyond the long, long shadow of the traffic cop, an obscene shrouded shape has risen, painted years ago by Chirico.

Or sit, as foreigners do, hoping to see movie stars, on tree-lined Via Veneto, site of the big hotels, the American Embassy, and the most elaborate arrangement of monks' bones anywhere; which set out to be Rome's climbing vinelike version of the Champs-Elysées and has turned instead into a street of shady deals and sun-back dresses; beyond the top of which, just outside those Aurelian walls you saw from the sky, the riding track in the Borghese gardens, called the *galoppatoio*, is strewn every morning with contraceptives. Sadness, ignoble disappointment, everything that is a little stale or tarnished stalk this so-called elegant street; something is wrong; Rome's real elegance was never on parade.

Or go up on the Janiculum thick with Garibaldiana — it is still a surprise, this Italy — where Lars Porsena had his camp and Cleopatra her villa, where the house-size Fontana Paola shows the baroque at its most loving and serene and the clarity of Roman light plays its most astounding tricks, and read the dirty and other scribblings on the lighthouse. "When graffiti are found in large numbers in one and the same place they gain the importance of a historical document" (Lanciani, 1891). The city, wonderfully flushed at twilight, is laid out beneath you in a perfection of worked enamel, a Cellini affair only the pieces live, the mountains with their winter snow might move; or as Dr. Arnold wrote of a neighboring height: "One may safely say that the world cannot contain many views of such mingled beauty and interest as this."

Another approach is through the keyhole of the Knights of Malta, on that religious hill, the Aventine. The piazza, designed by Piranesi, more like a little landscaped plateau, has a dead-end or Tibetan feeling well suited to the well-known property of the keyhole, which is to present, in miniature at the end of a telescope of pleached trees, the Dome. It is good Easter-egg magic, always a hit, and for good reason; the trickery is basic. The Dome, which has a way of following you around the town, proclaiming Michelangelo and the center of the world — whatever you think, that is what it proclaims — happens not to be visible from anywhere else on that street, and looks, through the keyhole, more like an image abstracted from the real thing and placed there by some feat of physics, so that you are surprised not to find some other basilica in the second keyhole in the same door. It is both real and not real, there and not there; and so an object in space clearly illustrates for you the trickery of all Rome, which has to do, as Pirandello was trying to say, with time.

You could start the long journey under the Dome too, or up in its lantern, but that is not wise. Better to see it from everywhere else first, in the various sizes and aspects it assumes: sentimentally in the best sense, across Corot's basin under the pines, looming like the giant at the top of the beanstalk at a certain turn of the river, small and with the late sun striking so fiercely through its windows, the top will be only a black shell sitting in the air; almost everywhere except in the middle-class district of Prati, one of the nearest to it. That quarter was designed in the last century by the Masons, who performed the odd stunt of blocking the view of Saint Peter's from all but a single street in the whole section; it was not the center of *their* world and they put real genius into ignoring it.

Any of these will do; the entrance to Rome is no longer a matter of geography. It is a place secret, sensuous, oblique, a poem

and to be known as a poem; a vast untidiness peopled with characters and symbols so profound they join the imagery of your own
dreams, whose grandeur also is of dreams, never of statements or
avenues; from which the hurrying determined mind takes nothing
but its own agenda, while the fearful logic and synthesis that were
there escape like a lion from the zoo.

But the Campidoglio is at least in the middle. It is also where
the most things happened over the longest time, and can give you
the most solid example of that four-dimensional art form that goes
by the name of the Eternal or even the Holy City.

It is true you are spared the baroque just here, and at a certain
moment a large part of the city suddenly wore that new expression, but if you brood a while on what does appear on this small
hilltop you will be pretty far over into the baroque as a way of
thinking, if not out the other side. The scorn of neatness, the deep
fantasy of juxtaposition are there, beyond the power of any poet or
period; nobody could be so ruthless. The author of this creation is
time, in collaboration with aesthetic judgment and energy, which
has smashed and transgressed in one way or another at every point
as art always does, until the fine and the atrocious are a joint
essence of the one always contemporary work, and the eye of the
beholder loses all independence from memory, which makes it
hard on us in these days who lack both memory and eye. The
humor of it too is beyond any talent; Parisian DaDa would have
made no ripple here. The combinations of cars around town, from
Fiat "little mice" that you could carry in a pinch, to the Vatican or
Diplomatic Corps Cadillacs, would look absurd anywhere else
but in Rome only fall in with the buildings and statues, and history as well; and that is only the matter of scale.

Not that the Campidoglio is all so funny; the parts are not.
Michelangelo's square, subtly enlarged by the trapezoid angle of
the side palaces and the views back from their ends, is the most ra-
tional in the city, a strong thrust, up through the night imagery, of
grace and mastery of form, as the Dome is or that other creation
partly from the same mind, although a mere private house, the
Palazzo Farnese. The proportions are exquisite, and to scale with

the human body; the three facades with their balustrades and statues — crochetwork of the aging Renaissance — the two side ones with their porticoes and the somewhat insincere elegance of their upper window columns, the Senators' Palace at the back presiding by reason of its clock tower and handsome double stairs, are a text of unity, a single, and considering the actual size, oddly spacious experience. But the larger design is something else; shabbiness, wreckage, unreason will pour in on you in a moment.

This gracious symmetry is crouched under the white cliffs of the Victor Emmanuel Monument, which ignored Michelangelo as he in his time ignored the brown naked medieval majesty of Aracoeli, a dress-pattern shape and one of the most poignant surfaces in the city, now wedged between the two. Not that anyone stops revering it for that, nor minds its having been a town hall as well as church for quite a few centuries; the civic and the supernatural never could stay separate on these hills, they were always rolling back into one; the church was named for an apocryphal tale conveniently linking Augustus with the coming of Christ, the stairs, from an ancient temple, were put up here for penance purposes to stop the plague of 1348, the most prominent of the miracle-working bambini is still there and still miraculous. These matters, along with the beauty of the facade, survive quite well in the lee of the monument — a confectioner's typewriter, some call it; and down in back there was always the Forum, a quarry and cow pasture, lazily creating its own derangement of the senses.

Among the characters present there is the same mutual obliviousness in everything: role, genre, epoch, scale, materials.

The central one, and so the Dome to the contrary the center of all Rome, is Marcus Aurelius on his famous plump-bellied bronze horse, whose forelock was going to sing to announce the end of the world, and may still: a statue described by a fascist-era guidebook as having had "a tremendous influence on all of modern art." Probably it did have quite an influence on other equestrian statues as long as the genre lasted. It is modest and grave and powerful, decent in scale and spirit; the horse, always a peculiar animal, is all fire and strength and seems restrained more by his own

sense of statecraft than by the rider, who in any case has no stir-
rups and is otherwise occupied, his right hand, palm downward,
being extended in a gesture that is of both command and benedic-
tion. If one should want to be so commanded or blessed, and aside
from the awkwardness of all official art, aside too from certain
reservations in one's feeling about this particular emperor, and the
fact that there was originally a bronze barbarian under the horse's
raised front hoof, this would be very fine. Anyway it is not hysterical; the father-ruler, you would say, had been caught here in his
last really appropriate moment, eighteen hundred years ago; at
least he could be nobly portrayed; and actually the person of the
father is not important in this case. The statue is of the blessing
and dignity of Roman Law, sunk so deep, both sculptor and model
can render it as their own most native truth.

This steed, however, stands in peaceful conjunction with two
others of a different condition and breed altogether. They are of
marble, and are there with their trainers the heavenly twins
Castor and Pollux, cracked, nicked, enormous, and beautiful at
the top of the Campidoglio stairs; heroic statuary borrowed from
an age Rome never knew, but the borrowings go deep; the
horses, like the centaurs and marine ones scattered all over the
city, are to be taken as literally as the emperor's or Garibaldi's up
on the Janiculum.

These are the *other* twins, the miracle-workers, with the
strength and wonder of the unknown in them, complement to Romulus and Remus. It is true there is something extrahuman in any
case, aside from the wolf in this notion of twins; the nation was
plainly announcing from the start that it was not interested in personality; but the indigenous pair, however unnatural, have only an
indirect relation to the supernatural. They are all flesh and blood,
strengthened with wolf milk and much oftener unpleasant than
not, whether in the way of virtue or vice. Roman Law or not, they
belong to the dark; in general one thinks of the beginning and end
of Rome's old power as pictures of a scary night, full of the terrors
of the fighting first, and more fighting and another kind of terror
afterward. But the Dioscuri stream with light like the saints.

That is the way they stand here by the stairs, and the way one sees them appearing out of nowhere to win the great Battle of Lake Regillus against the Latins and Etruscans, in 496 B.C. There is none of the later nervous glory of the empire in that story; it is all comfort and radiance, as though a pair of angels had appeared to push George Washington across the Delaware. A few minutes after the victory they were seen far away in the Roman Forum, showing signs of their great exertion but still, one imagines, walking in a golden light, with no expression on their faces — they never look at each other or at anyone, and are so beautiful you would not want them to; then they water their horses at a certain nymph's spring that is still there, which is appealing too, you would not suppose that they would need to, and quietly vanish.

There is no such lovely beneficence on the other side. The faces of the Roman twins are far from inexpressive, and where they come in things are usually grim, beginning with Romulus killing Remus for jumping over his wall. The illuminating thing is that Law, or the highest social reason, could emerge through these extravagances. The country is always in danger; there is a premium on psychological monstrosity, not always exempt from plain nastiness; and how new the tales of it sound now, as if some savage genius had just thought them up, with the dark circle of the unknown enemy always pressing close around. Consider them: Horatius at the bridge; Mucius Scaevola around the same time burning his hand off in Lars Porsena's camp; Virgilius stabbing his daughter, and dry-eyed Brutus, five hundred years before Caesar's friend, witnessing the execution of his sons; the mother of the Gracchi; M. Curtius leaping with his horse into the abyss in the Forum because Rome's dearest possession must be sacrificed to close it; and during the empire, in a time of famine, a lady could pull a stranded grain ship off a sandbank in the Tiber by tying a string to it and saying "Follow me if I am chaste." Human nature has never been so satirized.

There is the dark episode of the Gauls and the cackling geese too, which occurred in the citadel around the corner from the Campidoglio. That time the country was saved by a man named

Marcus Manlius, who as a result of political intrigue was ruined shortly afterward, like many national heroes before and after him. He was not executed just on this spot, because it was thought better in his case to do it out of sight of the citadel he had saved; however, there is still a live wolf there in a cage. The famous snarling Etruscan one, with a pair of Renaissance babies added beneath its udders, is in the museum on your left.

The collage continues in the courtyard of the right-hand palace, called the Conservators', where the central piece is a broken-off head of Constantine as big as a wine barrel, but that was normal. Augustus, who passed for frugal, had a bronze statue of himself 50 feet high in a reading room on the Palatine; one of Nero was twice that tall, the head measuring 6 feet; the Emperor Gallienus is said to have planned one of himself as the sun on the Esquiline, to be 219 feet tall or twice the height of Trajan's Column, which marks the height of the hill that was removed from there. Here there are other parts of the body or a body the same size lying around, a foot, a section of forearm; there has been a trunk murder between giants only there are two right hands, the forefingers pointing up, to what? — to something in the lucidity of that sky like a child's blue eye, theology or the glory of Rome or the memory of the marble murder, never to be recaptured though the fingers point till the next ice age. There is also a not quite typical scavenger's exhibit around the walls, the soil of Rome being stocked to a great depth with words, bits of architecture and sculptured limbs, tombstones and all the other compost of civilized time, for which there continues to be a brisk black market.

As for hawk-nosed Constantine, official bringer-in of Christianity, he may have been what the time required but it is hard to think of his great battle at the Ponte Milvio as instituting anything one would have cared to side with right away. A rather basic sentimentality is imperiled by this huge hatchet face; but that is Rome too, the danger is equal in politics, in art, in love. His lady mother Saint Helena never strikes one as very attractive either, with all her busy pilfering of holy objects including a whole flight of marble stairs from Jerusalem. It was in the tradition; Rome, never creative in mysteries, had come by most of her holinesses the same way, most notably the black rock or Great Mother, which Italy has never since been able to do without. Still, there is a particular note of the ruthless grabber in this other performance, whereby the blood of martyrs was both ridiculed and brought to serve its purpose, and the astral horsetamers, children of a swan, set out on their long dim way to changing their names and becoming really saints. For the time being, anyway, it was traumatic; nobody for a long time after the baptism of Constantine seems to have remembered anything that had happened before.

They were not even very clear about him. The bronze Marcus Aurelius outside was preserved all through the Middle Ages only because it was mistaken for Constantine, whose features would seem hard to forget, and there is something of the agony of the amnesiac in the legend about it, one of several of the kind concerning Rome, all with the same pathological anguish and terror in them. Its gilding, of which you can see a little now, was slowly returning, and it was when it was all there that the horse's forelock, which does look like a perching bird, would sing, and then would be the Last Judgment.

But memory did return, in its own good time; the monks and the river gods between them had been looking after it.

They are there too, those guardian rivers, as they are everywhere in the city, along with the tritons and obelisks and fountains and all the mythical horses, half human, or half fish, that are the poem's deepest imagery. You walk close to your dreams, and that is the sexual gaiety that rises from the streets. If all the crosses in this Holy City disappeared overnight it would hardly be noticeable, but if the obelisks or the river gods were gone it would be as if the city had had a frontal lobotomy, everyone would know that its deepest nature had been interfered with in some way.

The most famous of the three rivers here is the one in the court of the Capitoline Museum, called Marforio from the street where he used to be. He is reclining like an ancient Roman at a banquet as all rivers do, fat and lazy and with not a split but a fine full double personality. He is water, and that is Rome's element, and he is, or was, a wit, and that is Rome's character. Even now you hear him spoken of with special affection for having been involved, together with the Foot and some other statues, in the dangerous satirical dialogues started in the sixteenth century by the tailor Pasquin, who pasted the first lampoons on the lump of ancient sculpture since named for him; the *barbari* and *Barberini* pun first appeared there, one of thousands; there were not many popes, cardinals, or rulers generally who escaped, any more than they do now, but Marforio at least was moved up to the capitol to keep him quiet, as quiet as a river can be. His role, or rather both his roles, would have had to be more secretive anyway under fascism; now the political one has been taken over in part by the radio. *Moritur et ridet*, as some tourist said of the Roman people ages ago; they would laugh on their deathbeds.

There is another crucial figure here, a human, and speaking only of the visible ones. The rest are the long community of Rome in all its time, the one enduring present in which one moves, and which so strangely annihilates geography. Here or in the bald Mamertine prisons below or anywhere, the map on which you know yourself situated is rarely of Europe, you feel outside of that, but of centuries, and distances are in time; something that only running water can convey or make bearable, hence the fountains of Rome. But there is another character in the actual Campidoglio cast, of bronze, in medieval dress and less than life size, standing halfway down between the two flights of stairs, with the useless little third one beside him.

This is poor crazy Cola di Rienzo, the Tribunus Augustus, Knight of the Holy Ghost, and so on — there was no end to the titles he gave himself — in whom toward the end of the second dreadful night the nostalgia for light and the anguish of confused memory flared up most pathetically. Yet he was not entirely crazy; the yearning was so extreme, many could believe in him; even Petrarch, who had recently been crowned with laurel here in the square that preceded Michelangelo's, had thought for a while that this inspired man of the people, in restoring Rome's grandeur and authority, would save more than the country; it seemed the human

mind itself must be thin without that center. How the idea got per-verted in this instance is beautifully told by the historian Gre-gorovius, who only made the mistake, natural in the nineteenth century, of assuming that such weird resurrections had stopped with the fourteenth.

Marcus Aurelius and his horse were not here then. The statue, still thought to be of Constantine, stood in front of the half-ruined Lateran at the time, and when Cola, having bathed for mystical purposes in the font where Constantine was baptized, had himself knighted in the basilica on the old pagan festival of August 1 (Christianized) the people celebrated with a huge banquet out-side and the horse, instead of announcing the end of the world, was made to pour wine and water from its nostrils, while Cola conferred the blessing of Rome on the universe. The Roman people, the old SPQR as you can read it on all the sewer lids and urinals now, were going to run the world again, though at the mo-ment their monuments were fortresses, the roofs of most of their churches had fallen in, the pope was in Avignon, and the city of Florence among others had no intention of being run by them. Nevertheless they cheered while he had himself crowned with six mystical wreaths, then pointing a sword in three directions in the air cried three times, "This is mine!"

The scene occurred in 1347, or the year before the Aracoeli stairs were put up to stop the plague, though one version is that they were erected the year before and he was the first to walk up them. At any rate he was probably the first to roll down them without his head, having been literally torn to pieces on the Campidoglio. That was after seven years' exile and a triumphant comeback of two months, and it happened to the shout, as terrible as the war cries of the barons, of "Popolo! Popolo!" — the same who had drunk from the horse's nostrils, and who would die laughing; after which they left him hanging headless for two days outside the church of San Marcello on the Corso.

The pedestal of his small statue is covered with another of those assortments of ancient bric-a-brac plastered in every which way, perhaps by accident, through some workman's caprice, in imitation of thousands of house and garden walls in the city, and perhaps not; they would not have done it to a statue of Augustus, but then if Cola had not reminded them for a little while of Augustus there would not be any statue of him at all, and the mad little work of decoration seems touching here. But it is the right hand that is remarkable. It is extended, not like the emperor's in the piazza above but all the way, high and with the palm turned up and the rapt fingers wildly spread, and from each fingertip the man's visionary will seems to issue like a piercing scream, as though his volition alone would be a crowbar to move both heaven and the accumulated happenings of a thousand disjointed years.

The collection of right hands on the Campidoglio is altogether quite remarkable. There is this, and the sober, vastly controlling one of Marcus Aurelius or Roman Law, and in the courtyard opposite Marforio the two white right fists, with their giant enigmatic forefingers pointing up into eternity.

The Victor Emmanuel Monument, surmounted by allegorical chariots, which was inaugurated in 1911 and had taken twenty-six years to build, is of Brescia marble known for its cold and stupefying whiteness; you can judge by comparing it, as rock, with the Dioscuri. However if that or the Colosseum had to be bombed it might be hard for a second to decide; at least it has a peculiarly vitalizing effect on the Forum and Michelangelo; not that a good piece of modern architecture would not do the same thing much better or that there is really any reason not to tear the thing down, except that it is called the Altar of the Country and many Italians like it.

Another important point about the Campidoglio is not to see it when the sun is too high; the best time is early in the morning, though in winter there is more leeway. The piazza of the Quirinal on the other hand, where the second pair of Dioscuri are, in front of the barnlike president's or royal palace, comes into its color and its own lyrical majesty, so unlike what anyone comes looking for, suddenly in the late afternoon. Either of them, and even more the Forum, seen in the high flat hours, can put you in a far from gay or healthy mood. The composition disintegrates, the stones are dead, you and a million lizards move in a sun-split devastation where once, you cannot remember how long ago, there had been the good green of memory and Rome; it is all over forever; it was finished a million years ago. Actually the city is only having its daily nap and in a few hours, winter or summer, will be swelling every street with the crush and clamor of its daily promenade.

FOUNTAINS

YOU WALK CLOSE TO your dreams. Sometimes it seems that these pulsing crowds, with their daily and yearly rhythms established so long ago none of it has to be decided anymore, with their elbows and knees and souls and buttocks touching and rubbing and everybody most pleased and agreeable when it is like that, have fish tails or horses' behinds like the characters of the fountains. For the Anglo-Saxon mind, ruled by conscience and the romantic, rigid in its privacies, everything here is shocking — an endless revelation and immersion; this is the vocabulary of our sleep; and the key image is always water.

That is the great assault of Rome, and it is total and terrible. It is really strange that foreigners of the polite centuries always used to wax so romantic about the fountains of Rome, and the music supposed to represent them was such as any young girl could listen to. The truth is, they are extremely indecent, in various ways. Their number is indecent, much as the lives of the Caesars were; common reason expires here; it is of their nature too to make those lives quite ordinary, nothing surprises you beside them. Their settings are apt to be extravagant; they can have sprung up anywhere, be tacked anywhere on the sides of buildings or are themselves a whole house wall; and their details have the candid, smiling sadism of dreams. But the worst is the life around them, and their part in it. They are not only memory, or the living singleness of time, though they are that too and the city would have fallen apart under the weight of its past a long time ago without them; this is easy to see; you notice at once when there is a drought and the fountains become quiet and stale, or empty, how old everything begins to look. But there is another unity or community within every single moment to which they are essential, and that is where the real outrage comes.

The romantic, the idealist, the tender-minded of any vein dies a thousand deaths in these fountains; their every dolphin is his nemesis.

The very genius spent on them makes them shocking. They are not objets d'art held off from life and treated with respect as they would be anywhere else; there is a closeness, an imminence of touch around them that nothing in our life has except dreams and sex, whence the awful burden on those. They are always being drunk from and splashed in and sat on, everybody dips into them as into his own private memory and quite often they have all kinds of rubbish in their lovely basins, because although the street cleaners of Rome are many and hardworking they cannot be everywhere at once.

The churches likewise; it is all physical and close; God is not up in any Gothic shadows but to be touched and smelled and fondled, reached into up to the armpit. The Anglo-Saxon, hunting everywhere for French cathedrals, feels his mind threatened like a lump of sugar in a cup of tea.

The spaces are shocking. They are close too, and give no warnings, so that suddenly the Pantheon or the huge volutes of Sant'Ignazio are crowding right over you; you are not allowed to stand off, it seems you are not allowed to admire at all; it is as though a giant mother were squashing you to her breast. Besides those freakish squares and the narrow streets around them, most vividly in the old quarters, Trastevere and all the part between the Corso and the Tiber, do not constitute an *outside* in our sense, but a great rich withinness, an interior, and running water is its open fire. Even a tourist can tell in a Roman street that he is in something and not outside of something as he would be in most cities. In Rome to go out is to go home.

There are no sidewalks in these sections. The walls rise from the cobbles as from lagoons, only people are out all along them, under the laundry that is a drastic exposure in itself, more than for any Kinsey or Gallup, and unless they are playing football they are most often mending something. That is one of three occupations you see anywhere in Europe that are no longer known in America: people walk, they carry, and they mend. Not only women; men are mending too, in thousands of dark bicycle and mattress shops and tiny individual foundries opening on to the same streets, and which may be the family's windowless kitchen and bedroom as well. What makes these streets Roman, and not those of any old European city, is the demonic energy that goes into everything, and the divine disregard for any other form of life, especially in the football players; also an element of miracle in the way the motor-cycles and other traffic get through, shooting straight from hell, without anyone's changing his expression or pace or direction at all. If a Roman does have to move an inch for your car he looks at you like an affronted emperor, but on the whole American cars are objects of as pure a passion as Romans are capable of. "Oh, what a fine machine!" a woman calls out. "When Baffoni comes that'll be for me!" Baffoni is Big Whiskers or Stalin — but it was only a gaiety this time, at the sight of a Buick in her living room.

The big spaces are distressing too. There is nothing French about them, none of that spacious public elegance of the Place de la Concorde or the views up past the Tuileries. Big Piazza del Popolo, where the great political mass meetings are held among trees and flowing streams and Egyptian tigers, was even designed by a Frenchman, but the Roman look soon grew over it, like the weeds and wild flowers in the crevices of its twin churches.

Piazza San Pietro, so splendidly reasonable as architecture, if you forget the Viadella Conciliazione, is not a place for reasonable individuals to stroll with a happy sense of partaking in the achievement and somehow corresponding to it, as they would in such a square in Paris. It is a place for people to congregate in the terrific force of their gregariousness, their mass cravings, like cattle around a water hole; and when it is empty, when there is no saint being made or other spectacle, it is lifeless: very admirable in its lines but cold, with a hollow look, like the scene of a dream in which after standing with a great crowd one has suddenly been left alone. But then as suddenly you find it filled another way; another sequence has begun. It is a sunny winter afternoon, and now even this enormous space has become a living room, or public nursery. The Dome, announcing itself for miles around as the center of the world, is actually presiding like a hen over thousands of babies and mothers and lovers and very ancient people strewn all over the steps of Bernini's colonnade and the awesome area it encloses, not as if they owned it but really owning it. It is where they live. The fountains, those two high waving flags of world Catholicism, are as local as a barnyard pump. There is no distance, there is no awe of anything.

It is like a party all the time; nobody has to worry about giving one or being invited; it is going on every day in the street and you can go down or be part of it from your window; nobody eats alone in the cafeteria, reading a book. A sickbed is another public gathering; there is a ritual of moaning, question and response; everybody must crowd in.

Then there are the periodic Big Parties, a great deal older than their present ostensible occasions, dogmas, and the names of saints, so old that the tumescence of life they cause seems of an order with the habits of bees and the motions of tides. Everybody knows what to do, none of it is to be decided anymore, there is no question of having a good time or not; if that is what you are supposed to be having that day then you are having it. The strolling places are all big with motion; the main sounds are of laughter, easy as waterfalls, and motors, but the machines are not going out of the city unless to the beaches in summer; they are just expressing themselves. The little iron tables or big wooden ones with their scars and rubbings of so many other such days, or in some arbor restaurants the hideous cement ones like cut-rate tombstones, are each a domestic fragment of the one sprawling family affair — the material of the public table is of intimate importance in this form of life, more than a person's own last name; the children are in and out of everything, no distance there; other families, of four, five, six, rumble by packaged into one bulbous organism astride the family vespa; and at the proper hour it is all one mass exodus, to bed.

The honored personage, in any gathering, is the pregnant woman. She is exhibited, she exhibits herself, everyone feels happier and more important if there is someone in that condition at the table; and nothing can be refused her. If you refuse a pregnant woman something she wants you will get a sty in your eye, and her frustrated wishes will appear as blemishes in the child.

It is a deluge. You are in life way over your head, there is no getting out of it, except in the *beaux quartiers* that are not beaux at all but only pretentious; taste never functioned here on anything between the hovel and the grand palazzo. There are distances there but they are the result of a failure, not a natural way of being. Those sections are always sad and on the big party days, about a dozen a year though some percolate into a season of two or three weeks, seem marked more than ever with the black sign of the sickness of the middle class. The health of the city is elsewhere, around the fountains, where the private soul is in ceaseless disintegration; nothing is held back; the only secrecy is of the city itself.

Of course the fountains are not all for every purpose and time of day; it depends on the space. Piazza del Popolo is a fascinating crossroads, a place to sit awhile, but far too big and unprotective really to live in; the little square around the lovely Tortoise Fountain is more like a back stoop. For general all-day use, but especially at *l'ora della passeggiata* and in the evening, two of the best are beautiful Piazza Navona with its three fountains — "godless Navona" the angry reformers of the Middle Ages called it — and the cobbled square of Santa Maria in Trastevere, which is not much less beautiful although only one of its buildings is a true palazzo. But the others are massive and handsome too, of a comfortable height, and have the weathered stucco colors of embers, ochre to rose, darker under the ledges, that are the characteristic ones of the city and help to give the walls their mysterious organic relation to people, nothing one could think of clearing away in a hurry. The main beauty of the piazza, as of most of the others, is that in spite of its superb proportions it seems not to have been planned but to have come about as a widening in a cow path does, so that nobody has that unpleasant feeling of doing what is expected of him, though in fact they are doing in nearly every detail what has been done in the same place for a great many generations. The fountain here is large and central, as it needs to be. It is not a sculptured one but a high impersonal form, a real flowing goblet, chattery but serene, which both fosters and absolves all the immense amount of *being*, being then and there, not waiting, not conceiving or imagining, that goes on around it. All water has an aspect of holy water; you feel it most strongly in these unfigured basins, not shooting up great rousing banners of liquid light as at Saint Peter's but the stiller ones, especially where life is so thick around them. The main feeling around this one is of a perpetual wiping out of experience; continuity is all in the water.

The church is essential in the same way. It was the first one dedicated to Mary and has kept the modest, authentic dignity of its great age beneath its tatters and strange accretions — or not so strange: there has been no serious change since the twelfth-century square tower and mosaic across the facade. It gives the square its deep subtlety of color and line, and is part of its other spaciousness too, along with the moving water, and as a view of the mountains would be.

The place itself is voyage; that is why there is no restlessness. Neither is there anything for the tender heart, neither pity nor self-pity; for the delicate sensibility it is all scandal and continual death.

The most startling people are the children; no other Italians have quite that look. These are the boys painted by Caravaggio,

with all the tough seductive wisdom of the city, the toying challenge miles beyond any illusion, in their eyes; painted sometimes,
in their careless open shirts, as child saints, when all their sublimity is of the rock bottom. They have been spared nothing, nobody ever changed the subject when they came into the room; by
the age of seven it seems there is no human temptation or degra-
dation they have not walked through the boiling center of, no vice
they have not made up their own minds about, and they can have
the manners of mule drivers or of cardinals as they happen to
choose; only they cannot dissemble; they have the appalling
candor of all Rome, and when you see it in a child's face you do
not know if you are looking at fish or at angels. You see something
else in their eyes; it is themselves as very old men, then their children and great-grandchildren standing before you at the age of
seven and of seventy or a hundred, all with the same two huge eyeballs looking at you in what might be a smile.

The wonder, you might think, is that their fathers can be so
childish. The rages of these men are marvelous. A vespa brushes
with a filobus and immediately the two drivers are at each other as
if there had been a feud between their families for years. "HOO!
LA! HO!" "Ignorante!" "Fesso!" "Coglione!" They gesticulate,
point to their steering wheels and fenders, bring the city to witness;
the buses run from overhead wires so soon twenty are held up.
The owner of the vespa in his fury gets his front wheel stuck side-
ways and the motor going full speed makes the machine buck like
a wild horse; so the bus moves on but he catches up with it a block
later, plants himself square in front of it and begins shouting
again. The scene is mandatory, if you were in the wrong it is even
more necessary to make out that you were not; and inside the bus
everyone is pleased, more than they were already at being transported like a shipment of eels; they would have been cheated if
one of the drivers had not played his part. The most relaxed-
looking people in Rome are the bus conductors, patrons all day of
a kind of party that puts the public at its best and wittiest, because
the lack is not of sensibility, only of nerves. The Roman form of
serenade is to race a motorcycle motor under the girl's window,

but mufflers are not common in any situation, the only things as dearly loved as a good noise are breakneck speed and eye-splitting lights, preferably neon — all expressions of well-being, like a huge belly laugh.

The women are of the species. Foreign men who take up with them or try to are nearly dashed to pieces, which in these days is a common attraction. With their dumpy graceless bodies and an air of the empire about their beautiful heads and shoulders, their faces not marred but somehow made more personal and approachable by the extraordinary frequency of wens on them, these Roman women move in the blazing noon of a terrible cold sensuality that can kill because it is so truly gay. They are said to be the coldest women in Europe but they are probably also the most candid; they are no more nebulous than the sky above them, and seem incapable of the least affectation; and they lose not an atom of their tremendous inner conviction because their calculations have brought them to a prospect of doing the washing for the next fifty years under an image of the Madonna. Their power even takes on another depth of joyousness once that is settled. The drive of femininity, which is of the whole being and so just the opposite of nymphomania, never gives out; neither does the lung power; their voices carry like rockets across the square and in all the streets around, in a frenzy of anger you would suppose but it may be only to ask the time and in a moment will be as loud with laughter. With their children it is a torrent treatment that may go on for thirty years, or never stop, of huggings and slappings and spoiling and tyrannical ordering about. The American, reflecting on his own childhood, feels exposed as to a break in the Boulder Dam.

The guitar player at one of the two restaurants there on the square, in the aura of the venerable church, is something worse than shocking; it is because of the church, and the fountain, that he can be.

The restaurant has become rather fancy lately and the two musicians, who are the most talented of the kind in the city, size up their little audiences with a brutal shrewdness that could be mistaken for ridicule. Those knowledgeable children, after all, have not lost anything in growing up; these men know what they are doing, and for tourists they will play the worst of the Neapolitan repertoire as soulfully as anybody else. The guitar player, who sings, brings a look of longing into his big dark eyes, set in a leathery egg-shaped face, broadest at the bottom of the cheeks, which for those five minutes is all wistfully racked by the incapacity of any human art to express such beauty as the heart perceives; the beauty of the lady at the table is also too much; if he rested his eyes on hers for more than the duration of one yearning middle G he would have to stop singing entirely; when business is brisk he may have to be overcome by such sorrow twenty or thirty times in an evening, while the violinist, who is taller and wears glasses, keeps expressionless and a little in the rear, knowing that his face — this is *his* sorrow — is more suited to a comedian, and not wanting it to intrude on so touching a performance. The only thing is that their little routine bow at the end, acknowledgment of the guest's superior station and extreme kindness in listening to them, never gets quite finished; they had already moved on when they started it.

Their real songs, and any Roman's, are the long obscene *stornelli*, ballads with a Moorish twist and many verses rising in detail as they go on. One is about the prison of Regina Coeli — nobody is a true Roman who has not been there, the song says, but that is only the beginning. One is about the fountain at Piazza Esedra where the bronze naked ladies are kicking up their heels while the man at the center wrestles with a dolphin: "*Oh what is he doing with that big fish . . .*" A Holy Year one may have come out of mothballs: "*I sin all the year round, now I am making up my accounts for l'anno santo . . .*" Santo goes into a dozen or fifteen syllables, a long, spiraling, leering, eye-rolling cadenza as coarse as any of the items that follow; the violinist is not retiring at all now; his big comedian's face is crackling with obscene suggestion and the moaning of the strings has turned to a sly slithering and biting more skillfully dirty than any of the verses; and after this song the singer will have to get out his handkerchief though his forehead was dry enough after the sad ones, at which he seemed to be working so. But this is an act too and will not make you friends with them, though sporadically, depending on business and the sirocco, they may pretend so; friendship is an alien idea; sooner or later your feelings are going to get hurt, and then suddenly it appears that all this time you had not been where you thought at all, among the roots of your own memory, but in China. It is an oriental city.

The spaghetti and the beads hanging in the doors to keep the flies out, the guttural singing notes and sudden rests of Roman speech are Chinese; the reverence for parents, the bright-colored swarming streets, the easy talk of death; there is nothing here that you will ever understand.

In the cheaper cafés and wineshops of the piazza there is a commotion of domestic gatherings all mixed with undercover operations of every kind, sexual, commercial, counterfeiters, pickpockets, and the lower depths of the sports and lottery worlds. There are plenty of ways of getting into that typically named place Regina Coeli, but the murders of Rome, with some political exceptions, are nearly always of passion, and usually in the family. Considering the habits of the rulers for so long it is peculiar. Perhaps it is only that serious gangsterism would be too much like working for an idea and Romans care too much for their skin, but perhaps it is also because of the purity of the water they drink and see everywhere around them, water being the element of miracle and ultimate innocence, so that the wickeder they are the more they are only foundering in a state of grace. There is not even a concept of crime and so there has never been any detective fiction, it would not make sense; if a criminal is any good he is a *bravo*, a hero, but the really good ones rarely do come from Rome.

This is terrible; it makes for a terrible familiarity with holiness; you can treat it like a dog.

You can hear young men in these trattorie saying obscene black masses, sitting under the crowded little bunch of flowers and tiny electric bulb of the shop shrine or the shrine in the street, droning and chanting in excellent mimicry a liturgy of Roman four-letter words, and other customers will treat them to wine to hear it again. Italians from any other city speak of them as the scum of the earth.

Then they go off across the piazza, eight or ten of them, with their arms around each other and one perhaps with a guitar, and may pair off in the dark or be going to meet their fiancées or both, or there may be more interesting possibilities, princes or diplomats hunting in the quarter. On one excursion of the kind a Trastevere boy went along gladly enough, until he looked around his companion's fashionable bedroom. "Macché!" he said. "Are you a Turk? You have no picture of the Madonna here!"

The unmarried girls are on the whole still rather careful; the ones who are not write their telephone numbers on five and ten thousand lire bills; and here enters Dr. Strom, although there is more than one way of looking at him.

There are in fact two Dr. Stroms, Dr. Alfredo and Dr. David, specialists in venereal diseases, "sexual anomalies," and most conspicuously impotence, and in point of public notice they are by far the most outstanding men in the city. They advertise every day in the best newspapers, also on big signs set in the sidewalk beside all the important bus stops; the space must be rented by the city. There are many other such ads in the papers and on the insides of urinals; a dramatic one read BETTER HELL THAN IMPOTENCE and had along with the doctor's address a picture of a devil with a pitchfork; and there is one "sexologist" who advertises only in the communist paper; but none can compete with the great two-headed Dr. Strom. The only question is whether he really exists, and if he does, how he can make a living. However you take him, it is more of that blurting out; romance is impossible.

The very old are shocking. They are not left out, any more than criminals; there is no conception of an outside for them to be out in; the great living room with its flower and chestnut stands and shade or sun for summer or winter is theirs too; the fountains flow for them. It makes no difference how poor or sick or useless or disagreeable they are. The Eskimos on the other hand are said to take their old out and abandon them on the ice, with their own consent, and in America many of our best sociologists are working on this problem.

The beggars are worse. There are thousands of them as there always were, some with rented children smeared up for the job, some who are half dead and ought to be in institutions, some who are perfectly able-bodied and have simply chosen that profession, and most Romans who can will give to them, at least a few times every day. They do not give out of kindness or because anyone is deserving, there is no buying of conscience in it, they just give; it is another kind of flowing out, and if the beggar were properly taken care of, as has been tried sometimes, everybody would feel that a natural outlet had been blocked and they had been somehow shut back in themselves; it would be as if something had gone wrong with their speech, or one of the big fountains were dry. There is no more outlandish sight in Rome than an American refusing a beggar.

The trouble is, it is very kind, this flowing ritualized amoral and unromantic community, which did not have to learn not to judge one's neighbor; it seems never to have heard of the idea; and in which individual kindness is unnecessary and practically unheard of — what looks like it is often just genuine enjoyment of other people's business. That is what is terrible, it makes social improvement so difficult; there is not much room for busybodies or any false charity. The beggars know that their work has that profound use and dignity and would howl with derision at a Swede who tried to put them in an institution, but the Swede and the Swiss are the great comic types in Rome anyway. Better hell, or a home in the Tarpeian caves and a dog's bowl at noon at the back door of the monastery, than to be out of the big swim.

The urinals are shocking.

Go up the hill from Trastevere and sit at the Bar Gianicolo, across from the papal walls and the Porta San Pancrazio. That is the newest and dumpiest of the city gates, a petit bourgeois triumphal arch in stucco, still it marks an exit, and you are really in the country there; the bar is a village bar; the vegetation is thick and casual: trees, wisteria, an arbor to sit under in summer, azaleas on the roof, capers and other shrubbery in the city wall. But this can happen inside the walls too; it is another mysterious kindness of the city that for all its staggering recent growth and harsh new sections such as the one that begins a few blocks from here, in a few minutes from almost anywhere you can be in a country place, not parks, nothing kept up or planned, but real ones; real country lanes running between high uneven overgrown walls, with donkeys and troughs and bits of ruins left to themselves, and rough little eating places in a profusion of birds and greenery. There is no word for weekend; it is not necessary; you may want to get away from this city sometimes but you would never think of needing to get *out* of it.

Here across from the gate, also from an iron gate leading to Garibaldi on his horse — on the Passeggiata del Gianicolo — there is no fountain, only a spigot from a kind of hydrant that spills night and day into an old wooden tub and eventually down a drain. But there is another water aspect. Along the old road to the north that starts from here, the Via Aurelia Antica, that drowsy sunken lane that leads you out of the city as from a secret garden that you have come on by accident and will probably never find again, runs the aqueduct begun by Augustus to bring the water in from Lake Bracciano, and called at different times the Alsietina and the Traiana; then in the Renaissance when all the spigots and faucets began being turned on again it became the Acqua Paola, after the pope whose arch straddles the road with that charming Roman air of having a purpose, where none is visible or imaginable. The water, which is chalky and the least good of the Roman waters for drinking — but there is as much rivalry about them as over qualities of diamonds in a mining town and you never know whom to believe — runs in pipes under the road now, so the only practical use of the old arches is to frame one of the nicest views of the Dome: just beyond the pope's gateway it appears as a huge inverted and stemless eggcup resting lightly on a field of cabbages.

This aqueduct has not the grand haunting broken stride of the ones across the campagna. It stays close beside you all the way, familiar, the arches becoming gradually filled in and finally just fading out into a farmyard fence; but like the others it gives you an image of what the city's true defenses always were: not walls, Servian, Aurelian, papal, or economic, but running water and the mind's need of it; no army was ever as strong as that.

However, it has other functions too and so there have to be urinals, otherwise people would relieve themselves anywhere as they do of their feelings and as the children do. The café proprietor's grandson Rodolfo makes himself an object of delighted attention in the piazza because he has to go so often. "Why he's a regular little faucet!" his pretty mother says with hilarious gaiety, addressing everyone at the three or four tables outside the bar. "He's been five times this afternoon and I've only been once. . . . All right, but go behind the bush. Oh, look at him, he's doing it right here! *Five times!*" She goes off in peals of laughter, doubling over the table with it, and everyone falls in with her pride and humor; Rodolfo beams, finishing; naturally he is spoiled, being such a *wunderkind.*

The urinal here is the handsome kind with two compartments and the screens coming pretty well around, not one of the cheaper little open niches of the less important streets, where in any case just as much use is made of the corners provided by the irregularities of the buildings. It is right in front of the café, beside the hydrant and tub, where people stop to drink and bring their bottles to fill all day, so that especially on holidays there are two waiting lines or shifting social gatherings mingled there. It is the corner spa, one part of it for men only — indicating a certain archaism in this society, but that is deceptive; if there were any exclusion beyond mere convenience the men would button their flies inside the screen and not as they stroll away across the piazza. It is the whole cycle, natural and manifest as pregnancy or the flow of historical time; and this is happening all over the city, in combination with hundreds of fountains that are not just a public faucet such as this one but designed in a spirit as of the greatest cathedrals, if you could speak of such a thing as a cathedral here. The waters themselves so beautiful, even the less good ones being incredibly limpid, with no suggestion of transit, none of that half-dead look of most city water — all the millions of gallons of it seem to be springing just that instant from virgin earth — are among other things continually working their way, mixed with various quantities of wine, through every single intestinal and urinal tract in the human conglomeration, and thence eventually in their new chemical form out the great and equally visible end hole of the Cloaca Maxima, that anal opening on the Tiber that is pointed to with such intimate affection because it has been discharging the same substances as now for some twenty-five hundred years, and some excretion from every person's body in all that time had to go through it. It seems that past generations would moan and a million and a half people would start having gastric pains all together if it were blocked up.

There could never, of course, be fairy stories in such a place, any more than ghost stories; there never have been in the country but they would be particularly *de trop* in Rome. The nordic soul misses its yearnings and regrets. Here in the dazzle of physical facts it detects a ghastly blank, in which there resounds endlessly that terrible word *pazienza*, applying to all calamities and inconveniences of whatever degree and meaning not patience at all but an attitude as toward the facts of astronomy. That is the strange gaiety and relaxation of the piazza; only you, the alien, ever conceived of happiness; the assumptions in every one of those heads would make any of your compatriots commit suicide. The absence of friendship can appall you there too, more than when you suffer from it; it is all bump and flow, meet and good-bye, unless there is some motive for maintenance or ritual continuity, but the heart is all in the moment; the lasting, loyal heart is the one compounded from all their little ones, as Dr. Strom is from their fears.

The priests and monks and nuns are shocking: what is this vast population feeding at the expense of the other? So are all their expensive new houses going up on the Janiculum where they already have dozens, while the poor are still in caves and huts in the dumps, having to throw their droppings together with their garbage out the door. All those men and boys in their long skirts always seem to be walking on revolving paddles like little steamboats; and how pleased they are; it is only in the faces of the nuns that you see signs sometimes of great suffering.

There they all go, between the spa and the Bar Gianicolo, down over the hill into the fat arms of Mother Church, above which the Dome, the *cupolone* Romans call it, sits like a Paris hat. This road is the main artery between it and many of their houses, which are all the same — tasteless elaborate villas of which the only beauty is the flowers; the architecture is on a par with modern church music and the neon crosses that are going up everywhere now — and so there are processions of them all the time, of all ages and costumes and prattling in all the world's languages: the Germans most vain in their scarlet, others with purple sashes, Negro Jesuits from Africa, Chinese, intense young Dutchmen, Boston Irish not yet used to the soutane, cold-toed Capuchins in brown, Passionists with the heart of Jesus usually a little crooked over their own. It is like a satire of the waterfront of Marseilles; Rome is their port, and as long as they are together you would not think they could ever be touched by that other life thronging around them all along the beautiful ridge of Passeggiata. It is an element; they just paddle through it; and may well, being the *pensionnaires* of the greatest real estate firm in Europe. In return they provide a spectacle, a note of variation in the scene, and Romans will support anything for that. Their main hold, as a city sight, is as a tremendous sexual image in reverse, which would be sorely missed; even the smaller groups, and most noticeably ones of adolescent boys with tonsures, always leave a special animal exhilaration in their wake.

You can see another kind of procession here sometimes, aside from the permanent one of Garibaldi's soldiers in marble busts among the trees, down by the lighthouse. The young communists, because of that heroic association of a hundred years ago, tend to hold their parades and meetings in the neighborhood, and afterward drift about with a sullen, surprised look, all ready to pull some big handle like a brakeman's switch that will change everything and not seeming to find it in the piazza. If an American

makes the mistake of being friendly to one of them in that mood he is liable to get insulted; you can tell them from the young fascists by whom they pick on.

At the café there is a subtler play of differences, the proprietor and his sons, all at heart extreme right-wingers, having rather more incentive than the Senate and Chamber of Deputies to play up the common denominator. There is the royalist hobo who sleeps across the road in the gate and for a free glass of wine will tell tall tales of his courage in fighting communists; the scowling neofascist lawyer who explains the newspaper every day to anyone who will listen — he seems for some reason to have no family; the communist masons building the new monastery down the road eat their lunch under the arbor. There are the usual café "characters" too; the starving barefoot young man with black hair to his shoulders and a briefcase, who gave away an inheritance last year and thinks he is Christ; the old prince who comes up from downtown every afternoon and holds court at one of the rickety tables, leaving his car and chauffeur twenty yards down the street. But it is hard for eccentrics to be of much interest in Rome; they would be more talked about if they had kidney trouble instead.

At election times the walls are all painted with slogans and rival posters climb higher and higher on the gate. For the great election of 1948 many of the best of them, as well as the leaflets that floated down through the trees from planes and other stunts that may have swung the tide, were the work of an American publicity man hired late in the game by the Demo-Christians and who called himself the King of Contacts. It is touching; nobody had ever heard of him before, hardly anyone knew his real name then; like a mysterious knight of old, or Castor and Pollux at the Battle of Lake Regillus, he won that great victory practically singlehanded, then quietly disappeared, and perhaps now in countries far away mothers are soothing their children as they listen to the leaflets hitting against their windowpanes in the storm: "Ssh my darling, sleep; the king is watching over us. . . ." Here at that time a priest or two was slightly mauled in the piazza, and as before any election there was huffiness and occasional fur flying at the café. Then the day after the vote, although the wall writing never stops, the posters are scraped off here and everywhere, so that for a few hours the whole city is knee-deep in wet paper, which shortly ends up like all other good things in the ancestral sewer, and life goes back to its pazienza and its regular rhythms and its regular gas, electricity, and public transportation strikes whose purpose nobody attempts to divine.

The real common denominator of the section, and in a sense of the whole city because it is high over all of it like a shrine and the eye rises to it from almost everywhere, is just out of sight of the piazza, but the sense of it enfolds all the life there; everything would be more brittle without it.

This is not the Dome. It is the Fontana Paola, built to show off the new water brought in when Pope Paul V fixed up the old aqueduct down the road — the same water that provides that very different appeal in front of Saint Peter's and also supplies most of Trastevere. The fountain is often criticized as architecture; its curves are thought to be heavy and its proportions bad; its griffins and eagles are perhaps rather spiky for its sensuous lines, too much like gargoyles. But in the particular case this is caviling. It is not exactly that the building suggests a church, any more than a centaur suggests a horse; it is one; its typical baroque church facade, from which three torrents of water gush out into the large and similarly curving basin, belongs to it honestly; faith and the dream have assumed one image, in which the orphans next door do their washing and through whose three gaping frames, the church doors, you see an incongruous house wall and a collection of carpenter's rubbish, and nothing else could so properly stand over that landscape. The popes knew what they were doing when they engraved themselves as most of them did on fountains; for the mind bred on tension and principle nothing could be so disturbing.

But this is at the rim, up a way from the thick of things. It is in Pasquin's district, down across the Tiber in the neighborhood of another great fountain, that you find the truest Romans, though some will tell you that none are left in that category but the statue-wits Pasquin, Maroforio, and the Foot. "Noialtri siamo dei fessi.

All the rest of us are horses' asses." The central fountain of this district is Bernini's one of the four rivers in Piazza Navona. Many of
the streets around are named for guilds; they are of the butchers,
the bakers, and so on, and at the trattorie you are likely to come on
a tableful of carpenters or ironworkers having their evening wine.
A peculiar thing is how often they are talking about Rome and
themselves its inhabitants, in those terms; *i romani, noialtri romani* are like this or that, behave this way or that; there never was
a city at the same time so unexclusive and so fascinated by its own
character, although if it were threatened like Paris at the Marne it
is hard to imagine that many Romans would willingly give up
their motorcycles to help defend it. It would not seem very vital,
and by the same token the 1943–44 German occupation, which
was as vicious as anywhere else though in some ways no more
galling than the French ones of the past century, left no sense of
human breakage, none of that cracking and splintering that occurred in some places; and so the city was saved better than most
after all; there were not even many collaborationists; it must have
been maddening, more than Horatius to Lars Porsena.

The most conspicuous public character in the quarter is a
woman — a newspaper vendor named Carolina. It may be that the
real power is another woman, her friend, who runs a small café-
restaurant on a much more secretive little piazza, triangular and
hilly, back of Navona. This woman is massive in every way, having
some malady that has turned her legs to two barrels and in her strik-
ingly handsome face a power as of dynasties, and it is said that she
does reign over the section, arranging contracts and marriages and
so forth; to look at her she may well arrange consent or rebellion in
larger matters too and would not be anything for a tyrant to trifle
with except in his last panic. She is a whole other government,
benevolent it would seem, but incontrovertible. At closing time,
long after midnight, she moves slowly out across the cobbles on her
inadequate little feet, on the arm of a son or nephew, her imperial
head having no need of a basket of washing to keep it high, turning
once at the top of the square to acknowledge some last remark from
the attendants taking in the last tables. At other times she must be

capable of tremendous laughter; just now there is no occasion for it. Her regard, in which there could never be anything so undependable as pity, rests a moment on the scene much as it did a little earlier when the children were playing there; she murmurs goodnight again, not needing to commit anything of herself in that banality, which however she would not omit; then with another word to her companion to set them in motion again, as though a cortege were falling in behind, goes off down the flickering crooked street that is one of the corridors of her palace.

Carolina is of different material. She is not even the prime minister but more a scout and buffoon, who operates out in the large world, her occupation giving her contacts with most of the dignitaries who come into the quarter. She is the everyday link between the *rione*, or district, and the government, also the United States, Brazil, the movie industry, etc., and there is probably no diplomatic job in Rome more strenuous. Everyone knows her, she knows everyone; the better outdoor restaurants are her beat; if she sees glancing at a certain table that she has gone too far she will immediately pretend to be drunk, or silly, and begin talking about love. It is convincing because quite often she is really drunk. Even so she is very skillful in her improvisations of headlines that are never entirely absurd, although the main effect of them, always funny, is just to make hash of all public affairs. But there can be something of Pasquin's point in them too, especially on his original subject, the Vatican, which the postwar pious government brought to the front again; the ministries are called monasteries, the Monastery of Foreign Affairs and so on; the name of Mussolini's mistress, Petacci, has a letter added — De Gasperi's is named *Pretacci*, rotten priests. But Carolina is first of all an actress.

"All priests ordered to take wives!" she calls, waving a paper over the potted-hedge railing of the restaurant. "All priests must marry by Monday!" "The Chinese take Rome!" — meaning Americans; or she may be only making fun of all war. "Giuliano takes over the government!" "Scelba drowns in the Tiber! Terrible misfortune! The minister of the interior is dead!" At a table of her better acquaintances she will stop to toss off a glass of wine, standing and making longer recitations, in a mumble if they are risky, or loud enough to be heard all around, though she has the great gift of not eyeing her audiences; they always think she is talking to herself. Then she moves on stolid and thumping on her heels through the crazy streets, as though wearing a tiara of cabbages, to cry her crazy wares somewhere else. It is impossible to think of her growing old or having ever been young, and surely she was there once shouting: "Tarquin is sick!" "Nero gives birth to a frog!" "The pope chased out of Avignon! Everybody out to welcome the pope!"

She is the best Roman comedian of the present time; the only one in the theaters who is better is a Neapolitan and he is not concerned with politics. Besides she is making it all up, with only a hint of a gleam in her tough fifty-year-old gamin face, as handsome as her queenly friend's, but round and wicked, with a texture like an earthenware jug; and she is a power too; nothing will ever shut her up, though she might have to run a pushcart again if democracy failed instead of selling papers. "If I had only learned to behave myself," she says. "That's the way to be rich and strong. I never could behave myself."

But she can improvise just as well on life in general, and her own life, and in one way she certainly outdoes the great Neapolitan, Eduardo de Filippo, who is sometimes guilty of a real tear over romance, and death. Carolina's act stays pure to the end; her nearest approach to a real tear is because she has been sick recently and is not supposed to drink anymore, but this is fabricated too, she will do as she likes anyway. Around the time her friend is going home she can finally sit down at a corner table of the café in Piazza Navona, where they will serve her something free at that hour — it is one of the best cafés — and if there is nothing better to do she will advise young people to be happily married. Herself, so she says, she has had four husbands and been in love other times too but she never found, she says looking at you in her bold blank ingenuous way, the word coming right along, the ideal; she would always discover some horrible thing and it would be finished. The last one was the director of "my paper." She believed in him, and he was taking care of her, but then she found out horrible things and it made her sick, that's why she had to go away to the cure for four months. She was eating her heart out; so Roberto Rossellini who knew all about it went and spoke to the director, and he was really sorry, but still there were those horrible things she had learned. True love was what she had wanted; she has never found the ideal.

Out in the empty piazza two of Bernini's bold white river figures catch the light, one with his hand up in comic horror, the other hiding his head; the fountain's obelisk finishes in shadow, you can hear the water trickling over the marble snake and marine centaur beneath. Carolina is looking at you with wicked wide-eyed innocence; you are supposed to be moved by these confidences; she would not have been happy to end the day with a poor performance. At last she finishes her coffee, gathers up her few unsold papers, faces the sinister gleam of the piazza like someone setting out alone at night across an ocean. "Non ho mai trovato l'ideale."

The design of that fountain is Bernini's. Other sculptors did the river figures, representing the Nile, the Ganges, the Danube, and the Rio de la Plata, or the four corners of the world — good signposts to the esoteric expansion of spirit in the baroque. Most of their fingers were broken off by American soldiers for souvenirs during the war and the replacements are a little whiter than the rest. The favorite story about the fountain, referring to the rivalry between Bernini and Borromini, who designed the church alongside, is that the Plata is holding up his hand to keep the church facade from falling on him and the Nile is hiding his head so as not to see such a hideous building. Actually the church, though not Borromini's best, does a good deal for the fountain in the way of setting; so does Palazzo Madama, just visible on a parallel avenue on the other side.

A few other fountains:

Tortoise Fountain
At the edge of the Jewish quarter. Paths of royal gardens could have been designed to lead to it, but its Romanness and half its beauty are from the sudden little cobble-paved clearing it is in;

one thinks of the copies of such works put up in garden courts in the Berkshires in the 1890s, and how sad they have become. This has lost nothing. But it is alone in its genre in Rome, and too exquisite to be Roman; the figures are the work of a Florentine. The life-size bronze tortoises at the upper rim were removed for safety during the German occupation. The water moves up in two or three ways and down in three or four, through marble cockleshells and over the gleaming bodies of the boys, whose lifted arms and raised knees make opposing circular patterns through the water. The problematic part is their smiles; they are almost exactly that of the Mona Lisa; it is very striking.

Fountain of the Ponte Sisto

Formerly at the other end of that delightful bridge, at the head of the Via Giulia; built by the architect of the Fontana Paola up the hill. The shrine theme again, but this is more strictly a shrine, and really it is not very beautiful but it is tall and necessary and gives an impression of the beautiful. There is a crescent piazza there that is the formal anteroom or visitors' entrance to Trastevere and this requires a particular dignity of water; however, there is another such water shrine at the back of the district, where it is only a roadside one; like the Madonna, they could be anywhere. In this one water falls the full length of the recess, among monster heads and portaled by Ionic columns, a grave and pleasant concept, which has lent itself to various pompous imitations, notably in the fascist era. There is one parody of it, still with the imprint of the ripped-off fasci, out toward the Baths of Caracalla.

A large number of Christian martyrs were thrown off the adjacent bridge.

Face on the Via Giulia

A big ancient marble mask, picked up somewhere in the great junk pile; all these masks looked agonized, and now water gushes from its mouth and it has acquired from it an extraordinary black walrus mustache. The effect, a common one, is of a curious gaiety

of torture; any face made into a spigot looks tortured to the less
outgoing mind, including the more usual ones of tigers, griffins,
frogs, even the everyday dolphin. But around in front of the Farnese, the French Embassy, things are in a different vein. The twin
fountains there are composed of high fleurs-de-lis set in a majestic
pair of ancient bathtubs, from the baths of the Emperor Caracalla.

   The water coming from the face must be the Acqua Marcia. At
any rate for drinking people take their bottles instead to a spigot in
the courtyard of No. 147, the only one in the neighborhood provided
with the Acqua Vergine. Another faucet up by the Ponte Milvio is
much frequented because it carries the famous Acqua Acetosa.

   A larger grotesque in the genre of the face is on the Via Grego-
riana, a doorway, with the monster's forehead and eyes over the
door and his agonized mouth the entrance. The biggest and best
of all are a few hours from Rome, carved from huge rocks in the
woods of Bomarzo.

Barcaccia: Piazza di Spagna

A sunken boat, in the thick of traffic, co-image with the flowers on
the steps a few feet away; the traffic adapts itself to these reveries.
Water falls from various tongues and spigots in the boat, whose
stone is pleasantly corroded. According to one account it was built
to commemorate the naumachia staged in an artificial lake in that
place by one of the less appealing emperors, Domitian; a more
likely version is that it commemorates a flood of the Tiber in 1598
when a barge went ashore there. By the father of Gianlorenzo
Bernini, his only conspicuous work in Rome; and so provides a
happy notion of all the Bernini's luxuriant contributions to the city
having had the stone boat for their cradle; he was born in the year
of that flood.

The Triton: Piazza Barberini

Bernini *fils*; his best single street figure, possibly more useful now
among the billboards and traffic jams than it was originally when
the square was halfway out into the country. A true water creature,
man in spirit but with the vigilance and muscle of fish, who draws

up to a point there in the commercial hubbub the general human memory of waves and slimy deeps. It is where you most feel the value of sculpture, especially fountain sculpture, as a public antidote to introspection.

In feeling and workmanship a far cry from the Tortoise Fountain, and more typical of the Roman water art, the great fountain century there having been the seventeenth. The fountain figures, when there are any, are neither sensitive in the Florentine fashion nor academic. They are on the whole coarse, and have often a careless-looking air of not having quite left the state of raw materials — showing more plainly than dry sculpture the baroque derivation from late Michelangelo. Their subtlety is of the grand stride, the profound suggestion, the fantastical arrangement, for example the position of the obelisk in Piazza Navona. Bernini appears to have learned a great deal from the Apollo Belvedere in his youth, but the most obvious parentage for the Triton, who is more than anything a study in back muscles, is the Belvedere Torso, by Apollonius, son of Nestor, sculptor also of the bronze Sitting Boxer in the Museo Nazionale. It recalls Pasquin too, that nearly shapeless lump of marble out on a street corner, so hidden behind its other, satiric personality it is hard to think of as art, which Bernini is said to have called the most beautiful statue in Rome. Another round sinewy back, same masculine vigor and realistic modeling, just adumbrated now, and with a further energy from the activity, only to be guessed at, of the group it is broken off from. The explosive suggestion of these paraplegic stones, headless besides or nearly, was what genius in Bernini's own explosive time could use. The Triton is an athlete — of the spirit; no trickler; he blows his single jet of water straight up in the air.

That, and the place he is in, required that he squat on top of his shell, or it may be an ocean lily pad. The two tritons at the Bocca della Verità are holding up their similar basin from beneath, so that they are obscured by it and by the drip and the effect, just the opposite of this, is of drowsiness, another of the moods of Rome.

Acqua Felice

Another water first brought into the city by Augustus, this one for his baths, from the direction of Palestrina, and the conduits of which were restored by various popes, named for the friar pope Sixtus V, Fra Felice. This was the first deliberate showing-off of water on a big scale (1585–87); the water is the same that goes to the Triton, also to the dolphins and ladies of Piazza Esedra and others. Its charming name however is not what it would have been to Hiawatha or would be to us; it is rather sinister, like the Felix of Sulla the dictator. Sixtus, who got the same architect (Domenico Fontana) to raise the obelisk in front of Saint Peter's, seems to have been about the most hated of all tyrant popes, and in his portrait in the Vatican has about the most disagreeable although intelligent pope face. — The architect was apparently not much of an engineer. The story is that when the obelisk was half raised the ropes were about to break, and although silence had been imposed during the operation on pain of death, one of the workmen saved the day by crying "Water on the ropes!" The hero's reward was the privilege granted to his family of providing the palms for Palm Sunday in Saint Peter's.

The fountain is rather a fiasco. Its only beauty besides the water is the four Egyptian lions, comically excruciated as usual by their crystalline vomit; you have to imagine your favorite dog in this position; the only other fountain lions as handsome are the four facing out from the corners of the basin in Piazza del Popolo. But the worse brutality here is the angry blown-bellied dwarf-legged Moses, which met with such howls in its day the sculptor committed suicide; he had been telling everybody he was going to outdo Michelangelo. In fact the figure is so good a caricature of that other Moses it is as though it were meant as a tribute in satire, the deepest tribute Rome can offer, to the great artist of the cupolone. Something of the same self-mockery, the ultimate brutality, runs in all the fountains; there is always a catch; the most lyrical of them will always be made fun of somehow a little farther on; and the most ribald of all, the one in Piazza Esedra, so stunningly lit up at night, is really a satire on the whole idea of fountains.

Quattro Fontane

These are not very handsome either, with their jaded allegories, only they have a particular quaintness of unreason; you are back to the generic fountain feeling; some vast subconscious is at work, and you are a moving figure in it.

The sense of them at that spot is that if you could stand in the middle of the crosswalk without being run over you would have views of three of the most important obelisks — at Trinità dei Monti above the Spanish Steps, on the Quirinal, and at the back of Santa Maria Maggiore — and with its deep sense of propriety in symbols the city knows that the image of primeval power requires its counterpart; an obelisk without water near it looks unnecessary or bombastic like the little private ones in American cemeteries; so for even a distant view of such a cluster of them you are made to stand among fountains. There is no need to be particularly explicit about this; sexuality is general in Rome. These huge cold monoliths, stolen from Egypt, are affirmation and definition, the complement of water, and as Rome was as it has remained the least feminine of cities, the thefts, of an extraordinary number of the things and undertaken at fearful cost, were to satisfy a real necessity. They were its other most necessary image, and it seems an appropriate rumor that the largest of them all is still buried in the neighborhood of the Pantheon, as though the city were still keeping its most spectacular energies secretly in reserve. Most of the others are combined in some way with water, and take from that element of memory their vivid strength. — Of course in Egypt there might have been a different logic of feeling altogether.

Pantheon Fountain

The four great obelisk compositions are at Saint Peter's, in Piazza del Popolo, with Castor and Pollux on the Quirinal, and in Piazza Navona, but this is the most gracious and subtle in another scale. It is what makes the piazza (the Rotonda) a clubroom, and more a daytime one, and for men, not for the whole human show like other piazzas, and not political either — the public af-

fairs clubroom is a few blocks away in Piazza Colonna, around the
newspaper bulletins. The sense of touch is especially strong here,
the space being tiny in relation to the dark immensity of the Pantheon columns and their associations.* There is a jungle craziness
in the proportions, crushing on short acquaintance, of which the
modest obelisk with a cross on top and the water, the whole raised
by a few steps, are the secret balancing point. The basin is of utmost grace, with the usual sadistic details, little monster faces
cheek to cheek and upended dolphins — formal elegances of the
language, which is outside of pity, and the water keeps its peculiar
holiness. There is something of the sacred grove about this square,
which affects its more or less hobo occupants, and it was surely
from the sense of this that Piranesi gave so strange a perspective to
his best etching of it, putting the Pantheon off at an impossible distance with the little fountain grandly spreading in the foreground.

It would be somewhere here that that most enormous obelisk is
buried, if it is; the rumor, anyway, fits the feeling of the section.
The midget of obelisks is there too, next door in Piazza Minerva,
center of the ecclesiastical trade: stoles, chalices, plaster Virgins,
Catholic reading matter, etc. It is on the back of Bernini's marble
toy of an elephant, who is looking quite surprised to be so saddled
and is also peering around at the elephantine behind of the Pantheon, which in his tiny way he burlesques.

Another function of the water is to preserve from deadliness
the most impressive inscription in Rome: M. AGRIPPA L.F.COS.
TERTIUM FECIT.

Old Man with Barrel

This much-photographed character with his time-eaten face, who
is pouring water from a stone barrel, turns out not to be where you
would suppose from the pictures at all. He is tucked under a low
window ledge on a dim street off the Corso, and you jump when
you notice him. He is a bit part in the dream who somehow got
left behind there, like the Foot, a huge ancient sandaled one on a
still narrower street a few blocks away.

---

*Now ruined by traffic except late at night.

Tre Fontane

Miracles and saintliness, to be believed, require water; it was inevitable that Castor and Pollux after saving the nation should turn up beside a spring. Saint Paul's head bounced three times to produce these three wells, now in the charge of Trappist monks; there are three small churches there but the wells are all in one of them and you drink from only one of the three, out of a long-handled tin cup. This is the kind of thing that makes theological discussion in Rome so ambiguous. One of the miracle-working Madonnas of this century appeared in a eucalyptus grove across from the entrance.

Still, a few things did happen without producing a fountain — Saint Peter's chains from two different prisons miraculously welding when brought together (the joint ones are shown every August 1 in San Pietro in Vincoli, where Moses is); the Crooked Wall (Muro Torto) up in back of Piazza del Popolo bending in deference to Peter when he walked by on the way to his crucifixion, and staying that way in defiance of physics ever since.

Fountain of Trevi

The final fountain fantasy, and the purest of waters; called Vergine, formerly Virgo, for the girl who is supposed to have shown its source to some soldiers who were dying of thirst; an unlikely story but one of the waters had to be called that. It is a question whether it is thought to be the best water because of the name or vice versa, it is hard for anyone who smokes much to taste the distinctions, anyway it is a splendor to look at in its tumblings there. Yet the only miracle ascribed to it is quite humble and for foreigners, i.e. about the penny you throw in — a typical case of making the deepest mysteries practical and concrete.

The original channel, coming in up by the Porta Pinciana, was built as so much else was by Agrippa, Augustus's son-in-law before Tiberius, and was restored as usual by a pope. In between Rome had been without water for a thousand years and it is terrible to think of. At the beginning of the sixteenth century people were drinking the water of the Tiber, and from wells. On the campagna soldiers had been camping in the arches of the aqueducts, those sorry lines of blitzwork across the sorrier plains, whose spell is all of water; if they had been relics of some old grain-distribution system they would never have haunted the world so, though the shape of their arches might be as beautiful and the masonry as good. They were the world's broken memory, and are the memory of the break now; driving across that country in a car at dusk you have a clear impression of riding overland in a ship. But when the new channels came, all in a rush of a hundred years or so, it was all one growth with the old ones; there were miles of them that could still be used, with a little fixing, and it was the same water. It was only a matter of getting it back into the pipes.

The Fountain of Trevi is the final song of joy in this return of the waters. It was a big job, extending rather absentmindedly over the reigns of many popes and not pleasing everyone in the process. Urban VIII (Barberini) financed his part of it with an extra tax on wine, at which Pasquin commented bitterly on the pure water the people were going to have instead. It took its present form only a hundred years after that, in the eighteenth century, but from an idea of Bernini's. The spirit of the Triton and the Four Rivers was to be lifted to the scale of a public altar, big as a house.

An altar to be swallowed up by; the nature of all Roman fountains is isolated and magnified in this one; nothing in Rome is so offensive to the abstract eye. This is the last, royal chamber of the dream; the immersion is complete, more obviously so from the basin's being below street level like the boat in Piazza di Spagna; the stepping down is part of the imaginative process, such as the descent into wells and pools in fairy tales, after which you feel no serious distinction of kind between the ocean characters of the fountains and the promenade-hour swarms, thickest in summer because it is always cool there unless something has gone wrong with the pipes. The piazza is engulfed; the lower windows in the palace wall, which could have been a basilica instead, fade away at the sides among the fountain's cliffs and boulders. At the center rides the king, Neptune, whose palace is all motion and transformation; sea horses led by tritons are drawing him forward, and you think at first a hundred other sea creatures but that is an optical illusion, another of the attributes of Ocean; all the rest is rocks, caves, ocean flora, with the beautiful Acqua Vergine racing across them from everywhere.

The people might turn into tritons, and the tritons with no great trouble into saints in a church; the baroque fantasy and exuberance are the same, and the water, so much of it sprung on you in so sudden a little space, tremendous enlargement of the surprise of the Tortoise Fountain, has here more than anywhere the impact of the fullest, loudest "GLORIA!"

One of the most arresting pieces of social gossip told by Suetonius is about Tiberius, after he had been forced by Augustus to divorce his wife Vipsania and marry the emperor's nasty daughter Julia, Agrippa's widow; it seems he had been deeply in love with Vipsania, and when he ran into her once at the theater afterward he was so affected by it he nearly fainted. This is nearly the only love story recorded in all of Roman history that could be called romantic. But then Tiberius was everything the Romans of that time would not understand: rigid and economical in all his ways, conscience-ridden, overscrupulous in detail, given to solitude; he would not explain himself. Whether at the end he was throwing boys off cliffs and so on is not certain but the stories may have been partly true.

The fountain dispenses eighty thousand cubic meters of water a day.

Fountain of S. Onofrio

Under pines in the churchyard, on the Janiculum. A flat goblet basin, so like the one in the postcards and that Corot painted, just across the valley on the Pincio, it seems that if something were said over the Pincio fountain you might hear it even a hundred years later in this one; they are each other's echo and memory. But the feeling around all the fountains is of a memory much longer than that.

SALVATORE GIULIANO

The Education of a Bandit

THE INTERESTING THING about the death of the Sicilian
bandit Salvatore Giuliano was not so much the political use
that was made of the whole story, as the private uncertainty of
feeling about it. In Rome and thereabouts, hardly anyone seemed
to have a simple view of the matter, or if they expressed one you
felt they were not quite telling the truth; there was one set of
double meanings in the salons and another among the people,
and both had something to be said for them. The story itself was
not simple. However unpleasant most of his goings-on in his last
few years, the fact is that Giuliano, twenty-eight years old when he
was shot down in the first week in July 1950, was not a mere gangster type; he also had, as one of the most grudging Rome newspapers observed, "a certain virile beauty." But there was more to it
than that.

The story begins in America. Giuliano's parents had gone
there with the usual high Italian hopes, did not better than they

had at home, or perhaps worse, and just before the child was born the mother returned to Sicily and found work again as a peasant. The boy had the normal childhood of rural Italian poverty, a little schooling, a lot of farm and other work, a lot of slapping and laughing and making things usable that anybody else would throw away — under the thumb, in this case, of the world's most notoriously absentee and idle landowners. For all that, judging by some of his mother's actions Giuliano, known as Turiddu, would seem to have been something of a spoiled child; his good looks and general hold on people would have lent to it too, but it can be a far cry from a spoiled child to a juvenile delinquent and he was never that. Nobody ever accused the future bandit of having been, at that time, anything but a good boy; not wayward, vicious, given to drink or petty thievery or street brawls — none of the gangster build-ups. The trouble may have been rather the opposite; if anything, he seems to have been a little more austere than most, or at least more driven, more bent on whatever he was after, and you can believe this from the pictures.

It is to say the least a dynamic face: proud, ambitious, with no look whatever of ordinary criminality and a strong look of the unreconciled, of a superior energy that cannot help rising out of a scheme unfit for it. The best known of the pictures, one of the few in which he is not lying dead in a pool of blood or on the autopsy table, reminds one of certain faces in the earliest Soviet movies, or of those young Israeli fighters who were ennobling the rotogravure sections in Giuliano's time: shirt open at the neck; jaw round, hard, set, and well-covered; mouth full and firm; head raised with a somewhat posey vigor as though the shoulders were being forcibly held down, and seen in three-quarter view, to emphasize the look of staring high past all danger and personal concern, to the Goal. It is what you might call "heroic"; you might also call it anachronistic.

They said he went to the poolrooms now and then, but not much; his favorite pastime was hunting, and he was a wonderful shot.

At sixteen he got a job with the Sicilian telephone company, which was putting in the first lines from Palermo to the district around his hometown, Montelepre. No trouble yet. He kept the job, bicycling many miles to and from work every day, helping to support the family, until he was of military age, then having a passion for mechanics, got himself assigned to aviation, but before he had taken any part in the war came the Allied landings in Sicily, June 1943. "With this invasion," as a right-wing Rome tabloid put it, "there came disorder and hunger in Sicily." The telephone company stopped work on the new lines and the Giuliano family, like many law-abiding others, was reduced to black-marketing.

The trouble came soon, and considering the time, and the strength and high temper of the face, seems to have a classic inevitability about it. Turiddu and his brother had organized the traffic in grain among the towns around Montelepre, and one night in September, in a scuffle with a carabiniere who tried to confiscate a sack of grain that he was taking somewhere, he happened to kill the man. So far, a common incident; they were happening everywhere, these wretched little combats in the dark involving necessity and a fit of temper and no great intent of wrong, nothing of what went into the making of the big black-market fortunes. Only Giuliano ran away into the hills, and so became automatically a *fuorilegge*, an outlaw, in a land where outlaws are a common and ancient curse.

They said he should not have done that, it was not sensible; he should have given himself up that night and he would have had a few years in jail and everything would have been all right. Which may be, although the telephone company would not have been likely to take back a convicted murderer, and he can have had good cause as well as bad to trust himself more than the law — you could get a notion of it from the trial of his accomplices in Viterbo, and that was under a stable government, not like the tangle of power and intrigue and vice in Sicily at the end of the war. Death and mess had become the natural things, not legality; it would not have been the natural thing to turn to that; what was natural was to have black-marketed and killed someone by mistake and to be hiding in some hillside cave as the partisans were doing elsewhere, for other reasons and not always better ones.

There were dead bodies in the brush in many places; three or four years later they were still turning up. But there can have been some passion in this natural decision too. The accident may only have set off what had to come anyway: a sudden heaving up, a revolt of the whole spirit, as of some gross Julien Sorel, against all the known constrictions of a life and the prospect of worse, and even more against the assumption on the part of those who had it of their power over him.

Who would these people be? Fascists, foreign colonels, local politicians and officeholders frantically selling themselves to one side after another . . . Experience is bitter, respect impossible, the young man (just twenty-one then) full of the consciousness of his own worth and touchy Sicilian honor, and extremely ignorant. But you cannot speak of a natural propensity to crime; there is no sign of it. Even later, with many murders to his credit, there is always a desperate effort to make the extraordinary power he had achieved respectable, in the highest sense; desperate, and absurd, but really it is very hard to say who is less or more absurd in this story.

A year before his death, speaking to the one Italian journalist who ever managed to interview him, Giuliano said of this time: "I would have gone back to my mother's house, and gone back to work again, the way I had been before. But they came to look for me, and so I had to go on hiding." In a bit of diary given to the same journalist he speaks of having spent his time "in silence, meditating on my future course," and of how in those years hunger had driven many Sicilians to looting and to crime; "the roads of Sicily soon became a field of crime," and he adds that all the crimes committed anywhere began to be attributed to him. "But I was not embittered by this, because I had no feeling of being a delinquent."

At any rate his first moves as a registered outlaw were not criminal in the Chicago sense, but political. The Sicilian separatist movement was taking advantage of the Italian defeat just then to reorganize, and Giuliano, after conversations with one of its leaders, was made a colonel in the movement's helter-skelter and not-too-choosy military arm, called the Volunteer Army for Sicilian Independence (EVIS). He got into this, he says in the diary, "as a true son of Sicily . . . because Italy never considered Sicily anything but a mere province," which is the usual formula. His job, like the young Stalin's for the Bolshevik Party (there is a resemblance too in some of the qualities Giuliano later showed), was to carry out holdups and robberies for the party treasury. In return, "after the victory," he was to have a pardon and a deputy's seat in the parliament of liberated Sicily.

If such promises, and his absolute authority over a growing band of experienced roughnecks, should have turned his young and muddled head, it would be no wonder; but to accuse him of fraud in this alliance, of being moved by nothing but self-interest, seems presumptuous. Anything that offered a hope of pardon must have been seductive. Beyond that, all one can say is that if that noble-looking photograph is not entirely misleading he should have been born somewhere else, where a simple-minded young man of daring and iron will and the gift of leadership, out for glory, would not have to make such a mistake.

The Sicilian movement, never very plausible in modern times, was at that moment quite crazy; its leaders were being criminally irresponsible. After a civil war consisting of a small brawl, in which Colonel Turiddu killed another carabiniere for them, they were arrested, including the head of the movement, a man with the pretty name Finocchiaro Aprile, and sent into that mild form of Italian custody called the *confino* — enforced residence in a village away from their home district. They were all let out and pardoned before long, but Giuliano, having done their dirty work, was too compromised; furthermore, since they had no more use for him at the moment, it appeared that they were rather more anxious than the police just then to do away with him. He could furnish some nasty evidence against all of them if he were caught; and in fact he was said to have collected a number of incriminating documents concerning many of the leading men of Palermo, which he sent by his brother-in-law to America for safekeeping, but they were evidently never opened, or perhaps never existed. He had another enemy, of course, in the communists, always in more or less violent opposition to the separatists.

By this time he was twenty-two or -three and had come a long way, however dim the intellectual results, in human and political education. One imagines him at this juncture: with his power proved, his ego enflamed, his political illusions, entertained in whatever spirit, turned utterly foul; seeing the distinguished men who had hired him, and were now out for his skin, being taken back into the best society; with surrender to law and order offering no hope but of life imprisonment, and around him his colleagues in crime, most of them not nice or noble at all but ordinary thugs, as ready as anyone else to do him in if he should slip, and ready to work for him and feed his vanity if he did not. Straight banditry was the possibility that was left. In the young man's head, however, there was another development. Earlier he had considered himself, as he expressed it, a mercenary in the ranks of the separatists. Now he was a political power on his own hook, and the head of a private army. Unfortunately this meant that he had to do his own political thinking too, and being no better qualified for that than most other people in the world today, what he fell for was the widespread scheme to make Sicily a new state of the United States. There were manifestoes about it, signed GUILIANO, showing a little man with a sword cutting a string between the island and Italy, with another, very long string going presumably to Washington but actually ending up somewhere around Labrador. There were also various murky entanglements nearer at hand, and more in the nature of gangster politics in some cities in America.

On this side of things, and perhaps in his frequent attempts to obtain a pardon, for which he never stopped hoping, his chief aide was Frank Mannino, a handsome young Italian American who had been in the Foreign Legion for a while and was reputed to have been planted in the gang by the Mafia. He was the best educated and had the job of explaining the newspapers to the others. But Giuliano's real chief lieutenant, the only one who knew of his doings and whereabouts at all times, and whom he seems to have trusted absolutely, was his cousin Gaspare Pisciotta. They ate, drank, and slept together, and Giuliano once said of him: "Without Pisciotta, Giuliano does not exist." He was the only one who was allowed to duplicate the silver star that Turiddu wore on his belt as symbol of the Chief, *il Capo*; the others, even Mannino, were only fraction leaders, the groups and meetings of the top men being so organized that betrayal of Giuliano by any of them was nearly impossible. With several others besides these two, however, he made a real old-fashioned pact in blood — rather touching, considering the pattern of modern sophistications his rustic mind had become embroiled in; they would cut their fingers, mingle the blood, and swear mutual defense for life, unrelenting war on the carabinieri, marriage only with relatives or affiliates of the gang, and so on. Over all of them his discipline was austere and ferocious, which is probably the main reason why the band was so phenomenally successful, as against the thirty or so others operating on the island at the time.

Of the man he had become in the process, you can see something in the series of snapshots supposed to have been taken a month before his death, by Pisciotta. This is not the youth one imagines earlier, in the bumbling unhappy discovery of his great powers, nor the one of that earlier "heroic" photograph, though there is plenty of resolve of another kind, and more than anything, the kind of animal grace and ease that one associates with a person of steady peaceful outdoor life — a ranger, a rancher; the difference is in the eyes. The pictures were taken on his last hunting trip, in some high scrubby place, against a background of pleasantly desolate mountains as in Arizona or Idaho, and the only flaw in most of them is that the shoes are too polished and the trousers, a quite citified pair, too well pressed; he is also wearing a large ring, and the large gold calendar watch he never parted with. He had become something of a dandy, it seems, rather sensibly, in view of what he had gone without for twenty-one years. That "certain virile beauty" is in evidence, marred a little by the peasant chunkiness of body, with nothing high-flown or grim about it; this is just the young mechanic or movie star, possibly a war hero, serious and likable. Then you come to the eyes, first in a full-face view that is not attractive but suggests guerrilla fighting, or would except for the crease in the pants, rather than crime. There is only one picture that a gold-star mother would not keep on the parlor table — a close-up, curiously mongoloid, in which the fierce power of the eyes looking straight at you, combined with the full cheeks seen head-on and the terrific lift of the head, not posey here but the natural one of a dominating energy and will, make you feel the killer, which he was; which he had become.

Even that has nothing of the simple criminal. It could be the portrait of a precocious Chinese war lord or young mountaineer rebel in Turkestan, who might or might not use his forces on the "right" side and would in any case not be squeamish about the treatment of prisoners. But what is curious is to observe, as you look at it longer, that this is not a newspaper fluke but the same man you were looking at before, the one of the high misguided gaze, who was above all personal concern. The head has only turned a few inches to face you, the gaze has come down from the Goal to rest on *you* and you have this, the murderer.

Not an indiscriminate one. Giuliano's killing was always for a purpose, even if it were only to avenge his reputation. He had become very sensitive about that, and once on hearing that a certain small storekeeper and his wife, in one of the villages he bossed, had ridiculed him in public, he went in himself the next day and shot them both in front of a crowd of customers. But mostly there were more practical reasons, vendettas, elimination of police spies and such, aside from the political "executions" and accidents in the line of work. In October 1946, after sentence by Giuliano's tribunal, five young dealers in black-market soap, all under thirty, who were to be questioned the next day by the police concerning some recent crimes in the neighborhood, were waylaid on the road, ordered behind a thicket, tied together, shot, and left there. In that case Giuliano had acted on good information; but he had become suspicious and is supposed to have killed several men on a first hint of danger or disloyalty. According to one report, his method was to make them sing at the top of their lungs and then fire in their open mouths, announcing afterward to those present that he had acted in the name of God and Sicily. Such scenes are said to have left an indelible impression on his men.

This curious custom, of shooting the victim in the mouth while he sang, was also to be found among the partisans in sections far from Sicily. For the young employee of the telephone company, aside from the general education of the time and the particular bandit-lore of his native land, there had been an extra twist, easy to understand. It was something very like the American. process of hurling juvenile talent into sudden fabulous success, usually set off by some accident of publicity and in fields involving huge public applause — movies, orchestra conducting — from which they can never again extricate themselves until they have fallen either dead or on their faces. These boys too can have within a year the psychology of killers, though it happens to be something else that is expected of them; after the first wild triumph, as after the first murder, the quiet patient basis of everything up to then disintegrates; shoddiness sets in, under cover of a true gift, and more and more lordly behavior; as the public dotes on them more, their love affairs became shorter and more sadistic; before long they are having to make a desperate effort to look interested in the company of their best friends.

"Cara mamma," Giuliano is reported to have said to his mother once later, "I have just one friend: my gun" — so even Pisciotta was a bore.

It is true, anyway, that nearly all the band betrayed him in the end, insofar as they were able; all twenty-seven in the courtroom in Viterbo when his death was announced turned against him.

He had the family, however, he would never be cut off from that; the whole huge tight howling loving and hating indivisible Italian organism: brothers, sisters, cousins, nephews, nieces, in-laws, even a father somewhere, and at the center the ritual mamma (that is the word, *madre* is used only in hatred or speaking scientifically) who may be a nobody but presides nevertheless by virtue of that national charity that gives to all mothers, whether of whores, murderers, idiots, or just children, and whatever their own fault, a part and haven in the image of the mother of Christ. One imagines this particular one hearing that remark, or being driven in a jeep at night or waiting at home for all the other meetings with her son in those years, and in the meetings with the neighbors. There was a secret tunnel leading from her house to the open country, in which were found binoculars, a military telephone, and a radio transmission set, just as if it had been a center of resistance to the Germans; and in April 1947 there was a great festa in the house for the marriage of her daughter Mariannina to Giuliano's lieutenant Pasquale Sciortino, the one who is supposed to have taken the documents to America afterward. The ceremony was performed by the local monsignore; brother Turiddu was there, probably handsomer and better dressed than ever, and there was dancing and singing till all hours, while heavily armed guards kept watch outside. Sciortino, promoted from lieutenant to vice chief after the wedding, had been with Giuliano in the EVIS, and chose to stay with him later rather than profit from the general amnesty. These were the top ranks in the rebel army; the mamma like the others wore its insignia.

One sees her later too, being taken to jail herself as an accomplice, as others in the family also were; then in a still cleverer move by the police under their new command, being let out so that she might persuade her son to give himself up, but still refusing, for all her curtseys to the new police commander, the brave Colonel Luca, to make the least move or murmur against him. "Iddu knows what he is doing." "Iddu will have to think about it." Then at last one can literally see her in the pictures, standing strong and demurely smiling in one, with Mariannina and the new son-in-law, whose arm is around her; in the others, being brought to identify the body: a short, strong-featured old woman in dingy black cotton, a better dress perhaps than before her son was rich but still the same kind, her hair pulled straight back peasant-fashion, leaving vanity in the dawn of her history, the massive, shapeless, workmashed body bent into an arc of absolute grief; held up at the armpits by two young male relatives, yet with something about her, in the carriage as much as the rocky ledges of the face, that announces she will walk on her own feet till doomsday if necessary.

At the first sight of the body she shrieked and did faint, but had herself led back in a few minutes, while the comforting ritual of which she had always partaken came closer to infuse her speech: "Yes, that is my son, Salvatore Giuliano, born of me (*parturito da me*) twenty-eight years ago." Then she knelt by the corpse, and between whispers of prayer kissed the hands and face repeatedly; it was the handsome young mechanic, who had wanted to go into aviation and with luck could have been killed that way, but she had her own Sicilian pride in what he had done instead. "Oh my favorite son, what a terrible end you have come to. . . ." Outside, after screaming maledictions at everyone around, she fainted again. Her other daughter had just taken off one of her shoes to hurl at the press photographers, and went on furiously to denounce the traitors responsible for her brother's death. It seemed there *had* been betrayal, by whom was not clear until months later; some said the star-wearer, Pisciotta, who was still at large.

But meanwhile Turiddu had been what everyone knows, the "King of Montelepre" and of a good deal more than that, with a band formed in a system of cells like any clandestine army, and a network of agents, informers, and city and peasant lookouts over a large part of Sicily. It was not safe for archaeologists to study ruins in remote parts of the island without a safe-conduct from him, and it was said in Palermo that he could walk in the streets or sit in cafés there when he felt like it; nobody would tell, nobody tried to claim the price of thirty million lire that was on his head, whether more from terror, partisanship, or just native Sicilian mumness it would be hard to know. It would be as it was the last night, when he was found shot in an apartment court in the town of Castelvetrano; all the shutters stayed closed; nobody had heard anything. He could give orders to the so-called Sicilian Parliament, a body unique in Italy — something like a state legislature in the United States though not so powerful; still, it was probably useful to keep it scared. He could also exact tribute from all the lesser bandit gangs around, to whom he would give permission to pull off certain jobs; the recalcitrant ones were wiped out.

His own jobs were chiefly of a Jesse James variety, or something between Al Capone and Robin Hood, leaving out the modern-political complications. The steady work was made up of highway holdups, kidnappings, blackmail; on one occasion the band blew up a truckful of carabinieri, killing seven and maiming more; in the end some eighty carabinieri had been killed, plus an undetermined number of plain citizens. A fairly typical episode was the attempted kidnapping of a Palermo businessman named Antonino, in September 1946. He and his wife were being driven to their country house by a chauffeur, in the evening, when they were stopped by a taxi parked in the middle of the road; a group of men jumped out and tried to pull Mr. Antonino into the taxi, but being a strong man and evidently rather high-strung he struggled with them and so got filled with bullets instead. His wife was also shot, but not fatally; the chauffeur had fainted in the car. This assault was a failure; so was another on a jewelry shop in Palermo, in which the owner resisted and for some reason was not even shot. But the failures were few. Other incidents were more romantic: stripping the duchess politely of her jewels and later returning the volume of Steinbeck (his favorite author) that he had taken from her table, with a note: "I don't see why anyone as reactionary as you should have such a book, so I thought of not returning it, but when Giuliano gives his word he always keeps it."

In 1947 alone he was said to have carried out seven ransom cases, all involving wealthy men, and about fifty holdups, thefts of cattle and so on, with a gross intake of three hundred million lire, or about five hundred dollars. His figure per ransom at that time has been reported at between thirty and fifty million lire. What the total for the seven years was nobody knows, nor how much stayed in the hands of Giuliano himself, nor whether it is true that he sent a small fortune to be invested somewhere outside the country. The expenses, of course, were heavy; a great many minor people had to be paid, and the gang and their families taken care of — Frank Mannino, for one, is supposed to have become a large landowner through the business; and some of the profits were distributed among the poor.

Nobody knows how much that was either. It was belittled after his death, in official versions and among people of property in general, because they disliked the idea of it and also disliked the possibilities of a Giuliano myth; one figure put it at 1 percent of the total loot, but it may have been much more, or less. It was enough, in any case, to give a solid basis to the immense popularity of prestige he certainly had among a great many working-class Sicilians, too separatist in their views or too independent by nature to incline toward the Communist Party, and perhaps even some of those were as confused, for all the party line on the matter and Giuliano's warfare against them, as they were on the mainland. It would have been enough that in a country of such rabid social discrepancy he stole only from the rich; which is true, however little he may have given to the poor. On that his orders were absolute; the lower income brackets were not to be touched. One of his men once robbed a poor peasant — one who furthermore had a sick wife, as the story goes — of two barrels of wine that he was taking to town to sell, and Giuliano on hearing of it immediately shot him in front of several others: another of those "indelible impressions."

There can have been, of course, a consideration of policy mixed in with this furious homegrown social justice. The poor were his safety. In the end it would be love and not terror that would keep them mum, and keep them ready to shelter him for an hour or a night or for weeks as hundreds did, not only in the countryside; that was Colonel Luca's trouble in the last months; he was beating the hills but Giuliano was not there, he was in the towns, in one house after another. The poor were also his immediate public and applauders, the necessary prop, along with a string of women, for his conception of himself, though at the same time for both protection and applause he was beginning to look to larger fields.

In particular he seems to have had a great yearning, perhaps spurred a little by his family's inglorious retreat, to be admitted in America, not as a gangster, which he still refused to consider himself, but as a kind of foreign dignitary and equal champion of democracy; perhaps he had heard too of the political right of

asylum; his obsessive hope of pardon, together with his lofty notion of what he was about, led him to stranger fancies than that.
But probably piqued by the reception, or lack of it, of his state-
hood scheme, which he had taken great pains to work out so that
the United States government would not be embarrassed interna-
tionally (the Sicilian people were to ask unanimously for annexa-
tion), he became severely critical, not of America's social system
but of its foreign policy.

In a letter gravely and laboriously setting forth his views on the
prospect of war, etc., he described various aspects of current
Americans, including Truman, as ridiculous. "In my opinion
Truman has lost the race because I am sure that a good part of the
American people has already concluded that he is ridiculous as I
have concluded." The line of reasoning, rather obscure, had to do
with inconsistency in dealing with Russia. The idea of atomic control was also ridiculous, "for the reason that neither Russia nor
America is a house or a palazzo that you could easily control, but
are very vast territories where whoever wanted to could hide a lot
more than atomic bombs." The Atlantic Pact was an excellent
idea, but the Americans had not known how to "qualify the situation of their allies," especially France and Italy, which were
hotbeds of communism and in a war would become "a field of
treason or a field of fraticidal strife." He had decided that Italy
could be saved from slavery and ruin only if communism and cler-
icalism were both gotten rid of, and there were a government of
liberals and social democrats, divorced "from all ideology," and
that would put through "a truly social law."

These corner drugstore deliberations, amicably addressed to
the Italian newspaperman he had permitted to visit him, and
which after all could get by in many higher places, are semigram-
matical and have the frequent crossings-out of an unaccustomed
mental effort, but are written in a curiously rapid, unflowery, and
confident hand. The tone is engaging too, as of an informal mem-
orandum from Roosevelt to Churchill.

Another such leap into the grand impossible was his series of
direct communications to Minister of the Interior Mario Scelba,

pet anathema of the communists, proposing what must have seemed to Giuliano a plausible and intelligent horse trade, good for both parties: the government would drop all charges, and he would quietly depart, presumably to live somewhere on his savings. He had only failed to consider that Scelba, under several years of daily battering from the communists on just this subject, had somewhat more prestige than he to think of; every incident in the country's continuing civil battles, every death of a party member, some apparently engineered by the party itself, in strikes and demonstrations, had brought the same shriek and litany: Scelba, "assassin of the working class," could not even catch a bandit; the further implication was that he didn't want to, and was even using Giuliano to wipe out the Sicilian communists. So the only answer was a stepping-up of the manhunt. But for that proposal of Giuliano's really no special derangement was needed. The brigand and the minister of the interior did have that cause in common, and the young man's whole political experience, even more than that of young men in most places, had been of such deals and horse trades, often enough involving murderers. The best families of Sicily could have, and in some cases might have to have for their own protection, a son in the Mafia, whose Ku Klux Klan activities, beautified by no such aims as Turiddu ascribed to himself, underlay the nicest garden parties as they did the most legal elections. The distinction between his kind of power and the respectable kind must have seemed a little slim; and his power was at the moment enormous; he would have had to be more cynical not to think of a deal as natural.

In the furor of discussions of him later there were suggestions that toward the end he had even had some thought of a deal with the communists. It was possible; he might have come to need them, and thought he could use them; an ignorant country strong-arm man, however well-meaning, would not necessarily be above such recombinations, and for the party line it would have been routine: the "martyrs" are forgotten, the aspiring young working-class fighter, victim of the reactionary landowners and separatists and their ally the monster Scelba, carries the banner of the starving Sicilian proletariat, in its march for Peace. . . . But there may have been no such prospect.

As it is, his record in that direction is unswerving: the communists had deceived and betrayed the workers, Russia was going to bring on a war because it had the "megalomania of parties and command"; and he made quite a number of martyrs. The main engagement, and the cause of the proceedings in Viterbo, took place in 1947 in a town called Portella della Ginestra, when his band descended on a communist May Day festa: the motive this time was purely political, whether or not connected with some new separatist tie-up or illusion, but not all those shot were communists, nor adults. Also described at the trial, which was thought too provocative to hold anywhere in Sicily, were similar attacks on the Communist Party headquarters of five other villages in the territory Giuliano controlled. The accused were twenty-seven of his men, some of whom had been kept in jail three years before the case came to trial, and whose families were also being held; all denied any part in the "massacre," evidently on Giuliano's orders and in the conviction that he would rescue them, or out of fear of reprisals. The witnesses included a long list of the wounded and relatives of the dead.

One villager told at length how his horse had been killed in the Portella assault, together with nine other animals — horses, donkeys, and mules. "A few minutes later they were horribly swollen up, perhaps because of the heat." A woman whose twelve-year-old son had been shot spoke as follows: "Giovanni was almost a child. The morning of May first he was in bed when some friends came to get him to go to the festa; I didn't want to send him alone, so I went along too. In Portella, Giovanni left me and went off a little way to get some medlars that were there, and it was just then that I heard the first three shots; I threw myself on the ground, hearing the bullets whistle over my head; I called desperately to my boy; he came in a minute, terribly pale. I asked him what was the matter. 'Mamma, I've been wounded!' he said. I looked up at the higher ground where they were firing from, and saw the shadows of three heads moving; I screamed at the top of my voice: 'You murderers, what are you doing?' My daughter, who had come with us, bent over Giovanni and said to him: 'Don't be afraid, if you need it I'll give you my blood to make you well.' They carried Giovanni, who had his stomach torn by a bullet, on to a cart; barefoot, like a crazy woman, I began running behind it, until they made me get up and ride too. 'Mamma, I'm dying,' he said. 'Why did they shoot me? What have I done?'" (Weeping.) "They took him to the hospital; the bullet was a powerful one and had gone through his intestines; peritonitis set in; he died the next day." One of the older victims was a carabiniere whom the gang happened to meet on the road afterward, and whose body was found in a ravine forty days later.

Another woman, whose fourteen-year-old son was killed, after finishing her testimony turned on the prisoners' cage screaming: "I call for justice! Justice!"

In the midst of this the news came that Giuliano was dead. The twenty-seven prisoners, sitting as usual in chains, refused to believe it; his hold on them was so strong, it seems they could not conceive of any trap that could catch him, or that he would not bring them all through in his old style in the end; but they were shown pictures. "That's him! That's Iddu all right. He got himself killed!" and when they had had time to rest in their amazement: "And we're left here to take the rap!" Then they began to hate him and disown him. One said: "It's high time. All that delay wasn't doing any good, especially to us, sitting here in this cage all because of him. At least maybe they'll let our families out now"; and another: "He should have died twenty-eight years ago, he shouldn't have been born at all." Another, the oldest: "I wonder if they'll print the pictures of him, now that he's dead. I'd like to see him in the papers like that, the way they've fixed him now."

The woman who had called for justice was equally amazed. "Remember what I said here yesterday? A mother's curses never fail; mine reached Giuliano in less than a day!"

But in Rome it had been a different story; people were for him or against him, but it was not simple. For the great mass of the people in their great poverty it was not simple for obvious reasons, because he had been one of them and any revolt can seem better than none; he might even have won, got control of all Sicily and set up his own regime, and then everybody would have respected him. And for many others, not only and not primarily Italians because Italians do not get so excited as other people about criminals, the image was just as troubling. The guilt was too complex, the contrast too appealing with the little mangled timorous personality that seemed destined to become standard in these days. This was real, not an existentialist novel, and Giuliano was young and handsome, and in such an attractive setting; it was not as if he had had to do his shooting out of roominghouse windows. A Swedish woman journalist named Cyliacus had actually gone there and lived with him for several days; a picture of them came out later, she on horseback against those Arizona-type hills, he holding the bridle, smiling for once and looking terribly like any teenager's dream. There was talk of other girls from good families who had had the same idea; and boys and young men all over Italy dreamed of following Giuliano; one seventeen-year-old had given up his job in Rome and got all the way to Montelepre, because he had heard that the bandit had sent out a call for recruits. It really seemed that that subtle postage-stamp gum that makes faith cling to society and keeps the younger generation out of trouble and fit for war was very nearly licked off, in Italy as everywhere else. A great many husbands, earning a handsome living in some ministerial or commercial cubicle, felt themselves looked at in the evening as if they were hardly men at all. And the communists were laughing, insofar as they know how. The thing had to be exterminated.

Minister of the Interior Scelba, who had also instituted a big campaign against indecent bathing suits, was really on the spot by now, but the rest of the government were not much less embarrassed. Above all, it was not a spectacle to have continuing into Holy Year.

It was not easy. Colonel Luca, when he took over the new assignment, is said to have asked for a year to carry it out, and he knew what he was talking about, though actually he finished the job in ten months. He was a quiet, duty-minded, and by then worn-looking police officer, the son of a watchmaker, with some vein of restlessness and hunger for more than routine enterprise, which might almost have made him a bandit himself under different circumstances or a rebel leader in some colonial area, and which had given him instead a large experience in tracking down such characters. In Turkey, where he was called the "Italian Lawrence," in Rhodes and the Italian African colonies he had had, in the period after World War I, a string of boyish though deadly serious adventures, all very creditable from the old-fashioned or Kiplingesque point of view, and is said to have been greatly loved by the people wherever he went: the perfect missionary of Italian colonial benevolence. In Rome later he went out of his way to find jobs for the poor who were brought in to headquarters, instead of following the usual police routine, so that they began to come in voluntarily. It was not reported in the Giuliano period whether he also followed the line of duty in those early years with regard to opponents of the regime, anyway he seems to have gone on pleasing his superiors; a picture taken early in 1941 shows him in the full regalia, tassels, medals, feathers, of a high officer of the carabinieri, looking in fact very like Lawrence except for the stiffness of eye and carriage denoting the member of the corps, in whom thought will never come before discipline. But there was a limit; when the Germans came in he resisted all bribes and persecutions and chose to become, among other things, a repairman for the gas company.

Giuliano finally had an enemy his own size, and more; Colonel Luca, beneath his medals and whatever *his* crimes, would appear to have had real love in his makeup, the kind that is called a love of humanity though it may be only respect for it, so given equal tactical cleverness on both sides he was bound to win; Turridu had nothing but his own swollen self-esteem to oppose to that. A ghastly thing began to happen. Slowly, in one village after another, and although the communist part of the population was at least theoretically no more in favor of one than the other, the policeman began taking over the bandit's prestige. He became popular, he was trusted, he was also strong; it must have been a dubious shift of feeling first and at the end a landslide — even Giuliano's mother, though she would never play his game, spoke well of him to the neighbors, because he had been kind to her. People who had worked in small ways for the gang began to want, and dare, to do it for the other side; the network broke in a dozen and then a hundred unimportant places, and the ransom notes, in which the price had come down to a mere one or two million, were for the first time left unanswered. Giuliano was being cut off economically as well as in other ways.

He may not have been able to grasp how serious it was. Italians generally assumed that he would escape; he was known to have sent agents long before to feel out the ground in Tunisia and other places, and at the very end, two days before he was killed, there was a rumor around the country, received with a mixture of relief and admiration, that he had gotten out and was on his way to America. Locally, in the region around Castelvetrano to which he had moved from the Montelepre area, there was talk of an airplane that was going to come for him at night — and probably take him to America. America is bound to come into any such story, where a deus ex machina is needed; it is better, it is the machina itself, and had remained that, for all of Truman and atomic control, in Giuliano's mind too. He wanted to go there and exploit an invention of his that he was very proud of, and one feels again in both the desire and the invention the old humiliation of the immigrants who have failed, from whom no bounteous packages have flowed, who have not after thirty years come back for the summer traveling second class on a good ship, who lasted not even a year and came back, in shame, to what they had left. It would all have been wiped out; Salvatore Giuliano would have returned to America in glory. The invention was: perpetual motion. The mechanic in him was functioning to the last. Colonel Luca, who still fiddled with watches in his spare time, could perhaps have helped him.

The first official version of how he was finally trapped would have been appealing. It was said that Luca's men rigged up one of their cars as a movie truck, which they did but not with this sequel, and arranged to have word reach Giuliano that they were making a movie about him, which if he would agree to appear in it would have a huge commercial success — this too, in America; so out of vanity he fell into the trap. It would have been touching, like the pacts in blood and the fine clothes and his thinking he could fight the communists, or perhaps make a deal with them, all by himself; it would have been another innocence, with all the glamour he had, to have lost his life for the glamour of Hollywood; but it was not true. Then it was said that he was ambushed on his way to an "amorous encounter," but that was not true either.

Nobody outside Colonel Luca's confidence knew then what was, except that he was dead, and had been killed barefoot and without his gold watch, and at that time had lost all but two of his men; the last of the others to be arrested were said to have been Mannino and another named Badalamenti, one taken at a trumped-up appointment in a hotel, the other while riding hidden in a basket of tomatoes on the back of a truck; both had been sold out by other members of the gang. It turned out that not even the shooting scene in the Castelvetrano courtyard, which was blazed all over the papers for several days, was true. The body was there, and a companion was seen to slip away, and one of Luca's men, Captain Perenze, happened by some coincidence to be just in that courtyard, and fired, but Giuliano's gun, it was discovered, had not been fired and the seven bullet wounds in his body had been made several hours earlier, presumably while he slept, and Pisciotta was said to have been the only man who could have done that. Pisciotta's lawyer denied it, and quoted Pisciotta as saying he was going to avenge his cousin's death. Mannino and Badalamenti, who was known for his stunning gold teeth, also exonerated Pisciotta, each naming his own betrayer instead.

Anyway, the pictures seemed to be true. They show Turiddu lying as he fell or was dumped in the courtyard that night, looking except for the blood like any Italian boy having a nap on a hot afternoon, and then on his back in the improvised morgue at the cemetery with big blocks of ice set near him to keep him presentable, then with the local doctor who had been doing his part of the job, then with plaster of paris in his hair and beside him the local sculptor who had been making a death mask to be sent to the Museum of Crime in Rome, all of which was generally acknowledged to be for the best and was extremely gratifying to some people. There were speeches, congratulations, promotions; Colonel Luca was made a general and Captain Perenze a colonel; many husbands, officials, men of property generally could breathe easier, almost as if a whole threatening army of philosophical principle had been routed. It had really been too much to have this and the communists to feel oppressed by at the same time.

But there were other reactions. A woman who lived in the courtyard where the final scene took place said that some time after hearing the shots she got around to peeking out from behind her shutters, and saw Perenze and another carabiniere standing over the body, "looking sad." There were other people who looked that way when the pictures came out, because most had never seen a photograph of the bandit before and whatever they had expected it was not quite that; it was his youth that was startling. One had never quite visualized the great Giuliano, the terror of a population, as so young and so unterrible, like the best and the most popular in any Italian village, and this surprise came more from the view of the half-naked body, the actual young flesh and bone gone to waste, than from the face, though it was strange to find nothing "wrong" with that, unless you happened to see that one last close-up, with the eyes. It was perhaps what Colonel Luca felt too when it was all over, and perhaps he better than anyone could appreciate the juxtaposition of his own harried, guilty, aging features, like those of millions of men his age all over the world, with those of his young opponent. This is not the be-feathered and be-medaled functionary whose picture had been taken ten years before, but a man going bald, with shrewd but humble and deeply ringed eyes and his head, in violent contrast to that other, hunched down between his shoulders.

He looks very sad indeed, as though conscious of the poverty of his role, and of having much blame as well as credit in the whole long story. He did not lend himself to any publicity, nor proffer any statement at all — perhaps he could not, in view of the mystery around the affair; in any case for the time being he dropped back quickly where he had come from, out of the public view; and it might have been that for him as for many others the only true picture of what gave him his promotion was the black one of sorrow and despair, taken outside the cemetery in Castelvetrano.

It was a typical scene of peasant mourning, and could also be a scene from one of the Greek tragedies that are still produced on the island in the same theater where they opened two thousand years ago, and through which Sicilian peasants sit enthralled every year as if nothing were fresher; the patterns of feeling are the most familiar; their sorrow revolves around the same sense of harm prepared long ago, not to be averted. In this scene the faces of the two women, Turiddu's mother and his sister Giuseppina, are entirely hidden in their enormous thick black veils; they sit bent over on little straight-back chairs, clutching handkerchiefs, the mother with the other hand up to support her head and one foot hooked onto a rung of the chair, showing a length of wrinkled cotton stocking. The sister's husband sits looking toward them from the right, thick like a man of the fields and in a thick black suit, though it is July, with beside him his son, Turiddu's nephew and namesake, Salvatore, a boy of five or six, listless and slumped on the edge of the chair with his hands folded as though he had been waiting for hours. He is the only one who is looking out, straight out from among the black suffering figures that seem almost undifferentiated, a single pool of anguish, matching the two huge pools of the child's eyes as he stares at you from under the great burden of his solemnity and his weariness, not asking for anything now or for any other time. He knows; nothing was to be averted; nothing is to be.

The photographers, among other things, were not to be, the sister's shoe had not been enough; the mother, driven hysterical by them, tried to throw her chair at the cameras, and went on to the height of her primitive agony from that. "Oh my blood!" she screamed over her son's body. "Sangue mio! Sangue mio!" Then she insisted on going to the courtyard on the other side of town, and kneeling down, licked the pavement where his body had lain.

Outside the family, the story was not finished. At Viterbo, after the months of expensive preparation and the days of such questions as "Were you sitting or standing?" and "Were you in the army? Could you say at what distance the shot had been fired?" an exhausting legal dispute broke out, occasioned by the capture of Mannino and Badalamenti, or rather the announcement of it: it turned out they had been captured some time before. It seemed that if they were not brought to the courtroom within a certain number of days the trial would be invalidated, then when they were, it was invalidated by that. In the dark broiling hall of justice, a former church, the lawyers sweated, shouted, argued frenetically over points of this and that; there was talk of various kinds of procedure and why they applied or did not. It was all very complicated, and the heat wave the worst of the century in Europe, so when everyone was sufficiently worn out and exasperated the trial was adjourned, to be begun all over "as soon as possible," perhaps in the fall, actually after a year. The witnesses were sent home; they would have a new court to tell their stories to some day. The prisoners, unconvicted, untried, set off for another summer in their chains.

But as one of them said: "A bandit can't die of old age. Death or prison are always waiting for him, so whichever the end is going to be, it's better not to think about it; just keep smiling."

The communists meanwhile were equally busy finding a new line that would minimize any credit due to the government, or rather turn its belated success into new discredit of the hated Scelba. It seemed the authorities had been determined not to take Giuliano alive, for fear of the revelations he would make if given a chance to talk — revelations, it was suggested, that would show up the whole basis of the Demo-Christian regime if not of the Atlantic Pact besides. Furthermore it was not the carabinieri at all who had gotten rid of him but the Mafia; on which grounds a communist-line senator demanded that Colonel Luca, although deserving some thanks, be deprived of his promotion. This too, like the trial, would go on and on; even when it was known at last

that Pisciotta had done the killing there remained many political
obscurities to be capitalized on.

But for the people these ins and outs were too abstruse, the
communist explanations misfired; not that many of the faithful opposed the line on this question, they only ignored it, because at
least outside of Sicily they respected Giuliano for the same reasons
that made them communists, and what lived on, regardless of revelations, was only the sense of the man himself: a poor boy, driven
through no fault of his own to take power and make justice for
himself, and who had the strength to do it. "And besides, they say
he gave to the poor." As for murder, the party also went in for that.
There was for some months a little feeling of loss and vague depression when he was spoken of, broken only by the rumors that
kept arising that it was not he who had been killed after all; it was
as if there had been some obscure, intimate setback for all of
them, as if the very idea of "something better" — not only economically: some way of standing taller, having something to say
for yourself — had once more been proved untenable, and
stamped out like a brush fire.

In Sicily feelings were stronger and more specific, and another
fire, of myth and romance, began raging immediately, which it appeared that not even the great amount of enmity against Giuliano
on the island would check. The people of Castelvetrano, whatever
they thought of him, had to apologize to people everywhere else; it
was known as the Judas town, and the local youth all became ama-
teur detectives, reenacting the final episode in full detail night after
night in an effort to prove that the treachery really took place somewhere else. In Montelepre, when the news of his death arrived, the
village barber suddenly went mad and began yelling that he
wanted to go to heaven and shave Giuliano. There was another
kind of aftermath; a girl named Francesca di Maio from Castelvetrano, in the last stage of pregnancy, and who had known Giuliano,
after hearing with no apparent emotion that he had been killed,
went out and threw herself down a well on the outskirts of town.

In another town, a painter who went by the name of Corkscrew
had had within two days seventeen orders to paint the Giuliano

story on the sides of donkey carts, in place of the old ones of Roncesvalles, the death of Manfred, and so on. He was said to have turned them down because he would need more space to do the job properly, but other artists were available. The sober-minded editorial writers around the country were all remarking that with Giuliano's death there had been closed a "sorry chapter" in Sicilian history, also in postwar Italian history; it was the end of a period, fortuitously marked at the same time by the withdrawal, at last, of Allied banknotes: the disruptions of war had finally run their course. But they seemed to have reckoned without certain factors, though it was true that there was a slight lull in banditry; just for one thing, they were overlooking the donkey carts. The chief character in the sad chapter, being removed from all practical inconveniences, was already off on a new career, in legend; and in Sicily, as one of the Rome newspapermen on the case put it, "all of life is a legend."

A lone cart might even have turned up somewhere on which the painted hero was Colonel Luca, but that is hardly likely.

ROMAN JOURNAL I

*S*TREET OF IMPERIAL FORUMS
Designed in the '30s as a propaganda and parade street, and then called Via dell'Impero, Empire Street, in line with the fascist dream; the maps of the ancient empire in marble and bronze are still there, and a little of the hypnosis of archaism emanates from them even now. The problem goes beyond that; it is not only the original purpose of the street that is responsible for the depression one feels there. It is an age of platitude; the ruins were bound to be exposed and capitalized on in one way or another, and besides an avenue was needed, for modern traffic; the question is of the survival of imagination under any system in this century. However Empire Street happened to be made then.

One of the words that gained most in currency during fascism was the verb *sistemare*. The ruins among other things were systematized; they were made useful, not in the lusty old Renaissance sense of being hacked to pieces for building materials. They were physically propped up and clamped together and pasted over with patches of restoration until only a scholar knows and then not always when he is looking at the real thing. They were given a mental purpose. Not only here, although this was the center. There was not quite time to do it everywhere so there are still a few old structures with some of their old power of suggestion — the Portico of Octavia in the Jewish quarter for one, that is the best, and bits of wall or column here or there, but here and there everywhere is this other operation, not always macabre, sometimes only funny. A slick new apartment house has a surgical incision in its side, to frame an ancient column; dumpings of old brickwork are railed off like meteors in a natural history museum. Almost everything fifteen hundred years old and over has come in for a fury of exhibitionism.

Archaeology helped, and was helped by fascism with its particular propaganda needs, but it would only have gone ahead more slowly without it. The past, like love, was never so precarious and abused and useless; it was never so thoroughly investigated. The Forum, which you see in the old prints with the ground level halfway up the Arch of Septimius Severus, was bound to be dug out down to its last fact as dreams have been. The foundations are exposed, the temples identified, the lovely shapes defy you to be mistaken about them in any detail; if the guide or the guidebook is inadequate you can study the plaster model of ancient Rome in the little church of Santa Rita. In the imperial forums across the street houses flew, columns popped up, although sometimes there were only a few inches to work from; no ancient grandeur was to be left unused.

They were also building all the time, like Augustus, only the jobs went to the worst architects. In another country, another conjunction the buildings would not look so sinister; in Rome an offense in architecture goes deeper, and there is something in this one, wherever you meet it, like a tampering with the brain in totalitarian prisons. You feel it even in the brick wall across from the maps, nothing but a sustaining wall with a marble border but it is identical with the walls of dozens of large buildings, it being of the nature of fascist architecture to obscure any difference between a church and a gas company. Imagination had been killed; a strange air of the hygienic takes its place; the *piano regolatore* was being run by a bureaucrat, named Marcello Piacentini, who continued to function later in private and for the Vatican.

But on Empire Street the fascist operation is combined now with the others, which would have come anyway. The tourist buses are rolling along it; the Temple of Castor and Pollux, the beautiful twins, is on the travel and perfume ads; the Basilica of Maxentius is an outdoor concert hall and at night the Forum and the whole area are lit up like a movie set. The job is done by experts; floodlights are hidden behind casual-looking blocks of fallen architrave, behind bushes and on neighboring roofs; the place is crawling with wires.

The straight three-column piece (the Dioscuri again) is of course central, with beside it the little round white Temple of Vesta, more glowing than it ever was with the sacred fire or the thought of it; beyond is the billion-dollar curtain of the Palatine, with its rat-runs discreetly sketched in and its genuine bank of green shining like deep-frozen vegetables. Below the Capitoline cliff the originally decadent Portico of the Counsel of the Gods is brought forward for its decorative obtuse angle and the fine plastic contrast it makes with the massive masonry, anteceding it by several hundred years, of the Tabularium. The lighting fixtures are particularly thick here, and are turned on the cubicles of the portico in such a way you think the twelve gods must still be there but coming closer you find their places empty like a row of unused locker rooms.

It is all undeniably handsome, in the way of surfaces, but *the real thing* is precarious; you wonder, as in other matters, if there is such a thing; certainly the ruins are more shrouded in these publicities than they ever were by their vines, so much that at moments it seems they might as well be a genuine fake. They would be as decorative, and their old "awful grandeur" is gone in any case.

You discover them nevertheless, eventually. The stones are real, even though some have been pushed around; and in the daytime there is still the Roman light. There must be some meteorological explanation for it, aside from the lack of soot; and this is where it is most crucial. Nothing is static in that light; surfaces become depths, the relations of things are always traveling. The mountains around the city are sometimes low and distant, hardly a rim at all or even invisible, giving the place a free commercial look. Other days they are so high and precise it seems incommunicado, like a religious stronghold very high in Asia, and on those days there is a kind of ferocity of interrelation among the buildings; they belong together, and none with anything else.

That is when the Forum is most beautiful. It *is* still beautiful, in a very different genre of course from a hundred years ago when it was a cow pasture; it survives the Age of Platitude as it did the quarrying of the Renaissance; the night-lighting only exaggerates what is true. The depression lifts; memory returns. — There is a peculiar power in stones, which makes this little hollow, when one has begun to care about it at all, much more like a lake than the only real or real-artificial lake in the city, and Empire Street Rome's lakeside esplanade, and it is perhaps because one feels that power and experience in general most threatened just here that one comes to love the neighborhood more than most, and more than one would have perhaps in its old romantic look. It seems that the Colosseum at one end of the avenue and Trajan's Column at the other, although they have withstood every other threat, are nearly done for now; they could not possibly be there in another hundred years, if already it is such a struggle to see them.

It would be futile anyway to wish they had not kept up with the times, however destructive, when Rome's deepest gift for the imagination is in its having always done just that.

Colosseum
a) In 1855 there were 420 varieties of plants growing in the Colosseum; there are probably not more than 20 or 30 now. Many of the ones that were there were not to be found anywhere else in Europe, and were thought to have sprung perhaps from seeds mixed in with the fodder brought over from Africa for the animals. Myrtle, strangely enough, was not among them. The Baths of

Caracalla, when Shelley was being inspired there, were a forest of myrtle and clematis.

b) In 249, supposed to be the thousandth anniversary of the founding of Rome, there were celebrations here in which a thousand couples of gladiators fought, and the following animals were killed: 12 elephants, 10 tigers, 60 domesticated lions, 30 domesticated leopards, 10 hyenas, 10 giraffes, 10 wild asses, 40 wild horses, 10 zebras, 6 hippopotamuses.

But Statius tells in a poem about another kind of festivity, for the Saturnalia or in later parlance a Christmas party, held under Domitian, not long after the inauguration of the place by his brother Titus in the year 80; at least one can assume that this is the amphitheater referred to. The emperor paid for the party and it was evidently very gay. A rope was stretched high over the arena, from which "dainties" were shaken down among the people, including figs, dates, plums from Damascus, apples and pears from Ameria, etc. There were also bread and wine. The emperor himself put in an appearance, and people of all classes mingled in the scramble; as the poet puts it, "freedom has loosed the bonds of awe." In the afternoon there were combats of women gladiators, dwarfs, and others, and at nightfall prostitutes and Lydian chorus girls were brought on. By this time people were getting tired, but suddenly there was great illumination and a whole new show started, and they all revived. This was the most exciting part of all: thousands of exotic birds were released overhead, flamingoes from the Nile, pheasants from Phasis, guinea fowl from Numidia, and the people went wild catching them; the amphitheater held probably forty to fifty thousand people, perhaps more on that kind of occasion, and there were enough birds for everyone. Statius thought it had been splendid of the emperor.

There are other Roman amusements one thinks of, of different periods. In the Renaissance greased pigs tied on carts used to be sent rolling down Monte Testaccio, the hill made of ancient potsherds, and both aristocrats and men of the people would run out and try to catch them; the casualties were numerous. Another sport, begun in the fifteenth century, was the carnival races of Jews on the Corso, with mounted soldiers galloping behind; eventually the Jews got out of this by paying for wild riderless horses to run instead; other carnival races on the Corso were of cripples, hunchbacks, and naked old men, and part of the same festivity was the execution of criminals in Piazza del Popolo at the head of the street, with executioners dressed as harlequins, etc. Certain spectator sports, such as mock naval battles and more important public executions, required special stands to be built, even in ancient times when the permanent facilities for shows of all kinds were of fabulous size and number, and one of the recurrent themes of Roman history is of the collapse of these stands, it seems that for all their genius as masons they were not very good with wood; anyway the mortality rate in the pursuit of pleasure, taking a two-thousand year average, seems to have been about equal to that for war, plague, or politics, not counting the fatalities that sometimes constituted the show.

This is one of the places where the secret of enormity that characterizes nearly all the ruins, even now, is most perplexing. It has to do partly with the nature of stone, and in the Colosseum with the size of the separate blocks of stone; and the spatial relations are different from any of ours. The inside seems at first strangely small for the outside circumference, and as compared to our huge playing fields, but soon another impression of bigness takes over, from the height of the rim, the extent and steep slope of the seating area, the intensity of what was looked at, and the fact that so tiny an arena held that much attention and justified that much stone.

c) It seems the old explanation of the missing half of its rim is not certain; it was that a Farnese pope gave his nephew permission to take as much stone from the Colosseum as he could remove in a day, and by hiring four thousand workmen he reduced it to its present shape in twenty-four hours, to build the Palazzo Farnese. But the general idea is true enough. One sale by the Vatican treasury early on in the new building splurge, in 1452, was of 2,522 cartloads of travertine from the Colosseum, and there must have been many others; if all the material of several of the handsomest palazzi in Rome were to jump back into the hole it would be partly filled, with its original stone. The Forum and everything else was going the same way; it is said that except for one minor set of columns not a stone in Saint Peter's was taken from contemporary quarries.

A furious destruction, with crowbars, on what had lasted through centuries of being an armed fortress: what wonderful vitality there is in this image, of the people destroying, of the thing destroyed. But its broken profile would be wonderful anyway, unless it had been done by design.

d) It was in the days of easy horror and the 420 varieties of plants that people used to fall in love there in the moonlight; but then at that time, and until the mid–twentieth century, you used to be able to walk around in the arena; not that Rome has lost the trick of stirring up the most misdirected passions in foreigners. The view from the top is dismal. There is a strong smell of urine in the lower halls.

A minor beauty of the three tiers of arches is that their side columns have rising orders of capitals, Doric at the bottom, Ionic, and Corinthian, as had also been done nearly a hundred years before in the Theatre of Marcellus.

e) It is on the site, or part of it, of Nero's lake.

Three characters: Augustus, Christ, Nero — the psychological triad of all Rome. Everything forces you to think of them; there is nothing that does not seem to have its source in one or the other, though the source was only a culmination; three men who lived within thirty years of one another and have been running a good part of the world ever since.

It is probably this power of theirs, as images, more than our calendar, that makes one think of that period as a central point in time, as the golden pillar in the Forum was the focus of all geographical distances.

D. H. Lawrence would have written quite differently and perhaps not so well about the Etruscans if he had not been writing under fascism. He might have loved them as much but he would not have had to fight for them so against the Romans. But the irritability was natural; it became hard for many people to think of the original apart from the parody. Besides, Rome was putting on the first modern exhibit in practice of some of his own deepest inclinations, a good ground for hatred.

Not the plaster model in Santa Rita, only Piranesi tells the true surrealism of the ancient city; he had to be a poet and a little crazy to do it. He had to have an obsession and it was a moving and beautiful one: stairs. De Quincey described, not quite accurately because he had only heard about them from Coleridge, the stairs in Piranesi's imaginary prisons; but his sense of them was accurate, and they were the images of his own opium dreams. The dreamer is always climbing, with desperate effort and hopelessly; there is no top. Fantastic machines of torture, big enough for giants, are around him at every level. "With the same power of endless growth and self-reproduction did my architecture proceed in my dreams." In the imaginary reconstructions, of forums, streets, basilicas, the patterns of stairs long or low, hedged to infinity with statues of gods and emperors on high pedestals, are equally a hopelessness but without dread; the steps are to the scale of human legs but in their conglomeration are a mystery that appears soluble only to the statues, several times life size. Beyond the marble desert of a landing, too big for a walker ever to cross or a human crowd to fill although it may be vaulted and roofed, will be more steps, perhaps only three or four but leading to a new orientation in the architecture, which will have its end or point of pause in other stairs. In the images of death, sepulchral chambers or fantasies of tombs along the Appian Way, there are sometimes ladders instead or all communication between levels will have vanished, the final hopelessness, because the towering tombs are made of superimposed elevations, each of which with its statues and architectural detail invites exploration, only there is no way up, or if you were up you cannot imagine how you would get down. The power of the etchings is that you keep trying to imagine it.

The 124 marble steps of the stairs of Santa Maria in Aracoeli, beside the Campidoglio, were taken from the Temple of the Sun, built by Aurelian on the Quirinal. The peristyle had 44 columns, each 65 feet high and seven feet, eight inches in diameter.

Baths of Caracalla: Accommodating some sixteen hundred bathers at a time; one of the ruined rooms was the model for Pennsylvania Station in New York; another is Rome's summer opera house.

Baths of Diocletian: Built by the forced labor of forty thousand Christians; enclosing in their ravaged state one of the biggest churches, Michelangelo's great cloister and the Museo Nazionale, once a barracks for French soldiers; it could also have been a hanger for dirigibles.

In their present configurations they are two of Rome's best works of wit, which gives one a relation to opera and to sculpture unlike any other in the world. The opera house was started in the '30s, when the parades were most frequent down the Via dell'Impero, and cannot have been very pleasant in that association. Now that nobody cares what you make of it, the fact that the wings of the stage are *the real thing* is comical and magnificent; it is where the present Roman game, of true and false, belief and suspicion, is most a game and most delightful; when the lights come on after the suicide duet nearly everybody is smiling a little. The museum is the only one, perhaps the only one anywhere, that the statues and other works seem to have found their way to naturally, through affinity in time and the wisdom of accident; they live there, with the funny fountain of Piazza Esedra outside and in the cloister a collection of huge ancient animal heads sticking out of the clumps of box around the fountain, like something left by naughty prodigious children.

The power of these incongruities is strongest for the Greek works — the Ludovisi Throne, the Sitting Boxer — since they have suffered most in this age, not only from the plethora of reproductions. Nothing has become so cheap as complete perfection, in industry, novel writing, bathing beauties. Among the perfect forms of the Greeks we move like diplomats at a reception; or we may get down on all fours and bark at them like dogs, especially at the heads, an affront to psychology. The head has become a different order of thing altogether in this century. The gigantic Ludovisi Juno head that so enraptured Goethe affects one like a face carved in a mountain. When a piece is badly mutilated it is easier, it makes for a kind of rapport; a little fragment of practically nothing, for the imagination to work on, is the best of all. But you begin to tolerate something more eventually; it is the particular triumph of this particular museum. Roman sculpture, being documentary and decorative, loses somewhat by the same process; on the whole one appreciates it more when bringing less imagination to it.

Nobody loves the ancient Romans anywhere, though they may feel bound to respect them, but it is in the baths that you love them least. The impact is all of daring, energy, vanity, practicality, especially related in this case to the flesh. Awe is in proportion to the offense, unless it stops at the quality of the masonry.

Item: In the steamroom of a little private bath at Ostia Antica, evidently a gentleman's club, there are cartoons of Socrates, Thales of Miletus, and the rest of the seven sages of antiquity illustrating their theories on defecation.

Item: At the end of the empire there are said to have been 338 miles of aqueducts, providing Rome with a daily water supply of 1,747,000 cubic meters, or 1,800 liters per head. A large proportion of it must have gone through the baths, these two surviving monsters having been only two of many. There has perhaps never been a national craze to equal this Roman one for water.

In the Baths of Caracalla, where Shelley wrote about him, one is struck by the demise of Prometheus in the past fifty years. It is quite startling how suspect individual assertion on the grand scale has become: or perhaps what we are questioning more is the gift of fire.

In the Lateran Museum,* two roomfuls of mosaic athletes from the Baths of Caracalla: naked life-size figures with subtle flesh shadings and muscle shadows on a white ground, inside a delicately worked

---

*Now moved to Vatican Museums; cf. preface, "Return to Rome."

border of rope-twist motif. Another fine point of design is the cubist handling of the platforms, or abstractions of flooring, on which they stand. There is the same sophistication of eye and workmanship in the figures, making them more overpowering. They are that; no other work of the time has stayed so fresh or conveys so much of one aspect of the empire.

Brutality is not the word, although they are the utmost in that. There are boxers, gladiators, runners, and a few portrait heads, some of the managers instead of athletes, but there is not much difference. The bodies are grotesquely muscular, all a swirl of leaden swellings in calves, pelvis, shoulders, the pectoral pockets, although beautiful in their balance, and the faces are often the ugliest possible, as though the idealization were of that; because they are not satirized. The feeling of the work is of praise, almost a tragic love for these gorilla heroes, who represent the ultimate reduction of man to the strength of his own body and that is surely the most tragic state, though the portraits are meant as admirable, not to cause dismay. Their equipment is as ultimate: boxing gloves packed with metal to above the elbow, some with two iron prongs protruding from the fist; the fights were really to the finish. A few of the faces are handsome; all are intensely personal, real portraits, yet abstracted from the person too as the bodies are from their atrocious sports. They are not in repose, nearly every one is shown in a pose of full vigor even though a second's remove from action, but each is alone in the elegant aesthetics of poise and platform, a monstrous melancholy abstraction of brawn and brainlessness. No scene of violence could compete with them.

Their faces are melancholy too, and strangely without pride or boasting; they hold their heads like any sober citizen posing for a portrait, but the exaggeration they symbolize hangs heavy in their eyes. It took great art to convey it, and as far as one can tell it was never so conveyed again. — Possibly they were commissioned by the emperor, himself addicted to the lower forms of athletics.

Roman coffin subjects: Triumph of the legions and misery of subject peoples, Bacchic feasts, occasional Greek myths, grim conjugal rectitude, business, and agriculture. In the Museo Nazionale the prizes are two battle scenes, packed with figures in an unusually brilliant defiance of perspective; the soldiers are writhing and whacking and tweaking the beards of barbarians in a tangle of corpses and war-maddened horses piled from base to rim; in one a subsidiary scene shows a barbarian leader kissing the Roman general's foot while wife and child cringe in the background. But the worst are the married couples, lying tight-lipped on their elbows side by side or their busts protruding from a frame; everything is tight shut about them; they are air-pressured with virtue. The legions are not nearly so savage.

The portrait busts: "Le sot projet qu'il a de se peindre," as Pascal said of Montaigne. However, they preferred truth to flattery as a rule, or were enough in love with themselves to be flattered best by the truth, and so the result is admirable if not the motive, which in any case was largely funereal too. At a funeral the chief male mourner would be loaded down like a delivery boy with busts of his ancestors: no bust, no ancestor. They are also the novels of the time, and the one art that did not come back in the Renaissance; there has never been any general portraiture in Rome again, and there are no novels either; characterization, queen of luxuries, more insidious even than the baths, went down with empire.

Some Europeans like to claim that the faces resemble American ones. They do not resemble each other in any extraordinary degree once you get past the coffin attitude. Still, taking a year's newspaper photographs of successful Americans as against these faces you would certainly have something a good deal more heavyset and sentimental, more anxious to please, less mature. If you come out with any composite picture after looking at several hundred ancient Romans, it would probably be of a narrow and prominent bone structure, long nose, taut neck muscles, mouth sensuous but commanding or at least not inviting, shrewdness of eyes, conveyed by the socket, not the blind or hollowed eyeball, and a general look of bad temper. It is a question whether so many would seem to look like lawyers if one didn't know they were; in spite of that one gets a strong impression of rather exasperating honesty along with the self-appreciation. Taken all together they are less handsome than one would expect from the beauty of Italians now, death on fancy as one knew already, and alarmingly intelligent. In short, the noble Roman; his physiognomy at its noblest, the face of Julius Caesar.

Of the emperors one of the more striking is Vespasian, who began the Colosseum: small businessman's face in contour, very round splayed forehead, nose low over small chin, with rugged flesh drapery hiding the further jawlines; no great feeling of stature but the small commercial or family look is overborne by another, rather sad, of resolve and a high effort of decency. The Domitii (Nero) tend to a different heaviness of skull, square, beetling; tremendous power; tremendous appetites. America permits no personality on this scale, bad or good.

The Ludovisi Throne, so-called, probably an altar, and painted: Venus Anadyomene, rising from the sea that in her case is total submersion, with the help of the two now headless attendants; and in parallel poses on the sides, on their bent cushions, the tight-cloaked bride and the naked girl player of the double flute. It floats up toward you through the slime and familiarity, the pall of academicism, the reproductions. You see the smile of the goddess, if it is a smile; the abstraction of joy in the turn of the head to full profile, and the profile's appalling purity; the firm lifted breasts far to the sides; the abstraction of the sea in the thin peplums of the attendants, the most antisexual in line of all female garments, with the contours of thighs and calves and buttocks just shadowed under the flimsiness; the bodies caught in such a quickness of motion there is a continual transition in feeling between strength, the healthy physical strength of the gesture they are about to make, and balance; the stiff little pleats of the bride's undergarment, like the sound of the flute; the serenity in solitude of those two side figures, bringing their calm sufficiency of soul to the scene of action: action and repose are one theme, and so the central movement seems at the same time about to terminate and to be outside of time. From the coils of your anxiety, as if you had not seen it on a hundred jaded walls, you observe the deep subtle intransigent modesty of this piece, modesty literal as well as of feeling: a drapery, making horizontal folds as against the tighter vertical ones of the peplums, crosses below the goddess's navel, and even her upper part is clothed in some evanescent clinging stuff, chiffon or sea ripples. It is a dance, of joy: Venus's arms are lifted high, in the truest gesture of pride and gladness: gladness in the awakening; gratitude for birth.

The only other bas-relief in Rome as moving as this is the one of Orpheus and Eurydice, in the Villa Albani — a dance of slowness, reluctance, and grief.

The bronze Sitting Boxer, a Hemingway character and brother to the Belvedere Torso in the Vatican, grows on one in its unpleasant realism, as far from the earlier godly Olympic athletes as from the "heroism" of the Lateran mosaics. The modeling is superb, and so is the story of the statue's survival; somebody, in some moment of crisis, had gone to extraordinary lengths to save it from being melted down. It is thought to have come from the Baths of Constantine on the Quirinal but was found across the street in 1885, carefully packed in sifted dirt between two cellar walls of the Temple of the Sun, where it had been sitting on a Doric capital for a thousand and some years. In this connection the figure's realism, the bashed-in nose and weary animal patience, takes on another dimension. There is a picture of him taken on the day of his unburial, sitting with quaint pathos on his stool in a corner of the excavators' pit, looking around at the sudden light as he had been looking for so long at the dirt against his eyeballs and at the light before that — timeless naked man waiting dumbly for the next round; it is partly because there are so few ancient bronzes left that the scene gives one a special sympathy for him. — Usually the digging out was not so methodical, and sometimes the things were found at the bottom of the Tiber, where there are probably many still. Of the Farnese Hercules, the torso was found in the Baths of Caracalla, the head at the bottom of a well in Trastevere, and the legs on a farm ten miles outside Rome.

The headless and armless girl–Venus Anadyomene, in the same room with the Boxer, is as beautiful from the color of the marble as in the form and young lift of the body; nothing vivacious or electric; the truism is true; there has never yet been anything in human affairs more engrossing than the repose of these bodies, as strong in the discus throwers and even the tragic niobids as when the action is only breathing. As one contemplates them, slowly the human head loses its contemporary emphasis: our sickness, like the portraiture of the Romans. This Venus would be as beautiful with hers. — She was washed to light by a bad rainstorm in 1913, in what had been the baths of the town of Cirene, in Africa.

How knowing the Greeks were to associate love with water, and to have a word for it that would mean nothing else — *anadyomene*; the word turns and grows in the mind. Venus is born from the sea; nobody would have thought of questioning it. It would have done a violence to any imagination to stand her on dry land, though in the statues most often she is in the homelier and equally profound act of stepping into her bath, or has just been startled out of it. She makes the immemorial gestures of modesty, or in the immemorial pose of beauty, curse of ten thousand movies, lifts her arms to wring the water from her hair. Venus herself, the original.

In the Lateran Museum, a copy of Myron's statue of the satyr Marsyas, who has just been frightened into a backward motion in the act of picking up his flute from the ground; tension with diagonal; the grotesque satyr face vivifying the little tough exquisite body — a very important experience in sculpture; and nearby, by the window, one of the most beautiful of Greek female heads. The male head, as representing ideal beauty, remains intractable, something of a blank, but this of course is not true of Zeus or Heracles.

Apollo Belvedere (Vatican): Like a Greek god.

In the cellars of the Vatican, as narrow and winding as catacombs, there is a strange enormous graveyard. It is of parts of ancient statues, thrown on the ground in a rough classification, feet in one heap, then knees, then whole legs, and so on. There is something particularly poignant about the fingers and elbows.

There are also parts of dogs and wild boars, and once the head of a
Parthenon horse was found there.

There are many dismal images of the fall. One is the statues from
Hadrian's Tomb being thrown down as ammunition against the
Goths, until the pieces of them were all mingled with the real
corpses and stray limbs and heads below. Another is the little
huddle of spectators scraped together for the last games, under
Totila, in the Circus Maximus; there were perhaps three or four
thousand, where there was room for seventy to ninety thousand.
But the worst is the stopping of the water.

It happened all in a day, during the Gothic siege. The aqueducts were blocked up so they would not serve as passageways into
the city, and with one or two minor exceptions they were never
used again. The rooms of the baths, of which a part of one is sufficient for the world's biggest opera stage, went dry like a little
household tap waiting for the plumber; they became in one day,
in all essentials, what they have been ever since. The hyperbole
had collapsed.

Ostia Antica

The nature of reality, of these realities, continues to be troubling.

The excavations of Pompeii and Herculaneum in the eighteenth century, Piranesi's time, brought forth a whole new impulse
of creative life, of which the direction and exuberance spread from
Italy throughout the West. The excavation of Ostia Antica, begun
in the 1930s, brought forth valuable sociological data.

Complete picture of a commercial (port) city from late Republic to late Empire: leading citizens, sewage disposal, apartment
houses, lares and penates, export and import companies, improvements of harbor basins, public latrine, temples, imperial inscriptions, a very pretty theater (restored).

Largo Argentina

The little republican temples were excavated behind a high
fence during fascism, and a story popular at the time was that

Mussolini wanted some ruins there and had a lot of old stones dragged together to make them, but this was carrying the natural suspicion too far. It seems they are real, more or less. The Senate House where Julius Caesar was stabbed was near there, not the one in the Forum.

Roman Forum
a) The plaster model in Santa Rita gives a misleading impression of spaciousness in the Forum. The widest open area, between the two confronting basilicas, is no wider than a standard main street and that only for the length of a city block. The place was packed like a moving-van; from their front door the vestal virgins cannot have had a view of anything but the temple across the street. In Piranesi's reconstructions of such places (as distinguished from his views of the ruins) there is even more spaciousness, but it is poetic and accurate; the buildings and statues were certainly very powerful.

b) The rump-size paving stones of the Via Sacra, in their value for the mind, are among the finest stones in Rome, not excluding sculpture. They are fine even in themselves. A later and higher Sacred Way, reportedly far inferior in construction, had to be dug out to expose this one. A remark of the archaeologist then in charge (this was at the turn of the century) has an ominous ring: "You see, the earlier you go, the better the workmanship."

c) Temple of Saturn, or Kronos, or Time, who ate his children: "the only honest parent," Kafka spitefully called him. Dedicated 497 B.C. in honor of the happy communal society or Golden Age he established in Latium after he had vomited up Jupiter and been thrown out of heaven by him. The symbolism of all this is very fine, allowing the mind to accept any number of mutually murderous authorities: the essential difference between the ancient and the Christian world is perhaps nowhere more clearly defined than in this matter of fallen angels. Lordly Jupiter Capitolinus, the practical one, looked right down on his ejected parent here from the top of the hill, but of his temple there is nothing left. It is impossible to take sides in such a story; yet Kafka to the contrary there is a certain deep and happy propriety in its being Saturn's temple that lasts, eight granite columns and a podium anyway, which gives one a special tenderness for that piece of the Forum collage. Besides, it is one of the handsomest pieces. Appropriately, the stretch of some seven hundred years between it and the nearby Arch of Septimius Scverus is one of the hardest to take in, they look so well together; one keeps wanting them to preserve the homogeneity of an air view, but they will not.

d) The Rostra. For political speeches but none that anybody would remember. The great speeches ended with the Republic, when the platform was over at the side and not decorated with fancy honorary columns like this imperial one. It seems the tomb of Cicero.

e) The Curia. A modern restoration of the latest imperial restoration, under Diocletian. An earlier systematization of it had been by Julius Caesar, when he turned the Forum around on its axis, as Valadier later did to Piazza del Popolo.

f) Lapis Niger. Time take the longest plunge here; the empire is a scarcely discernible glimmer in the future, the Republic too; you are back before the building of the Servian wall, already a high point of sophistication. All the wars of that time and before, comprehensible enough to Europeans, seem bound to be fumbled by the American mind, no matter how instructed; it has been our innocence, not always charming, to think of war as an outrage and "somebody's fault." The Punic Wars can be grasped on other grounds perhaps, although aloofly: the Carthaginians are not obviously evil or unattractive, nor are most of the qualities needed for conquest any pleasanter than usual; still, the outcome imposes itself on certain high grounds as well as low. The earlier wars against strong neighbors in every direction, even the single fact of there being no rest from them whatever for several hundred years, strike too deep into the confusion of our distaste for militarism. "That the regal period laid not only the political foundations of Rome, but the foundations also of her external power, cannot be doubted. . . . Certainly great deeds, uncommon achievements have in this case passed into oblivion" (Mommsen). The lay of the land and the river, a few cistern walls and other rocks contain the time, and it is the most heartbreaking, as Virgil knew. Centuries of Romulus and Mars, a warrior darkness, as the end of it all would also be. — The Black Stone is only a section of marble paving put down to mark an earlier tomb, perhaps not of Romulus; it may only represent a desire of those days of ancestral sentimentality that there should be a tomb of Romulus somewhere, otherwise there would be no past; or it may have had nothing to do with him, if there was such a person; and below that is the oldest known Latin inscription. The oblivion is relative; the conquering and centralizing process, with its necessary accompaniment of myth making, is fairly clear, and inspires such melancholy, one feels more like turning the reel still farther back, undoing Roma Quadrata and the Latin League and all, rather than struggle on through so many other wars to Caesar and his product, Augustus. One yearns here for wilderness; it hardly seems at the moment that Rome was worth it.

There is a character of another kind around the Lapis Niger — the archaeologist Giacomo Boni who discovered it in 1899 (it was he who uncovered the Via Sacra too), a great name in modern Forum history and of a race now in danger of becoming extinct. Anatole France made him the central and most gracious character in the group gathered beside the Forum in *Sur la Pierre Blanche,* a narrative of a journey of the mind into time past and (not so successfully) future; the point is that Boni, a scholar, presides over it with intellect, imagination, and love, and it seems this more than the innocent socialist illusion that makes it a period piece. Another, by Maude Howe:

"Signor Giacomo Boni, the architect in charge of the public buildings of ancient Rome, has a rival terrace on the roof of his house: we went to see his Japanese lilies the other day. Fancy, he has a cherry tree with ripe cherries on it, a peach tree with peaches, a tame starling in a cage, and quite the most wonderful collection of plants and flowers I ever saw in so small a space. Signor Boni has planted on the Palatine, in the Forum, and in the Baths of Caracalla, the flowers and shrubs mentioned in the classics as growing in those places. The good work is beginning to tell already; now there are roses and fleurs-de-lis growing in the Forum" (*Roma Beata*, 1909).

g) "*Basilica*. — Fem. of adj. basilicus, royal. 1) Anc. hist. Orig., a royal palace; thence, an oblong building or hall, with double colonnades and a semi-circular apse at the end, used for a court of justice and place of public assembly. 2) A building of this type, used for Christian worship; improp. applied to churches generally. . . .

"Basilical. — Kingly, royal, regal. 'Basilical rule of any other temporal sovereignty'; 'Up wells this basilical word *must*'" (Oxford Dictionary).

Basilica Julia, Basilica Emilia, Basilica of Maxentius (or Constantine).

h) Column of Phocas. Another of the most disturbing Forum pieces; erected in 608 in honor of that hateful eastern emperor by the exarch of Italy, and one of the few objects that went on sticking out as the ground level rose, only the pedestal was buried so it was not identified. Then with the rage to know the dirt was shoveled away and the fact came out: by the year 608 nobody remembered how to make an honorary column, or statues either; they dragged a column here from some old building and made it do. The old statues had begun having their heads changed long before that, but in this case there is some question whether even the head had any relation to Phocas. The perfect image of amnesia, especially taken together with the superb spiral reliefs of Trajan's wars on *his* column out across the street — a specious art but art nevertheless.

i) Vestal virgins. Suppressed A.D. 394, after having flourished for eleven centuries. Powerful ladies of the best families, who can return to ordinary life after thirty years if they choose. An interesting provision is for their being buried alive if found guilty of intercourse with a man, called "incest." It is a day of general mourning. The victim is carried to the place of execution in a cart, then with the Pontifex Maximus and other officials standing by she is dragged or escorted, depending on her mood, to the top of the stairs leading down to the crypt but no farther, because it must not be said that a vestal was put to death by force; it would not be proper for her to die of starvation either, so there is food in the tomb for several days. She walks down the stairs by herself, they are pulled up after her, and the masons quickly wall up the door. — One such execution, of a high matron of the order, under Domitian, sounds like a frame-up, as the vestal herself claimed; there might perhaps have been trouble over Alba Longa, site of the original fire of the vestals, which the emperor desecrated by building a huge and vulgar villa on top of it. What makes the story upsetting is that the emperor was also Pontifex Maximus.

j) Triumphal arches. An unpleasant idea. Of the three extant (including Constantine's out over the hill) the only one that is beautiful as architecture is the little single one of Titus, with the reliefs inside of the seven-branched candlestick and other trophies from Jerusalem, taking its whole life span probably the most execrated object in Rome. The two triple ones are rather ugly and nearly as nasty, and that of Septimius Severus carries a precise commemoration of a murder (by Caracalla of his brother Geta, whose name he had scratched off it); it also had golden chariots and such on top. Their beauty is all acquired — a delicate principle. The Arch of Augustus, of which the base was excavated well up in this century, beside the Temple of Vesta, was evidently the biggest of all.*

k) Mamertine Prison. On the edge of the Forum, under the little church of Saint Joseph of the Carpenters. Two tiny superimposed cells; in the bottom one, perhaps originally a cistern, enormous stones, well in the floor, entrance hole in the ceiling, exit to the Cloaca Maxima; stairs now for tourists. Upstairs, a list in stone of the more famous Christian saints "who left from here for the triumph of God" from the time of Nero through the third century; and another of political and military figures tortured and killed there, including Vercingetorix, the followers of the Gracchi, Sejanus, "and many others obscure or less famous, fallen among the whirlpools of human hatreds and events."

The other churches around the Forum are a main element of its plastic beauty, as of its depth, through incongruity, and so are a

---

*There have been important Forum diggings and reevaluations in the third quarter of this century.

main reason why Empire Street failed in its purpose. The straight line from S. Francesca Romana at one end to the Temple of Saturn at the other involves more turns than the lifetime of a fish; it would have taken much longer really to dry it up; not that it cannot still happen. The parts of the composition belong together, but one church keeps its old special power, or seems even to have gained more of it in contrast to the exposures around; that is the horned one with the dark temple base, of Antoninus and Faustina, and the sun-charmed other name: San Lorenzo in Miranda.

Piazza Navona: elliptical, 240 meters by 65, having grown out of the stadium built there by that ubiquitous and untidy character, Domitian.

The Renaissance and baroque scheme: imagination; sudden openings, narrow approaches; this particular triumph of the conception was a creation of, roughly, 1500–1650.

The fascist scheme: statements; avenues; horror of the imagination. Under the guidance of M. Piacentini, who had similar plans for the rest of Italy and carried some of them out, they designed a thoroughfare to run the length of the piazza, splitting it open at both ends, and started; an end building was torn down and the deepest current of Rome's life seemed to be flowing away through the gap. It was too much even for some party members to stand; it had to be stopped. The building was replaced.

No "intellectual life." There is another operation of clarity, or else none. Sometimes in the neighborhood of Piazza Navona you pass the entrance to some inner garden court that in Paris would set up a vague cerebral excitement, the trees by the apartment windows seeming alive with some *intellectual* history. It is blank — just life and architecture. You move on disconsolately.

Cristo Re: the biggest fascist church, built in the '30s on the Viale Mazzini, in the sprawling middle-class or Risorgimento quarter upriver from the Vatican. Of brick, with alternating indentations; like an observatory behind and something in Albany, possibly a crematorium, in front. The architect had been visiting Nazi Germany and shows it; the expression is a dogged and profoundly un-Italian one, of sodden weight, which is what makes the building somewhat more offensive than the big turn-of-the-century ones, the Palace of Justice and Victor Emmanuel Monument. Inside, a colossal representation of Christ, with the attitude and muscles of a fascist orator.

Nero has been called the Haussman of ancient Rome; it seems the fire was the only way to push a city plan past the vested interests. Among his improvements: a huge city market in the neighborhood of the present church of S. Stefano Rotondo. Among his projects: a canal across the isthmus of Corinth. Among his most hated innovations: public poetry contests.

Nero: Natura il fece, e poi ruppe la stampa — Nature made him and then broke the mold; said also of various other Romans.

Julius Caesar: "My aunt Julia was descended, on the maternal side from a race of kings, and by her father, from the immortal gods."

Augustus: "My father, the divine Julius . . ."

In one of his letters to Trajan in Rome, Pliny, then governor of Bithynia, writes to ask if it would be all right to allow an association of volunteer firemen in a small town in the province, where there had recently been some bad fires. The answer is no; such associations were apt to prove subversive. In another the governor apologizes for sending his wife by the Imperial Post to visit a dying aunt, without first asking the emperor's permission; there would not have been time to get a reply before the old lady died. In answer to another question the emperor states that local Christians are to be tolerated unless they become an obvious threat to public stability, or as it would eventually be defined, a clear and present danger.

Signor T., of impoverished gentility, sore pride and low IQ, emerged from World War I with less prospects than ever, but happily found his way into a menial job with the young Fascist Party, which he continued to serve with steady devotion and little pay after its victory. He asked for little or nothing for himself but his fidelity was noted through the years; he became a carrier-out of orders, on a slowly rising level. Eventually he had a desk in a ministry. He was loyal in thought and deed. When trouble came with England he told everyone: "There have never been poets in England. Shakespeare was born there by mistake." In connection with a party scheme to raise money from among the ranks he moved into a small new apartment at twice the rent he could afford, of which he would become owner at the end of ninety-nine years.

One day he met Mussolini in the hall of the ministry. The Duce said: "Why aren't you married? All good party members are married." In despair, Signor T. reported to his mistress; the arrangement had suited them both for some years; they had no desire to marry and could not afford it. They married. A year later he met the Duce again. "Why have you no children? The national policy . . ." Signor T. began producing children, he had several, though not enough for a cash prize; the triumph in Abyssinia was reward enough.

In the manpower confusion at the beginning of World War II he was slipped by mistake into a high post in the Ministry of Marine, and was responsible for some serious naval losses. On the day after the Italian disaster at El Alamein a nonfascist relative who had given up following the news visited him at his office to ask a favor for a friend. Signor T. was pale, distraught, speechless. "Why are you laughing at me?" he suddenly shouted. "I'm not laughing." "You're laughing at our defeat." "What defeat?" "But you'll see, England will pay for this. A country without poets!"

His nerves were more on edge because he was hungry. Through the whole war he refused to allow his wife to buy food on the black market; party members must give an example of principle in all things — in this one he was unique, his children became ill; his wife nearly died of starvation. He continued to pay on the ninety-nine-year lease. Then there was a worse time after the final defeat, of country and party, but still he kept the faith; only death, which had a good deal to recommend it at the time, would part him from it.

He became one of the top men in the reconstituted Fascist Party, or MSI (Movimento Sociale Italiano); its rise in membership, after a period of public noncommittal, was enough to repay him for all his sufferings.

Foro Italico
Once called Foro Mussolini, and the obelisk-type honorary column at the end of the esplanade still reads, downward, MUSSOLINI DUX. Built in the '30s; a multi-unit splurge of sports fields, as the ancient baths had been, and actually from a little distance the stadium, with its sixty-five colossal statues of athletes, is a hallucinating image of imperial Rome. It was dedicated to the conquest of Abyssinia — the longest inscription is to that effect (May 9, 1936, fascist year XIV); it calls on all Italians to raise their weapons, flags, and hearts to salute after fifteen centuries the reappearance of empire on the "fateful hills of Rome," the same language Cola di Rienzo used before he was decapitated and strung up by his heels on the Corso. After a similar finale, there were still many people who saw it as the pride of the city; the neanderthal statues are dedicated to the main cities and towns of Italy and almost any day there will be groups of visiting provincials proudly finding theirs; it is quite rare to hear them not being proud of it, although if they chose they could go and look at the Sitting Boxer or the mosaic athletes in the Lateran. On the bridge leading to the place are reliefs of battle scenes, sanctioned by the finest of ruins and sarcophagi, only there was no talent to hire for one thing and for another the enemy is not barbarians, nor Ethiopians; they might be French, or English or Italians in a different uniform. It is just rhetoric, equating sports with war and fascism with the Roman Empire.

The main pavement inscription, black on white mosaic, appearing all over the place in blocks of twelve and sixteen, runs as follows:

DUCE DUCE DUCE DUCE
DUCE DUCE DUCE DUCE
DUCE DUCE DUCE, ETC.

Another, quite frequent:

> MANY ENEMIES
> MUCH HONOR
> MANY ENEMIES
> MUCH HONOR

Many others, some rather long-winded, are strewn among the picture mosaics on which you walk:

> DUCE OUR YOUTH
> TO YOU WE DEDICATE

Another, from a liturgy for mass meetings, at which the recitation would be answered by the multitude, "I swear!"

> I SWEAR TO CARRY OUT WITHOUT DISCUSSION
> THE ORDERS OF THE DUCE AND TO SERVE WITH
> ALL MY POWERS AND IF NECESSARY WITH MY LIFE
> THE CAUSE OF THE FASCIST REVOLUTION

At the meetings it was fairly common for young Romans to shout after this an obscenity rhyming with the answer "Lo giuro!"

Some are just offhand bits of fact or slogan dropped in among the illustrations, as if the workman's brain had been so stuffed with them they fell out uncontrollably anywhere, for example, between Neptune and a group of fascist workmen who are building something:

> ITALY FINALLY HAS HER EMPIRE

It is like hearing a troubled person talking in his sleep; you would like to help him. A group of soldiers riding in a truck are shouting, in a comic-strip balloon, the really very odd slogan of the time, "Me ne frego!" — *je m'en fous*, or to hell with it. One that appears more often, in blocks of sixteen and other ways, is the well-known yell:

> DUCE A NOI DUCE A NOI DUCE A NOI
> DUCE A NOI DUCE A NOI DUCE A NOI
> DUCE A NOI, ETC.

The pictures are a no less troubled hodgepodge of pagan deities and other images from the past together with contemporary occupations; heroic caricatures of athletes and workmen in industry, building, agriculture, or even, most pathetically, doing just such artwork as that in which they are represented — with huge fists and hammers and stepladders, on figures five times as big as themselves. But the prize examples of this cynical thugwork are the statues.

They are of all kinds of athletes but with a preponderance of boxers and wrestlers. Their muscles are anatomically impossible, foreheads low, jaws out Duce-fashion, genitals in line with the virility policy whether behind tights or jock straps or (until Holy Year) bare, gaze either belligerent or loftily dedicated, beneath collie-dog brows, hands the size of fur muffs and tending to hang to the knees. Where possible it has been arranged to have whatever they are carrying, poles or tennis rackets or lion skins, cover somewhat their private parts; others in rear view show a painful-looking string drawn up between the buttocks. One of the best specimens is the skier, in the group of fifteen or twenty more around the sunken marble theater. There is a soldier in the same style but even bigger over by the tennis courts.

The tennis courts, swimming pool, fencing quarters, etc. are all excellent.

A Roman countess, indicating the spot on her chest: "During fascism I felt free *inside.*"

Piazza dell'Imperatore Augusto
One thinks continually of Virgil; that he should have written the empire's official poem; that he should have wanted it, at his death, destroyed.

This dreary piazza is another fascist job, which caused about as much destruction as the Via dell'Impero, for the same reasons. The central symbol had of course to be the tomb of Augustus; Rome's handsome and only adequate concert hall had been mercifully on top of it for some centuries; that came down, along with a great deal else. The tomb, a big sad bump of brick and earth-work, was isolated, and ringed by the neoclassic variety of fascist office buildings, the most pretentious, with facade color mosaics in the swimming-pool style: hips for women, fists for men, you never can tell just what they are supposed to be doing. Across one facade is an inscription: THE ITALIAN PEOPLE ARE A UNIVERSAL PEOPLE WHO ALWAYS FIND A SPRINGTIME FOR THEIR HOPES FOR THEIR PASSIONS FOR THEIR GREATNESS. On the river side a semi-open pink and white pavilion (but the pink has been painted out now) also suitable for a swimming pool, or an unloading station for trucks, houses one of archaeology's proudest finds. It is the Ara Pacis, Augustus's Altar of Peace, consecrated 13 B.C. on the emperor's return from Gaul and Spain, in honor of the peace he had established in the empire. Earlier efforts to dig the best parts of it out from under a palazzo on the Corso had failed; under the desperate prodding of the empire-urge it was finally accomplished in 1937–38, by installing an electric plant to freeze the whole underground area.

Here, says American Professor G., who has not quite lost his German accent, we are faced with many unanswerable questions; many things we do not as yet know; unfortunately this morning there will not be time for him to go into these questions, he can only call them to our attention. We circle the marble enclosing wall of the altar, the main exhibit here and perhaps of Augustan art in general — "note the floral decoration"; the altar inside, it seems, is just an altar, although there are minor reliefs and more floral decoration inside.

On the entrance end, which may be called the front, two legendary scenes: the Lupercal, or wolf scene, in the other Aeneas sacrificing, in the presence of the famous sow, also of a figure who may be his faithful friend Acates: "Or who may not," says the professor triumphantly; we are already stumped. Another question: there is the sow, but where are the piglets? they are there in Virgil, they should be there; another triumph; no piglets. On the other end, two allegorical scenes — so now we have two of the elements of the work: legend, allegory. On the right the goddess Roma, or so the figure was deduced from the bit of skirt that was found; on the left the crux of the whole matter, to which we will return; briefly, it is a lady sitting on a hill (Mother Earth?) among contented babies and animals; on her left a lesser lady, evidently a nymph, riding though not very high on a swan (Air?) and on the right another on a sea monster (Water?).

With this in mind we proceed in mounting suspense to the side reliefs, both showing figures in a procession, facing the legend end; in other words they are not going around and around. Here the professor is at his pinnacle; he can hardly wait for the masterly strokes he is about to give to our perplexity, but this will be so delicate an operation he must pause a moment, hands clasped, to arrange the coup and let us observe in his features the welter of *other* considerations that he has had to find his way through, in order to bring us these. First question, one of the greatest — remember, there will not be time for him to discuss its many fascinating aspects, he can only bring it to our attention, and so he does: are there *two* processions, or two parts of *one* procession? No answer. We are dumbfounded. And that is not all, not by any means. On the right or street side we are obviously seeing the members of the imperial family, men followed by flamens in front, women and children behind; after some buildup of the supposition, which the professor discounts as highly insufficient — we will just have to take his word for it — he points out the head of Augustus; veiled, meaning that he is officiating. We consider the various portfolios religious and otherwise that the *princeps* had managed to get into his own hands by the year 13 B.C., because the altar was not dedicated until 9 B.C. and we are presumably witnessing here the earlier ceremony; but at least on one count the mystery only thickens. Augustus's head is there and part of his arm, which is slightly extended: then blank, the piece is missing. What, says the professor slowly, his glance traveling among us to bring us the full weight of the inquiry, is Augustus doing with his right hand? Stumped again; we can only imagine; probably he is holding something. And that is still not all; it is scarcely the beginning. There is another veiled man behind, requiring a judicious

preamble to identify, although only tentatively, as Agrippa; if he is
Agrippa the woman behind him *may* be his wife; the emperor's
daughter Julia (later to be palmed off on Tiberius) and the child
hanging on to both of them *may* be their child: it is just a working
hypothesis, no more, still there are many arguments in its favor.
The one figure we can relax over is the empress, Livia. However
we revert now to our original question: are there two processions?
or two parts of one procession?

We give a more cursory study to the magistrates in the other
procession or other part of the same procession, and return to the
crux: the lady on the hill. Here we are at the very heart of the
meaning of the Augustan Age, not to mention the purpose of the
altar, which by this time we had quite forgotten and are about to
again, there are so many intervening imponderables.

It will be the professor's ultimate aim to convince us, in spite
of the handicap of the time allotted him, that the lady *is* Terra
Mater; who else she might be we are left to guess. The exposition
takes a more whimsical turn, supporting the allegation of allegory, for which we had only taken his word until now; the cow
and sheep, as we can readily see, are much smaller than they
would be in real life, ergo, this is not realism; even more ir-
refutably, in real life ladies do not ride on swans; a motorcycle,
quips the professor, would do; and so on; so it is allegory. And
what female figure, so obviously representative of fertility (babies;
flora and fauna) could be so central a symbol, sharing as she
seems to with the goddess Roma the full brunt of the credo of the
new (and riskily established) empire? We come to it eventually,
breathlessly. The professor avoids the word breasts, he even manages not to call attention to the lady's bosom but it is remarkably
full and might be taken as a cogent point for his thesis. We are
convinced, although it is sad to have to ignore Venus, who was
after all the one who cared about Aeneas, and was central enough
in Virgil's version of what the empire was about; she was always
the antithesis of her brother Mars and was even in one of her attributes Venus Mater, and the swan is her bird; the professor was
so tickled by the motorcycle he forgot to mention this: why a

swan? why not an eagle? But never mind; Terra Mater it is, in the sacred trinity, Earth, Air, Water.

But a dreadful blow is in store. Professor M. comes out with it later — a bombshell; why, he proposes to Professor G., doesn't he break down and call the figure Pax? Ovid in describing the ceremony explicitly says that *Pax was there*, so if that is not she, where is she? Professor G. has a little sidestepping to do to get this in his stride but he manages, that is he stays on his feet: he is willing, he concedes at last, to call the whole composition Pax; yes, that far he will go, but not the lady herself; on that he stands firm. He is not present when Professor Q. blows in from Oxford for his Christmas vacation and blasts even this edifice to smithereens. "Nonsense. She is Italia. Roma on one side, Italia on the other. Perfectly simple."

Whoever she is, it is an altar, and dedicated to Peace. There had been wars for seven hundred years, and now a thing was made of lunar marble with all those important people carved on it, called the Altar of Peace; at which by decree of the senate there was to be an annual sacrifice attended by the chief magistrates and priests and the vestal virgins. The murder of Cicero is nothing in comparison; the senate is content to be reduced to such decrees as that; the empire is secure; the long agonies of civil war are over; the lady on the hill need be nobody but Joy, and so must contain at least a touch of Venus. Peace would be no good without her; there would have been no Rome without her, so Virgil says: besides the Julian family claimed to be descended from her. There can be love, earth, all goddesses together; peace among the elements; peace in heaven, reflected up from the earth's new golden age, established not by Saturn, old Father Time, but by a hard-bitten teenager named Octavius, later Augustus.

Yet one keeps thinking, sadly, of Virgil. The poem really did not come out quite right; it was a little late in the day for the kind of epic that would please the administration, although he had honestly wished to do it, as he had wished to love the emperor. Something else comes in; you see it a hundred and fifty years later too in the faces of the mosaic athletes in the Lateran. The mind of Rome is called on for simple enthusiasm and simple pride in the national destiny, when what it truly knows is in sophistication and melancholy; grateful for peace, it can give itself wholly only to the human, not the national fate. Aeneas, although so strong and attractive a leader, is a man of pity; the whole poem is of pity — for the victims, for the ox whose forehead is crushed by an athlete's fist, for those who have grandeur forced on them, for those such as Turnus who in all the wars of the world have been heroic on the wrong side, for Venus who is the power of love continually outwitted and defeated even when her cause has seemed to win, for the fathers who are no longer simple enough to care first for victory, most terribly for Dido, and for all the dead. The poem breaks after Dido, or at least after the arrival in Latium; there are moments of splendor later but the driving, unique genius is gone. The official scheme that could be rendered with such grace in marble — legend, allegory, religious sacrifice, floral decoration: no problems at all — is death in words.

Virgil proposes to go to Greece for three years to "polish" the manuscript, meets the emperor almost at once, returns with him, ill, and in a few days is dead, having ordered the poem destroyed. He had tried to accommodate his great humanity and miraculous gift to political pressures, in which he believed; it had not worked out. He may have known the emperor too well, and been glad to die finally because of it; or perhaps he was seeing farther than that; there was certainly no happiness in looking back, to any immediate past. There was really nothing to say but what the sculptor said better: Rome, Augustus, Peace. It made a splendid if somewhat chilly altar; for a poet it was hardly enough.

On the outside of the pavilion, toward the tomb, there was reproduced in bronze letters the so-called Testament of Augustus, in Latin, covering the whole wall. Including this very expensive lettering, the piazza must have cost about as much as draining the Pontine marshes. — The second bridge up the river from there is named for the socialist deputy Giacomo Matteotti, who on June 10, 1924, was waylaid in the vicinity by five government strong-arm men and beaten to death. Not a great orator; an intellectual parliamentarian with a knack of asking questions on the floor of the house; ten days earlier he had made a carefully documented speech summing up the violence of all kinds beginning with murder that had characterized the blackshirt campaign in the recent elections. The Duce, shortly to be made an honorary member of the American Legion, was driven to frenzy. On June 6 he rose in the house to shout: "There are excellent masters in Russia! We have only to imitate what they're doing in Russia! [Applause, noise, exchange of epithets between extreme left and extreme right.] . . . But don't think we lack the courage. We can still act in time. And perhaps sooner than you think!" Four days later Matteotti was dead. That had not been the plan; he was only to have been given "a good lesson" but things got out of hand. Mussolini, who had ordered the lesson and was fully informed of every detail of the outcome, publicly promised the widow to use all the government's power to solve the sad mystery. It is curious to compare this bumbling, primitive affair with the techniques developed by the same government later and brought to their ultimates in Germany and the USSR.

Ardeatine Caves

On March 23, 1944, the forces of resistance to the German occupation blew up a truck in a small street in the center of Rome; thirty-two SS soldiers riding in it were killed. The following evening 335 Romans or people then in Rome, somewhat more than the stated reprisal quota of ten to one, were taken out to this bleak country place a little beyond the biggest of the Christian catacombs, shot in the nape of the neck, and dumped into a pit at the end of a series of caves. The sides were blasted in but people in the neighborhood knew of the event, and a few weeks later when the Germans had retreated the bodies were dug out and could still be identified. Most of them had been in prison for racial or political reasons; there were a hundred Jews, twelve foreigners, a boy of fourteen, doctors, teachers, electricians, men of many occupations, married or not; no women.

The place is a shrine now, and a cemetery; a cross and a Star of David are on the rock ledge over the entrance to the caves, an inscription written in the first person plural tries to give in the voice of the dead some common meaning to the common death. It speaks as unrhetorically as possible of democracy and the dignity of the human being; it indicts the twenty years of fascism with silence. The caves are a big mole-run; there is a small chapel and another small altar, not much, and in the end cave where the bodies were there is nothing, only two bronze gates designed by the sculptor Mirko are across its openings, in respect for a purity of horror. But the main work of commemoration is a slab of concrete outside, and what is under it.

It was bound to be false. From outside, the plain tremendous roof, raised just a little off the ground, seems only an abstraction and appropriate, with nothing under it. The coffins are under it, row after row of uniform stone caskets with names, snapshots, short biographies, and incongruous messes of flowers brought by relatives. Sightseers troop chattering through all day and a guard shouts at them please to remember that it is a cemetery.

It is considered by many people the most moving war memorial in Europe; perhaps it is; it also represents a small part of the price of the Via dell'Impero and all the Augustan revival, though not as movingly as the Matteotti Bridge. The great sorrow and meaning of this event refuse to be pressed into such generalities. One of the men buried here, named Finzi, had been a high fascist functionary, partly responsible along with others for the murder of Matteotti and helpful in covering up the crime afterward; one might say this had been expiated by such a death; it would be hard to know. Many of the men with whom he is now linked in one symbol to the end of time had probably had some notion of the dignity of the human being and risked their lives for it from the beginning; for others it may have been largely a matter of accident, although presumably there was some reason to suspect them all of hostility to the Germans. They may or may not have sympathized with the act of blowing up the truck. In any case, the specific occasion for the monument is just an enemy atrocity; you are meant to be appalled; it is rather debilitating, and so something of a crime against whatever true dignity and will were shuffled in with the pack. This was the more serious German crime; to have left heroism all over Europe mixed up with self-pity, and courage of mind with emotional excess. The answer under these conditions keeps slipping into what it answered: these caves and graves are not likely to put anyone in a particularly "democratic" frame of mind.

There was not even any vocabulary left in which to do honor; that was a part of the fascist part of the crime. To express their abhorrence those who came after had to borrow from what they abhorred; they could not remember anything else; it was all a confusion. There is an unjust heaviness in this pitiful place — the heaviness of fascist building and the fascist mind. The stone of the coffins weighs like a slogan; the concrete lid over them must weight twenty tons; not thugwork; a far better imagination went into it, but not a free one. Such as it is, it is counteracted by the huge statue of comradeship at the entrance, a work of sentimental realism. The bronze gates, a tortured abstraction, are the most genuine part but nothing else bears them out. From the top of the little hill behind you see across a sad stretch of campagna to the most haunting of fascist buildings, very white, designed in imitation of an ancient columbarium for what was to have been the Exposition of 1942.

But there was no vocabulary anyway for those happenings. One has not even the imagination to know if it would have been better to say nothing.

Piazza Vittorio

Thousand of cats; a city of cats, as of fountains and churches, and as naturally. Most of them are not even roaming but in definite asylums, which were never planned any more than the piazzas were, or seem to have been, for human use. They just come about. The cats are drawn for some reason to one place or another, which may remain the haunt of their descendants for centuries, and people come there to feed them. It is not that Romans really consider them a sacred or even superior animal, or think about them much at all, yet some ancient habit of respect seems to apply to them, giving them a unique position among the public cats of the world. There are not many private ones — a Siamese in the house is apt to be a sign of neurosis or international marriage; normal Roman life has no more need or use for pets than for similar attachments within its own species. The cats, like people, are mostly strays, and after their great number the striking fact about them is that very few are thin.

In the old days their most famous spot was Trajan's Forum, this of course before the cleanup of the imperial forums, when that one was not the propped-up showpiece it is now but a weedy ruin-strewn pit sunk among tenements, with the triumphal column bolt upright in its old-style grandeur at the end; the cats looked natural there. Sometimes the government saw to feeding them, other times just the neighborhood; at night there were the usual backyard screechings multiplied by a hundred or so but when the city authorities, before the final overhauling of the area, tried to remove the nuisance there was such protest from the people they had to back down. But then the tenements went, the excavations began; the jig was up; such an avenue could not be desecrated by cats; anyway the garbage supply had been cut off. Another place used to be around the Pyramid of Caius Cestius, beside the non-Catholic cemetery, but that district finally became too unresidential too.[*]

One of the smaller ancestral centers that remains is in back of the Pantheon where there is a colony of twenty or thirty, most likely of Renaissance origin. Another is an alley running from the Via Giulia to the rear of the Palazzo Spada, which some people consider rather sinister, probably because the alley is narrow and barred and usually in shadow and the Council of the State meets in the palace. The cats have a barricaded look; the council sits beside the sinister statue of Pompey that Caesar clutched when he fell. But by far the greatest cat congregation of present-day Rome and possibly of Western civilization is in the huge market square on the other side of town from these two — Piazza Vittorio so-called, really Vittorio Emanuele, for the Piedmontese first ruler of a unified Italy (1870).

---

[*]Not anymore; cf. "Beside the Pyramid."

The name happens to suit the architecture. It is of the early House of Savoy period, airy, sensible, and bourgeois, the colonnades around the square are not of any Roman style that survives though in the ancient city there were miles of them; the quarter around has a solid and quite pleasant middle-class look of its era. It is all most un-Roman, except as Rome like an insectivorous plant can take in anything, even Turin, and make it Rome. Pines and palms grow in the large parklike center of the square, inside the roaring double ring of the market, and from the middle there is a long lyrical view, from Santa Maria Maggiore to Santa Croce in Gerusalemme, and way beyond that, clear as angels and snowy sometimes in winter, the peak of Monte Cavo. There is a high jumble of ruins back of the fish stalls; a set of cabalistic carvings on a door nearby from nobody knows what or when, said to contain a formula for making gold; a baroque fountain of stone corroded to an even wilder appeal than usual; and about a hundred and fifty cats.

They are of course at the fish end, and the ruins, of third-century brick, are their backdrop. They never go far from there, or not for long; it is not necessary; an invisible line around that corner of the square marks their precinct, they have made their own atmosphere there, and prefer it.

The ruins have a connection with water, which the cats in their own way keep vivid. The building, big enough to have been a three-story villa or public library, was a monumental fountain or show-off point for the water of one of the big aqueducts coming in through the quarter, and a gaudy show it must have been, from that height. Now it is a craggy rambling mass with a suggestion of enchantment though of the wrong color for a fairy tale, and the cats, who cannot get inside where the keeper of the garden lives, in their idle hours wander and drape themselves over all its levels and sketchy escarpments and juttings, all the way to the top — unhurried, unchased, wonderfully at home and regal in all their motions, not having to play up to anybody. The choreography is excellent.

In a little window at the very top, opening on to nothing, a cat framed in vines lies like a princess drying her hair; another is oddly reclined below on top of a cluster of sharp posts that are end up; somehow in the mercurial way of cats she has made herself comfortable. Others are stretched or curled in the flower beds and on the chunks of fallen marble cornice and Corinthian capitals lying around, or in favorite dents like couches under the bushes. This will be early in the afternoon when they are not hungry anymore, although the market has not yet folded up. They are more or less sated; not groggy, and not really sleeping, because there is still a sense of opportunity in the air at this time of day but they have only half an eye open for it. A calico tom with a black neckline like a court decoration decides to investigate a bloody scrap of paper in which there are still a few scraps from one of the meat stalls, pulls his paw across it languidly a couple of times, and saunters back to rest among the zinnias. On the first shelf of the ruin two kittens, one white as a sacred calf, box a moment, not having learned to gauge their desires, then in disillusion move apart. Here and there older cats take a swipe or two at washing themselves or each other, and are not too drowsy to have their feelings hurt; obscure episodes of pride and disgrace are taking place all through the happy scene, but that is not the fault of Rome.

Nobody is even watching especially. The cats are taken for granted, as many holier things are; besides in the pace and gusto of its own life, in extent too, this is the Saint Peter's among markets. The fascination is general.

You can buy almost anything there — live fowl and any other foodstuff, leather goods, clothes, toys, stolen bicycle parts, and everybody is head over heels in the business not so much for the sake of the business as of life. An aged woman with two teeth, selling carrots, detects you smiling a little at her bellow of publicity, the same tremendous voice as the others but sharper from age, thinks for a second you wanted to buy, then perceiving that you were only laughing at her goes off in a fit of gaiety herself: "Ah, old age! . . . CARROTS!" People go out of their way to touch a midget for good luck, and down a side street a man keeping up a brilliant monologue tells fortunes with dolls that rise in a jar of water that he carries on a peg and white mice running up a string outside. Several of the young girls selling vegetables are of typical

Roman beauty and aware of it. There is much too much going on for the cats to be a center of attraction.

Nevertheless they do have a special part in the show, more than if anyone were paying attention to them, and not only through the spectacle they provide. There is something else, something in the apparently offhand human treatment of them that takes you way outside of commerce and common sense, not to religion, not to charity. It puts a bargain in another perspective.

Perhaps in the Roman feeling about the species there is some dim recollection from the days of popular Egyptiana in the city, around the time the present ruin was going up in all its watery glory; or it may be only that cats are a mysterious animal as everyone admits, and Romans are alert to mysteries outside their own nature and fall easily into ways of propitiating them. Or perhaps they came into honor as a check to rats carrying plague in the Middle Ages and after — a kind of honor that only the Roman mind would perpetuate, because if they were of any use in that way it would have been the same anywhere in Europe, and no other city has such sanctuaries or would take them as such a matter of course; there would be societies for preservation, committees for extermination, propaganda for equal treatment of dogs or birds, Malthusian editorials, etc., or somebody would decide they ought to be somewhere else.

Not in Rome. The regard they are held in is general and careless; the problem, if there is one, solves itself. No doubt there is some element of primitive religious sense, or call it superstition, at the root of the matter, there usually is in tigerology, but it would be hard to trace. There is no particular emphasis on the animal anywhere in Roman culture ancient or Christian, either as good or as evil; they were never deified, nor the familiars of witches, although at one time there were plenty of witches; they are not even liked for their company; you never read of Roman old maids being found dead in a house with seventeen cats, and nobody goes pussy-pussy, meesha-meesha in Italian, indiscriminately.

But there they are, not worshiped or pampered or feared or in any way consciously honored, but honored just the same, rather as the fountains are; with which after all they do have one function in common. They are a link with the past, that is with all time, having kept a clearer set of original instincts together with more various personality than any other tamed animal. There is nothing transitory about a cat, aside from the individual knack of survival; it is the most ancient of our animals. A dead cat never has the look of finality that a dead dog does; neither does a dead Roman, which is why you never see many people bothering to follow funerals there. The eye of a cat is an eye in the forest and in all time and so even the stupidest cat seems to *know* more than any dog or horse; it knows history; you do not have to believe in the transmigration of souls to feel that a living knowledge of Agrippa continues in back of the Pantheon just as it does in the fountain in front of it.

In any case, what with the view and their numbers and the strange beauty of their dwelling, the cats of Piazza Vittorio have all the look of a sacred colony even if not officially sanctioned like cows or monkeys in other parts of the world. It is not as if they were scavenging all over the market, or in captivity like the wolf on the Capitoline or creatures in a zoo. There is an air of pleasant natural concord all around, a credit to man and beast and not very characteristic of either party in the case. Romans are not notably kind to other animals nor of any Franciscan spirit in general, and cats are not a usual symbol of the earthly paradise. They simply happen to hit it off; they understand one another; consequently the cats are the most civilized in the world.

They are also of the most extraordinary colors. It is a botanical garden of exotic furs, in every combination; marmalades shading to bronze, orange in trout specklings on gray or black, a single contrasting or striped forearm on a monotone coat, every kind of bib and dashing including the common chest triangle, often only one perky ear of solid color like an insistent strain of nobility through the conglomerate birth; but they are all aristocrats though of dead-end breed, even the ones with backsides and front sides of two utterly incompatible schemes, blue-gray and white in front and black with orange behind, like a blue-faced mandrill or a polychrome bust from the late empire; or say a pansy bed took to

sprouting mammals, some plain white with only the golden circles of the eyes or all black as pansies can be, which now stalk or
rest among the other furless flowers that they would never permit
themselves to break any more than if they were of rare porcelain
on a mantelpiece.

They have neither the hyper-dependence of house cats nor the
fears of alley ones. They are free of the two greatest sufferings of
the species, hunger and loneliness, also from the ravages of
human temperament pro or con, not to mention surgical abomi-
nations. It is much as humans have imagined heaven, only the
cats run no danger of spinelessness; in fact the spine, their most
distinctive piece of anatomy, and muscular development in general are spectacular in these cats. Among domestic felines only
purebred Siamese leap to such marvelous heights and distances,
and they have become a race of neurasthenics. In Piazza Vittorio
you are seeing cat life at its healthiest, at least the healthiest possible in such a millennium as ours, but for that matter there can
never have been such a sight in the wilderness either. The cats
have reverted to true tiger prowess and beauty of form in action,
but without ferocity. The ancient jungle gym they have taken over
is ideal for all the play that cats must have, watching, stalking,
springing, etc., and at any hour there will be a few engaged in it,
acting as usual on primeval urgencies but with a look more of
Greek athletes, especially in the prowl and the slow gallop, two of
their most becoming sports. They have lost the jitters of wild life.

They seem to have lost some of their vices too, though not at
any cost to individuality; if you hang around a while you will see
them of every character, from pussy willow to the sphinx. But
there is not much stealing or fighting. They would not risk approaching the tubs of squid and other heavenly slobber that lie
around them on two sides, but they are unusually well mannered
among themselves as well; you see hardly any chewed ears and
bloody noses. When a passerby or one of the fish vendors comes
over with a package a dozen or two will bound for it, like planes
bouncing in to a landing, from their various marble roosts or solitary promenades, but if they are too late they leave quietly; there

will be more later, and not only refuse. The big scene is when the government feeder comes, a woman usually, and familiar with cats; otherwise she could be terrified.

They come streaking from the lower branches of the trees and all the heights of the ruin and everywhere around, leaping over the flower beds and fallen fluted columns, and champ and mew and race scratching up to other branches to leap down on her shoulders; in a few seconds there will be seventy or eighty with their crazy coats all in a roil so you would think they would come out of it with somebody else's markings, and their whiskers aquiver like telegraph wires, but there is no real frenzy; they all get something in the end. A high-strung bronze-and-black, leaner than most, stays on her shoulder trying to snatch at the basket from above; she lets him stay, and in fact though fierce of eye he is all humility in his claws — one of the grieving type, who are more anxious to be grabbed from than to grab and will stay thin all their lives; a more politic black one waits alert with neck stretched from a tree trunk; off on the other side a small white baffled Persian that has somehow joined the flock or perhaps was left there and is not yet used to its ways, tries different approaches, then stands at the rim anxiously lifting one forepaw after the other, his eyes following the whole course of every morsel from basket to the final dash for privacy; he was fed alone by a butler until recently. When it is over they nearly all follow the woman as far as the gravel path that nothing prevents them from crossing but they stop there, and little by little disperse, only to be shot into action ten minutes later by another event: rain.

A cloudburst; there is a human rush for the colonnades; with a subtle shuddering motion the market folds in on itself like a bird into its feathers; tarpaulins appear from nowhere over the destructibles, certain tender points are whisked in altogether, the vendors pull back under their awnings meant for protection from the sun.

This time the motion of the cats is not centripetal. The lines they trace are as fast and straight as before but all in a criss-cross as of night projectiles over a battlefield. It is each not to the nearest cover but the predetermined one, which may be halfway around the ruin or all the way across the lawn, one way to some nook in the structure, another to the sheltering brown pantalettes of a pygmy palm, so for a few seconds the whole ground is a contradiction of flying cat furs, which resolves itself in a moment without collision or argument or even a swerve of line unless a particular place were taken, when the latecomer shoots off by the same mystic geometry to the nearest alternative. Then there is no further move. Only nursing mothers have stayed where they were, having already chosen some fairly safe location, from which they view the sky's performance with gentle sorrow as others will when all of it comes down.

The rest are watching too, in a different way. There is really no inside room for them at all; they would rather drown in a place fit for guarding than follow the humans into the exposure of the colonnades. They are crouched under every little brick eave and in clusters under the low-branching pines, all in the same waiting posture and perfectly still, hind paws invisible, the front ones in a plumb line with their noses and shoulder blades, not to spring, only to guard. They will not begin to lick themselves dry until it is over, which is in a couple of minutes.

The sun bursts out; the market is bustling again though not for long — it is nearly packing-up time. Greenery and every kind of impedimenta around the northwest corner begin slowly discharging cats, which revert to their individual natures and ways of doing things and soon are all over the place again with their sinewy purposeful activities and delicate affections; a hundred and fifty personalities, although sooner or later all must dry themselves, at once and thoroughly like fussy housewives or in wayward licks and spinal doublings after racing back to some lone preeminence. Meanwhile they take stock of the damage. Many of their beds are puddles, certain surfaces untrustworthy; even the flowers have become inimical; there are many little new arrangements to be made.

They have another job in common, more than to look after themselves. They are about to be in charge of the empty square, as one cat may be of a grocery store but here it is not so much a question of mice. There is nothing left to attract a mouse. It is astonishing how fast and utterly the enormous market takes itself away; the fantasia of human commodities, wearable, edible, combustible, aesthetic, hygienic, and vehicular, the gamut of man's utensils, and all the push and pleasure of life that went into their changing hands, are suddenly gone; booths turn into carts and men into cart horses and everything vanishes. Piazza Vittorio at first glance is a big undistinguished place of northern design, with a park in the middle, where you would imagine little scenes of provincial longing and escape to the movie house. But there is something more.

One cat may be dying. Some will be conceived tonight around the fountain ruin with horrible shriekings as from the victims of emperors or emperors meeting their own ends, which the people who live above the colonnades will scarcely hear; if they do hear they will turn over and sleep again like children. A more fearful continuity has sprung up where theirs left off; a hundred and fifty charms are working for that neighborhood alone. The cats are not idle at all now, and not playing. Among the vines in the highest window of the jungle palace an eye burns that no human ever saw; between screams a furry figure is caught a second in the streetlight's gleam, in midspring, with claws bared to the root sharper than any doctor's tool, plunging to silence and the dark. No troop of Swiss could guard these mysteries.

The market will be back in the morning; for another day Rome is safe; if all were quiet, then you would stay awake.

> *The resounding Albunea, the headlong Anio, the grove*
> *of Tibur . . .*
>
> — Horace

PART II

HADRIAN'S VILLA

To F.E.B.

Animula, vagula, blandula

*Y*OU WALK UP THE LOVELY cypress alleys, planted by the
eighteenth-century owner of the place, whose life, one
imagines, must have taken on a strange dimension from his
having such an affair for an orchard — but probably not. At any
rate he had an appetite for statues. People had already been digging them up there for two or three hundred years but he found
plenty more, poking around among the olive trees — there had
never been such a cemetery for statues, and the best, everything
that taste and the imperial budget could collect in the second century; then filled up the holes so as not to interfere with his
plowing. His name was Count Fede.

Now the cypresses are among the most ancient anywhere, so
tall and old and thick, with such a looping and braiding of time in
their silk-gray trunks, you feel as close to Hadrian as to their infancy, and the busloads of tourists are being herded up the alley

ahead of you, looking blanker than anywhere else.* They have come farther, their feet hurt more, they will get more misinformation prattled at them, and all for rubble, rubble. But at five o'clock the horn of the last bus blows raucous and bossy from the parking lot and the last of the crazy hunters scramble down the hill, leaving the place to the twitter of olive leaves and the buzzing of flies over the brambles. Down at the end of what they call the Pecile an Italian mother will be sitting out the late sunlight with her children, and under the vaults of Hadrian's big or little baths a Swiss in shorts and rucksack reads aloud to his wife from the guidebook. Or in the fall there will perhaps have been no one, only a silent keeper or two, shepherds of ruins, and the big, definite clouds blowing over.

They are very important, the clouds, and so are the mountains and the beauty of the land, but most of all it is the hallucinatory quality of the light, as in Rome, and the depth of the shadows in it that allow you to go past the dismal surfaces, slowly, as you would enter a long poem. December is the best time; the shadows are long all day, there is nothing to hurry for, and the few people you see, if you see anyone, have a way of disappearing in a moment, quietly, without seeming to notice you or each other. They are intent on something else, like people on the edges of a dream or fishermen that you might glimpse here and there along a riverbank; they are quietly fishing for whatever it is that interests them, and all of them look as if they had been there for days.

It is the saddest place in the world, gaunt as an old abandoned graveyard, only what is buried there is the Roman Empire. There was a good deal more of it after that — the "noble" Antonines and the rule of the soldiers and so on, before Constantine packed up for Byzantium, but one feels this, wandering there, as the end, the delicate ghastly moment of the turn; there was never such a fling again, thought and the arts fell fast from then on and power slowly after them. Jack and Jill had lost their pail of water.

And one wonders if at that point anyone really knew it; did Hadrian, of all people? The decay of morals, waning *virtus* were

---

*For present entrance, see preface, "Return to Rome."

an old, old story by then and not too interesting; morals in fact were about to have a fine new heyday, glum, smug, and bourgeois; nobility of that kind had not been so hard to retrieve, and the empire, just then after Trajan's death, was at its grandest. No new conquests were planned. The Jews were making trouble again, for the last time, but on the whole in his thousands of miles of travel in Roman territory Hadrian the elegant, the sophist, met with no great unpleasantness, unless he should have minded all the scraping before himself. He could indulge the building craze peacefully everywhere. Something else was at the turn; for one thing there had been no poet worth speaking of for a long time, but that was only part of the subtlety of doom, of something else — you catch your breath thinking of it, wandering through the tragic heaps of masonry that loom still so huge over the olive trees, presenting a razor's edge of history and a character more complex than any in Proust.

Complex: but perhaps not, after all, so "enigmatic." The word got stuck to him some time ago, perhaps mainly because he was not wicked, at least not in the gross way of the century before; but one knows the face only too well, statues of the emperor amounted to a plague in this case, and there is the villa; it is his memoir, no matter how wrongly its courts and rooms and gardens came to be labeled. The idea was that Hadrian had recreated there the spots that had most attracted him on his Eastern travels, and so some very unlikely names were pinned on the ruins and scholars sweated over resemblances. It is not important. The fantasy is clear enough anyway, and so are the scale and the location; and how much too familiar one is with the brainless, incredible beauty of young Antinoüs, dead in the Nile, the new Apollo for this time that one thinks of as a fin-de-siècle of giants, a tremendous mauve convulsion that afterward was immediately hushed up and patched up as if nothing had happened. He is the other character among the ruins, poignant enough, but not heart-breaking; grandeur is missing in that story.

As for the location, various practical reasons have been suggested for it; the emperor needed an enormous space for his buildings, Roman villas were often on plains, or he wanted the hills of Tivoli at his back because of the prevailing winds or something of the sort. But that is not enough and the guidebook's description of the site as a perfect haven of tranquillity and philosophic contemplation is ironic. The world was his, he could have built where he chose, even allowing for his not being a thief or a firebug like Nero, and the noble villas in the vicinity were all on the hillsides; the lower land may not even have been very healthy, though up a way from the campagna proper. The point was the feeling of it, which was certainly not lost on Hadrian.

It is a subtle brooding piece of land, chosen by a man worshiped as a god over half the world and to whom elevation must have been insufferable. One thinks of the horrid glee of certain types of people on reaching the tops of mountains, and how for such a man as this the only equivalent pleasure must have been to tuck himself under the brow of one, especially if the nobles, whom he must have despised, could look down on him from it; a poor satisfaction, no doubt, but something, and in any case he was still high enough, though just under the view of Rome. The drop of the land on that side is theatrical, startling after the gentle and somehow insidious outlook toward Tivoli, where the slip of valley, with its suggestion of a moat or a gauze scarf, keeps the hills in spite of everything at their distance and the emperor's inner life inviolate; at any rate the inner life is what you think of there, with a strong flavor of insult about it too. But cross the palace, walk down that gorgeous marble portico, that now without its facing and its colonnades is only a very long and horribly straight brick wall five or six times your height, with round beam holes all along nearer the top — the paths on either side two desolate avenues of the mind — and there across a lovers' leap shored with slave quarters is the whole sweep of the plains some twenty miles to Rome. Actually to Rome now: if the air is clear there are two little jigsaw pieces of it there where the sun slips down, the cupola of Saint Peter's and the exposition building of 1942. But in Hadrian's time there could not have been anything high enough to show. The bankers or courtiers, whatever they were, up behind him, could look over to the white, wonderful city, but the emperor, who could only play at privacy, had had the caprice of putting himself just an inch or two below the horizon.

And there on his intellectual plateau, so lofty in its discretion, he spread out his stately pleasure dome, to put it mildly. "It goes on and on," you hear one of the tourists say — that is the usual remark. You can walk hours without seeing it all. Sumptuous country villas were an old commonplace to the Romans by that time, but except on the Palatine there was nothing to approach this, and the comparison with Versailles tells very little. The Roi Soleil is too simple, the childish whimsies of Marie Antoinette unthinkable in this atmosphere; with Versailles you associate a certain worldly statecraft, society flutterings, and a most grandiose toying with nature; Hadrian's game was with death, he would not have stooped to a pretense of wildness in his parks. Or so one gathers. It appears from the rubble that what nature he cared about was all brought indoors, that is, left in all kinds of strange ways and places under the sky — the sky was his intimate — but subject to a labyrinth of endlessly varying walls and colonnades, so that the whole area gives just the opposite impression from Versailles, where one simple architectural unit has connected with it a few lesser ones sprinkled around the grounds. Here there are no "grounds," unless the unexcavated part back of the palace on the east had some such purpose. All the rest is built over, with extraordinary terracings and underground corridors and linkings of one architectural fantasy to another, all crowded and shining as Rome itself was at the time, and turned in; nature is entirely dominated by geometry.

It took years to build, naturally, and Hadrian was not even there very much until nearly the end of his life, when his only desire was to die. He is supposed to have started it soon after the beginning of his reign in 117 and to have gone on until his death, but most of those twenty-one years he was traveling, seeking "into all curiosities" as somebody put it at the time, also looking after the empire. He was a public servant, trained under Trajan; he knew his duties; he had been a soldier and governor of a province. But something else was always driving him, not westward as people are driven in different times toward freshness and new lands, though he did his stint in Gaul and Germania, but east to the old and defeated ones, to art and symbols and the oldest mysteries; everything else was too easy, and in any case the thing was to keep moving, keep inquiring, otherwise every day would be a new boredom and life intolerable. Virtue and vice had stopped meaning anything, the oracles had gone dumb, the gods were part of the game to be played, he being one of them and for most purposes the chief one; he outdid all his predecessors in that, nobody had ever been worshiped in so many places, and he was not averse to it, which was perhaps another reason for going east: they did that sort of thing so well there. But worship does not fill up a crack in the soul.

So he came back to Rome now and then and would be off again before long, like a butterfly, really like a cargo of elephants, with all the world whispering about it every time. But it was not for him to feel weighted down by the thought of his baggage, or the thousand or ten thousand men who might be carrying it and making the arrangements. In that respect he was as free as a hobo, and could devote himself, among other things, to the serious profession of architecture. That was his passion, his true work, and it must have made up very often for the terrible absence, though not in the beginning, of love. One imagines him working late over the plans, furious at interruption, missing his meals like someone in a garret. Unfortunately Nero only fifty years before had done the same, to practice on his lyre, and had had the same appetite for the East, especially Greece but the rest of it too, where he had been adulated just as if he had not been a monster. But the times were not so simple now. Greece was everyone's Paris, that was inevitable, but Hadrian would never steal from it; the statues he could not buy he would have copied, there were plenty of artists for that, and he would make Greece more beautiful than ever. That was the compact: he, god, and Rome his instrument would glorify the spirit, which is beyond nationality.

The spirit was a little too subtle. The truth was the water was running out of the pail, there was not much time; pretty soon no-

body would know how to do anything but copy. Meantime, however, the fine new temples were being strewn over Greece and
Asia Minor, many dedicated to the emperor, and cities that he had
beautified were being named for him all over the place. He flitted,
with a sure hand however, with all his baggage trains from one
place and project to another; it was Olympus on the move, shrewd
and mobile as a newspaperman, subject to fits of melancholy. His
taste ran to the ornate, and his sense of scale, rather naturally, was
bizarre, though not peculiar to him: bigness was in the air and was
expected of him. Even so, his Temple of Venus and Rome over the
forum was really overbearing, and it seems the great architect
Apollodorus fell out of favor for caviling at Hadrian's designs for it,
one of his objections being that if the gods stood up they would lift
the roof off. Another important project was his tomb, across the
Tiber from the tomb of Augustus and more splendid, to be decked
with statues like a Christmas tree. But the great toy, or piece of
autobiography, the true private and desperate expression of the
man, was in Tivoli. It is there among the brambles that you get the
only real glimpse of him, standing between the glory and the dark,
like a colossal Des Esseintes studding the back of some impossible
tortoise, to be defeated in the end by what he must have hated
most: smug virtue, and common sense.

You have to imagine two things first: water and marble. Water was
a prime element in architecture, here as in Rome, an element to
be given shape, form, like other materials, subject to conceptions
as varied — left flat and still or used in the other simple ways on
occasion, but probably more often elaborate in its faces and kinds
of motion. It is the element of distance and the undefinable, co-
medium of flight, serving purposes of luxury that later, when indoors was really indoors and glass was better, were taken over by
wall-length mirrors and crystal chandeliers. From Renaissance
gardens you get a notion of it. The long pools of the Villa d'Este,
back up the hill, have their suggestion of infinity, and something
else, properly hallowed by cypresses, those elegiac trees; with the
multiplication of distance, three-dimensionally, comes a relaxation

of the formal statement, not *dolce far niente*, which never existed, more the *divin imprévu* of the artist, a sense of the lovely fruitful uncertainty whose gamut is from sleep and death to the brightest gaieties. A three-sided dressing-room mirror gives a little of it, or opposing mirrors in a ballroom; but water is deeper and wittier. A long curving staircase in the garden of the Villa d'Este has two streams running down its side walls, falling through a succession of cockleshell basins to disappear at the bottom in a pair of those funny, tortured heads typical in fountains of the time — the only use ever found in Italy for the tragic muse. The delight of it is beyond design; you have dreamed exactly that, or should have: to walk in stateliness down garden stairs whose banisters were running water. It is not the only one; there are smaller staircases on the same theme, one of them enfolding in its running double curve a large mosaic floor, patterned with mythological creatures seen through an inch or two of water; down the longest alley water spouts from the points of alternating obelisks and fleurs-de-lis, formally opposed in all their extent to a falling sheet and a slow trough; water spurts from the nipples of a sphinx, and the now corrugated mouths of monsters lurking behind an accretion of green slime; it forms as a backdrop to the great pools a giant cascade with as many parts as a symphony, and trickles and tumbles in grottoes, whose fake rusticity is the final worldliness in this dangerous decorative game. Pattern is motion, and you walk on the edge of dreams; another turn of a path and art might vanish and the flood rise over your face.

But this is all in the garden. At Hadrian's Villa the garden is the house, and it is a pity not to know what growing things there were in it. The right kind of literature did not exist to record that, or whether the Romans counted plants for much among their luxuries; it hardly seems so, they had too much nature in themselves to become fanatical over its vegetable refinements as Anglo-Saxons do; the point was always decoration. But they must have noticed the rarer possibilities for that sometimes, or perhaps Hadrian the aesthete might have been the one to think of it; perhaps the flowers here were as exotic as the stones, orchids big as pumpkins and var-

ious as African marbles, little botanical delicacies and live aphro-
disiacs from the East, each court and banquet hall having its own
schemes of plant color and perfume, as it had its fantasy in water.

In this house you would have lived with water, not gone out to
see it, except as the outside is part of the conception of the house
itself. There must have been a sound of it almost everywhere; you
would have moved from room to room, taking various kinds of
spaces as rooms, through the flash of crystal and pull of narcissism,
among thousand-faced mobiles or clear shallows where perhaps
fish from the Indian Ocean moved in stigmatic flickers of
turquoise, silver, and pomegranate. Versailles could never have
been so bright or so profound. And it seems the imagination was
as inexhaustible as the medium; it needed only more space, more
time to produce still other poems in water.

The most ambitious were the big nymphaea — three or four of
them, one in the heart of the palace, a whole liquid salon, whose
bottommost basin still shows some of its ancient coating of sky-blue
paint. One or two of the others may have somewhat resembled the
Fountain of Trevi, though the fake boulders of the baroque are
hardly in character for Hadrian; nor is the grotto idea, so dear to the
Madonna-ridden Italian heart and chronic in Renaissance land-
scaping; a dripping through moss is not his style. He had a few such
places, you can see them, but on the whole these waterworks,
though accommodating nymphs, must have had more of a formal
elegance, and one imagines running surfaces more in the style of
fluted columns, with all the varieties of cross-motion, however,
playing over and around the dolphins and tritons and sea centaurs
and marine divinities that are part of the game and its suggestion.
Some of the other arrangements are very quiet in their extravagance. There will be a small canal lined with marble, a sudden
pool-lit corner; down below the Stadium, near the Pecile, there is a
shallow garden basin of sedate geometric design and with a curious
illusion of great distance across it, where the boy with the dolphin
might have stood; and the four-leaf-clover end of the Golden Court
has niches at the four corners free for fountains, but surely there
only a falling, not a shooting or spraying up, of water, probably with

goddesses shining above, clear and single at the summit of motion, like Brancusi's bird: this is where one should have seen the Capitoline Venus, though it happens she belonged to somebody else, but some other product of Athens or Aphrodisias was surely here. In the banquet hall too, most fittingly, there is a mystery of water, perhaps separated from the diners by glass: one side or end of the triclinium seems to have been all fountain, which if the meal dragged on after dark must have played like sprayed neon in the light of the high candelabras. Then the strangely named Maritime Theatre,* with its strange exquisite moat; and the long canal of Canopus. These and dozens more, big and little, roofed or under the sky, without counting the baths.

Aside from the glory of it, what a pensiveness there must have been around the house from all this water: nothing lazy, but the repose of spaciousness that even one little garden pool can give, or a brook going past the house, and that the whole area has, its one and sufficient fortune, from the waterfall at Tivoli. Nothing else permits such voyages of the spirit, nothing gives such largesse of suggestion and of time present and past. A person of restless mind could go mad in dry country, unless he were always moving toward water like an Arab, and it is right that Hadrian, the burning incurable traveler, should have had it as his most extreme luxury.

It would have been richer than jewels or stones, but he had plenty of them too, and the most beautiful. It was of the time; in general the stones used during the empire and the workmanship spent on them are a continual ravishment, hardly credible: delights of a Dorian Gray, magnified to the superhuman scale of everything in Rome.

You see them in the museums, or scattered under altars — the thick porphyry tubs and urns and basins, sometimes with gold trimmings or more rarely the deep crowded reliefs of the period, but the best of them simple, their marvelous surfaces unbroken except by some light abstraction of handles, rings, or heads, at the ends. One of them, the tremendous shallow cup in the Sala Rotonda of the Vatican, like a birdbath for egrets or great white

---

*Now called Island Nymphaeum.

herons, or a goblet for heroes tall as mountains, is adorned by nothing at all. It is made from a single piece of stone, cut with what hideous labors from the quarries of Egypt and carried somehow to Rome, polished to a smoothness of silk and carved to pure form, as cool and elusive in all its tonnage as any Mona Lisa's smile. Not far away is a large bathtub of alabaster, a curdled, decadent stone much prized at the time also by certain early Christians, and farther on six more, very moving in mass and texture, of basalt and oriental granite. One is rose granite; in another the gray has a deep dusting of black, but sometimes the flecks, hardly visible, are as though scattered from the plumage of tropical birds; or the thing will be all taffeta-black.

Hadrian was surrounded by such objects; there is a sumptuous cup or basin of his nearby, of rosso antico, and at the door of the Sala Rotonda are a pair of telamones from the villa, of peach-red granite. In many common doings his fingers, when not touching precious metals, would have passed over rock surfaces as rare as these, of every vein and shade; he would have cared for gorgeousness in his toilet seat, as for spells of unnecessary hardship while traveling through rough territory. But the wonderful stones were not only in tubs and tabletops; they were everywhere, the materials of architecture; columns and walls and floors were made of them, acres of surface were coated with varieties of marble, some of them as hard to come by as malachite and lapis lazuli.

Now what is mostly to be seen is the sad, dull underpinnings, bricks, tufa, and cement, and in many places a facing of little mousy stones in reticulate, which at an earlier time would have been tile; it seems there was a bottleneck at the kilns at this time from the splurge of imperial building, so the little stones came in. There is anyway something peculiarly mournful about them; they are so sober and tidy, you feel the hand of the workman in them more than anywhere else, the little individual moment of skill and patience, and probably haste too — the drive behind it all was so impetuous, as though prophetic — spent on something never meant to be seen, and that never was seen again, once the workman was through, until the whole tragedy had been finished for so long the place was anybody's to go picking around in. You would like to cover them, pull the weeds and brambles farther up over them. Now it is as if they never had been covered; as if the stroke had fallen just that much earlier and everyone had begun drifting away or died, leaving a great half-built scrawniness to stand against the sky and go to pieces before the life had ever come into it. Yet like all things Roman it was made to stand forever; the materials have interpenetrated each other more every century, creating one gray-brown substance that at the tops of the broken walls becomes round and furry-looking, or like an icing of horsehair, though nothing is so hard.

But some of the final magnificence is still there too, tons of it if it were all put together: sheared-off columns, and whole ones, and pedestals of whole colonnades with only a few mutilated columns, fluted or plain, standing on them or dragged there from somewhere else and made to stand on them — there is an aching hypnotized look about some of them, as there must be in ruins in the desert or any place where no human voice has intruded since the catastrophe, for all the crazy hunters and even the popes and Count Fede: the place is still entranced — bits of architrave; the egg and dart and the acanthus leaf lying foolish as broken teacups on the ground; the black-and-white mosaic floors, too many for people to steal or care for, you can pick up handfuls of the loosened chips at the edges; and in patches here and there the other floors in opus sectile with their airy designs and lovely colors. So many stones and colors you would not think geology had such invention, and gathered from so far and in such quantities, not only by Hadrian, it is as though they had meant to finish off their world in a great frozen bonfire of marble. Then before long even the names of most of them were lost, and some are known now only by color-words with the adjective *ancient*, dismissing them forever.

There is giallo antico, one of the commonest and varying greatly, sometimes not yellow at all but a hovering sunset-pink; dove-pink pavonazzetto, rosso antico of solid blood, portasanta veined like steak, and africano with its more criminal red in smudges on black, also the gamut of porphyry from mourning purple to a bright grapejuice smear; several greens — malachite as strong as emeralds sometimes, gloomy speckled serpentine, and verd antique like old grass. In many there are wide differences in degree and kind of veins, from total batique to the simple tone with just a molecular infusion of something else, not for pattern but depth: with most of these stones the effect is not of looking at them but deep into them. Blue is missing, but there are blacks and grays and various whites: Carrara once paper-white, now blackened by its peculiar disease; a rich oriental white with a velvety thickness of pore unlike any from Italy, most wonderful in the weight it adds to massive columns; and various cipolini from glove-gray to Wordsworth's sky-green, one with twisting black streaks like a moving of heavy liquids. But there is an African granite better than any marble, so beautiful it is not enough to look at it, there is a compulsion as with certain trees to pass your hands over it and even so you cannot take in the bulk of the pieces that are there; you would expect a paperweight's worth. It is an angry sea-gray, close to gunmetal, with little micalike flakes very thickly strewn through it, only the shavings are so hard and the light plays off them so, they are more like diamonds, especially on the unfinished surface of a broken piece; on the polished ones it is like a section of dark ocean seen close to through binoculars, with all its points of scintillation held still; and of this marvelous rock, an unshakable profusion of jewels, Hadrian had columns three times as wide around as the clasp of a person's arms. It was a setting for angels.

Not the white and gold variety, however, though there was white and gold too, and not anything that taste now would conceive of any more than it conceives of the Renaissance, but that is only an indoors problem; here the challenge, or the offense, is everywhere. The place burned with color, rich and intricate as Chinese temples; the stones burned on their juxtaposition, the statues were paintings in the round; of the columns, some were painted or gilded only to half their height — this comes back in the churches — and the gray ones would sometimes have had white orders above them, also a ground for more painting or gold.

Everybody knows this but nobody sees it in the ruins, the great
past as it becomes that fades into the general gray of dreams and
photographs, with a touch of Pompeian red in Pompeii: who
thinks of Hadrian's color sense. But to be an architect was to think
in color, and the East more than Rome was his home; no verd antique or rosso or giallo antico for him; he would have known all
the names, as many as North American birds, and the varieties of
each, and chosen them with the petulant, fussy eye of an interior
decorator, though never forgetting grandeur and the grand line.

It would have been devious, all this, still not basically oriental
at all any more than he was himself; there are no Persian
curlicues, no minarets and candy stripes. The heart of the matter
is Greek, and more; there is a functionalism as of aqueducts beneath the complexity of forms and effects; and the floors are still
strangely pure to our eyes, the stones subtle and distinct on neutral
grounds, never overloaded or ugly-rich; no running together of
streaky slabs as on the walls of Renaissance chapels, which have always something of an undigested meal about them and perhaps it
is true of that too that nothing is more admirable than the pieces;
nor the primitive, somewhat chunky effect, excellent though it is,
of Cosmatesque work. These designs, the best of them variations
of leaf figures, suppose an eye for abstraction that the Church
would never recover. But better even than the opus sectile are the
black-and-white mosaics, or black and white with a discreet
touching in of one other color, and of these the most splendid are
not the figured ones. They have their greatness too, in the calm of
the spacing and the strong eruptive grace of their semihuman
characters; but the ones you can never get tired of are the others,
the orphans of ancient art, things so common nobody bothers to
speak of them anymore; imitations of third-rate statues are far
more discussed. However there is nothing to stop you from
looking at them, and in Hadrian's diminutive guest rooms, called
on the Italian maps the Ospitalia, you can see a series of ten that
are perhaps the most satisfactory floors ever made, at least it is hard
to imagine anything pleasanter. They are only squares — the three
bed-size wings of the rooms are left white — filled with abstract

tracings in black, so various and graceful and pure, with such a rightness of tension in the lines, like the final sublimation of a world's delight, it is very hard afterward to shake yourself down from the effect of them; the thin patterns hold the mind like a string quartet.

As against this, you remember the colored statues of the time, hideous enough with their porphyry flesh and yellow draperies or vice versa: the goddess Roma as so rigged up is the dream of an Abyssinian housemaid, and could no doubt have had a place of honor almost anywhere in Hadrian's house; she is what is known as savage. But even she falls in after a while, among the vases and the bathtubs and the gold; how thin and wintry we have become. These things were not meant to be seen in isolation, bright spots in a Gothic waste. They are part of a terrific game of color, dangerous as the fountains, dangerous as any bold, loud affirmation of life, in which the senses are not meant to be tickled or soothed, but expressed in all their range; in which mass too plays against surface, columns against paint, gold leaf or fabrics or stucco relief against solid rock. The literal depth of a color matters, and the depths of the surroundings. It is not certain there were paintings along the Pecile, that high brick wall ten times as long as the Greek one it is supposed to have been named for, but if there were, or whatever things in color were there, they were framed by mountains and fountains and the endless fancy arcades or columns of the double portico, set in a careful rigging of morning and afternoon sunlight. Outside or in, you started with the whole scene and smack in the middle of the palette: a strict and subtle game, Hadrian's own, and he played it to its finish, with all the might of his nature and the last taste left in his world. The color of most of the villa now, which is also the color of historical memory, or the sole of an old shoe, is probably the only one you would not have seen there at the time; or if you had it would have shone like silver.

It goes on and on. He could not stop building, he was still at it when he died, pushing the villa still farther out across the hill or adding to its heart, thinking up new and more perfect shapes and fancies for it though by that time he could hardly have cared; and in all of it that is left you feel his presence. Elusive as they say, but so strong, you feel always on the verge of knowing the whole truth of the matter; you think with just a little more silence, the suspension of a bee's humming, you will have it. It is not like a place that many people have lived in and added to so that it comes to contain mainly an epoch and a tendency, though there is that about it too; there is nothing else on this scale so packed and crackling with a single mystery, or tragedy, as you choose to see it. Who was this man? What on earth was he thinking about all that time? The questions become obsessive, the drama is so unlike any other; and most of all you wonder as you snoop and pry in the desolation how much, being both agent and victim on such a scale, he knew of what he represented. A good deal, probably, too much; which makes it more poignant for him to have gone on creating this fantastic dragonfly of a place that in no time at all would be nothing but a white elephant. More cruelly than in most things, what it is now was contained in its beginnings. He himself, in a last-minute fling of grandeur or irony, sealed its destruction, to delay the destruction of Rome.

Yet it had its moment; you have to start from that. They say that in the last few years, when he finally stayed there, there was a constant round of theatrical spectacles, ballets no doubt, re-creations of historical scenes, perhaps even of great naval battles, for which the Romans had an odd weakness, but they liked anything that splashed. This side of it all is not too interesting and the spectacles would have been less so; there was no talent; literature was all grammar and rhetoric, and the historical scenes must have been dead as doornails. But Hadrian was no force of nature himself; he would have liked a good doornail as much as anyone at the time, if not more, and probably he did sit through an awful number of them, in the pleasant little theater down below Count Fede's house and the erstwhile big nymphaeum. He would have come to them in relief from the great revolting shows demanded by the people in the city amphitheaters and the howling of the Blues and Greens in the circus: political necessities, not to be fooled with though he might mitigate some of the horrider aspects. For his own taste the thing would be learned, precious, antiquarian; he was hardly in a position to appreciate satire if there had been any, and there could not be much of anything else.

The theater, anyway, was charming; it was as if architecture in this case fed on the putrescence of thought and reached an eerie brilliance now just because the whole show was so nearly over. It is a Greek theater, rather dead at the present time from all the looking-at it has undergone, though its corridors remain — the count or somebody has used them for stables — and the high narrow stage with the space for the chorus below; if you try you can provide it with the appropriate masks and muses. But the theater is the least of it; there are many other units more original and probably more stunning in their time, the Pecile for one, which you come to next, up at the end of the cypress alley. There may have been something of the San Paolo colonnade in that, but it is impossible to think of, and surely it was saved by the single line and the lightness of the columns; it seems there is a notion of infinity built into it, taking it together with that view, the whole reluctant, half sleep-dredged spread of the campagna that even then had memories over it everywhere ready to rise up like birds from swampland. Or so it affects one now, which is perhaps misleading; there would have been more distraction about it then, in its elegance. Now it is one of the most beautiful walls in the world — immense, drab, useless: it encloses nothing, and never did; it connects with nothing, the path goes all the way around it, such a distance, that in itself is an image of infinity, or despair; and the round regular holes along the top, being far over your head and exposing what you will get to anyway if you follow the path long enough, are sublime. So perhaps one feels too much about what it used to be, all painted and perfect; at any rate Hadrian is very much there, not an academic creature as in the theater; it is one of the places where you feel the connection most personally.

See it with birds, fruits, and flowers, real ones, painted ones on the wall. There are myths on the wall too, antique rape and godly binges and cupids serving wine, and a thousand mythological animals, while in one of the gardens alongside a live peacock slowly spreads his fan a yard and a half high, exhibiting for a moment at its center a turquoise heart. The emperor's own face is not above malice. Besides, the walk is only a cloister without confinement, looking on infinity, and this at times will torment him more than any cell and all his fountains will be like dishwater. Nothing but the sea can cure him. He will thrash about in his malaise a few days or hours, then will be off again like thistledown with his forty tons of baggage, to come back nobody knows when, full of wit, state-craft, and his own glory, with a new load of statues for the villa.

But there is none of this in the two baths. If there is any character there it would seem to be the empress, poor thing, with her ladies; whose husband intends to outshine Augustus, while she with all her determination and advantages has never managed to be Livia or anything like it. Her intrigues are halfhearted, her influence nil, her body, her virtue, and her mind wasted and misinterpreted; she has been portrayed in marble as Venus, and will be remembered as the world's greatest sexual supernumerary. Her most intimate failure becomes a public cult. Yet one can imagine a certain social rapport between them, and he is perhaps not unkind, or not willfully; he may even have designed the little baths for her, where she can steam away some of her frustrations in a flawless sequence of caldarium, tepidarium, frigidarium, etc. without retracing her steps: that is what the building is known for after two thousand years, though what strikes one more is the grace of the proportions, and the marvelous ingenuity as well as the beauty of the vaults, looked at as a problem in building. Not that they are more marvelous than many larger ones, only they are better preserved than most, and one is more likely to think of construction on a small scale, that is in tranquillity.

There is nothing tranquil about the big baths as they are now, partly because of a particular accident of decay. A tremendous chunk of masonry has fallen intact from the north side where it lies like a meteor under the broken arches, blocking the way, spoiling the view, more moving than any perfect temple. There is a savagery of time in it. The ancient cypresses shoot down to nothing around it, a hundred cycles of them are undone by this huge shapeless mass of stuff that is so victoriously unaesthetic, so like a natural obstruction in a jungle though it was no cave it fell from. Hadrian dwindles; you lose interest in him, except as a figure to give scale. The sense of the place is of appalling struggle, art against nature, art and empire together against time, worse than any affair of armies, and when that bit of roof crashes — you hear it — it is like the whole ocean lifting back to pound against cliffs in a storm. It is the place in the villa that most loudly imposes the thought of love, compels it, and it will be terrible; lovers and nonlovers alike will know it; even two strangers left alone here, ugly, mismatched, the fat Swiss and an aging maiden college professor, could throw down their guidebooks and afterward not know what monster they had mated with, or remember nothing of it, though they will never feel the same about history again.

This can happen because the place was utterly trivial in its use; what went down in the awful struggle was not gods or the soul's courage but only some rooms where people washed themselves as pleasantly as possible, at various temperatures — the old Roman story. There is no such dreadful ecstasy in Hadrian's library, nor in the Temple of Serapis down beyond over the hill. Serapis, or Isis; and probably Mithra was around somewhere, and certainly others more obscure, one after another. They were coming in fast from everywhere like schools of fish or psychoanalysis in season and Hadrian, that busy intellect and connoisseur of every *dernier cri*, would be trying them all out and enshrining them for a time, reserving his distaste for Jews and Christians, political nuisances both, an obstruction to his liberal program, and something worse: enemies of art. His own contribution would be the new Apollo; he would cram beauty down the world's throat and make it worship as it gagged; beauty is truth, at least they are not to be thought of separately. But you will come back later to this wide valley of uncertainties and the so-called Academy beyond, where in Count Fede's time it was no doubt the thing to picnic in peasant costume while real peasants danced for you among the ruins: such a pretty pageant, that, so melancholy and grotesque; and how one is *schooled*, as Goethe said, by these reminders of antiquity. There seems to have been a whole other palace started, or even finished, out in this direction, and that would be likely; probably there were too many people around the main one, too much going on all the time; there would be no place to be alone; and the drive was always for more, more space, more kinds of space, more marble and fountains; nothing was ever enough, or big enough.

But there was not time enough either, so there is only a square mile or so of actual palace, up across the fabulous runways and cellars, past the praetorium three stories high, from the top of which you have one of the few views there are of the whole expanse of the place, immense and cryptic, not desolate, only like a city on the moon if there should be there such greenness and humanity. The bathhouse fit is over; you hardly want to go on from here, it is so good, but this too is all depth and motion; nothing is static. The ruins with their angry heights and furry edges stretch out before you in such a bigness of size and time, the landscape, itself so reflective, seems really to be riding on the surface like a duck in repose; and there is that other, plastic depth from the shadows, sharp black lakes that slowly travel and bend, erasing or restoring this or that part of a construction according to the hour.

Sometimes even the Pecile fades out, you hardly notice it; but more often it stands out as a fierce overpowering discord on your left, a great clash of straightness, with its blind lacy eyes open to the sky. Straight ahead of you is the high point of the whole, the section back of the Court of Libraries, a meccano-set Matterhorn all in a jumble and that refuses to fall; and very demure but arresting, between that and another sensational wreck called the Hall of Philosophers, the tight little circle of the Maritime Theatre. That is the center; you feel it even from here, though the moat and the island are hidden and you only observe the curious shelteredness of it; and its time, when the maze was all filled in, even that much could not have been seen from anywhere except on top of it.

It is like music, so much that you seem sometimes to be hearing the buildings more than seeing them, as though at some level of the brain the eyes and ears functioned interchangeably. You feel it right away coming in around the back of the Golden Court, which is usually the last place seen but that is wrong. It should be the beginning; it is the key, the place where the scale and whole tone of the place, the kind of thing it is, hits you most strongly. There is first the vast sweep of the court, the largest in the palace, staggering when you remember the colonnade around it all and the ornament — the richest of everything was found here, the marbles and granites, statues, bas-reliefs, the great intricate architraves — then right away that other exigence, of the forms. The uses of the buildings are not of much interest. They are first of all creations in space, necessary as expressions of a personality, or rather one expression: a long Mozartian invention that will never run out of motifs — again, the fountains — but that has one generic quality through every part. That is an extraordinary grace and lightness; the enormous hulks of the Golden Court are all *up*, poised like a dancer.

It is the lightness, however, of something massive and solid, never scatterbrained. The grand approach rules, a little too grand: it is stated in the formidable apse or half-dome that forms the back of the piazza, like a great shell drawing into itself all the secret and disparate lines of the rest of the palace, and in the other huge hemisphere facing it over the far entrance too; but this basic majesty of line is firm enough to stand an endless bubbling up of minor themes, and even a kind of general playfulness — "pleasure in the wind, the sunlight, and the sea." The secondary dome, over the vestibule, is itself playful as well as imposing, with its octagonal vaulting and the devious pattern of interlocking chambers around it; and the other great shell, that could so well loom over the soberest decisions of empire or justice, has under it that charming four-leaf-clover fountain arrangement, with a related fountain basin, deep and curved, as the backstop. Other rooms, symmetrical and evidently rather dark, open off from either side of this lyrical and quite feminine place with its awesome roof, with still more off at an angle once on the valley side; halls run back of the portico the length of the piazza; and at the far end, toward the valley, through a bouquet of tight little rooms of interesting shapes, probably at least one of them a toilet, appears the backside of a further apse, which while embedded like a barnacle in all that pattern and splendor, stubbornly faces off all by itself over the gulch to the mountains. The gulch, incidentally, is known as Tempe, after the Grand Canyon of Thessaly: one of those jokes or errors that the place is littered with.

The details are typical. The apse, the juxtaposition of straight and round, the double walks, the complicated bunching of small units around large ones, are motifs that recur continually; and the way the last little apse is stuck on, or stuck in, is typical too. You will see everywhere such flowerings out of minor themes, self-contained but held tight to the larger one, and the central ones too are only outgrowths from one another. Almost nothing stands separate; nothing ends; and there is something young and joyous simply in the creation of such a continuity, the sheer skill and tire-lessness of it. There is a certain sense of fearfulness in it too, a suggestion of a dread of exposure, which you feel more later but there is enough of it in this little barnacle affair, clever but after all rather freakish, as though designed by a man who would not sit with his back exposed in a restaurant.

But for the time being what matters is the invention, which among other things involves a relation between different levels, as complex as the other. Hadrian, for all the ground he covers, is not a horizontal man. The conception is always in depth; the tunnels and sunken passageways that twist about like mine shafts are not all mere conveniences; they are part of the design, an essential expression like the rest; or there will be a seeking out of the most impossible terrain, as in the praetorium if it was that, strung out in tiers across an artificial cliff as though on purpose to keep the soldiers or whoever lived there from having a back exit. The more spectacular case of that is the so-called Hundred Roomlets, four stories of them with balconies and insulating space behind, covering the whole arch of the cliff under the Pecile, in the manner of Trajan's recent markets in Rome, only bigger. If the main entrance road passed here, as it seems it did or may have, you could have been half hypnotized before you knocked at the door by the mere daring of the thing; and can be now, looking up from the field where the great white oxen seem equally hypnotized at their plowing, as if the same pair had been at it ever since the rooms were built. That is a firetrap too, a mistrustful place — it could not have been pleasant to sleep in; yet it is awesome as architecture, very like the Colosseum in its effect of weight and power, though at the same time delicate; with its balconies it must have had somewhat the lines of a snow crystal under a microscope.

The other striking thing about the whole creation is how public it all is. Aside from such windowless rooms as these, evidently meant for menials, and the even more stifling cubicles of the guests' dormitory, there seems to be no private space at all, at least it is hard to imagine a private life in any of it, unless the places called libraries and their ruined upstairs were for something of the sort. Almost everything else is either too light and big or too dark and small, and all of it pours into the hemmed-in outdoors, as in a hopeless cross between claustrophobia and agoraphobia, so that the whole place comes to have the feeling there is in the communal guests' latrine, of an endless roiling togetherness. It is the normal Roman business of building around a court or atrium, and the proportions are the proper ones for a gregarious balcony civilization, in which the dark airless retreat is good enough for what little privacy is needed. But there is a snake in the case this time, which leads you on through space after hollow space once designated for every kind of social going-on imaginable.

There are two other theaters; a couple of gymnasiums; a third bathhouse; several libraries, or so it appears, and banquet halls for different seasons; a regulation-size stadium, or garden in the shape of a stadium, anyway the obelisk now on the Pincio is supposed to have stood at its round end, not the biggest known obelisk but good enough for a country house; many, many porticoes, aboveground and under, too many for one owner ever to have strolled in, especially an absentee one. Nothing is missing, except as it seems the basic necessities: garbage disposal, food storage, stewards' quarters, butchering plant, and a hundred other simplicities

that must have taken a lot of room and made a lot of noise, but
have vanished; nothing looks poor enough for them; the music remains very fine and tense and grand in every part, as though life
could be a long pride of elegance suspended in the air, but what
you feel more is again the primacy of the forms. It is all a playing
with space; whatever goes in them is an afterthought.

The two most beautiful now are relatively small, though they
seem large in their different ways, and both are more or less
hidden among high walls that keep their moods intact and separate from the rest; beyond this they have not much in common.
The first is the swimming-pool court, between the stadium and
the boxlike building called a barracks, which you can cross to
from the back on leaving the Golden Court; of all places in the
villa the most shocking to come on without warning, as you are
likely to, thinking you were on your way through looking for something, and instead you find yourself intruding on a spectacle of
stupendous energy, something unnaturally proud and lofty, and
awake. It really seems that you have no right to be there, that some
terrific motion was stopped by your coming in. Not that the pool is
any bigger than a normal Hollywood one, but its few relics of
columns, on the raised platform of the upper portico, are extrava-
gantly tall, and so white they cast a sheet of black into the blue of
the sky behind them. Under them, all the way around at floor
level, are a series of eye-shaped and otherwise eyelike windows
that look out from under the ceiling of a crypto-portico, one of the
cleverest in the palace and the most subtly bound in with the rest
of the conception, at the center of which the pool, for fish or
aquatic plants or perhaps really swimmers, is suspended. The
compound effect of lift, of an upward-tending in the actual stones,
depending on an incredible rightness of proportions between the
columns and the two rectangles, of basin and court, with the
crypto-portico giving the extra, needed weight at the bottom, is so
strong it seems more like a product of religious exaltation. Unfortunately it is too good; with its modern duplex design and its
Corinthian profile against the sky the place is ripe for Technicolor,
unless it should more luckily fall into a sudden heap first from its

own intensity; but up to now it has kept its young, ferocious look of being beyond intrusion.

The other present glory is the one court of any importance that seems never to have had a fountain. That is the nearby Hall of Doric Pillars, once a two-story open court of fancy design — probably resembling those cloisters in which a lacy ground-level colonnade appears to hold up architectural blocks several times as heavy. Now it is a little walled-in desert, with a vast and windswept look, where a number of travertine wedges on short mushroom stems, all exactly alike, are lined up facing a group of light splintered columns, and there they all sit in a conclave of silence, a perpetual, petrified noncommunication. You can enter this court from either end, but you have a distinct impression when you are in it of its having no exit and no memory of one.

Next door is the big nymphaeum with the blue trough; enough water if it were put together differently for a small navy; then after an empty green stretch, along the rim of the terrace over the Court of Libraries, comes a collection of rooms, in which you begin to be conscious in a new way of the terrific complexity at work, not only of design: of the man, Hadrian. There was an earlier villa there to be incorporated into this middle section of the palace, and here and there you can see signs of the patching-up and adding-on process, whether around that or not; but that is not it. The real nature of the place is not accidental at all; it is as if it had been made by highly organized insects, and if all this had been destroyed it would have had to be put up again with the same complication somewhere else; it was a necessity.

The rooms there are the most fragile of all, with detail so fine you are likely to trample through without noticing it, especially two small adjacent courts forming with their two patterns of pillars and columns a lovely conceit in marble, square against round. But you find that this shimmering affair is to be taken together with some gloomy and cavernous underpinnings, not delicate at all though as ingenious, and specifically a great vaulted tunnel making four sides of a square some fifty yards each way, hacked deep out of bedrock under the terrace. It is one of the many; back under the baths you will have seen such places laid out as for a main subway junction, and there were once mouths of tunnels at nearly every sloping down of the land, sometimes several in the same area, as toward Tempe; it is not beyond Hadrian to have made his guests, or some of them, enter his palace through some such stygian channel, even by boat, as though to ritualize their departure from the other world, or pretend to: it would have been a pleasantry. But what is piquant about this one is that it seems to have had no point except as a promenade; it is a kind of garden path or conservatory, a place to stroll in the dark or almost — there were a few light shafts, mostly blocked up now — with painted walls and its vault lined with pebble mosaic, rustic but rare, which you can look at now with a flashlight and it is the most intimate and troubling piece of ornament in the villa: thousands of little stones searched for on the seashore, culled over for size and color, and patiently put together at last to please, you would think, an imperial turnip. But no, it is the emperor himself.

The most affecting of the serious mosaics found in the place, the three of the masks in the room named for them in the Vatican, were not far from here, in the pavilion over the valley. You know the others too, elegant and almost always a little sad: the dove perched on the edge of the basin, as though suddenly oppressed by its absence of brain, the Watteau-like landscapes, the fierce fighting animals snarling out from a romantic realism that makes them first cousin to the dove. But some higher genius made the three small plaques of the masks: violent, beautiful faces racked by their own unreality, thrown down or propped up in a landscape peopled only by inanimate and unrelated objects, a musical instrument, a fragment of architecture. That was the sense of the world, and it is wonderfully familiar; you know where you are. You stand on the ravaged roofless upstairs of the little pavilion, which is perhaps a place to dine in summer, two to a couch, while from two points in the canebrake below there may be rising a shrill antiphonal song, from voices never quite human: something else enters into them, a too vast remembrance and something like the pain of a birth, at the moment of the singing; and have a weird but

tonic sense of walking through an imagery that you have always
known. You are perhaps making the whole villa up as you go
along; certainly there is something between you and it at moments very like the passion of those masks.

But first there is one of those minor mysteries that have a way of
catching at the imagination as you go by, more vivid sometimes
than the grand lines. It is nothing: just a row of recesses above and
at the back of the guest rooms, where the windows are supposed to
be, and instead there are those high little alcoves that seem clearly
to have been strung together like beads by a stream of water, and
perhaps by a pipe too a few inches higher; the connecting walls
are pierced in that way; very curious, and why has no one ever
mentioned it? — the guests are perhaps played to as they sleep by
musical instruments run by water, or perhaps they are not guest
rooms at all. There are two more vaulted halls side by side, semi-
tunnels, one of them plastered carnation pink, between there and
the pavilion of the masks, and off to the left more rooms, another
court, another porch with bits of trimmings lying around as sumptuous as anywhere else, quite impressive enough for a main entrance, though you thought you had left that a mile back beyond
the baths, and you seem to be starting all over, hearing the main
theme again from the beginning, with variations. It is a chronic
impression.

However you return, moving toward that modest circle over by
the Pecile, into the Court of Libraries, with its two huge multi-
storied and indecipherable buildings, one of them evidently a sky-
scraper as things went then. They stretch out and out in back too,
growing no clearer, great battered rat-runs that you can make
nothing of; and now a reminder of certain other houses keeps tug-
ging at your mind. They are those enormous country mansions of
the past century in America called Follies, never finished and
never meant to be, that on the day after the owner's death were dismissed as impractical for orphan asylums. But nobody dared tear
them down, they were so big, and so you remember them: utterly
personal and monstrous places, though they too share the style of
their times and at first blush will have seemed no different from

what everybody else was doing. Usually the owner was a spiritualist, a theosophist, a dabbler in cults and magic, who built a hundred guest rooms while arranging not to be exposed too much to his guests, because these are the people for whom no human touch is ever right, who in their craving for society lock themselves up against it, and live in a long fury of hide-and-seek. The places are always labyrinthine, and sometimes nearly everything in them will be under lock and key; at the lowest there may even be practical jokes built into them, which are serious too, but these are refinements. The main thing is to keep building, for one's very point of rest to be always in motion, a thrusting-out of the ailing ego that must have recognition and more and more is forced to make it for itself, in its own empyrean; if it stopped building its own temple it would die. The spirit that was to be glorified has become indistinguishable from the *I*, and the threats to it have multiplied accordingly: watch out for open spaces, steps in the hall, a too familiar valet; listen to the warning voices; protect, protect.

But this is scurrilous; there is a small difference, enough even if there were no other. The place is beautiful. It will be fourteen hundred years, all the way to Bramante and Michelangelo, before you see again such harmony of great and small, of ornament and purity of structure; before anyone knows again this trick of tension and great scale without any pressing down into the earth or too flighty leaping up, and how to extend horizontally without sprawling, which is harder. The madman adds patch to patch, pushes his private doodle this way and that, with no center except in his own mind and doing everything to conceal that. This is the opposite. Every radiation is held within the pattern, instead of leading you cannily away, is an addition of strength and repose, being only in spaciousness, and for this the word is genius. Not, in this case, the communal genius of a period, which makes the greatest architecture, but that other of an artist contradicting his time a little, pushing against it at one point or another. There is a good deal that is not classic here: the reminder of mosques in the aggregation of domes of various heights and sizes; the flamboyant use of upper stories, especially in this court, almost as though the

great upflung tower building were meant to be seen against particular cloud formations; even the general layout, which is on several
axes, always an invitation to disorder. The whole sense of the place
is individual, violently so; it is the expression of a single artist,
straining away from the standard so far that with the least slip of
taste it could fall into freakishness or vulgarity and that achieves
greatness instead: a tour de force, certainly, like a Turner or
Tiepolo sky, but convincing, through sheer personal brilliance.

That is the passion in these ruins: a creative one; and the appli-
cation is not so startling, not necessarily. Hadrian is one of the
richest as well as brightest men in the empire, which is how he
happens inevitably to be at the head of it, whatever else his cousin
Trajan might really have preferred; and one of the most cultivated:
he has been to the best schools, entertained the best philosophers
and probably subsidized quite a stable of them. There is no need
to imagine him skulking around his marble labyrinth. He is as busy
as the president of the United States to begin with, the hundred-
year rampage in the wake of Augustus being finally up; he has all
sorts of things to see to besides architecture: codifying laws,
building the first wall across barbarous Britain, like patrolling the
Arctic now, pulling in the empire on the east to a tenable line,
pushing reforms for slaves and prisoners past a grudging if more or
less powerless senate, stamping out Christians, and so on; in short
delivering the new golden age, and in his leisure time exempli-
fying it. It was never more proper to do so: for the head of the state
to stroll in brilliant company through the most magnificent of
country houses, concerning himself with love, cooking, and the
things of the mind, while beyond the fountain at the edge of the
cypress grove a favorite peacock pecks for grub. The obligations of
the ruler in this age are not simple, when half Italy is studded with
villas and Herodes Atticus, a private citizen, can build cities as
splendid as Hadrian's. And he has other passions too, especially for
hunting: he can work off his conflicts in that.

Nevertheless there is a sound in the place that leads you past
the forms of art, and like a mosquito in your ear drowns out the vis-
ceral struggle of centuries that came forward for a moment in the

big baths. It is a very modern sound: the scream of the *I*; the geometry of these vast courts is all a dialogue with self; they are not
public at all but private as a dream and whatever company moves
in them will also be a projection of the dreamer's mind. What is
shared with Versailles and the palaces of the Czars, the lavishness
and the arrogance of the dimensions, becomes something more
insidious here, not the simple effrontery of despotism. The thrust
is obsessive. The rooms high as Grand Central Station, the maze
of half-lit halls and those others where slaves must have hurried
with torches at high noon — containing without knowing it the
end of all the emperor's culture and mystical experiments — the
feminine niche in the liplike fold of a garden court, the honey-
comb guardhouse and more secretive cliffside burrow of the Hundred Roomlets, the playing with planes, pure abstraction, lined as
with fur with every voluptuary fantasy, the tiny tight theatrical
center of it all, the impossibility of an end: all are the innermost
statement of a mind, a true Folly, just the opposite of innocent
Versailles. And when you are this far into it it is not sad, nor even
particularly ironic; it is what they call entertainment; you want to
know what is hidden in the Maritime Theatre, so valuable that it
has to be protected with a moat.

It is at least clear that you will not find simplicity. This is the
house of a man who will always seem false, and most when he is
not; whose anger is less offensive than his kindnesses; from whom
the simplest goodness comes out as the worst ambiguity. Between
him and shrewd, goodhearted, ambitious Trajan, his guardian and
predecessor, who liked the company of honest soldiers, it must
have been a more ticklish business than anyone now knows; there
will have been a moat there too, and a wretched effort to cross it
going on perhaps for years, until the issue could only be decided
on the basis of rank power, perhaps even the rankest or almost,
everything short of murder, while on both sides the heart was still
crying out for confidence. The pattern will be repeated many
times, when it is not broken off sooner with plain hatred. This is
Hadrian's curse, and he will build it into his villa, along with the
shiny, shifting dreamworld in which for a moment at a time the

self finds its comfort and revenge, never imagining the portrait it will have left. It is a clear one, however. No man who was loved, or who was easy in the lack of love, could have built such a house; among the gods and temples strewn about the place there is one real invisible altar, and that is to romantic sexual love, which is a version of the glorified Self.

It is in the neighborhood of the libraries that you think of Antinoüs, because they are the only places that look like bedrooms. There is more to the story than that, even an extraordinary perception of the future, no more perverse than most at the time. It is an age of anxiety. What will roll into the dominating force of centuries is popping up in all kinds of clownish, incongruous forms like a boxful of Punch-and-Judys whacking each other over the head, and the beautiful boy from Bithynia, Hadrian's love, has his place among them. But what his statues announce and glorify is sex, and less a fulfillment than a long languorous exacerbation, a voluptuous delay such as Tivoli had never heard of before. A new kind of experience has come in the romantic obsession, and wrapped in a sensuality the very opposite of Roman; this sultry shepherd child could only have come from the East.

Look at him in the little Sala Rotonda, that wonderful room with its niches and cupola and the great porphyry cup, so much in Hadrian's spirit it might almost have been arranged to commemorate the love affair; you even enter it at either door between pairs of objects from the villa, the Egyptian telamones at one and herms of Tragedy and Comedy at the other. Antinoüs is there twice: in the bust whose gaze ironically crosses Hadrian's past the chunky primitive bronze Hercules, so strangely solid and out of place between them; and as the full-length Bacchus by the door, with the old sexual symbol of the pinecone, turned now to what unfertile suggestion, on his head. It is a good place to see him. The beautiful mosaic floor too could as well have been Hadrian's; this was the grandeur that was left, of architecture and objects; it is in such rooms as this, and some twenty times bigger, and among such furnishings, statues, gods and all, that the boy, probably only twelve

or thirteen years old in the beginning, leads his short domestic life
with the most powerful man in the world.

The rest of the setting is there too, sketched in in a few strokes .
around the walls, the whole lurid story from five hundred years
back, with it slow merciless progressions of power and belief, the
whole dynamic tangle of causalities in which for a moment there
occurs this particular twist; and who would dare to assign responsibility among them? The great Jove from Otricoli is there, the
deep-bearded bull-like bust, five hundred years old in Hadrian's
time, shown in all the raging fullness of his power as Michelangelo would have done it, with his hair like the sides of a cavern
and the middle of his forehead thrust out so far with the power he
has over the world it is nearly bursting; no sculptor was turning out
anything like that anymore; divinity has dribbled away — you can
see it in the room — among the emperors, everywhere, and the
emperor himself is the chief loser. Who will now be father to him?
Certainly not the people; he has been turned loose among the
horrors of infinite possibility, everything depends on a mere trick
of disposition. And there is the terrible strength of Roman women,
the good and the wicked, beginning with frigid Juno: no romance
there, nothing at any rate for the anguished mind of these times to
look to. It seems that this sad ponderous image of Antinoüs was
what had to be created; it has the same dead weight of inevitability
about it as Augustus; and he is undoubtedly handsome, even if the
statues are not.

It is a lush Middle Eastern handsomeness, even rather gross,
and more than anything, empty; you could take him for a young
Armenian rug salesman, or for King David, and this is curious because the shape of the face is new, and unique; you would know it
anywhere. It is rounder than any classic face though the nose and
forehead line is still nearly straight, with more cheek space and the
eyes farther apart, so that it is at the same time softer and more an-
gular, more the face of a specific person, although idealized; only
blank, as though the artist had not quite known what was expected
of him. But this is corrected by the pose, more or less the same in
all the statues, at least all that one is likely to see; there must have

been thousands once. There is no confusion there. His head seems nearly too heavy to hold, not with the physical weight of the skull but the vague burden of languor, conveyed in a nuance; it is just that the old divine self-sufficiency is gone, the picture is of indeterminate sorrow and a life that has meaning only in sensual rapport. The face, crowned with the richest ringlets yet seen in art, bends just a little downward as in the resignation of the captive, nostalgic for a happiness he is no longer fit for and can scarcely remember; playing Bacchus, he holds up his grapes, or flowers or thyrsus, in a mood that could not be farther from Bacchanalian: deadly serious. The spring and tension of the perfect body have vanished; this one would change its pose only to sink, to fall, though in build it suggests great strength, more than any Apollo; it is broad shouldered but passive as a plum, close to fat, with untrained muscles and a succulence of flesh at the breasts and armpits; no little sleeping hermaphrodite, but a power to be shown on a scale with Hercules, a subtle and murderous triumph of the female principle.

It is the natural thing; it was to be expected, especially taken together with another of the busts in the room, his perfect antithesis: all strength and what Protestants call character, enough to have pushed the empire through a delicate moment, yet securely, even massively feminine too. This is no poor brittle Sabina. It is Plotina, Trajan's wife and Hadrian's adoptive mother, the one person who can perhaps have given him, and for many years, the sober intimate sanction he needs, and he does need it. He is not a person who can easily stand alone, though in fact he does more and more; he would wish for the security of general love if that were possible, but it is not, except from people too simple or silly to see into him at all and with them he is at his most gracious. The rest he alienates when he needs them most; he exposes himself on all sides, he who cannot stand it on any: that is not his kind of courage. This powerful woman is his natural counterpart too, and it is only after her death that he has his revenge for the lifelong devotion; it could have been told beforehand.

You could tell it even from the official face, bearded but so unfatherly and not handsome at all, which could so easily have lent

itself to caricature; and in fact the whole story was probably better
drawn in the back alleys of Rome than in all the solemn nudes, as
Mars or Jupiter, and the portrait busts that must have had all the
sculptors in the empire working like scriptwriters. The face asks
for it, aside from anything else. Everything in it is a little exaggerated, including the conflicts and irritability; the look too of
having a marvelous gamut of expressions if they could only be
seen, though you would never guess the great charm of the man
— it must have been one of the main points, it would all have
been so much simpler without that — from these features. The
eyes are much too narrow set, and have something a bit weaselish
about them that jars with the noble, overprotuberant nose; the
hair is combed down nearly to the eyebrows across a low forehead
as though in a chronic urge to concealment but perhaps really
more out of vanity, not to leave too exposed the long bellying ill-
proportioned cheeks, which are not cushy like the boy's but more
rankly sensuous, swollen, and stuffed-looking; and in his expression too there is something of the captive, but only of his own
mind. His preoccupation seems real, not the kind so shrewdly
wrapped around the tricky, neurotic features of Augustus; this is
Hadrian himself, but the preoccupation is not quite pure, though
it creates threats as chimerical and aggravations as real as if it
were; and his majesty, which seems also entirely native, is more
of the man of wealth than of the thinker. Yet he thinks, continually; that could have been made to look very funny too.

Especially as his vice is mental, not the mere physical indulgence so easily tolerated among the Romans and by now such a
worn-out theme as connected with emperors. It is the mental trappings, the lack of promiscuity in this case that will offend; the romantic agony is having its first tryout; the individual soul is
asserting itself in strange and dangerous fashion, in fact in a way
that seems to make even power secondary, a most un-Roman business, particularly as so entwined with the highest and rightest national aspirations. Still, the process only makes Antinoüs more
flagrantly a sex object; when you break the official pose in the Sala
Rotonda, animate the marble, release the hidden humorous

glance — across Hercules — there is only one scene you could precipitate; no royal amour ever had such candid immortality.

It leaps out from the rubble of the villa, everywhere, but most at the center, inseparable from that other sensuality. There will be pinchings and beseechings, little cruelties and caresses slow enough to hatch a peacock's egg. In such an armpit a lover might hold his fist all night and imagine he was not yet born; or he might lie all afternoon holding a real bunch of imported grapes above the sleeping face, furious at the intrusion of a fly. In one of these rooms, perhaps the one called the Greek Library, there will be over the favorite couch a mosquito net all of gold thread with a blue serpent embroidered on one side, and from under it suddenly comes wild laughter, as of two children. Here, and here, the step sounds most loudly afterward, the loss is most horrible: but where? It hardly matters; the whole place is at times one yawning Turkish couch, enough to smother in, and it may have been only a moment of good spirits in the triclinium that nailed in the incurable devotion. On the other hand Antinoüs is often sulky; he likes the notoriety but his role palls, his heavenly languor as he grows older becomes shot with spite; he pits his power against the emperor's and plays the little cruel games of a stupid person testing his hold over a bewitched intellect. His delight then will be to break, snarl up, confuse, before he becomes available again; in his dull oriental mind there are canny resources beyond the range of that other, aching intelligence, and in them lies his revenge for the intolerable romantic burden he is made to carry. On one point, however, he can always be had: he is not unwilling to be a god; that is an aspect of imperial favor that is bound to appeal to him; he believes in it, they believe in it together. They are bound in a joint megalomania, strengthened by contemporary ideology, which from everywhere at once is proposing the ancient theme of sacrificial Death and Resurrection; astrologers, oracles, magicians are all busy as ants too, putting ideas in people's heads.

Consider Canopus, that long phallic valley south of the baths, with the room-checkered canyons along the sides and the

Serapeum wedged tight and round in the cleft at the end. There
used to be a canal all down the middle and booths and shops, it
seems, leading up to the temple, all copied from the place outside Alexandria where worship went on amid scenes, as the books
put it, of unbridled merriment, but what seems unbridled in this
one is only gloom and apocalyptic confusion. The head only half
knows what the rest is doing, which is to strike down among the
oldest sexual symbols, water and the inside of the earth, for its
new verities. That is the power that Jove had lost, the profound in-
stinctual hold, and it is here that Antinoüs most truly dies, though
it happened in Egypt. Among the fakeries of this valley one thing
is clear: there can be no new principle without a new injection of
ultimate seriousness; the castrated priests and devotees of Attis are
nearer to the truth than those who continue to sacrifice with the
blood of animals, but even that is not enough; and now the old
craving for mystery, the air of obscure meanings and explorations,
still clings around the place. You feel it as you walk toward the
temple with its fallen portico, filled in to a third of its height now
just as it was two hundred years ago when Piranesi was playing his
grand poetic game with all these buildings, setting his pensive
doll-size hoboes in front of them for the effect, which was certainly splendid. But now one would want the figures as large as
possible, anyway the buildings create them that way, people five
times as tall as the roof of this temple, which even so, and although you are six feet closer to the ceiling than you should be,
looks larger than it is.

The mystery gathers inside, as though something of violent
import had been done or said there not long ago. It is in the central shrine, set deep at the back like an egg, and the two tall thin
brightly painted rooms that curve close around it and were literally heated, and the great tunnels opening out from behind it and
at the sides too, which seem for once to be incidental; they are
only pozzolana quarries, but the effect is right; that is the true picture, and the little version of Canopus in the next valley over —
both valleys are artificial — has real underground passages for its
enclosing arms. You can crawl through them on your hands and

knees, where once perhaps you would have gone in a little canoe; there is no telling what this place is, though its stones at the center are those of a grotto, but there is the same feeling of the lonely intellect, perhaps only idling here, as in the other. In these biological shapes and engineering stunts, adorned in the first case with the Vatican's entire museumful of Egyptiana, you seem to hear a groan from the world's most terrible search for gods, and the great shapeless nugget from the roof that has fallen at the entrance, nearly like the one in the big baths, is like a piece of the soul's highest yearning turned to rubbish; you can kick it, nobody cares; yet there is a part of Christ too in these mystical tunnels and merriments.

In the particular case the idea happens to offer also a fine perception of romantic love: in death Antinoüs is perfect; and the alternative is dismal; he is already twenty years old. No one could hesitate. Probably Hadrian did just the same; his mysticism is not quite pure either, his senses do not always go along with his generalizations. Osiris is no comfort under the mosquito net, though it might have been just there that the idea took hold; it is in sex that the need for an ultimate truth will be most imperative. Nevertheless, he is said to have wept like a woman when the body was brought out of the Nile, and of the story up to that point that is the only known fact. Antinoüs might even have acted on a chance remark, some idle dropping of intellectualism never meant to be taken up; or perhaps he was pushed, or slipped in the mud, though it seems not, or was caught in some explosive muddle of ideology and personal despair. Hadrian can well have worked himself up to the sacrifice and understood nothing but the anguish afterward, as many Romans had lately been doing every year after the rites of Attis; and it could be true, as some thought, that that life had only gone to safeguard his, on the advice of an astrologer.

In any case a new star appeared at once in the sky, which he was pleased to have pointed out to him as the boy's soul; the divinity was proved; and shortly afterward when he killed a lion while hunting in the desert, a poet in the company claimed to have found a new kind of rose growing in the wound, which was also called Antinoüs.

You have come to the Maritime Theatre, the jewel-like heart of the villa and one of Hadrian's loveliest works, so drab now you could walk through without thinking about it; six columns of the colonnade around the moat are left, half of them minus their capitals, and a couple of others and three clumps of masonry on the island. Probably it was built much earlier, but it is now that you can understand it; it goes with the image of Antinoüs, it comes from the same need. Ordinary love does not build so tensely, it needs no protection, it can set up its cerebral center like a tent anywhere; but then the whole drive and character of the house, all the luxury and torment of it, come into their own at this time. The ego that everything combined to swell and sicken has now at one blow been nearly severed from the real world, which more and more becomes only an intrusion and a threat; true communication is with an image made flawless by death; the playboy side of the man has come into its grandest justification, among the mysteries of afterlife.

The artist keeps up with it; the wonderful private poem goes on growing, in marble and water and gold, but tight at the center of it remains this little moat-bound shrine, one of the most splendid toys in architecture, linked in all its substance to that sacrifice in the Nile. The Temple of Venus and Rome above the Roman Forum could have existed without Antinoüs, but not this. But the colossal statue of him as an Egyptian god would not have been here, there is no room for it, and it is not necessary; perhaps it is in the apse of the structure called the Vestibule, below the baths, or more likely among the fancier trappings and richer waterfalls of Canopus, to be approached by boat down the canal: it is that kind of game, as if nobody were looking, and the little round marble island far away in the palace is part of it. Hadrian is playing Robinson Crusoe, as everyone does in childhood and longs to do forever after; the island is the oldest, most necessary image, older than the Dying God; that is the true romantic impossible, to be separated from the rubs and nudges and impurities of society by the primordial, deathly medium of water; the perfect assertion of self and the regions of the dead are alike surrounded by water. Of course it is a game; in reality Crusoe goes crazy; but the poetry is true, and the form in this case charming.

The touch has been kept light. The whole affair is in a tub: a high circular wall and portico held up by forty columns of Ionic order; then the moat, crossed by two playful wooden bridges that swing open or shut along a semicircle — every intelligent child's desire; and within, unassailable as a foot-high fortress in the sand, the tiny elegant palace, complete, at least for the purposes of the game, with the design of some diminutive four-petaled flower. It has nine more or less open roomlets, one a little bathing place, all scarcely big enough for an adult chaise longue; and an exquisite atrium, decorated with marine figures in marble, the four sides curving inward, in a graceful scalloping edged with small columns, toward the centerpiece. That is not Antinoüs; it seems not to have been a statue at all, though there were surely some around in the niches; it is just a fountain. The whole beautiful fantasy, set like the soul's treasure at the center of acres of methodical flamboyance, brings you to nothing but that. A real toy; just a marble gazebo.

Archaeologists a long time ago hit on the idea, and have stuck to it, that this is where Hadrian came to "be alone"; they like the thought of him swinging the bridges to behind him and welcoming the Muses, that is concerning himself somehow or other with music, painting, and so on, while affairs of state wait across the moat. It won't do; he is not that kind of charlatan. It is more likely that he comes there to cut himself off from women if anything, there is that feeling about it, but that too is only part of the essential poetry of the place, in which it is hard enough to imagine anyone listening to a record player, let alone drawing up plans for a temple. It is in the middle of everything, utterly exposed, in spite of the wall, and Italians were never quiet; it could hardly give him much peace to station guards at the entrance to shoo off the guests and servants, he is far too irritable not to notice, he registers everything, and not like Julius Caesar; besides, there are the threats, more and more, to be listened for. But the place in any case is too theatrical; its seriousness is only as a poem; in real life, since he is not actually mad, far from it, the first thing he will do is what anyone else does on an island, that is to ask someone over, even if he is not very fond of them. He will have his after-dinner coffee there, an apéritif perhaps, with an acquaintance or two, among a few favorite objects; he can treat it lightly, and must if he is to be there at all; it is not adapted to anything else. For work there will be the neutral place, nothing that involves the eye or spirit, and a serious, not this fake, isolation.

What is not fake is the expression; the need is real; one symbol of purity, one fountain indistinguishable to the public eye from a thousand others must be conceived of as unapproachable, beyond the touch of the commonplace. Certainly the gesture is theatrical too: to have literally built the island, actually played out the game; but what in the villa is not? This staginess is of his deepest nature, the very stuff of his genius. Everything in him, the grand and the tawdry, the terror and the boredom, requires to be turned into a visible object; if he does not express his perceptions in architecture they will grow to madness, and the deepest and most private will be the most urgent; he has to build himself a plain of philosophy, a valley of the dead guarded by a stone Cerberus; if he is not on a stage he is nothing, he will lose all belief in himself.

But on this little stage, this island, he invokes his purest part. It is the other side of the shameless public bombast that goes on around the dead Antinoüs, by his orders and with his inspiration. It is not enough for him to glorify his private experience to himself, the whole world has to be brought into it. The resources of the empire must be lent to the apotheosis of his love. Slaves sweat, ships scurry about the seas getting stone for it, the priests have to be dealt with, threatened if necessary, the public initiated; the shrines pop up in a dozen countries; the city of Antinopolis appears on the Nile, whose inhabitants will be scurrilously linked forever with those of the cities named for Hadrian; the statues for which gods are stripped of their symbols right and left roll out of the workshops by hundreds. You would think it would sicken him to have thrust at him from everywhere, wrapped in every atrocious hypocrisy, the face that he had known in ecstasy and sleep, to whose risky eyes he had entrusted all that is most secret and true in himself. No; he demands it. The world is his stage too, and on it through any loathsome obsequiousness, to be valued by volume, he is paying his most sacred debt, more sacred because of his guilt; such a man is always guilty toward those he loves, even if he has not killed them, it is the same; and so he calls for more and still more of the cringing adulation, refused only by Rome; he exposes himself more recklessly.

Especially after his last return; that is when the real outrage comes. But first he manages to linger on in the East for four more years, probably having one of his best creative periods as artists generally do after the tragic end of an impossible love affair; there is as much relief as grief, the dead and idealized love really suits him better than the rather embarrassing live one, and that will be part of the guilt too. He is perhaps in Athens, his true home, which he continues to beautify as though imperial handouts could restore the living spirit; it is Athens that he has wanted to give to the world, it will be the place for him now in his cruel detachment. There is the Jewish war now too, a nasty business, perhaps more than necessary; and why not: that single jealous god could never have been so repugnant to him as at this moment. But the real enemy is waiting for him at home, and is deadly; it is virtue; a horrible pedantry of virtue, always the Roman forte, is slowly closing in on the creative imagination of the world. You will see it soon in Marcus Aurelius: the fear of passion, the hatred of art, the scorn of life itself, that other, more hateful egotism of self-congratulation dressed as humility; and against that, Hadrian when he finally returns makes his last heroic, ridiculous gesture in defense of a world that is already in smithereens. There is perhaps some mysterious personal loyalty in it too, which would be like him, but it would not be only that. He appoints the worst of all the possible candidates, his friend Lucius Verus, as his successor: the perfect playboy, rich, dissipated and astonishingly beautiful it seems — almost to be deified for nothing but that — an expert in sensuality, poetaster, and inventor of a certain meat pie, probably a good talker; nothing else. It is not certain he was not the emperor's illegitimate son; he was at any rate all that his bright nervous world — of joy, of wanderlust, of the mind's daring — could offer by way of an heir.

It is Hadrian's last great insult to Rome, the final alienation of all those right-minded men he has never really been able to do without; and Plotina is not by him now. That is when the madness sets in. He becomes a murderer. Not for the first time: he had always had his suspicions, his spies, had been to quick to look over his shoulder, though he had sometimes exaggerated in forgiveness too, but now it is different. He strikes out among his relatives, friends, anywhere, until nobody is safe near him, nobody is left who ever assumed a relation with him; if he refrains from poisoning his wife he will be accused of it anyway, it almost seems that she manages to die just then so that he will be. It is as though an ancient nightmare, a poetry of horror established long ago, waiting to spring forth in every scene and circumstance of his position, had finally found the crack in him to flood through and become reality, and he had no choice but to be its agent. Nero and his crazy Golden House are very close; there had perhaps not been so much difference after all. The real world is very dim.

But now go down the path that leads off from the beginning of Canopus, through an olive orchard where turkeys greet you like watchdogs and lambs are bumbling around — one of them half an hour old looks at you in astonishment and you feel an awful responsibility — to the Tower of Roccabruna, perhaps the ugliest of the buildings in its time and the only one of any importance set off by itself, far from any other, though it is connected by an immense job of terracing with the remote Little Palace, or Academy. This is the place you are drawn to now, that fits this part of the story; not that it dates from that period necessarily. Hadrian seems to have been building additions to the main palace now, the Golden Court, perhaps the Pavilion of the Masks; he is still studding the tortoise, still, in this howling darkness, dreaming up his most daz-

zling extravagances, settings for every kind of fun and social graciousness. But it is in this lonely stubby ruin, which was used as a
barn a couple of hundred years ago, that you can feel the impact
of that return to Rome: without Antinoüs, without hope.

The building itself you are free to imagine as almost anything:
a love nest; a lighthouse; an observatory; a mere pavilion, something to give an end to the long garden in back; there is perhaps a
secondary entrance leading past here to that part of the villa and
this is the gatehouse. In any case it lacks the usual lightness of
touch, though its forms are interesting. Only the square base is left
now, with the inevitable array of niches inside, for gods or art or
water, but you can see traces of the heavy portico on the north side
and the complicated upper story, round with engaged columns on
the outside and octagonal inside, above which there was perhaps
another more elaborate cupola; there seems to have been a balcony too, which must have given it an ungainly bulge around the
middle, though the arched marble supports that are left are
among those objects in the place that have taken on the most
moving life of their own, as things in a country junk heap do. The
whole affair is squat and heavy, with features of a little Pantheon
and a general effect of Grant's Tomb; it is the only thing in the
villa that sits on the earth in this solid chunky way, but aside from
pressing on it, it is literally huddled up against it. It is not on the
high point of the land there but a few yards away over the drop of
the hill, so that from the terrace side only the top half is seen; a
nice problem in design, and the kind of use of terrain that appeals
to Hadrian, but here it makes you physically uncomfortable. You
would like to pull the building out; there should be one at last,
among so many, that would stand alone and free.

But it could not. Scholars have labeled this an imitation of
Timon's tower in Athens, but a tower, it seems, is exactly what
Hadrian cannot stand. You see it clearly now, how protective it all
is, how everything backs up into something else, architecture of
the earth; the site of the villa itself is low — it was not only caprice
— and nothing is exposed; the compulsion is the opposite. He
digs down, he makes valleys, he pulls up the mountains around

him, a well-known phenomenon. This is a man who will go mad without shelter, and now he has stepped forward and made himself vulnerable on every side; he is being cursed by all Rome, and for once there is no way out. His voyages are over. That is the really desperate fact of the matter; motion was his sanity, motion of wheels, motion of water and of ships; now he is too sick to go thrashing off anymore, anyway he has used it all up, all the strange places and gods, the foreign luxuries and exciting little hardships, and has come back to be trapped in what was never meant to be lived in: it was always a poem, as anything he built must be. It lies over there on the right, enormous, a setting for angels, but for him more like the Hall of Doric Pillars today, or a bright-colored fish that has been dead for a week.

The rest of the view from this corner of the land is terrible too. It is superb, it is wide, it is by far the best there is of the mountains, which everywhere else are obscured by buildings or seen from a less effective angle, but it is terrible. Perhaps the place is actually a lighthouse and at night, with stars, the long landscape not flat from here but heavily rolling on your left and the black choppy surge of the mountains on the other side do offer a release and mystery, as of the sea. But in the daytime and especially in the sunshine all that distance, very different from the one at right angles to it, from the Pecile, only drives you back into yourself; it invites you out into it, but to nothing, it is all made up of more and more of what you know, and what you know is blighted in a matter of seconds before it; you turn back with no inclination for anything. It is one of those deadly views known as peaceful, only the most stolid personality could enjoy it; not Hadrian; certainly not now, when he is making his last stand in a setting of just such despair.

But then something happened; within a year Verus was dead, possibly of venereal disease. His next and final choice is Antoninus Pius, of all Rome's rulers up to then perhaps the nearest to a saint.

The land rises in one last green sweep south of the tower, the part farthest away from the entrance and the parking lot and the overtrodden cypress alleys, before sheering away to its precipitous end, which almost seems to curve in under you like the stern of some huge silent ship riding at anchor in a green cove. It is the Little Palace, not often visited and never owned by the state, so that it has a different quality from the rest, more what it all was for Count Fede. You go back from Roccabruna or scramble up behind the Serapeum, through mud and nettles and barbed wire, and find yourself after a while in a court probably as rich and glittering once as most of the big palace, but so tangled and shady and still now, it is as though somewhere among the olives you had crossed a line beyond which the tremendous tensions of the villa have no more hold; they have snapped away from you, and you have moved on in a sudden lightness and peace to another kind of place. The ruins do not stick out here; a single dead pine towering over the grove, a shiny skeleton without a green twig or a stitch of bark left, which ought to have toppled years ago, has far more rage and drama. They have given in; their geometry is dominated by trees and innumerable birds, thrushes and all kinds of little field ones and nightingales, and over your head the roots of other trees push clutching and fearfully exposed, like the minds of sleepwalkers, down the ancient walls.

They are most beautiful in this state, with all their insistence gone and their secrets taken back into the larger course of things, the sick screaming *I* was transcended ages ago, leaving only a suggestion as spacious as the rest but gentler — a charity of time, beyond tragedy and beyond respect. They do not ask even for that, and though there must be a little or they will disappear, it is the violations of them, as in Rome, that are most moving: a tremendous speckled pig wallowing in a stubby relic of one of Hadrian's buildings, off by itself in the sun-speckled orchard beyond the farm that is a little farther on; the farm itself, more charmed and still-looking than the ones on the other edges of the land, being so far away and without any visible road leading to it; and in this first court, the most entranced of all, a high pointed tower of a thousand and some years later, already in the groaning stage, its wooden stairs inside too rotten to risk: it rests on, or seems more to have grown up in an inevitable, vegetable way from the three tall arches of the end building of the ancient court, but the splicing point has gone dim and the two epochs have become one substance, as if the thousand-year misery between were nothing at all.

It is misleading, though not entirely. Hadrian comes closest of all here if you let him; from beneath the thick protective bangs, sticky now with fever, the narrow eyes look out at you with a sick hatred that in a moment will have turned to some sharp gay disposal of life and his own state, some Parisian quip, before the dull intolerable load, which must still be tolerated, settles back on him again; the big muscular lips move as in a separate delirium of their own, like a mouth floating on the ocean, remembering their own sensuality. Everything is finished; virtue has won, he has bowed to it; now there is nothing but pain and more horror, until he manages to die, which will not be in Tivoli or Rome either; naturally; a haven or point of rest is what he could not bear, and he happens to be in Baia at that moment, the Bar Harbor of the time but richer and more insidious — he could get at least that far — where he dies in a last agony of silence, living out his curse to the end, in the arms of that noble stranger, his heir.

Virtue, or call it the genius of Rome, which was his own too; the enemy could not really strike except from within himself; and in the end there was nothing to believe in but that: the greatness of Rome. He has acknowledged it, has risen at the last to an act of simple moral splendor — one imagines it done with a sigh of exhaustion, but this is also when one sees him for a moment as most tremendous, not with all the baggage and scintillation of his state and the tonnage of his temples, but stripped to the moral bone: a lucid melancholy figure standing tall as Paul Bunyan against these mountains and against his century, with at his back the derelict shreds of the world that he has loved with such passionate extravagance, and that still shoots off its most brilliant rays behind his head, and far off under his gaze the dull seething movement of the barbarians. Or not so far; it all happens terribly fast; but he has delayed it, providing the empire with not one but two generations of everything that his deepest nature rejects: altogether some forty more years of commendable not to say unheard-of decency, dignity, and security before the thugs and the military take over, and perhaps there were some who thought it would be four hundred, or eternity. And for this great gift to Rome, which is also an act of self-condemnation, he will be more suspect than he had been as a murderer; he is surely used to it by now.

It can all be slurred over a little; there are ties, which perfect the irony. They go through the same forms, he and these Eskimos, these noble Stoics; they meet at parties, invest in the same businesses, have the same views of statecraft and the same kind of country houses generally speaking; it is a gentleman's world and they are the gentlemen; and Antoninus will be as great in loyalty as in wisdom. He, a man so unworldly he hadn't even wanted the job — you can tell the species from that; who in a reign longer than Hadrian's will not once travel farther from Rome than to his nearby country estate, will use all his power afterward to rehabilitate the hated name of Hadrian, and will build to him the temple that is now the Stock Exchange and the tenderest monument in Rome. The Castel Sant'Angelo was only one of Hadrian's splashiest tributes to himself; the temple is one of the world's enduring tokens of respect, or it could be of love, from one species of man to another, raised over a bottomless hollow of noncommunication.

There are ties with his further choice too, young Marcus Aurelius, intense and willowy at the time and probably with a certain adolescent leaning to the abstruse, which he will outgrow shortly: his patrician mother had made part of her fortune selling bricks for the emperor's villa, and for his building in general. But this youth who also professes loyalty is a different kettle of fish from Antoninus; many hundreds of years later he turns up as the white-haired boy of a self-interested bourgeoisie very like the one that Hadrian despised, and every worthy maxim he gets off will be a crack at his imperial grandfather; that great and various nature seems to taunt him so from the grave, he cannot leave any part of it unpilloried: boys, building, art. Yet there were statues of him in the villa, the count and the others found them, and so one imagines him stopping off now and then at the crazy old place, in the triumph of his survival and the safety of an unimpeachable character: uncomfortable, out of place, jealous as a Protestant minister, and with a worm of ecstasy in his heart from the contact with what he condemns. Still, he was a good ruler as opposed to a wicked one, very good indeed; Hadrian had chosen well.

There were other posthumous items too, before the Vandals came through; the place was not quite uninhabited. There are touches of restoration from later in that century and the next, and it can happen, though this is the rarest thing, that in one of the fields near the palace you will pick up a little fragment of pottery from a still later time, left by some caretaker or squatter on the land, or perhaps the retinue of the captive Queen Zenobia. Some of the soldier-emperors will no doubt have used parts of it for a weekend camp — there was every facility for keeping fit, after all, and those who felt like it could amuse themselves in the evening knocking the noses off the statues. But really it had ceased to exist long before, and before Hadrian's death; he himself had condemned it. It had been many things, many kinds of expression noble and ignoble, but it was always, along with the rest, his private work of homage to a civilization founded, as on a rock, on the knowledge of the world's beauty and delight, and it ends, as if he had ordered its literal destruction, at that great moment of his defeat. There are no theatrics in that; he rises for once in all simplicity, and for that one last second you can see the whole villa strewn twinkling and absurd around his ankles, already old hat, the sense of it simply gone; then the nightmare closes over him again and he sinks back to wait to die.

Not patiently; he is still in character, irascible, scathing, spoiled; he longs for death with the same passionate appetite he has had for everything else, only he cannot bribe anyone to kill him and is evidently too weak or not quite willing to do it himself; there is a touch of the old game again in this, his passions have always bred their own negations. So he lingers on with his horrid disease, dropsy, in such suffering it will become a legend for generations and is thought to give him powers more miraculous than any he has as emperor; the physical pain alone is punishment enough, but the rest is worse — for him there can be no resolution

— and it is just here on this last gentle hill that one imagines him then. It is the natural retreat, or seems so; the main palace will be too ironic now, though he is still adding patches here and there, and really this far place is neither so different nor separate from the rest; the torment if anything is only clearer. The most monstrous of his crypto-porticoes, the one called a little too literally his Underworld or Inferi, is here, and the biggest of the theaters; none of it could stop; he spins down through the crack in the split world, in all his agony, with the whole show still raging.

There is a strong touch of comedy in it, of course. Those once famous Inferi, out in the big field beyond the farm, are as stagy as anything else in the place, and in fact seem to have been connected underground with the theater; the thing is a splurge of gloom in the Max Reinhardt manner, and could hardly have been made more serious by having a Cerberus at the entrance, if it did; very likely it was a place for the emperor's well-dressed audiences to stroll in bad or hot weather, though it looks more like something made by some huge prehistoric mole. In any case the staging is brilliant, is and no doubt was; nothing else could be so shocking after the grace and restraint of the Academy, could so pitch you forth into still another emotional area, when it seemed no more was possible; it is the grandest effect of them all, the most violent and the funniest — and always missed. Nobody but an occasional archaeologist ever comes this far, and of those perhaps not more than one in two or three years; it is off the guidebook map, and if you do get there you are not sure to find it. The place is not even a hayfield; there are a few trees, scrub, a few figures of peasants near or far gathering brush: a proper setting for this hilariously macabre affair, so much more sophisticated than any niche or statue.

The wonder among others is that it is still not filled in, or not entirely; the round skylights are still open, and are marked, as you discover eventually, by the bushes growing out of them regularly all along like clumps of hairs from a nostril; the pines too follow the lines of the tunnel, which traces out an enormous trapezoid, so although you could hardly get in, or rather out, without a rope ladder, you can lie on your stomach among the bushes at various points and look down into a construction that brings you back not so much to the other underground passages in the place, however bizarre, as to the Golden Court. That is the scale; they are of the same stunning exorbitance, the dark and the brilliant making one entity; this is one man's alley, not the Saint Gothard, though the effort must have been equivalent to a good piece of that. It is fifteen feet across and with its four sides nearly a mile long, cut deep out of bedrock, and for no practical purpose at all or none to warrant such an enormity. One of the smaller passageways leading off from it had opening on to it a series of small chambers taken to be wine cellars, but there could be no such reason for this, and besides it was decorated like a salon, with paintings and elaborate stuccos. It is a necessity of another kind, like the island, and as genuine: a fantasy of dread made literal and elegant, normal enough in the general poem of Rome but that shakes one nevertheless in this context, in spite of the comedy, like the sound of a splitting skull. Not that it was conceived of, it is what everyone conceives of: this too is one of the oldest images; but that it was built. It is the necessary complement to Antinoüs, the rest of the twin metaphor love and death, and the only other perfect denial of society. The bonds are broken; the individual soul lives with its own heaven and hell, staged in this case with all the impudence inherited from some of the world's leading criminals, which only gives it a greater charm of familiarity now. And this is the mind that has made its peace with the sober citizens; you can imagine it.

But in the Academy there are only the forms. They are Hadrian too, and they emerge gradually from the tangle, purer, more with an illusion of music in the composition than anywhere else; or like an image handed down through many centuries in sleep; because in that first central grove there is a familiarity far stranger than the other. You come on it with a sense of return and comfort, as though some part of your mind had been deprived of it for a long time; the forms are exactly right, as though remembered; the proportions could not be otherwise. There is another of those long straight useless walls, the side of the now imaginary court, actually a very high class of fence, that is, leaving passage all around, in a wood imprinted by marble centaurs; there is no doubt about the centaurs, you can see them in a museum and this is where they were found. At the end, grown in with the tower, are the three sober arches, the eternal triad, holding the key for the romantic and slightly irregular triplet on the other side. The center of that one is a two-story vaulted hemicycle, roofless now and one of the loveliest shapes in the villa, set up as for some solemn tribunal of dreamers, behind whom the two rows of windows gape in a majesty of blankness on more of the same hanging, twisting, living furnishings that are inside. The window pediments are of two alternating forms, rectangular and arched as they will be again in palaces of the Renaissance, and the two smaller rooms winging this beautiful center space are eccentric, the larger one consisting of a hemisphere that proceeds out of a half-square; the smaller leads back — this would never stop either — to a little group of satellite rooms, in one of which you find some midget niches halfway up the walls, and for a moment their particular mystery and the load of life in it excludes all the rest; what on earth were they for?

In the court beyond, what is mainly clear is the four graceful and tricky fountain corners, the inner sides of four triangle buttresses that would have taken the weight of the roof, leaving the colonnade inside deceptively light. Of that there is only a suggestion left, a few rough strokes on the ground, for the mind to complete. But all of this place has something of a sketchbook look quite different from the furious desolation of the rest, as though you were seeing not a thing undone but one never developed, a Leonardo's notebook of forms in a wilderness, with the mystery of their origin still hanging about them. It is the creative imagination that comes close here, in all the abundance of its energy, its playfulness; Hadrian's sufferings, his tortured disagreeable face fade out; they were only a condition, it seems, for the birth of these lines in stone and brick, which keep bringing to mind in such a happy way the word *civilization*: a meaning of it that can only properly present itself nowadays in overgrown places. It may be that the finished product had this gay serenity too, more than the rest of the villa; certainly the scale is more respectable; the over-bearing note is missing, the effects seem less strained after. It is all ingenious and difficult, but also profoundly natural; which may only mean that this section was built not later than the rest as you would imagine, but earlier, before power had worked too much on the source.

Early or late, it is Hadrian, the part of him that one sees rising at the end through all the wreckage and pathos, a thin clear light, something like the upward jet of a single fountain, that somehow disengaged itself from the appalling mesh of pomp and person-ality, and hovers behind the grim jumble of the human mind a thousand years, waiting to be known again. Its sound is the sim-plest note of laughter; its spring you have seen; it was horror.

But that is not where you stop. From one corner of the field in which you trace out that mammoth tunnel, looking back toward the villa, you can see over to the mysterious little canal parallel to Canopus and ending in a grotto, which has been taken to be the main entrance to the Inferi though it is hard to see why. Whether it was or not, it stretches the fantasy out still farther. It is another shape, another meaning, so out of the way and suggestive and sad-looking as it lies there now, like a toy that has lain twenty years out in the rain, all the complex of feelings built up from the beginning suddenly resolves itself into a rush of sympathy — or call it love, for this imagination that could not repeat itself and that nothing could stop, and the whole wonderful joke of the place is there for you, as fresh and bright as if it had been scribbled across the field that moment. You are in it, you understand it finally, and all you can express it with is a little echo of Hadrian's own laughter; which returns in a moment to silence. The joke was serious; and the great and sorrowful scene you glimpse briefly in the theater — going back now toward the farm, and you must not be in a hurry — is of Hadrian the lover of the past, the playboy diver into every dread and flaunter of every glory, dividing, as he dies, with a suc-cessor he cannot speak to, a future they both despise. They con-tain each a part of it, he with his mysteries and his poet's anguish and Antoninus in the goodness of his heart, as much as any Christian martyr, and both are of such stature it seems the stage, though it has stood for two thousand years, will not be able to hold up under the spectacle, which all of Rome sits watching. But it is short, and very quiet. The body is carried off, to be hidden until the hatred of the senate subsides, and the silent chorus and the other actors follow, leaving for a few seconds, until they are removed, those disembodied masks you saw before, with their refugees' eyes and their great open mouths that birds could nest in or that could be spigots for fountains.

The theater is much bigger than the Greek one down by the entrance, and the proscenium and the off-stage quarters in back are still in fairly good condition; the rest is only a green bowl now, which has kept its shape however, although the pines are thick around it. The two tallest of them are at the back of the orchestra, the highest point, with a little temple of some kind between them, and right there is where the land pitches down, so that from the last row of seats you could topple over backward out of the villa. The whole place is an island, you can see it now; it rises out of the valley like an atoll; only on one side there is a more gradual slope, around the big curve that embraces the Inferi, and out there are the remains of an aqueduct, of course: all that water had to come from somewhere.

PART III

MIDCENTURY JUBILEE

*W*HEN THE PRESSURES and processions of Rome's midcentury jubilee, or Holy Year, had joined the many others of the kind in the past the whole show began slowly to be visible, as it could not be while it was happening. It could not have been clear beforehand either how much of the disturbance of an age Rome would once more bring to focus; in most quarters it was perhaps not even clear just what was wished of the year and its ceremonies. *Something* was: anticipation, some of it adverse, grew very great in Rome in the months before. There was to be a big show, with behind it a big effort, only by a stretch of unimaginativeness to be summed up as all mercenary or political; something would be formulated; some large power would be brought to cohesion in the course of the year, or would not be. Whatever it might be or do, it was properly heralded.

That is the right word. The ancient Jewish jubilee, from which the Roman one rather obscurely derives, was announced by heralds with trumpets, and this became the practice in Rome during the Renaissance, as Holy Year observances gradually took shape; the first jubilee, proclaimed by Boniface VIII in 1300, had been an unplanned event in which nobody was quite sure whether there was any Christian precedent for it or not. But the main announcement was with bells, as established by the Borgia pope in 1500. For three days before the opening of a Holy Year on Christmas Eve all the church bells of Rome were to ring together, not all day but long enough; and so they did again. They rang and rang; a shattering experience. It was like the Last Judgment as seen by Rome's poet, Belli, in the nineteenth century. "Four huge angels with trumpets in their mouths will start blowing, each from his corner; then in an awful voice they'll begin to say, 'Step up!'" Only it was not Judgment Day, only a preparation for it, and the awful voices were of the bells. The Holy Doors of the four jubilee basilicas were opened; the sins of the world, the sinners willing, were to be washed away in the waters of spiritual regeneration, the same water that Moses struck from the rock. Everybody knows that Rome is a city of bells, only usually they have their own gentle anarchy of hours and messages; when they are going all together they are not good music; most of them are not even of good metals; there seems to be too much iron; anyway it is no comforting Angelus call that comes from them. They ring of battle, fire, interminable crisis, the bells of Saint Peter's like the rest only a little slower and deeper, but still more iron than silver or bronze; they have the raw crash of history in their choppy rhythms, with some other sonority always nearly there but never quite coming off, which seems the voice of some terrible vast patience and control. This was the opening music of Holy Year, at noon on the day before Christmas, 1949.

Around 6 P.M. the first German pilgrims began their procession in Santa Maria Maggiore, of the four basilicas the most obviously beautiful in interior design and the one supreme on that night, being dedicated to Mary. Later one became used to the processions; at the end of the year there would be six or eight going on at once in any of the basilicas. At the time this one was startling. There were perhaps two hundred Germans following the standard wooden cross, men first, women after, chanting as they made the slow round of the church, which at ordinary times looks so splendidly secular under its gold-coffered ceiling: the perfect ballroom. They had the grimmest set of faces seen in Rome since the German army left, only the determination in this case was aimed at the other world, less in penance, it seemed, than anger; their eyes never wavered from the cross or the air ahead of them; their ramrod righteousness would have suited the faces called American Gothic, if for those other certainties there should be such a symbol and capital as Rome. It was an aspect of the city's power not usually in the foreground, the churches and papal ceremonies showing themselves more as accumulations of custom and art ordinarily, to those not bent on the Catholic core beforehand. Another Roman history was being shot into prominence. But the particular tone of that one group of pilgrims never became the general one of the year.

A few hours later in the same place the foreign rage of penitence was lost in the shuffle. The church was very differently crowded, as always on Christmas Eve, lit to the limit and strung with loudspeakers. In the genial crush and clatter a treasure of early Christian art could finally be seen: the long series of mosaics above the columns of the central nave. The basilica's most revered relic was carried in procession, in a huge elegant Renaissance container of silver and glass shaped like a soup tureen with a silver baby kicking up his heels on top. "You see?" said a Roman in the crowd as others were saying too and do every Christmas Eve. "It's the actual wood of Jesus Christ's cradle." He crossed himself, cheerily talking on as it went by. "A real piece of it. . . ." All through the year one would be seeing this total and strangely procreative misalliance between local and foreign versions of the faith.

Another work of art, usually recessive, seems to flare forth from the apse and fill it all on that night. This is the large concave mosaic of the Triumph of Mary, by one of the greatest mosaic artists of his time, finished five years before the first Holy Year; no little town of Bethlehem there; nothing that to the Protestant mind was ever Christmas; Christ is crowning his glorified mother, as they sit splendidly robed on thrones with their feet on gold-embroidered cushions and the stars beneath; two royal personages but very much larger than life and of a better than earthly power. The dogma of the year, another affirmation of Mary, would keep it emphatic even when not so lit up, and enhance the basilica too if that were necessary. Since added to and beautified by many popes, it was built in the fifth century under the inspiration, it seems, not of the marvelous snow of legend but of the Council of Ephesus, which granted to Mary the title of Mother of God. It was the beginning of the long slow ascendance that has risked turning Protestants against the ideal of any motherhood, and in Rome has helped to keep Christ so inconspicuous except as an infant.

He is certainly not much in evidence along the pilgrim route. Saint Peter's with all its range points up first of all the power of Christ's vicar on earth — of the four big basilicas the one closest to the original meaning of the word. Saint Paul's Outside the Walls, a modern reconstruction, the old church having mostly burned down in the last century, turns the mind vaguely to martyrology and very precisely to a point in geography; even more than Saint Peter's it seems to ring all through with the right of Rome to her preeminence, because of what happened or is supposed to have happened not exactly on that spot but near it, not Christ's teaching but the apostle's being in Rome is what it tells you; furthermore it is a pagan edifice, inside, pure in form and awesome in scale; what moves the heart in its dark forest of immense ancient columns is again not Christ but the long vitality of Rome in all her time, which Paul and Christ through him served. Saint John Lateran, inside the most awkwardly redecorated of the four, is the hoariest with church politics beginning with Constantine, with another infra-orthodox lesson in the name of the ancient Roman family it has kept and whose baths are visible under the Baptistry. The last basilica is Mary's, pilgrim palace of the great mother-image that dominates all the religious life of the city as in some form it always did.

The basilica was not more crowded than the others during the year. Nevertheless Holy Year was Mary's year and plainly marked

as such, not only in the HAIL HOLY VIRGIN placards across the ra-
diators of the pilgrim buses. But it was even more visibly the year
of Pius XII; there was perhaps never a Holy Year so stamped with
the character of a pope.

The event in its general lines and most of its details as well was
by now an old story — the twenty-second occurrence of it, not
counting the many special jubilees called in connection with various joyous or dire happenings. In the nineteenth century the tradition suffered badly from political developments in Europe, only
one Holy Year, in 1825, was held in the century. But from 1475
when the twenty-five-year period was settled there had been no interruption in the series of jubilees for three hundred years. The
one of 1775 was such a success that D'Alembert prophesied, a little
too hurriedly, that it had delayed the revolution for twenty years;
according to Voltaire, another such Holy Year and philosophy
would be finished forever. There were surmises along the same
lines, pro or con, this time. Many in the series of jubilees had
been designed as rallies of Christendom against the Turks; others
were meant as a counterblow to the Reformation; there had not
until now been another such enemy and immediate danger. How
far the 1950 jubilee would strengthen the world against communism was one obvious question; for non-Catholics another was, at
what price. In any case, the very questions might be taken as
bearing out the worst delusions of grandeur of the people of
Rome; their power, in contributing or not to the success of the
year and therefore to the world's devotion, was once again enormous, as it had been a hundred years before when they helped jar
loose the foundations of the Papal State.

Of the symbolism and essential procedure of the year there was
nothing left to work out. Pope Pius, reputedly both learned and a
stickler in matters of ritual, was not likely to overlook any of the gestures long ago become traditional for the year, for all his knowledge
of electronics and welcoming of television. The idea itself of a periodic pilgrimage to Rome seems to have existed, although un-
clearly, long before the first jubilee. The Jesuit scholar Thurston
tells of a man a hundred and seven years old, whom Pope Boniface

questioned after seeing him carried into Saint Peter's in January 1300. "I remember," the old man said, "that at the beginning of the last century my father, who was a laborer, came to Rome and dwelt here as long as his means lasted, in order to gain the indulgence. He bade me not to forget to come at the beginning of the next century, if I should live so long, which he did not think I should do." He added that the indulgence he expected to earn by the trip was "a hundred days every day of the year." Other centenarians told similar stories of the "hundredth year"; it was a scary number, in the apocalyptic thinking of the time. The Vatican researchers, put to work on the subject, could find little to go by, but pilgrims, most of them poor, continued to flock in of their own accord, moved also by the awakening wanderlust of Europe; and in February Boniface issued his famous bull, putting the seal on what was already happening. "The Church has never been more understanding than in this consecration of adventurous curiosity" (T. S. R. Boase). "And great treasure was accumulated for the Church," according to a chronicler of the time; the attendants at Saint Peter's were seen pulling in the pilgrims' offerings with rakes — presumably just such heaps of tiny coinage as those mainly of paper that littered the base of the high altars in 1950 and were oddly stuck in the heads and hands of many holy statues too. But there were also heavy expenses. Of the value of the jubilee indulgence, "not only full and copious but the fullest possible," the most moving testimony comes from Boniface's worst enemy, Dante. Of the angel who carried souls to Purgatory from their assembling place at the mouth of the Tiber, he has a friend who had been one of them say, speaking on Easter, 1300: "Truly, for the last three months he has brought anyone who wished to come, in perfect peace."

Adventurous curiosity was not the whole story. The great indulgence had to be earned, not only through the hardship of travel although that was important. True contrition was required; and it was a long way between basilicas, although only those of Peter and Paul were on the list that year; the visits had to be repeated every day for fifteen days and most of the pilgrims were on foot. When the Lateran had been added in 1350, and Santa Maria Maggiore a little later, the distance was over eleven miles, to be trudged over every day; a group of newshawks measured it out with a chain one night in the seventeenth century. The now forgotten obsession with pilgrims' feet, and the much publicized ceremonies in which popes and nobles washed them, had to do with a point of real anguish, as much as Christly precedent.

There were also dangers, and recent or impending disasters to shadow all the early Roman jubilees, and further justify them; expiation seemed in order. At the time of the second one, in 1350, the pope was in Avignon, Rome was a shambles, from the neglect and the wars of her leading families, with half her churches roofless and the Lateran half wrecked by fire, and all Europe was still reeling from the horrors of a two-year plague. "All Christendom flocked to Rome to gain the indulgence." It is reported that every time Veronica's Veil, supposed to bear the imprint of Christ's face, was shown, such crowds gathered that many people were trampled to death. Petrarch came "in a spirit of fervor, because I wished to put an end to the sinfulness of my life, which overwhelmed me with shame," and held the blessing of that visit far higher than the exercise of "a poet's curiosity." War or the prospect of it was everywhere, but the pope had managed to secure an armistice for the year between France and England.

The plague theme recurs continually, but the most chronic nightmare note in the long succession of Holy Years is supplied by the Turks. The papal bull of 1470, concerning jubilees, speaks of the ravages of schism in the Church, continuing: "The terror which had settled upon Western Christendom when, by the fall of Constantinople, the Turks gained a footing in Europe; the alarming outbreaks of pestilence and finally the havoc which ceaseless wars had wrought in the moral life of the Western kingdoms, led men to turn their eyes to Heaven, and showed that in order to arrest the chastening hand of Almighty God it was needful that all should tread the paths of penance." War, plague, schism, Turks, finally the Reformation, but most relentlessly, one generation leaving its dread to the next and that again to the next as though the same people were living their lives over and over, the Turks: at every Holy Year's opening these themes were heard again in the iron brawling of the bells of Rome.

When the pope opened the Holy Door at Saint Peter's, open only for the one year in every twenty-five, he was repeating a gesture established through ages of such peril and crisis, the fact of there being by then any door to open might convey less a sense of the Vatican's practical genius than of its truth in the matter of miracle. Current peril and crisis, not at all dimmed by any analogy, were meeting a power mercifully transcending current confusion, even regardless of any transcendence in the creed. The opening of a door is the natural symbol of such consolation, most of life being a wish to find some door or other that will open: to get out, to be let in, to find elbowroom that is not lonely and meaningless. The pope did not literally open this one. The brickwork had been replaced ahead of time by a light screen, on which he knocked with a hammer made for the occasion by a Spanish jeweler and given by some of the faithful of Spain — not by the Spanish government, whose representatives caused a good deal of trouble in town when they did turn up to "do" their Holy Year, as the phrase was. Then to the accompaniment of prayer and song, with cardinals, diplomats, and other worthies looking on from the special stands set up for them in the portico and throngs of ordinary people waiting on both sides of the door, workmen lowered the door filler and tried to get it out of the way. There had been some rehearsal but not enough; the pope had forbidden it, not wanting to trifle with the mystical significance of the event; consequently there were some hitches in the proceedings and Pius was seen to become somewhat irritated, before the space was finally cleared and he was able to lead the year's march of the Catholic world in to the deeper symbols of the water and the rock. In the Holy Door the Church had opened, in her terminology, her treasure of grace and pardon, "the fountain of living Water," radiant as on that bright windy day the two high fountains in the square. In many minds the opening was also, however dimly, to a hope of peace — worldly, unmystical peace, between countries.

Nothing in the door ceremony was new; only in earlier centuries the actual unwalling used to be part of the scene, a tedious operation, which caused many deaths in the public scramble for a piece of the sacred masonry. There was nothing new either, generally speaking, in the Vatican's work and appalling expenses in getting ready for Holy Year, though of course there was less scope for architectural improvements than formerly. With all their troubles the popes spent enormous sums outdoing each other in the splendor of their Holy Years and in beautifying the city at those times. The fountains outside Saint Peter's were put up in anticipation of one lavish jubilee, in 1675; another jubilee work, two hundred years earlier, had been the restoration of the ancient aqueduct to bring the Acqua Vergine to the Fountain of Trevi, and the beautiful Ponte Sisto was built for the same occasion. Bridges and street widening were always a main concern, because of the crushes and casualties of early Holy Years.

The main restoration to be completed for 1950 was of Rome's only great cultural loss of the war, the ancient Basilica of San Lorenzo, almost totally destroyed in the bombing of the nearby railroad yards; it was a marvel, of modern expertise, that all its frescoes and early sculpture were not lost; a great deal was put together again from their Humpty Dumpty state. Meantime and throughout Holy Year some of the thousands of Romans whose living quarters had been bombed at the same time were still among those living in cardboard shacks, in caves and reappropriated schoolhouses, ten and twelve to a room. From the caves where they were likely to be seen by the city's visitors, under the Tarpeian Rock, they had been removed at the beginning of the year. Several new monasteries were finished in a rush, some of which served as hospices for pilgrims. But the big jubilee job was to finish the extension of Saint Peter's square, at the end of the new thoroughfare leading to the river.

The work had been dilatory. The two end buildings, linking Bernini's colonnade with the avenue, had stayed half finished for over two years and were not ready for the opening of Holy Year; it was something of a scandal, but a minor one in that particular picture. The architect was Marcello Piacentini, who in his earlier fascist role had destroyed the old crooked approach to Saint Peter's and put through instead the present pompous avenue, the Via della Conciliazione, named for the Lateran Treaty of 1929. Suddenly Saint Peter's had dwindled; the colonnade looked arbitrary and a little tawdry, without the old ragged asymmetry it had opposed and with its outer ends dangling. Even Piacentini himself seems to have been partly aware of the damage; all the proportions had been spoiled; the avenue was obviously too wide; he rectified it in time for Holy Year by lining it with two rows of imitation obelisks, the laughing stock of Rome, through which the most revered church in Christendom can now be approached like a pavilion at a World's Fair. About the two end buildings, which finally did get finished and for the rest of the year housed two huge exhibitions of Catholic art from all over the world, there was nothing to be done. For what was to complete a picture made by Bramante, Michelangelo, Raphael, and Bernini at least some small talent would have been needed; not that it was lacking in postwar Italy — only the Vatican did not hire it. A further mistake was made in exhibiting, as part of one of the art shows, photographs of the old approach together with the new one.

Of the two exhibitions, the one of primitive or "missionary" art was better to an embarrassing degree than most of the work by civilized Catholics, but that was not the fault of the pope; the quality of the painting was probably not related to his fairly liberal pronouncement, placarded up around the lobby, on the proper subjects and spirit for Catholic artists. Rouault, a few other artists of stature and long standing, seemed to have given their canvases to a ward bazaar. Another exhibition of the year was of life-size waxwork scenes illustrating the history of Christianity, beginning with martyrs in the Colosseum.

Among the more curious jubilee measures, in collaboration with the Demo-Christian government, was the addition of plastic fig leaves to the marble athletes in the Foro Italico and the removal to less conspicuous spots of the Dr. Strom signs. Also removed were several casefuls of saintly relics from a much frequented chapel in the church of Gesù, chief temple of the Counter-Reformation. They were the usual skeletal remains, in this case mostly hands and forearm bones, richly encased and labeled with the saint's name; nothing uncommon except their number; it would have been unthinkable and physically impossible to play down the necrology of Roman churches — a very important aspect of the city's "holiness" and undoubtedly a great drawing card for many of the faithful in 1950 as it always was. Yet about this one display there seems to have been some uneasiness; it was so concentrated, and hands and forearms with their split structure are not as attractive as a simple shinbone or piece of rib, especially when they have turned black and even when they are silver-plated; there is a certain desperate look of continuing will and struggle in them, that might turn a northern stomach, or frighten a northern child; Roman children play games around the cases while their mothers pray, as they do in front of whole skeletons dressed in brocade and cheesecloth, as if it were a natural history museum. So only a few were left there; the corners of the chapel where the rest had been were covered for the year with pastel paintings such as one might find in a parish church in Chicago.

Just before that chapel is the most magnificent of all baroque altars, a swirl of gold, silver, angels, and lapis lazuli (the biggest known piece of it in the world), with a jeweled and silvered figure of Saint Ignatius represented in a mighty upward swoop of glory between two gold-ribbed pilasters. The altar railing is an elaborate one of wrought bronze, featuring cherubs, one of the handsomest works of the kind in Rome, and for 1950 it had been dusted. This was not a minor item; it had been coated with dust for at least three years before and quite likely longer; understandably, when one considers that the present religious sense of Rome is the one set by the Counter-Reformation, and that the visible expression of that movement was the baroque, and that the formal essence of the baroque is the curve as opposed to the straight line and the unbroken surface. The amount of curved and broken surfaces inside and out that the Vatican has to keep clean, not to mention crannies such as those of several million angels' feathers or the trompe-l'oeil overhang of the ceiling figures in the church of Sant'Ignazio (companion to Gesù), is truly formidable. What was more awesome was that every curve and cranny, every crystal chip in the lovely chains of chandeliers in every important church seemed to have been scrubbed and polished for Holy Year. Miles of red damask pilaster strips, gold-edged, used only at special times, were put in condition and hung; miles of wax candles had to be laid in for the year, even though most of the candles like the church organs are now electric; endless big and little repair jobs on leaky roofs or art treasures were done, all at once. It is unlikely that many living people, even living in Rome, had ever seen the churches so beautiful — assuming one considers them beautiful at all, which people of Gothic or modern-function taste rarely do.

Then they began to fill with pilgrims, at least the main ones did — the absence of curiosity among the mass of pilgrims for anything off the prescribed beat was very striking, not only with regard to pagan Rome; they missed half of Christianity. For the first time one seemed to be seeing the big basilicas as they were meant to be, swarming not just for a big event now and then but all day, every day. It drastically changed one's sense of their origin, and of their art. There were no more of those cold unmystical emptinesses that make Roman churches the great tourists' chore; no more remote acquisitive stare at what was meant for a clutter and closeness; not the eye or the mind, the whole body must know a Roman church. It was possible now; you could know them as you know a New York subway; it was only then that one was beginning really to know their beauty, or the religious meaning of so disturbing a work as Bernini's Saint Theresa. The statue, or scene rather, happens to be in one of the tiniest churches, but the spirit of it, no more than was called for by the deliberate, orgasmic sensuality of the Counter-Reformation, transformed all the largest basilicas too except Saint Paul's. This was also the time when torture paintings, as frequent as bones in Rome, became most ghastly and prominent; the ancient Greeks would have scorned such emphasis on the body; the mind swam among physical extremes, pain and ecstasy becoming one, breast milk and decomposition alike serving the rapture of faith. Such places are not for solitary inspection; they need the humdrum physical bustle that the smaller churches do have but that can be kept up in the big ones only in a time of pilgrimage.

In the streets one was mainly conscious of the foreign influx, and the word *pellegrini* became a rather derisive one in Roman mouths. In the everyday scenes in the basilicas the tone was set by Italians, largely from rural places, who made up a big majority of the year's pilgrims: over 70 percent in the final figuring. Their adherence may have had something to do with the falling off of communist prestige from its high point before the Italian elections of 1948, but the Church had also done itself some harm at that time; many people not communists at all had resented the political pressures applied from the pulpit and in the confession box, as they did the later bull of excommunication of communists. It was and is a common state to be both in some way communist and in some way Catholic; and the time of highest communist influence was also a high point in visions and miracles, most of them not sanctioned by the Church — appearances of the Madonna to children, holy statues breathing, corpses said to have been found perfectly preserved after many years of burial, and so on, along with a sharp upcurve in miraculous cures.

The greatest phenomenon of the kind, then and for some years past, had been the repute of the monk known as Padre Pio, inmate of a monastery near Foggia, said to have the stigmata and whose miraculous powers, aside from the common one of healing, were believed to include the gifts of ubiquity, prescience, and in certain categories omniscience. He was the object of constant pilgrimages, not only by the poor; he had a following comparable in fervor to Rasputin's among the rich and the nobility, although on those levels he attracted perhaps fewer Italians than foreigners, especially English. Whatever his real psychic powers, and wherever else he might be at the same time, he stayed, unlike Rasputin, in his monastery or the church nearby where he officiated, and was quite an embarrassment to the Vatican during Holy Year. The

Church was not willing to commit itself on the subject, but in the summer finally felt obliged to publish a statement that a visit to Padre Pio was not a required part of the Holy Year pilgrimage.

In Rome, the atmosphere was far from visionary. The collapse of the monarchy had brought the city back to its old single source of pomp and ceremony, and for all the private sardonicism of the Romans, the endless religious processions were bound to be a success; with no rival on the Quirinal the Swiss guards and other handsomely uniformed Vatican corps were exciting as they had not been in three generations; the cardinal's cloak, the bishop's miter seemed actually supreme again; and the local concourse, no matter how complicated, was bound to look simple to the world. The insides of the churches had an element of a big show too for most of the Italian pilgrims and they were not too rapt to take it in. The foreign groups were little islands of intensity in the general chattiness, which made Saint Peter's most of the time seem more a mirage of an ancient basilica, a huge place of business, with people scooting every which way among the statues and arcades, men hurrying somewhere with briefcases, little groups standing in conversation or interrupting it a moment to run over and be touched by a penitentiary's wand, cheerful penitents in procession breaking off their hymns to ogle the sights.

They were also packed three and four deep around the crypt rail saying the requisite prayers, and as the year wore on Saint Peter's bronze toe was being rubbed nearly to knife-edge. For a particular celebration the statue was dressed in a miter and vestments from the Vatican treasure, thick with precious jewels, and as a precaution a wooden railing had been put around it that made it hard for people to reach the foot. There were swarms of aspirants in front of it all day, laughing at their failure to reach far enough across the fence, beaming congratulations at the few long-armed ones who succeeded, and who would then pass the touch around to their companions' fingers, for them to cross themselves with. "Bravo! He made it!" It was like a trial of skill in an amusement park.

But such crowded scenes were not the rule early in the year. The city was full but not as had been anticipated, and not at all by comparison with many earlier Holy Years. It is true that Rome did not become a very big city until after the end of the Papal State and the jubilee "multitudes" need not have been very large to cause all the tramplings to death and cavings-in of bridges that are recorded; still the figures are impressive. By the middle of 1950 not a single bridge had collapsed; there had been pilgrim deaths but not from asphyxiation; it was disheartening.

". . . and finally the havoc which ceaseless wars had wrought in the moral life of the Western kingdoms, led men to turn their eyes to Heaven . . ." It seemed for a while that the present moral havoc was too deep even for that, assuming the unique propriety of both heaven and the particular approach to it in question. Toward the latter, Holy Year invited inevitably, from friends or enemies or plain witnesses, a new scrutiny. Havoc moral or physical need not imply a retrogression of intelligence. It was right to wonder if the legitimate anguish of the time could be met by a dogma so arrogantly out of line with modern thought as that of the bodily Assumption of the Virgin, and by the canonization of an eleven-year-old girl who happened to have been killed resisting rape; because although there were other canonizations and beatifications during the year, there was no such stir and propaganda for the others as for little Maria Goretti, and not many saints had been officially recognized so soon after death. That and the dogma of the Assumption were the two great themes of Holy Year; neither would have been out of place in 1300. Other questions were raised by the pope's famous encyclical of the year, *Humani Generis*, which furthered the alienation of important "relativist" or liberalizing groups within the Church, and as an appeal outside it scarcely seemed aimed at any but the saddest victims of contemporary havoc. To all appearances, the true meaning of Holy Year was as the opening blast in a new Counter-Reformation, a calculated and skillful challenge to the broken heart of the world, modeled on that last great triumph of the Church by the method of the intellectual backtrack. It was to be seen how far it would work.

Judging only by numbers, from midsummer on it seemed to be working very well. Huge as it is now, the city did become jammed, and at night along innumerable shadowy outlying streets the pilgrim buses would be parked like sleeping circus elephants, who would not get nearly the rest they needed before the next day's performance. There are said to have been three million pilgrims by the end of the year; it seemed more like twenty million. A great many of them, foreigners too, were very poor; of the foreign countries Ireland naturally sent by far the most per population, and most of those were of course poor; they had taken on extra work and hoarded their savings for years to go to Rome. In that sense for many the journey was still a hardship and penance worthy of the great indulgence; and then in Rome the last of their savings vanished at a furious rate. A dramatic aspect of all the earlier Holy Years up to the nineteenth century used to be the exorbitant amount of charity given to poor pilgrims in Rome, however much profiteering was going on in the city at large; hundreds of thousands during the year used to be fed and put up free by various religious organizations. If any were this time the fact was not conspicuous. The one group of pilgrims that came from Australia went away complaining bitterly that their purses and watches had been snatched from them in public places; most were impoverished in more legal ways. There were certainly many individuals of more Christly inclination in the religious boardinghouses, but they were not responsible for the setup. The cut-rate services that were provided for pilgrims, as by monk barbers, annoyed the local tradespeople and were another great source of profit; nothing was free.

On the pilgrim side, whatever the financial sacrifice, the signs and attitudes of the old-time penitents — sackcloth, tears, bleeding feet — had gone quite out of date. It was front-page news when a pilgrim arrived on foot or as one did on horseback; many came by plane; the eleven-mile trek to the basilicas, to which only one visit was now required, was done by bus or taxi; one heard nothing of the once traditional humiliation of the powerful before the poor. It was rare to see middle-class or rich pilgrims departing in any way from the customary foreign scorn of Rome's great natural charity, they were apt to be as harsh toward the beggars as any other tourist; and a good many seemed less bent on the "reform of life" that Holy Year was supposed to induce than on other possibilities of the trip. It was natural. Rome is famous for its strange sexual effects on foreigners, and with the human crack-up so intimate, devout people were as likely as anyone else to succumb to that other power of the city, in some cases more so; the churches themselves are part of it, as much as the fountains; not to speak of people who came for convenience as pilgrims without being particularly devout.

Still the Vatican was the thing; many seemed never to have heard of Rome as consisting of anything else. The Museo Nazionale did no more than the usual seasonal business and often was practically empty; the Vatican Museums were a cattle-run all day every day especially in the last half of the year. There was traffic control, with a new one-way route of an extra half mile or so to the Sistine Chapel, and stop-gates set up throughout the museum; herds of pilgrims with their bags piled up behind them as at a slaughterhouse, then they opened and there would be another onward push through a Raphael room or the more dangerous bottleneck of the Apollo Belvedere. Some wore beautiful costumes — peasants from different parts of Europe dressed for all the stay in Rome in their holiday best. But the greatest number was always of Italian peasants, whose physique a century of democracy would not be enough to lighten into a likeness with any other class; it would take more ease than that to smooth away the coarseness of arms and legs and the rough wide beauty of face that seemed so out of place in Rome, although this was the very backbone of Holy Year: young girls, marked off more than by their dress and cheekbones, by the depth of their poise among all the city sights; greatgrandmothers wizened to a little brown fistful of features under their shawls but with the same indomitable profile. In the animal room at the Vatican two men from the country were discussing a piece of ancient sculpture. "Look, what a beautiful rabbit! You'd think it was alive. That's by a real artist, you can tell." "It's beautiful but it's not a rabbit. It's a hare. Look at its ears. Who ever saw a rabbit with ears like that?" "I tell you it's a rabbit. Look at its paws! I caught one exactly like it just the other day, not a mile from the house." "It's a hare!" "It's a fine work of art and it's a rabbit." "It hasn't even got the expression of a rabbit. . . ." The argument goes on as they are carried forward, between pagan gods and busts of emperors.

The story of the child saint of the year, Maria Goretti, was in some ways a natural one for this public, for whom chastity had not altogether lost the hold of a life-and-death conception; it has other kinds of appeal too, aside from dramatizing several of the main virtues stressed by the Church, especially obedience, to parents, the Church, and God. The child, stabbed to death by an evidently psychopathic youth in 1902, had been of the poorest peasantry, living at the time on the edge of the dismal Pontine marshes, near Nettuno, and her canonization, which took place in June and was the biggest event of the year, was a powerful gesture of sympathy toward the poor. Furthermore her mother, *la mamma*, apparently herself of the highest dignity and beauty of peasant character, of the old-fashioned or pre-marxist variety, was still alive and could be present at the ceremony — the first time in history that any mother had seen her child raised to sainthood: a very old woman, who had loved her husband, dead of tuberculosis and overwork fifty years ago; who had had to work in the fields a large part of her life; who taught her daughter such love of "Christian purity" she had seen her murdered for it; who with all her great load of suffering, this more than anything, had forgiven the murderer. So had the child before she died, a crucial point, the miracles required for sainthood having all been postmortem cures of people who had prayed to her; or all but one; the first "miracle" was the repentance of the murderer, after she had appeared to him in a vision in jail with her arms full of lilies. He served thirty years, and then became a gardener in a monastery. Purity, forgiveness, repentance: these were the essential story; for Holy Year purposes the apotheosis of motherhood was a not much less important part of it, and it was perhaps of some value too that there was a Goretti brother in America, who also went to the canonization. There was another side to it in the parades and exhibitions of the waxed-over body, looking closer to

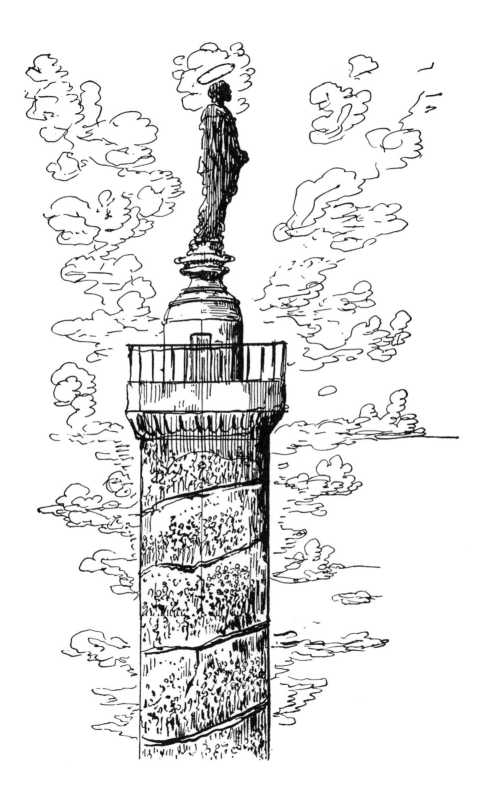

forty than eleven years old, minus the bones that had been taken out for relics. The huge portraits of the saint of the day that hang in Saint Peter's for any canonization are always the same, saccharine representations that compare poorly with even the worst of American commercial art, but the permanent paintings in that basilica are not one of its strong points either.

It seems obvious that the main purpose in making so much of the Goretti story was to attack the "sexual laxity" that had been alarming the Church as it did other social guardians and for an extra reason; which was sensible, and no reason to suspect the pope's plea for "purity of heart." The story itself was moving in that way; the child seems to have had really a rare grace of spirit, however one may interpret grace. Whether it could have kept so orthodox a form, among the acid choices imposed by intelligence and even by plain generosity later in the century, particularly in such a world as hers, is another question. Her mother was nearly ninety then; the best of the young men still accepted their absurd and tragic lot in her time. So romantic a glorification, in 1950, would no doubt have some appeal for adolescents and even more for the world's sophisticates; rather ironically, since the story on the face of it seemed most adapted to Italian peasant mentality, it seemed to misfire there more than in other circles. In the villages the subject was apt to bring a shrug, from people not averse to saints and miracles in general. "What did she do? Cos'ha fatto?" There were more marvelous legends of saints in the neighborhood; there was perhaps also a clearer knowledge of modern life, quite aside from political urgencies, than in the Vatican, shut off behind so many screens of hierarchy; the sinfulness of the young now was not that simple; they knew it.

For export purposes the movie made from the story, with Vatican approval, was unfortunate. Its best scenes were of the wet eerie landscape and the atrocious poverty of the peasants; as a story of grace it fell into even more than the usual commercial confusion. The episodes were those stressed in factual accounts of the girl's life; in one she was shown fearlessly killing a snake, symbol of evil not always free of deliberate confusion between original sin and any sexuality evil or not. Most of the movie was more explicitly sexual than that, to a point that would create panic in Hollywood. All its suspense was in the growth of the young man's bestial craving, which came to a climax in the scene of the girl's first communion: her face transfigured by religious ecstasy, he goaded by her rapture to still more violent lust. It closed with a spurious scene of mass recognition around her deathbed. There was a greater scene in the story as it really happened, but that took place many years later and was not shown.

The arguments for the dogma of the Assumption, as for the earlier one of the Immaculate Conception, suggested something of the same physical obsession, but were hardly a surprise; the ancient preoccupation with Mary's body, traceable to the days of the most ferocious sexual frustration in leaders of the Church long ago became second nature to Catholicism; and if Christ's mother were free of any "taint" of sex it was logical that she should not be contaminated by worms either. The furor in the Anglican Church over that Holy Year dogma seemed curious, unless inspired merely by its being the only one so far proclaimed in the twentieth century. In any case it was inevitable, and the only pending dogma important enough to bring out in 1950. The scathing attacks on the proclamation by biologists and others seemed for the most part weak, if not rather ludicrous, as though one should take exception to a single thread in a rug. Inside the Church the dogma had been growing, as the Church puts it, for a long time, and was as much a grassroots movement as a Vatican decision; there had been Marian congresses on the subject, petitions by innumerable bishops, etc. Most people were only surprised to discover that it had not been a dogma all the time.

It did, however, serve to dedicate that most ambitious Holy Year to Mary, under whichever of her names one might prefer: the Blessed Virgin, the Blessed Mother, Our Blessed Lady, or as children call her, bringing their tons of white flowers on December 8, Feast of the Immaculate Conception, to her column outside the American Express, *la madonnina*. She takes care of them all, and of their parents too; she thinks about them, she takes them to herself silently in their sorrows, having herself suffered more than any; she is everybody's most perfect mother, and the Church's most perfect counterforce to the crimes committed in its name, as well as to other hostile powers whether organized or only in the nature of men. No amount of supposings of theology have yet managed to lessen the power and comfort of this great image, and nothing else just then seemed likely to lessen people's need of it.

The power that gathered all these elements into the greatest religious demonstration of the century, which is not to say that the century has been a very outstanding one in that line, was Pope Pius XII. At the end of the year, when all over the vast spaces around the high altar in the basilica of Saint Paul you had to pick your way among kneeling pilgrims racing in Latin through their rosaries, the whole Vatican hierarchy was said to have been dizzy with success. Such numbers! such response! nobody would have dared to hope for anything approaching it. If the pope cared to consider his efforts as anything more than an operation of divine truth, he might well congratulate himself; many people had wondered if he would survive the strain, healthy though he appeared to be, until the end of the year.

For all the interest of Boniface VIII in the first Holy Year and his fame as the originator of the tradition, he was outside Rome the best part of the year, busy with diplomatic crises and in preserving the lull in his war with the Colonna family — who were excluded from all the benefits of the jubilee; remission of sins was not for political opponents. Others in the series of jubilee popes after overhauling the city would attend the most important ceremonies and let it go at that. Pius XII was dedicated body and soul every minute; even at his summer residence in Castel Gandolfo there was scarcely any letup in his exhausting number of private audiences, and he continued to appear twice a week in Saint Peter's for the mass ones, which drew a near-capacity crowd every time; this on top of twelve beatifications and canonizations and a number of large special occasions, such as the epoch-making celebration of the Greek rite in Saint Peter's, at which he assisted in December; plus the regular political, financial, and theological business of his huge, peculiar empire. The "Mystical Body of the Church," on which he had written an encyclical in 1943, depended by definition on the health and participation of all its members. An impression even more striking than the aesthetic one from the year's exhibit of missionary art was of the ubiquitousness of that body; jungles, lake dwellings, obscure Asian plateaus were suddenly to be seen, really seen, not just known about, as parts of one organism with Rome; an unfriendly term for the impression would be tentacles — in those rooms the word lost its pallor from overuse, the image was brand-new; the head with its never-sleeping eyes was a block from where one stood. In orthodox imagery the body is more like a human one, and no sacrifice undergone by any pilgrim could have compared with the grueling labors of the pope in giving it its year-long blood transfusion, and making unforgettably dramatic for every partici-pant its fabulous unity.

The most publicized fact regarding his mass audiences was that he was able to address the pilgrim groups in five or six lan-guages. It was impressive, but no more so than the welcoming gesture of his arms, alternating to left and right, as of a dancer, and his keeping that and his thin earnest smile, as he was borne across the "sea of faces," from becoming mechanical through so many repetitions. The great slow single wave of cheering that breaks around the progress of all popes down that aisle is a stan-dard awe-rouser; in this case there was uncommon personal charm at work too, whether or not it were felt as emanating from uncommon holiness; it had warmth and what seemed even a real humility, not incompatible with an autocratic office and a char-acter suited to making the most of it. But that was not the main point. There was one grandeur in these enormous gatherings that was not a matter of taste or opinion. It was a fact, for this century the most thrilling possible. For an hour each time many thou-sands of people, of many nationalities, stood together under one roof and were not asked to make war on anyone, neither a com-munist nor a Colonna nor a Turk; the pope's little speech of wel-come and blessing, addressed to each group by name and repeated in all the languages he could pronounce, contained not a word of anything but affection and respect for the whole human race. It was moving; it was queer; it produced goose pimples. It was likely to blind many people to various practical activities of the "Mystical Body," aimed at binding the whole human race with something more dependable than love. Nevertheless for one hour of their lives people had heard the words, and stood together hearing them; they had had at least one experience of peace, perhaps strong enough to turn some of them someday even against the Church if the memory were betrayed; the pope had risked that, perhaps more than any of his predecessors.

According to reports, he was truly convinced of the spiritual benefits of the year, whatever the worldly one might be, and truly grieved when the day came at last to close the Holy Door. The wooden stands were up again in the portico; only now there was a trowel instead of a hammer. Inside, Saint Peter's was lit up, not with the big vulgar lights of some churches but very beautifully with a Milky Way's worth of little ones, drawing forth other golden reflections from the tremendous barrel-vault ceiling, less Gothic, more celestial than ever, from the ribs of the writhing baldachin pillars under Michelangelo's dome, and the huge sunbeam horse-collar ring, Roman archetype for all holies of holies, around Peter the Apostle's chair. His bones had been found down below, it was said, during the year; it was important that they should be, to settle any lingering disputes about the vicarage, and the excavations in the Vatican grottoes had been too extensive not to come up with them if they were there. Through the golden haze the inside of the dome was sufficient for the eternal glory of papal architecture whatever might be added or taken away, if only that were left, with its thin rib lines gathering upward toward the lantern modeled on the eye of God; outside for miles around, appearing in all its uncanny ways and perspectives, it was proclaiming, aside from what it always does, the triumph of this particular jubilee. Another work by Michelangelo but of his youth, not yet Roman, the dead Christ and mourning girl-mother of the Pietà beside the Holy Door, the only great work of pity in all Rome, looked utterly forgotten and dismissed afterward, with the door-rubbish heaped up around it. There had been signs up for several weeks, there and in other basilicas, saying that one could give money for a brick for one of the four Holy Doors, which would be removed on Christmas Eve, 1974.

It was not a golden day, as it had been a year earlier when the door was being opened. It was chilly and gray; in fact it had been raining most of the time for two months, which is not the kind of thing anyone seems to report about the Holy City. There was only a loosely formed little crowd in the square, carrying umbrellas, waiting to make a dash for the upper corner where the parade of the guards would pass, and another one back to the center to cheer the pope when as the really last gesture of Holy Year he appeared, a small figure in the white high above them, at one of the Vatican windows. With the mystique of numbers still not altogether superseded, some might be thinking more of the year 2000 than of 1975, possibly with something of the terror that the world of the Middle Ages felt at the ending of the first Christian millennium, and with somewhat better reasons.

Holy Year had certainly been a success in one way; it had shown the Catholic Church to be more of a going concern than many of its members might fully have realized before, and that alone was bound to strengthen it further, at least for the time being. The number of pilgrims who left Rome disillusioned was probably small; there were more charms working for the Church there than it was responsible for, and its own are considerable. The number whose lives were morally changed by it was probably also small; the havoc of an Age of Platitude was not likely to be so easily cured. The year had not been intended by its masters of ceremonies as a patching up and holding fast; nothing defensive; it was to have been a spiritual revival, a restatement of ancient creed in its strictest form because that alone would tear it away from all dangerous or halfhearted, half-energizing associations, and bring to the old formulae the drive and spirit of a new belief. There seemed no sign that anything of the sort had taken place; numbers of conversions are no measure of it, not acceptance of the Virgin but the health one brings to her would seem the question for the

Church's ultimate vitality. Not that the deeper failure of Holy Year, if it was that, need be a source of cheer to communists. The jubilee undoubtedly did undercut communist power to some extent, even if not very lastingly, not by creating new energies, but because of the joy of a past alive in symbols and in gestures made so many times before, and the love of travel, which people under communist rule cannot have. Its closing piece of pageantry ended with a sudden downpour, just as the other four doors were opened to let the crowd out of Saint Peter's, so they all put up their umbrellas and for a few minutes formed a stream of black inhuman creatures being belched out as in a parody of the Last Judgment all over the square.

There was another scene that became related to Holy Year, although it had happened long before; but nobody made much of it; it was not generally heard of. The murderer of Maria Goretti had asked her mother for forgiveness, and received it, by mail. Years later when he had finished his jail sentence he went to see her, only once, in the family's original village to which she had returned and where there was now a chapel and shrine to Maria, already treated locally as a saint. He came without warning, on Christmas Eve; somehow everyone in the village knew who he was immediately; he knocked on the door and was let it by an old woman, Maria's mother. It seems they did not try to find anything much to say, but she urged him to stay to supper, surely not with any thought of an effect or thought of herself doing anything; it was only another natural sorrowful thing that she must do. She cooked the meal and served it to him, and later he went to midnight mass with her and sat at her side, beside the chapel to her daughter whom he had killed with a knife. For thirty years he had been a name of horror in the village; it had been a terrible excitement to them that he had come; now suddenly the old woman in her charity was stronger than their rage. They began to lose their curiosity, and after a while there was no more hatred in the church.

ROMAN JOURNAL II

*J*F ONE COULD SEE, really see, only two buildings, the Cancelleria and the Palazzo Farnese, one could begin to see all the Renaissance in Rome — furnishings, philosophy, and all. It is a temptation to call these two buildings perfect, though in other surroundings they could no doubt look as vulgar as our imitations of them, or nearly: the real thing being real is important. But this is where our atrophy of the eyes is most critical and the operation on them most slow and painful. You can sight-see these two buildings a dozen times and not see anything but the marketplace between, Campo dei Fiori, picturesque, so full of life, and in fact beautiful in itself. Really the point is what the life and the buildings are doing to each other.

Le Corbusier, in conversation: "Rome has nothing to offer me."

Communist painter Picasso, returning to Rome after many years for a peace congress, was taken by communist painter Guttuso to the Vatican; the only painting that interested him was Michelangelo's Last Judgment.

Between communists P. and G. there is a crucial difference, corresponding to their difference in age. P., of the sentimental marxist period, was a painter who happened to be a communist, which he could be because he lived in a free country and his medium was not words; paint as he used it required aesthetic, not intellectual honesty. He was right about the Last Judgment; it is the greatest "modern" painting in the Vatican, built not around an objective harmony but subjective breakages of forms. Guttoso, of the bureaucratic marxist period, was spoiling a considerable talent by trying to be a communist *in painting*; he was pretending to have the objective vision of Raphael.

Le Corbusier was speaking admirably too; all that Rome offers was taken into his own great creativity long ago. What is depressing is the number of our own fine arts or architectural school graduates who are either arrogant toward the past because they are creative, or respect it because they are not. The first category is bored in Rome, the second makes even Rome boring. Another possibility is to have studied with Gropius and out of starvation or perversity later to care about nothing but baroque, which in such a case has to be taken in stronger doses all the time.

The city makers: Bramante, Sangallo the Younger, Michelangelo, Raphael, Peruzzi, Bernini, Borromini . . . and around them, necessary to them, dozens of others, as many as movie stars now. They were doing just that all the time, making not a work of art here or there but the city; the suction of it on all the genius of the country was irresistible; they came from everywhere, rarely from Rome, and were sucked into the one great work of architecture, the city, which required painters and sculptors and hydraulic engineers as much as architects. The painters were decorators; the outside walls were forming the piazzas; it was a tyranny of collaboration. And so one tends to think of Rome as a city very poor in painting, because the pleasures of painting are not separate as they are elsewhere; the galleries are the worst hung and probably the worst in general in

Europe; everything was to be lived with, in houses or churches. Everything was architecture, and we are only used to looking at, or looking for, canvases. The typical experience of art in Rome, indoors, is not of great paintings but of great rooms in which great or sometimes only ordinary painters worked; outdoors it is of the relation of buildings to what is around them. The Cancelleria and the Palazzo Farnese are more beautiful for being neither adjacent nor far apart and having that particular marketplace between.

"Ecco Roma!" . . . Where? which Rome? who is seeing it? at what time of day?

Leaving out the Last Judgment, which is outside its time, nothing is so hard now as the Renaissance — so concerned with being, so unconcerned with "truth"; it explains nothing; it is without tragedy and without love. We bring to it all our self-seeking, our loneliness, apathy, and need of love; we see it in bursts of traipsing between sieges of boredom and melancholy; we are looking for ourselves and are given — decoration! This nebulousness of ours is very time-consuming. The most impressive thing about the travel writers of the old days is the amount they could see and do in twenty-four hours. It is perhaps connected with their enjoyment of the company they were in; they are always referring to their "charming companions." Nowadays most people seem to travel either alone or with companions that they are not finding charming at all. It might be that if we saw more truth in decoration we would not need to expect so much of it from our acquaintances.

Many Roman palaces might have been somewhere else, but when you think of Roman palaces you think of something that is not anywhere else. This is apart from their associations, which give the iron bars across the ground-floor windows a different weight for the imagination than other grilles have. The palaces are massive; they are secretive; they are elegant. The Louvre is extensive rather than massive, and not secretive at all; it shows what it is right away. Roman palaces, even aside from their dinginess, have a way of

hiding their distinctions like cottages on the main street of an English village. You have to pry them out. On the other hand they are
not monolithic and quickly spoil one's taste for medieval towns.
The creative spirit was moving too fast to become repetitive — a
motion toward outwardness nearly from the beginning, which
would take its time arriving at the baroque. The Cancelleria, finished in 1511, is not of the world of the Farnese, begun in 1514; windows have become dominant and the window pediments, like all
the ornamentation, have begun to push out. The houses, with a
few exceptions, go on following the basic plan of a square around
a court, but it is not defensive or brooking; the court is another facade, another elegance, and often another place of trees and water
and worldly charm, like the street.

But they could never be merely elegant. A French traveler,
shortly before Bramante's and Cesare Borgia's time, remarked that
Italians always had a rule and compass in their hands. Most of
them seem to have had a volume of Vitruvius too. In Rome, besides that national fastidiousness, there was fearful pressure from
other superlatives than in mathematics; it ought to have been
crushing. The Colosseum and the Theatre of Marcellus, Vitruvius's models, might be torn apart physically but they could not be
violated in spirit. The palaces had also to be Rome. The city could
never break into the glorious facetiousness of Venice, any more
than it could develop much gift in color; one always thinks of extremes of chiaroscuro there, never of the range of the palette in
the Venetian sense.

Perhaps the most peculiar effect of Roman as against other
palaces is windowphilia. In the churches the windows are nothing
to notice — no Gothic splendors there; they are made as inconspicuous as possible and are apt to be common kitchen glass with
common kitchen curtains to draw when the light is too sharp. In
palace design they are central and bewitching in their variations.

Palazzo Farnese: ground floor, low rectangles; piano nobile, alternating triangular and segmental pediments, with side columns;
top, triangular pediments over arched opening, with columns.

Palazzo Madama, where the senate sits — perhaps the most

beautiful windows in Rome, in a four-story design: plain rectangular (as always, behind the bars); segmental pediments, with a
break by means of balcony and surmounting pediment figures over
the portone; triangular, with the base of the triangle broken, enclosing fleurs-de-lis; attic, small, square, with sensuous underframe,
the squares being a countermotif to the frieze that they interrupt.

And so on, up to the breakup of all the nonessential forms, verti-
cally and in depth, in the baroque. Above the ground floor the windows are apt to have painted wooden slat shutters and they are
always appealing, there or anywhere in Europe; they suggest a
warmth of life behind, that would not go with too much perfection
in art or efficiency; they are part of what keeps a Roman palace from
looking like a museum or an embassy although it is probably both.

The facade of the Farnese, which became the French Embassy by
having passed to the Bourbons, is a natural for a movie set and has
been used as such very often. A character with a sword and a
plumed hat was taken some fifty times one day, swashbuckling
from the right-hand fountain across to the portone, where at the
end of the sequence, over and over, two sixteenth-century guards
got out their cigarettes and collapsed to torpor, waiting to grab
their halberds and jump back to life again at the cry of "Lights!"
which however would not bring the hero any farther across the
threshold than before. The whole Renaissance was gasping to be
known but it was hopeless; the scene always stopped at the same
point. Inside in a similar hopelessness, at grips with a bit of France
in Rome as all Rome used to be with the French troops, a man
driven mad with waiting for a visa at the proper door bribes his
way in through the front and gets a foot inside the inner door of
the consulate. "I have waited all week, every day. I ask merely for
information; they tell me I must ask inside. *I can't get inside!*"
"Monsieur, je regrette. You must wait your turn." "My business
can't wait any longer! I have to leave for Paris tonight! I am a busy
man. . . ." "We are all busy, monsieur; *comme vous voyez.*" The
door is closing; he sobs, heaving his body against it. "If you will
wait your turn, at the other door . . ." "I tell you I have waited a

week at that door! I have important business, I must be in Paris to-morrow! . . ." He is physically overpowered; the door is shut. "Un fou. Si on devait faire des exceptions pour tout le monde. . . ."

Palazzo Venezia: Begun 1455, for future Pope Paul II, from design attributed to L. B. Alberti; with crenellation, the only medieval touch on any palace, and Mussolini's balcony. The unfortunate match to it across the square is a late copy.

Cancelleria: Begun before 1500; attributed to Andrea Bregno although it calls up inevitably the name of Bramante, who may have arrived in Rome in time to help with the cortile. There is a smaller replica of it, of the same period and perhaps by the same architect, down the street from Saint Peter's.

Palazzo Farnese: Begun 1514, for future Pope Paul III; by Antonio Sangallo the Younger, and after his death Michelangelo; finished by Giacomo della Porta.

Palazzo Orsini: Set in what was left of the Theatre of Marcellus, begun by Caesar, finished by Augustus, dedicated to his dead nephew. Palace possibly by Baldassare Peruzzi, one of those who had learned most from that ruin.

Villa Farnesina: B. Peruzzi, 1508–11; for Agostino Chigi the Magnificent.

Piccola Farnesina: A little house, with great charm and a loggia over the street, rare in Rome. 1523; attributed to Sangallo the Younger; facade done over much later.

Palazzo Massimo alle Colonne: Down the street from that and from the Cancelleria — on one of the nineteenth-century avenues that caused such grief at the time but the buildings have stood it. B. Peruzzi, 1532–36. Hides itself more than most; with remarkable front curve and columns and ceiling of the upper portico of the court.

Palazzo Antici-Mattei: Back-to-back with the Gaetani Palace, which also used to belong to the Mattei family. Sixteenth century. A few steps from Tortoise Fountain. Particularly anarchic and pleasant collection of bric-a-brac in the garden and portico.

Villa Madama: On the hill above the Foro Italico. Early sixteenth century. From designs by Raphael, but never finished. Sad garden, once beautiful; sad house. Bad copy of Bramante's spiral staircase in the Vatican.

Villa Medici: 1544; since Napoleon, the French Academy. Overdecorated rear facade, toward the wonderful garden inspired in part by Michelangelo. Beautiful careless stucco front, crucial in views of Rome from almost anywhere.

Villa Giulia: 1551–53, for Julius III, now the Etruscan Museum. Severe Renaissance facade, last of its kind and excellent but it misses its old life. Architectural court and garden fantasy by Vignola, with collaboration from Vasari and Michelangelo.

Palazzo Cenci: No special genius; only the rise of the hill, a fountain, the good Roman shape and feeling of the building long since a tenement, the remains of the Theatre of Balbus underneath and more visible ones down the street of the Portico of Octavia, also Augustan; and the story. Young Beatrice and the others were executed in 1599; her wicked father had probably not had the house much over thirty years.

Palazzo Chigi: Sometime Foreign Office; begun 1562, by Giacomo della Porta, finished by other architects. The windows are the best things on Piazza Colonna after the column itself.

Palazzo Laterano: Attached to the basilica. Sixtus V built the present one; 1586; by Domenico Fontana, architect of the Acqua Felice and, for the same pope, of the *other* Sistine Chapel, in Santa Maria Maggiore.

Palazzo Borghese: Called from its shape "The Harpsichord"; begun 1590. One of the biggest and shabbiest and most affecting, in the best shopping center, with the most DaDa garden.

Palazzo Rospigliosi: Quite incredibly enormous, and over the old enormous Baths of Constantine. 1603; for Cardinal Scipione Borghese; enlarged by later owners, especially Cardinal Mazzarini (Mazarin).

Casino Borghese: Now the museum; also built for Cardinal Scipione; 1605–13.

Palazzo Barberini: High baroque, and showing better than the churches the rigor and propriety of form maintained through that flowering outwardness. 1625–33; Carlo Maderno and Borromini, central part finished by Bernini. The inner court plan has been cut in half, leaving the center exposed, with wings. To be considered together with the Triton in the square below.

Palazzo Altieri: Hidden by heavy traffic and cheap shoestores. Begun mid-seventeenth century, enlarged by Clement X (Altieri). With the Cenci-Bolognetti palace across the way, of the same period, and the somewhat earlier church of Gesù, it forms, when one manages to see it, a very handsome opening.

Palazzo Doria: Also enormous; front on the Corso, back to the Jesuit Collegio Romano. Eighteenth century, but the beautiful arcade court was modeled after Bramante. Disastrously hung but large collection of paintings.

Montecitorio: The Chamber of Deputies. Begun by Bernini, 1650; finished by Carlo Fontano of the fountain family (this one made the shrine fountain by the Ponte Sisto). Should be appreciated first in Piranesi.

Palazzo Spada: On a line with the Farnese; begun 1540, restored by Borromini. Most heavily decorated of palaces, with stuccos and friezes: Roman heroes outside, gods and myths in court, with garlands.

Palazzo Doria-Pamphili: 1650. A very important piece of Piazza Navona.

Palazzo Braschi: A huge trapezoid, late eighteenth century; its back is another important piece of Piazza Navona. For nephews of Pope Pius VI (Braschi); the last palace of a papal family.

Palazzo Lancellotti: Another piece, lower and earlier, forming with the above the end of the square.

Palazzo Madama: An important piece of perspective for Piazza Navona, back on a parallel avenue, a cross slice of its beautiful windows and portal to be seen from beside the river fountain. Sixteenth century; facade seventeenth; named for Margaret of Austria who married two Roman princes.

Quirinal: Begun 1574, over an old villa; worked on by half a dozen of the best architects of the time; portone by Bernini, finished under Clement XII (1730–40). Summer residence of the popes until 1870.

Palazzo della Consulta: Also for Clement XII; 1734; in its more obvious elegance (symbolic figures, roof balustrade, heavy window pediments) an excellent foil and companion to the barn-like Quirinal, also in color; the third piece of the enclosure, to which all Rome opens itself in the sunset, this one deep red and set below the brow of the hill, is the so-called Papal Stables. Castor and Pollux were already there; Pius VI added the obelisk, from the mausoleum of Augustus, and Pius VII the fountain basin, an ox trough from the Forum. One is struck most of all here and in Piazza Navona by the deliberate part of genius in these sleepy-looking arrangements; they were not making statements but releasing images.

Palazzo Colonna: Built over older buildings in the fifteenth century and rebuilt in the eighteenth; comparable to Grand Central Station in size and ground-floor elusiveness; offering no perspective at all and incorporating the grandiose church of the Santissimi Apostoli, which offers little more.

Villa Albani: 1760, for the cardinal, for whom Winckelmann built up the famous collection of ancient sculptures, mostly stolen by Napoleon, later repleted. The city at its most petit-bourgeois has grown out around it; it belongs to the most hated landlords in central Italy, the Torlonias, and can only be seen with their permission although no one lives there; which helps to give the museum and beautiful garden a morguish air. As in many old places in the world but few in Rome you fall between the two realities of then and now; from the old prints it appears that the building was one of the finest of its century.

The Vatican: Little fifth-century house (Pope Simmacus); restored twelfth century; after Avignon (1377) became the papal residence, the Lateran being a shambles; courtyard plan, 1450; Sistine Chapel 1473; big push by Bramante, for Julius II; Pauline Chapel by Sangallo for Paul III; and so on through sixteenth, seventeenth, eighteenth, and nineteenth centuries. About 1,400 rooms, including chapels; not including gardens, covers about 55,000 square meters, of which some 25,000 are taken up by some 20 courtyards. Any genius involved anywhere in the city was first of all involved in this.

And many, many other palaces. All down the Corso for instance, or narrow cobbled Via Giulia, which was put through
around the time Farnese, backing on it, was begun, and was then
the grandest street in the city.

> Considering that each of the places mentioned has its
> own special literature, forming altogether a library of
> several hundred volumes, it would be futile to enter
> into details.
>
> — Lanciani, on the Renaissance in Rome

The palaces are shocking. They were built through nepotism and
are still maintained by a version of slave labor; the noble families
whose names they bear have for the past century or so been of no
use whatsoever in art, commerce, or the state, and did nothing to
oppose fascism, although some members of them eventually fought
the Germans. The buildings are half rented out as apartments and
even so mostly depend on American, South American, or Milanese
money, acquired by marriage. The Roman noble of the present
time, speaking of men, is apt to be an insufferable boor and a high
percentage are homosexuals and dope addicts; some are harmless
playboys made more arrogant by good taste in art; others are just
mildly cultured and gently melancholy; a few examples of great personal dignity on occasion can be found in all these combinations,
but if an aristocrat distinguishes himself in the country he is almost
sure to be from somewhere else, not Rome. Nevertheless the enormous rooms — marble floors, painted ceilings, brocade cuffs for
manservants — have been kept alive and therefore beautiful, since
they were that to begin with. It is partly due to the presence of two
full diplomatic corps in what for society purposes remains a small
town, but that is not all. There is something of the tough gaiety and
grace and wit of the piazzas on that side of the walls too, along with
the stupendous luxury and frequent depravity — they were only
rulers before, not leaders, except of armed bands in the baronial
days, so they have not lost much. And the candor of the piazzas:
"Who is that hideous old woman over there?" "My wife really wants

to commit suicide." "In this house you meet the stupidest people in Rome." "All the men in this family have horns." A novelist who has written a blasting satire on his hostess thinks nothing of discussing the book in front of her. "That woman? oh, she's my husband's mistress." "One always gets a stomachache in this house, the food is too rich." "If my husband weren't impotent . . ." The rooms are the other part of the one organism, the one big indoors.

There is the same passion for American cars, the same scorn of government and quick satiric tongue, the same lack of affectation, the immersion in life; only the women have become through international marriages less handsome than women of the people, and are supremely well dressed. The best of everything that is missing on the Via Veneto, even intellectual life as it is, is in the palaces.

These are of course not the *old* Roman families. Those were all killed off or sold into slavery, or ended the line by becoming martyrs and saints.

The two most valuable contemporary records of Rome in the sixteenth century were written by two Florentines: Macchiavelli and Benvenuto Cellini.

Medieval Rome. It is commonly said that there is nothing left of it. It is true there is only one medieval house, the Anguillara in Trastevere, but there is an immense amount left in the churches, and a few towers, two of them back of the imperial forums, the Torre del Grillo and Torre delle Milizie; there used to be another right beside them in the Forum of Nerva, the Torre de' Conti, much higher and considered one of the wonders of the world. The main fortresses are all there; they were the ruins: the Colosseum (held chiefly by the Frangipani family, who also had the arches of Titus and Constantine and outposts on the Circus Maximum); the Theatre of Marcellus; the Baths of Caracalla; the tomb of Cecilia Merella (Gaetanis); the tomb of Augustus (Colonnas, who also controlled the height that is now Montecitorio and all the deserted ruin-strewn area between Piazza del Popolo and the Quirinal);

Castel Sant'Angelo (Orsinis, together with the Vatican territory and Monte Giordano, from which they kept Dante's hero Henry VII from crossing the city to be crowned in Saint Peter's), etc. It was over these that Cola di Rienzo spread his hysterical fingers, appointing himself the new Augustus and Knight of the Holy Ghost, just a hundred years before Palazzo Venezia. But most of all there is the nature of Rome with regard to time in general, which keeps the Middle Ages more fresh there than in any well-preserved medieval city; they become the news of the day, and about as edifying. Coherence begins with the Cancelleria — the first palace that is not a fortress, although the windows are small and far apart.

Gregorovius, who was partial to the Goths, dates the beginning of medievalism at the overthrow of the Gothic kingdom established by Theodoric, in the year 553, or sixteen years after the stopping up of the aqueducts. "Classical civilization then perished in Rome and Italy."

More vividly than in their extant works, the Middle Ages present themselves in the absence of works that to one's mind had been so vividly there. The gilt bronze roof tiles of Hadrian's Temple of Venus and Rome, which had been spared by the Vandals, were carted across town in the seventh century by Pope Honorius for the new roof of Saint Peter's, from which they were eventually stolen again. The Pantheon also had gilt bronze roof tiles, which were taken away by Eastern Emperor Constans II when he visited Rome in 663, but he was murdered on the way home and the loot was taken by the Saracens. The Theatre of Marcellus began being demolished in the fourth century to repair a bridge.

The owner of the only remaining medieval house, Count Everso dell'Anguillara, was known as the worst baron of his time. Among other things he coined false money and controlled the road from Rome to Viterbo.

Cola di Rienzo: "Where are those good old Romans? Where is their lofty rectitude? Would that I could transport myself back to the times when these men flourished."

Petrarch, on Stephen Colonna, four years before the Colonna family was ruined and nearly wiped out in the fighting with Cola (November 20, 1347): "Great God! what majesty is in this old man! What a voice, what a brow and countenance, what manner, what energy of mind and strength of body at such an age! I seem to see Julius Caesar or Scipio Africanus before me, only that he is much older than either. . . ."

Like the palaces, many of the happenings in them could have happened somewhere else than in Rome, but when you think of a number of them together they are not anywhere else. Not that everything was happening every day, there are dull generations in any family. But stories are not remembered unless they are images of a general truth of a place, as for us George Washington and the cherry tree, Priscilla and John Alden, Colonel Astor going down on the Titanic, Daniel Boone, John Jay Chapman holding his hand in the fire, the Collyer brothers, J. P. Morgan and the midget. The images in the palaces contain more murder than is usual but that is only part of a more comprehensive Roman truth — what Symonds called "the impulse toward the illimitable." Its virtue would have to share the character of its wickedness, its private ambitions that of its God, and the picture is always superlative. Julius Caesar may have fallen because he was too modest; Mucius Scaevola by holding *his* hand in the fire was probably as responsible as anyone for there being no civic sense in modern Rome at all.

Agostino Chigi the banker, in his beautiful Villa Farnesina, designed by Peruzzi, decorated by Raphael and others, as one of his "magnificences" used to serve his guests on gold plate, which was then thrown into the Tiber. However he had a net there to catch it. At his banquets for Pope Leo x the gold plate was engraved with the coats of arms of every guest, and each was served with food from his own country, for which messengers had been sent to what were then known as the four corners of the earth. Chigi had bought his way into the aristocracy, as the Torlonias did most recently; as a Roman historian observes, "A golden key has always had the power of opening the most obstinate doors of a Roman palace." Cellini says that he used to go to the villa to study Raphael's Cupid and Psyche frescoes, and the owners, like others in their social position, "plumed themselves exceedingly when they saw young men of my sort coming to study in their palaces." But the banker's son Lorenzo was "prodigo e furiosi," so the villa passed to their neighbors the Farneses in 1579.

The Cancelleria is said to have been financed by one night's gambling winnings, by a pope's nephew from another pope's nephew.

In 1512 the boy Federico Gonzaga of Mantua, in Rome to perfect his education, was taken to see the dismemberment of a priest who had been convicted of several murders; the quartering took place in the church of Aracoeli.

At a feast for Eleonora d'Aragon, on the Capitoline, the bread was gilded, the dishes were in the form of mythological characters and from one of them a poet stepped out reciting verses. This has something in common with the meal described by Petronius.

Pope Paul II, born in Venice and for whom Palazzo Venezia was built, was so fond of his own looks he had to be dissuaded from calling himself Pope Formosus. It was he who instituted the carnival races of Jews as well as horses down the Corso.

One of Cesare Borgia's governors held a page over a fire with a poker. Like Augustus's friend's feeding slaves to his lampreys, this was not generally approved of.

Not long after the Massimo family had moved into their new palace with its lovely curve and entrance columns (Chigi's architect again, the brilliant Peruzzi) a son and heir of the family died, at the age of fourteen, and was brought back to life by the family's spiritual adviser, Saint Philip Neri — founder of the Oratorians and himself noble, as well as learned, witty, and kind; "he did not discourse; he conversed"; he is outstanding among Roman saints, most of whom were of earlier times and distinguished themselves by extremes of asceticism. The rest of the story, as told by Mrs. Jameson (*Legends of the Monastic Orders*): "'Art thou willing to die?' asked the saint. 'No,' sighed the youth. 'Art thou willing to resign thy soul to God?' 'I am.' 'Then go,' said Philip. 'Va, che sii benedetto, e prega Dio per noi.' The boy sank back on his pillow with a heavenly smile on his face and expired." This happened on March 16 and every year it is still commemorated; the boy's bedroom is in a part of the house now rented as an apartment, which has to be vacated annually on that day.

The chief Borghese family pope, Paul V (Camillo Borghese), responsible for the palace (the Harpsichord) and the family fortune, has one of the least attractive faces of any pope on record. He is represented in marble over his tomb in the chapel named for him in Santa Maria Maggiore, amid appropriate luxuries of art, gold, and marble, kneeling in prayer; the face is fat, piglike but authoritarian, shrewd, with a look of rabid highhandedness that seems to have been comically interrupted, at the moment of the portrait, by an effort to appear spiritual. He was in fact unusually direct and sweeping in the matter of enriching the family and in exalting papal prerogatives, which involved him in many disputes with territories of the Church and nearly brought on war with Venice; he finished Saint Peter's and enlarged the Vatican and Quirinal. Most conspicuously he immortalized himself in the Fontana Paola and in the inscription across the facade of Saint Peter's: PAULUS QUINTUS BORGHESIUS ROMANUS ET SEQ. — the only one that in pomp and power comes close to rivaling Agrippa's on the Pantheon.

There is a strong family resemblance between him and his nephew, Cardinal Scipione Borghese (Palazzo Rospigliosi and the Casino Borghese), of whom there are two busts by Bernini in the museum. This one seems a shade more genial but like his uncle has the kind of flesh a cannibal would not like; worldly bossy sensuous intemperate clever men both of them, with no humility it appears, except that which gave them good judgment for the art that would perpetuate their glory.

The Torlonias increased their banking fortune in the past century by lending vast sums to the bankrupt Vatican treasury at vast interest, and along with the Villa Albani acquired sixteenth-century palaces, one of them in the thick of town, across from the

Hotel d'Inghilterra. A recent prince of the family kept a riding stable in the inner court and issued forth to his riding followed by mounted grooms. On the walls along the family estate nearest to Rome there have been painted off and on in our times in letters a yard high, such legends as DEATH TO THE TORLONIAS! A young prince of another branch of the family was wounded in an assassination attempt by one of his farm employees in 1949. Their vicious maladministration of their huge estates in the Lake Fucino area made their name one of the most politically crucial in Italy, and caused the communists to profit greatly from the government's strange reluctance to carry out its promises of land expropriation there.

The Cenci story comes out far better in Stendhal's narrative, sophisticated version than in Shelley's dramatized and romantic one. To begin with the central fact of incest was awkward for the stage, more so as mixed with every other "impulse toward the illimitable" of Roman Renaissance life; but in any case the Romantic vocabulary ("O, world! O, life! O, day! O, misery!") always ran into trouble in Rome. In that treatment the story is now sadly outdated. For a matter of gratuitous horror (Francesco Cenci) and outraged innocence driven to crime (Beatrice was fifteen when she took charge of murdering her father, sixteen in the painting long attributed to Guido Reni before her execution) hell gapes, the heavens ring, etc. The Cencis have become rather absurd.

In Stendhal's version they make a brilliant subject of what would now be called existentialist literature, only the work far outranks any modern novel under that heading. As a parable of good and evil, enmeshed with political meanings, it is a striking corollary to *Billy Budd*, only the connection of private with public necessity is more explicit. It might have been still more so. The Captain Vere in this case is the pope, Clement VIII, for Shelley another force of evil, for Stendhal or at least for his narrator a man "kind and merciful," obliged to act against humanity in the interest of higher justice: and it seems to have been true that the Cenci children and their stepmother, all of whom had suffered intolerably from a character whose wickedness was well known, would have been pardoned if another case of patricide had not intervened. What is omitted is that Clement was largely responsible for both the incest and the murder, and less directly so were several of his predecessors, none of whom was known as bad. If Cenci had not bribed them one after another with enormous sums he would have been executed for his crimes long before; Clement had been deafened by cash to many pleas from the agonized family, although he had arranged for one sister to escape through marriage. The fortune that enabled the monster to survive so long had been amassed by his uncle, according to Stendhal his father, Cardinal Cenci, in his capacity as minister of finance under Saint Pius V. Another point in the drama might be Clement's seriousness and ability as a diplomat.

But Stendhal's villain is excellent — a Don Juan he calls him, not in Byron's meaning but the one expounded in the aftermath of the last war by Albert Camus. He had been born in 1527, year of the sack of Rome by the constable of Bourbon, which had left as much moral as material devastation; and had seen the severe inquisition-minded Pius V (who however permitted that colossal graft) impose an inexorable and terror-haunted morality utterly out of the nature of the people. "'Well,' he must have said to himself, 'I am the richest man in Rome, this capital of the world; I will be the boldest too. . . . How can I startle my stupid contemporaries? How can I give myself that keen pleasure of feeling myself different from all this vulgarity?'" There is nothing likable about him; he is not "a man of good company." The Roman Don Juan has no pleasure in human sympathies or "the illusions of a tender heart"; his pleasures must be triumphs; he has no confidant, none of the charms given to the breed by Mozart and Molière. "He spoke only those words that were useful for the *advancement of his aims*" — which were of depravity because he saw no cause for ambition. His one pursuit was novelty of sensation, and he brought to it intellect, singleness of purpose, and strength of passion enough, without the twist, to have made him a famous ruler or the founder of a new heresy. Beatrice the pure and innocent, in her fearful fortitude during the murder and later under the tortures of the Inquisition, and on the scaffold, was plainly her father's daughter.

An item of interest in Stendhal's version of the story, but not in any other, is that when it was announced that the youngest brother, Bernardo, had been pardoned, all the sympathy of the crowd flowed toward him because this was proof of his "grace"; later he was taken up to the scaffold so they thought at first that he would be killed after all and had lost his grace. Another, which the author has his narrator refer to as a "frightful heresy": Cenci told his daughter that the children of such incest were automatically saints, and that all the great saints of the Church had been of such origin. In fact one or two may have been, as it appears, and it might be that Cenci, who built a chapel to Saint Thomas in his palace, was not without some belief in what he said, if he said it. But Stendhal is evidently making fun of his narrator's simplicity, and putting in the villain's mouth a rather profound comment on an aspect of grace in Rome. — The famous portrait is now in the Corsini gallery, opposite the Farnesina. A mass of suffrage for the family is still celebrated every year in the little church near the dilapidated palace.

There was another important execution five months later (February 1600) also under Clement. It was of the philosopher Giordano Bruno, who loathed Aristotle and was burned at the stake in Campo dei Fiori, between the Farnese and the Cancelleria. There is a statue of him there, put up by anticlericals late in the past century, with the strange inscription: "To Bruno the century by him divined here where the pyre burned."

The eyes of Santa Maria Antiqua.

At the edge of the Forum, under the Palatine cliff, in what was perhaps a palace anteroom. Said to have been the earliest Christian church built in a pagan edifice, which seems unlikely, they were springing up everywhere; anyway the later functioning church was cleared out in this century to expose the earlier one with its paintings: a stunning collage, of several hundred years' worth.

All Byzantine eyes have that directness, but there is more in these, from their being just there among the fallen temples and palaces, in the hallucinating Forum light. They do what present-day advertisers would like to: it is a communication, to *you*; you have to go into the walls with them; desperate, breathless transitions are kept alive in their pupils — as if a cat should be walled up in the building of a house and centuries later come out snarling. They begin to come out at you from everywhere. First the long rigid row of Fathers of the Church with Christ at the center, down the left nave; badly damaged but the eyes, or sometimes only one eye or half an eye, are alive. Another is following you from where there seemed no painting at all; then another pair high on your left. No emotion, no personality, only message; of all periods in Western art this is one of greatest communication in face. A Madonna and child stare out at you with the same intensity at the right of the apse, painted before the apse was cut, and flying toward a collision with them an angel of two or three hundred years later, when such eyes were outdated and painted out; the angel is in profile and of great sweetness of line and expression; the truths have unbent, liquefied . . . In the apse an enormous ruined Christ, more eyes, and like worms over the plaster little iron keys to hold it there, crawling over the huge gaunt inchoate face. Eyes of the fifth century, seventh, eighth, tenth; they are alive; they have a right to your memory; they demand it. All the ages of Christianity are to be lived through.

In one of a series of little smudged scenes Christ is carrying the cross — unbearded and with what appears to be short black hair; it is touching to think of the time and effort it took to settle on a likeness. The only one that one can react to as a painting is the crucifixion at the end of the left nave; with Christ not in the loincloth of later times and the spear wound made central, but in a blue garment hanging straight from the shoulders and the arm-line straight across; no body-slump; no pain; the soldiers and the mourning women are rigid too and expressionless, and the hills stylized. But the most affecting is the little triple Madonna on the other side, Elizabeth, Anne, and Mary each with her child — same frontal assault as the Fathers; twelve eyes;

the dreamlike insistence of this triple image pursues you through every other church in Rome.

Beside the little pool, still fresh, of the nymph Jugurtha, where Castor and Pollux watered their horses.

Across the Forum, the church of Saints Cosma and Damiano, twin Arabian physicians martyred under Diocletian; with sixth-century absidal mosaic, only God was originally a hand holding a wreath over Christ's head, the old-man image not having yet developed. The nimbus, borrowed from Apollo and the deified emperors, is as yet given only to Christ, not the saints. The site had previously been that of Galen's house and a meeting place for doctors.

Across the Palatine, the church of Saint Theodore, persecuted under Maximian, at Amasea in Pontus, for having "in his zeal" set fire to the Temple of the Great Mother, Cybele; he was wasting his time; that image could not be defeated. The church was supposed to have been the Temple of Romulus and Remus; mothers were in the habit of bringing sick children there to be cured, and with the marvelous intransigence of Roman custom went on bringing them to the new tenant of the same place, Saint Theodore. From this fact one could deduce a good deal of the essential history of Roman Catholicism, beginning with the inevitable reappearance, after a fairly long struggle to the contrary, of multiple altars.

It is perhaps because they release the mind from absolutes that these continuities are so moving. It is not pomp or corruption but mere history that seems to make Rome the least likely place for conversion in these days, and makes visiting converts always look a little pathetic or absurd.

Conversation with a Roman: "Conversion? You can't be converted to Catholicism. You just start going through all the motions, confession, mass, everything, and the actual process becomes interesting, like any other. It is like making a chair. You become interested in what you are doing." "But in making a chair you would know beforehand that you would have a chair at the end. In this . . ." "You will have a Catholic experience."

You feel the absence in Rome of Saint George and his prototype Perseus. Chivalry could never get anywhere there; it was the Greek popes who promoted Saint George, and it is in Florence that you are suddenly reminded of Perseus. And yet the martyrdom of Saint George, under Diocletian, was of a kind that ought to have appealed to the Romans. He was subjected to awful tortures, during which an angel appeared and took him in his arms, causing the conversion of the Empress Alexandra. A gigantic stone was put on his chest; he was torn by an iron-toothed wheel and spent three days in a burning lime pit; he was made to wear red-hot shoes, and given magic poison, all to no avail, so he finally had to be beheaded. Up to that point it is said that he was still able to overthrow the statues in the Temple of Apollo merely by speaking to them, and to restore the dead to life.

Saint Cecilia, patroness of music, martyred under Marcus Aurelius, was nearly as hard to kill; she survived three days of suffocation in burning steam and other trials of the kind before being beheaded. Her church in Trastevere, possibly on the site of her husband's palace, although a rather forlorn exercise of the baroque inside, is altogether among the more gratifying of the churches that have been processed by almost every century from the fifth to the nineteenth. The statue of her by Stefano Maderno under the altar, lying as she was seen when her coffin was opened in the seventeenth century, hunched up on her side with her long dress bunched around her and the thin mark of the ax around her throat, looks embarrassing enough in the souvenir shops where it is such a favorite but there in its right place seems neither vulgar nor sentimental. The beautiful Roman cantharus serving for a fountain in the courtyard has something to do with the statue's being so improbably genuine in its pathos; it is of a young and gracious girl, who should not have had to suffer so.

Saint Agnes was martyred at the age of thirteen; Saint Pancrazio at fourteen. Both their churches (S. Agnese Fuori le Mura, that is, not the one in Piazza Navona) are of that lyrically accretive kind — like many others but not like the big ones although those represent as long a working of time. There is a simplicity of hoariness in these; things have grown in them and stuck to them as on the shells of very ancient South Sea turtles. Not that S. Agnese, which has its own catacomb far away from the main catacomb area, has really accreted much; it is still largely as it was left by Honorius in the seventh century. Little Saint Pancrazio for all his youth took over after death a hard and not necessarily Christian function; he was supposed to bring down the curse of heaven on perjurers and the most sacred oaths were taken by his grave. His neighborhood is around the Bar Gianicolo, across from the city gate named for him.

There is a fairly full catalog of martyred saints, with data and succulent illustrations of their tortures, around the circular walls of the most Chirico church, Santo Stefano Rotondo, possibly but not probably a transformation of one of the buildings of Nero's food market there; in process of restoration.

One of the chief martyrs under Hadrian was a lady with the same name as his wife, Sabina. Her spacious church on the Aventine among other excellences has columns from a temple there, perhaps of Diana, and the only full set of entirely beautiful church windows in Rome, of selenite. There is also, on top of an oddly sunken ancient column in the church, a plain field rock that the devil threw at Saint Dominic.

Among the thousands of paintings of martyrdoms in the city none is more repellent than Nicholas Poussin's of the disemboweling of Saint Erasmus — in the Vatican Pinacoteca, and in a part of it particularly plush with such scenes, all seventeenth century (the fountain century) as are those in Santo Stefano Rotondo. There are two other saints writhing on a rack nearby, and a crucifixion of Saint Peter, always a risky subject, by Guido Reni. The remarkable fact is that when the Poussin ceases to be a canvas, to be looked at as such, and becomes integrated with the architecture of the time its character changes. The mosaic reproduction of it over an altar in Saint Peter's is strangely impersonal and unprepos-

terous; it is in the spirit of the surrounding interior decoration and only proves that that spirit was much better expressed in sculpture and architectural forms than in painting. About Poussin, of whom it is most uncharacteristic, it only proves that the influence of Rome at the time could lead to some powerful aberrations.

For relief, the tidy little Masolino frescoes of the life of Saint Catherine of Alexandria, in S. Clemente; with their fine strict design, when it was still possible to use the color pink and put the same character in two or three places at once. And the fine twisted monumental and incongruous figure, which seems more a Masaccio, on the outer arch of the same chapel, of Saint Christopher carrying the child Jesus.

Two of the most continually satisfying of the small ancient churches are those of the sister saints, Prassede and Pudenziana, the second perhaps on the ground of their Roman father's house. The famous little chapel lined with ninth-century mosaics in S. Prassede, called "the garden of paradise," is more like a jewel box and more instructive than illuminating. The mosaic that has perhaps the fullest power as art of any in Rome after the absidal one in S. Clemente is in the apse of S. Pudenziana; fifth century; with Christ vivid in gold and the great beast symbols of the evangelists swimming in the bright streaked sky, above Giottesque architecture, and saints. — Lovely comfortable places, that one keeps dropping into again, if they are open or the janitor can be found, as one might stop at a bar or go swimming in the country, for refreshment. But one is much more closely entangled with religion in the big baroque ones, whether grown from an ancient structure or not, especially in the early evening when the pleasure of the promenade-hour life outside has its counterpart in them — S. Andrea della Valle, Gesù, the ss. Apostoli, the Chiesa Nuova. There is a magic for the senses stronger than any Gothic exaltation, and that makes even history weak.

Saints Onofrio; Alessio; Clement.

The first two involve one in the longest journey, of spiritual speculation, which they would not be likely to do if one were not cohabiting with them, in Rome. The virtues of solitude and self-abnegation have never had a more grotesque embodiment; these men were heroes of personal filth and general uselessness, the self-centeredness of the fifth-century Christianity appears in them quite stripped of all the residue of institution and art (Subiaco, Monte Cassino) that permit a certain evasiveness or dishonesty of feeling about Saint Benedict although his impulse was the same; and it is just because they are so stripped, and ugly and ludicrous, that their gradual triumph over one's disgust amounts to a revelation, one of the most crucial in Rome, even if it should be only historical.

Alessio was of "a rich and noble Roman family" (the usual opening of such biographies) with a palace on the Palatine where the church named for him is now — between Sabina and the key-hole of the Knights of Malta. Smitten at an early age with religious fervor and "disgust at the profligate ways of his companions" (also standard) he vowed to dedicate himself to God. In order not to be guilty of disobedience toward his parents (sic) he married the girl they had picked out for him and walked out on them all the same night, and proceeded to wander around the Mediterranean with no money until he was a physical wreck. Then deciding it was better to accept charity from his family than from strangers, he returned to the palace, hardship having made him unrecognizable, and lived as a beggar under a ladder in the cellar for seventeen years, hearing his virgin wife and his family weeping for him upstairs. As he was about to die the family and the pope, who were at mass in Saint Peter's, were struck by an illumination and rushing to the palace cellar found the saint wreathed in heavenly light and holding some kind of paper of identification in his hand. The odd object hanging over his tomb in the church is a piece of the ladder; there is a ninth-century fresco of the legend in the lower church of S. Clemente; the story is untainted by any suggestion of Christian charity.

The story of Onofrio, a Theban monk of the fifth century, is painted in childish pastel with a touch of William Blake in a series of frescoes around the monastery cloister connected with his church. It is a story of grace. As a baby, on the devil's advice, he is held in a fire, which refuses to touch him; eventually one sees him as a little boy monk, offering bread to a painted child Jesus, who accepts it; he refuses to become abbot of the monastery (wicked conniving monks are stock characters in these accounts) and begins instead a long life of solitude in a rather charming desert, with villages in the background, sleeping shepherds, etc. A palm tree and an angel feed him, and every Sunday the angel brings him the Eucharist, leaving him in ecstasy for the rest of the day. He wears a G-string of leaves, grows an immense beard tangled with briars, and is caked with vermin. At the end he is visited by another hermit, Paphnutius, who when Onofrio dies sees his soul depart in the form of a white dove, surrounded by cherubs; the next picture is a very pretty one of lions coming out of the woods to lick the dead saint's feet, and then with their paws helping to bury him. Then the palm tree dies, the fountain fills up, the shack collapses or disappears; Paphnutius goes away.

In the portico outside, opposite the lovely fountain basin under the pines, twin to the Pincio one across the valley but not so disturbed, are inscriptions from Saint Jerome's letters to the virgin Eustochium: "Oh how often when I was alone in the desert in the company of wild beasts and scorpions, half dead from fasts and penances, still I would imagine myself among the delights of Rome and the choruses of dancing girls." Saint Benedict had trouble with sex too and had to roll naked in a thorn bush to get over it; as various angry rationalists have pointed out, human beings could not be impressed long by a conception of religion that proposed to save their souls at the cost of exterminating the species; one might say at the cost of developing such tormented imaginations.

In this century, though we can't tell about the end of it, the bizarre but only refuge of human dignity in the fifth is bound to strike one more sympathetically. The desert must have been lived with as an image for a long time before anyone actually moved to it.

Clement, Bishop of Rome, author of the Epistle to the Corinthians, is exposed behind glass in the only rococo church, the Maddalena, as the central exhibit in a particularly florid necrological collection. The church named for him, seat of the Irish Dominicans, remains in spite of some ugly plaster work upstairs one of Rome's best thrillers: twelfth-century upstairs, with the best mosaic, the best scholar cantorum (carved from fifth-century marble), the best interior forms, the best (almost) disparate ancient columns of different circumferences and stones, a ceiling as bad as Pius IX but which happens not to be; then literally down down down through time made easy (partly through the archaeological initiative of a Prior P. Mullooley) but thrilling nevertheless, through superimposed caverns, the Middle Ages looking like a basement for YMCA theatricals, darkly aflower however with distinguished oddities, down through sounds of trickling water behind republican walls, to where at the bottommost bottom the empire lodged a cell of its disease in the Mithraeum, chamber of the bleeding bull, cold as a butcher's icebox all the year round.

The rites were probably going on there while Clement celebrated others as strange on the other side of town. He was perhaps of the imperial Flavina family and could have had stones and statues as good as any; instead he forced the good Emperor Trajan to send him off to the quarries of the Chersonese (Crimea) where he was followed by many converts and made more with his miracles. The convicts were dying of thirst. Clement prayed, and was led by a lamb to a spot where striking the ground he caused a fountain to appear, more powerful than all the fountains in the villas of emperors. For this he was thrown into the sea with an anchor tied around his neck, but in answer to the prayers of his followers the waters parted, revealing a little temple where the body of the saint was found.

The frescoes of some eight hundred years later, in the lower church, are of another part of the story, along with the ugly tale of Alessio: both are equally of grace. Sisinnius, prefect of Rome, comes to arrest the pope, Clement, while he is celebrating mass but the prefect and his servants are struck blind: in one little Punch-and-Judy scene, smacking of the triumph of God, they are shown dragging away a huge column under the impression that it is the pope. But the more talented painting on that time level is on another wall and seems much restored but the outlines are probably authentic; it is of two symmetrical and intense groups at the right and left of a higher crucifix, toward which the central figure on each side is fiercely pointing. One hears this being much admired for its "modernism" by tourist-students who have learned to look for nothing else; and in fact it might almost suggest Picasso if you forget the idea being pointed to.

S. Maria in Aracoeli: Some objects of superstition affect one most of all by their value for human continuity, so that without literally believing in them one takes parasitical profit from other people's belief. Others are offensive only intellectually. The miracle-working doll here, packed like a papoose in a solid swathing of votive jewels — rings, necklaces, bracelets, earrings — is one that offends more deeply. To see the devotion it inspires can fill one with loathing for every aspect of the religion of Rome. There seems no Catholic dishonesty more guilty than that of intelligent Catholics who separate themselves from this willful infantilism while accepting dogmas that could not have been propagated without it. But what seems dishonest in an Anglo-Saxon mind often does not in an Italian one.

S. Maria del Popolo: First built in 1099 to exorcise the ghost of Nero, who had been blowing around the place for a thousand years. Nero was anti-Christ; in the power and perseverance of that idea one seems to touch the essence of the dramatizations necessary to Catholicism.

S. Francesca Romana: Another place of lazy refreshment, of a worldlier kind; it is only that it is so beautiful, in its complicated grace and elegance on the rim of the Forum — a lake pavilion but the pavilion has also its depths of memory, and this, which used to be called Santa Maria Nuova, is just across from Santa Maria Antiqua with its eyes. One begins in such places to feel an insidious, or it may be only healthy, distrust of the products of thought arrived at in ugliness and frustration; which undermines one's distrust of the thought embodied there. — The saint, born in 1374, is the only other prominent Roman one, with Saint Philip Neri, distinguished in the love and neighbor side of Christianity, and she too was of noble family: the charity and humility of the poor are not legendary material. The legend in this case is a valuable one of good works, inseparable from its other part of ecstatic trances and miracles, and undoubtedly does its work still in the real secret charity of Rome, but the story itself is too theatrical to seem quite pure or be quite pleasing; one effect of it is greatly to increase one's sympathy for Alessio under his ladder, not that contemplation is necessarily any freer of self-dramatization than good works — Saint Francis of Assisi is even farther from the Roman makeup than Saint George.

The life in the churches would surely be quite different if they were something to see from all the way around outside like French churches. It is of their essential character that for the purpose of art they are only a front wall and an interior; everything draws you in, and once in you are not in something of which you have a three-dimensional outside sense. The perfect opposite of them is Bramante's Tempietto.

Palaces: stairs and ceilings.

The stairs are important because they are stone and you apprehend them with your feet. One of the saddest losses in our civilization is of city stairs; we have lost all pedestrian sense of our buildings, except in outmoded ones, tenements and such, where in any case stairs were something to be fitted in like toilets and closets. Otherwise they are where the fire hose is kept; you could easily go through a busy life of extreme ups and downs without knowing what a flight of city stairs looked like. But then we have lost all conviction about our feet even on the horizontal; they are another pair of eyes, which have atrophied. So this is a most important and exciting thing about Roman palaces. It is how you first know and know in the most unforgettable way their great dignity — from the operation of your feet on the hewn rock of their great stairs, worn down to a slope in the middle by all the other pairs of shoes that have worked with yours in the channel's erosion; if there is an elevator you will still have to walk down. The experience contributes more than anything, far more than vision, to one's sense of the outside dimensions of the building, and keeps anything inside from ever looking frivolous although it may be so in itself; whatever is seen, everything is felt against an experience of solid rock, and as related to that unaccustomed use of a part of your body.

We are not used to having the focus of a room over our heads either. Not that it always is; the coffered ceilings and more neutral representational ones keep the upper surface only one of the working elements of the room; even so they involve one's body in an upward relation as strong as the horizontal one and so are vital for one's entering into the full-bodied and extroverted Renaissance use of color. One is apt (looking for walls and canvases) to think too little about the genius that went into avoiding the pitfalls, or updrafts, of this work, especially where the ceiling painting was to predominate; it neither sits on you nor sucks you up, nor in the best of them do you feel that the painting would be easier to look at on the wall. It is done most often by treating the surface in depth as sky, but there are dangers in that too; it must not be too convincing; there must be a basic playfulness, even when the subject, as in a salon of the Palazzo Torlonia, is God the Father — among cupids, garlands, naked ladies, cockleshells; not, presumably, that anybody was trifling with God but the point was to decorate a ceiling. In that case the figure of God is less important than the molding motifs that keep the walls from ending too abruptly; and the walls, there and in the adjoining rooms, are plain, lending majesty to a work (the rooms) in which all that seems to stand out (the ceilings) was done by some fairly run-of-the-mill followers of Raphael. They are comfortable rooms, that is, they invite a high standard of strength and imagination, and make unnecessary the pathological slump we have taken to calling relaxation.

Of course in the Sistine Chapel God is everything, because it is a chapel; but that room is also canyon-shaped and in other ways outside a consideration of living quarters. Nobody could live under a Michelangelo.

The most dangerous playfulness was painted architectural perspectives, especially with marble beside real marble; horrid examples in the Casino Borghese (done over in the eighteenth century) and upstairs in the Farnesina; the rooms are swollen and reeling. Yet the same notion gave Raphael his most impressive distances in the tapestries — bringing in again however the Sistine Chapel, which they were meant for. At their best in private places the painted masonry, vaults, etc. are subtly theatrical and always on the comic side, with among others the serious function of bringing the indoors outdoors and vice versa. It could of course go much farther in a villa, where the painter was in strict collaboration with a landscape artist, and it is only in villas too that the ceiling sky is made vivid.

Villa Madama: In the wide three-part portico designed by Raphael, the quite incredible stuccos of Giovanni da Udine, which could have been done with little difference of technique or vocabulary (gods, nymphs, shells) in the empire. The depths of perspective achieved in an inch of literal depth in the material are astonishing, and can afford to be because this is the end of the garden, or the junction of garden and house. It is kept livable by there being no question of "meanings"; the themes are all a conceit.

In the little parkish Buoncompagni villa, Casino Aurora: Guercino's flying luminous Aurora ceiling — this too an entrance hall, otherwise the terrific soaring effect, the motion of clouds and horses and the clarity of the sky, would have been extreme. In this trade Guercino was perhaps after all a little bit "divine" (the author of that however was speaking of his canvases).

Another Guercino, very different, in the upstairs portico of the Palazzo Spada: the painted sky serving as a clock; through a little opening the sun's rays travel across a geometrical heaven decorated with signs of the zodiac.

In the Farnesina, another flying ceiling, the Constellations, by the architect himself, Peruzzi; stiffly excellent; with Raphael's

bright ocean-blowing Galathea beneath it. The room opens on
the garden on the Tiber side.

But the ceilings in Rome that most change one's life are
Raphael's of Cupid and Psyche, in the other great room of the
Farnesina, and after that, in a different way, the Carracci Bacchus and Ariadne in the Farnese across the river. — It is perhaps
because they help attach one's head to one's shoulders where it
used to belong, as the stairs bring back one's feet, that they are so
moving.

Renaissance mystery no. 1: The love and destruction of antiquity.
You imagine the stones from the ruins being carted across town to
build the Farnese and the Cancelleria, while the architects pore
over Vitruvius and passionately measure whatever ancient walls
and columns and arches they have not yet destroyed. Of all the
images one can find of that age of genius none is more splendid
than this. They could afford their passion for antiquity only because the age was also half criminal: genius with its own native
awful protection against sterility, the crowbar counterpart of
poison in politics, but guaranteeing in this case that they would
never merely copy, no matter how much they did copy. The only
real tyrant was the creative imagination; you needed stone; you
took it where you found it; you tore your love to pieces to have it;
the point was the capacity for love. Of course the priests had been
wrecking things for a long time, in a different spirit, to have stones
for the churches.

Item: The barrel-vault vestibule of the Farnese, by Michelangelo — granite columns on ponderous pedestals, vault coffering
in the style of triumphal arches or the Basilica of Maxentius (or
Saint Peter's) — gives a more accurate impression of ancient
Rome than the Colosseum.

Item: A contemporary epithet for Bramante was the Wrecker. In
drawings made partway through his beginning of the restoration of
Saint Peter's the basilica, which had not been in bad shape before,
looks definitely tragic. There is something of the accomplished
assassin in all the great builders of that time, even sweet-natured

Raphael. Not just what any artist needs; these Roman outrages had certain repercussions.

Bramante

Of all the great makers of Rome he is the least conspicuous, almost as though one knew nothing of Bach except as some haunting majesty and presence in the works of his successors. In the Vatican and Saint Peter's, where he was most active, he breaks into a general shrapnel of research and gossip; other giants in art slide to the front wherever you look for him. Other designs for the basilica, beginning with Raphael's, slide over his (it was to have been "the Pantheon on top of the Basilica of Constantine"); his Greek-cross floor plan alternates with a Latin cross half a dozen times before the building is finished in a flourish of baroque. He is nearly as elusive in the Belvedere Cortile although his designs materialized there, connecting the Vatican with Innocent VIII's little summer palace, but too much happened on top, some of it right away and necessarily; they say he was a bad builder; his foundations were weak. The later clutter of S. Maria del Popolo, although one of the more rewarding clutters, makes it difficult to take in much of Bramante's apse.

But there are three works in Rome, all three compared to those other vast projects in the nature of toys, where the genius in the case can been seen and felt intact. The cylindrical staircase at the end of the Belvedere wing — one of the most beautiful constructions in Rome and not shown to the public; the Tempietto in the court of S. Pietro in Montorio on the Janiculum; the cloister of one of the tiniest churches, S. Maria della Pace.

It is curious that in his earlier work, in Milan, Bramante had had a lively sense of ornamentation, not as added but essential; in these three Roman works the majesty is all of forms; a talented blind person could very likely take in more of the beauty of the staircase than anyone seeing it. The ramp, rather; it was made so the pope could go upstairs in the summer palace on muleback, and from the outside looks like an abandoned grain chute; inside it is nicked, battered, windy, unvisited. The ornament is minimal:

rising orders of capitals, on the Colosseum formula; the simplest
edging to bind the rough brickwork of the floor strip, under a plain
iron railing. The rest is proportion, a balance so delicate of the
parts of the spiral that as you walk up or down or even standing still
you are taken into a development of volumes that seem capable of
turning themselves into their equivalents in music and leaving you
in the air. It seems inevitable but was not; in the imitations the
whole idea becomes an expense and a fanciness; the parts stick;
the flow is lost.

The two other themes are of more obvious classical derivation:
the two-story Roman court, the round temple with a dome suggested by the Pantheon — the Pantheon was as persistent a haunt
as Nero. But this is a new version of the monumental, less ram-
pant, more amused, although the Tempietto marks the spot where
Peter was supposed to have been crucified and the shabby little
yard it is in, which adds so to its toyishness, was to have been fixed
up accordingly. ". . . as nearly pure volume as a Greek temple.
Space, that all-important ingredient of Western architecture,
seems here defeated" (N. Pevsner, *Outline of European Architecture*). Still there is a play of space, strictly calculated for the quality
of Roman light and shadow, in the round portico, with the complexity of the inner wall surface helping to keep the light broken.

The court or square theme seems more peaceful. You are
plunged in repose there, coming in from the beautiful baroque
stage work of the little piazza, built around the facade of the same
church; you have dropped a fearful distance, into pure peace.
That is a complexity too, with the in-sloping pavement of the
court extending the play in depth of the porticoes. The peaceful-
ness, really more a lordly calm, is from the center imposing itself
so unquestionably, as it does also in the staircase and the temple,
and in that sense it seems true that space is not active, as it is in the
piazza outside and would be for Borromini. The terms of definition tend to be reversed, and what is most engrossing is that both
are involved in Saint Peter's. — But these three toys, almost more
beautiful when one is only lying thinking about them in the dark,
are also and more plainly of the world of that forbidding gray

palazzo the Cancelleria, which Bramante may have had nothing to do with but he could have had. It is in his "style," as the Farnese is in Michelangelo's.

There is a curious thing about the Tempietto, or rather the spot it is on. Peter may have been crucified there, there is no proof that he was not. Yet the Romans, who are ready to believe all sorts of miraculous things about both Peter and Paul and worship accordingly, are not interested in this place. They seem not to believe anything about it in spite of the temple. The only possible explanation is that there is no fountain.

There are stories that make Bramante appear rather unpleasant personally, jealous of his supreme position, even mean. Still it was he who appointed Raphael his successor for Saint Peter's.

Raphael
Died aged thirty-seven, of overwork.

In the Vatican, tourists of every nation with their Babeling guides are being squeezed through the Stanze. It is an awful rush, to get your money's worth in paint, philosophy, allegory, and general information; you should be able to recognize every ancient philosopher in the School of Athens (*and* the famous self-portrait) and every poet in Parnassus (and know why Apollo is looking up in that idiotic way instead of so much more handsomely down as he was in the original sketch) and which pope and what pupil and the difference between Prudence and Wisdom. Furthermore the crowds are terrible, you are lucky if you can see anything or get close enough to your own guide to catch one word out of ten of his broken Swedish or whatever he is being paid to talk. Room I: Fire in the Borgo, there really was one, he has put it together with the burning of Troy (Aeneas, Virgil, Rome, very interesting); never mind the rest, not much Raphael there (note portrait of Charlemagne however). Room II: this is the real nut to crack; if there were only the four or rather three main walls, but the lunettes! the ceiling! — almost all Raphael too, the room he did first, before he was all worn out and having to run a factory to fill his orders: Original Sin, the Judgment of Solomon, Temporal and Spiritual Justice, Apollo and Marsyas (Apollo used to be a demon but now you see he is not, it gives you a feeling about the Renaissance), a sibyl showing the Virgin to Augustus, sounds strange but it makes a link, like the Borgo or the School of Athens — you have really got the whole Renaissance right there in a nutshell if you could get it open, architecture too, see the compass and the basilica, everybody studying; they call it a Dispute on the opposite wall but as you can see it is not one at all but the contrary, earth and heaven, the pope and Jesus all in Christian harmony, that's what Apollo and Aristotle meant without knowing it — fine work, splendid design, note the prophets and portraits (Bramante for one, perhaps). Room III: Heliodorus; brilliant work wrapping the Mass at Bolsena (Corpus Domini) around that window, across from Saint Peter in prison and the angel with three different lightings, one two three, two angel, three moon. Room IV: Constantine beating Maxentius up beyond the Foro Italico at the Ponte Milvio but never mind this, Raphael was already dead. Now the loggia, "Raphael's Bible," he had the ideas for it anyway. — Madonnas? no, not here; not many in Rome, different type of work; there was one back in the tapestry room (Madonna of Foligno) along with his Transfiguration with the epileptic boy seeing the whole thing, interesting idea; those were his tapestries (cartoons in London); he was building Saint Peter's too, and a couple of palaces, and a chapel in Santa Maria del Popolo and doing some frescoes for Santa Maria della Pace where Bramante did the cloister but you can't see them now, somebody should put in an electric light but you can't expect them to worry about every single Raphael.

Back in Room III a gentle ravaged guide of indeterminate nationality wedges in with his American charges who have not fully responded to his efforts under the historico-philosophical strain of Room II. Of course there is always the man in the party like the one in the skiing class who wants to be important with the guide and will say something every time, about the design or the idea, something, but on the whole they didn't seem to be looking much, just glancing around not even tired; he did better with them in the Sistine Chapel. His English, however, is not too bad.

"Here we have something different — drama, *action*" — they pick up a little; that was the trouble in the other room, all ideas, no action, and that foolish Apollo with the lute in his lap practically. But there is not much time and there are two other parties at it in the same little room in French and German. "This is a historical scene, a contrast, all action. It refers to Pope Julius II and the enemies of the Church. Heliodorus is sent away from the temple — temple, angel, Heliodorus, being sent away." Hurrying, he scans the nearest faces without really seeing them or wanting to, to see if he has given their money's worth. As a matter of fact Heliodorus is in a ghastly situation, sprawled headlong on the temple steps with a knight on a charger after him and two others, perhaps angels, bearing down on him with scourges and fury in their eyes; he cannot possibly get away, the horse's huge front hoofs are just about to break every bone in his body. The guide is perhaps conscious of a certain discrepancy. He glances back at the picture and then with a sudden strange reflectiveness at a spot of nothing, his mind seeming to have snapped momentarily under the awful burden of his work. "Sent away," he murmurs dreamily. "Yes . . . sent away . . ."

Poor Heliodorus; he took another beating in the factory process; that heaviness in it all, those dull bronze tints never came from Raphael unless he was having a terrible week; as bad in its way as that famous triple lighting in the Peter scene or the lower half of the Transfiguration. One thing you have to say, he had queer taste in pupils, the Giulio Romano touch confuses everything. The Christ, though, with his strange gray cheeks that are not gaunt but almost fat in an unhealthy way, rising in his blowy nightdress with his bare feet dangling, looking up almost at the same angle as Apollo and about as foolishly — that's Raphael, that's what Picasso was not interested in, nor anybody else you'd have cared to know. No *terribiltà*, no torment, no "truth." None of that strong inward *square* feeling that gets you in P. della Francesca (square shoulders, the square regard of truth, sleeping soldiers in a square around the heavy rectangles of Christ's tomb; that's a real Resurrection, "the greatest painting in the world").

Not here. Poor old superficial Raphael-Heliodorus, a decorator, all curves, evasions, obliquities.

Or call it perfection again; worse than the Greeks, although Professor L. who gives courses in the matter in America will tell you Raphael went in for "ideal types" (the tapestries?) according to the professor. The portraits? — ah portraiture, a different problem; still you will observe there are not many wrinkles, it is not real realism. But there are other opinions, libraries full, on all his phases from Perugino to Michelangelo (only Beethoven changed that much and he lived much longer) and on the authenticity or not of every little bit: don't, for instance, bother with anything but the Three Graces in the Cupid and Psyche room (not a room then but an open portico, the end of the garden) that he did for Count Chigi the banker in the Farnesina; they say all the other flesh in the room is too heavy and the sky too flat a blue. That's the kind of order he was filling, all the time. There was a duke up north who had one in, for a portrait or a Madonna or something, and sent his agent down to Rome in a rage early in 1520 to hound and threaten Raphael for being so late with it; he was tired of his excuses; let the pope wait; the duke wanted his money's worth, at once. The agent saw Raphael, and became embarrassed; he wrote daily difficult letters to his employer, suggesting that soft tactics under the circumstances might be more effective than the kind he had been ordered to apply. Raphael himself wrote, gently, promising to finish the work at the first possible moment — it seems he was never angry, nor was anyone else in his presence; he can hardly ever have been alone, there were people around him all the time, bosses and agents and pupils, and he had a strange effect on them, true to the name Raphael, meaning in Hebrew "God heals." Everyone said that, that there was always somehow a great sweetness and harmony around him, in all the fury of the work. But the duke never got his picture. In a week or two, on Good Friday, Raphael was dead.

No tragedy; no "soul." Not a breath of cynicism even, to liven things up; probably he was lucky not to have lasted for the horrors of the sack in '27 when the bottom dropped out of everything, though if he had there would have been a different sequel in art. They called his architecture cold at the time; you can see why in the two tall triangles of the chapel (this also for Chigi) in S. Maria del Popolo. The Jonah there that he did the drawing for is frigid too, is it not? — that is, it misses being a Michelangelo, there is no astonishment in it. He seems not to have had any in his makeup; it is as though he knew no evil. He solves the window problem in the Mass at Bolsena, mystery of the bleeding wafer, by putting some calmly seated officials, one of them glancing out for his portrait, down at the right, as if they were listening to a speech in congress, with the sharp design of their clothes the only emphasis, and across from them a group of women looking after their children: if there were only some stiffness, something the matter with them! — nothing; they are only a marvelous counterdesign, more circular forms, more blocking of color than on the right, and drawn furthermore from a humanity that you would have to call cold, it is so untroubled. There is no mystery in Raphael. There is no pity. It is most strange that he should make you think so much of Virgil, the greatest poet of pity.

No, it is not real realism, not at all. The tapestries are full of grotesques, and of violences held in a weird suspense; the great stone about to crash down on Saint Stephen will never fall although the ideal type holding it has the muscles and rage of a Goliath; the violently conceived gnome of a cripple on the end wall will never be cured by Saint Peter, his deformity belongs with the vista of giant twisted columns such as Bernini would draw on later for his baldachin. Designed for thread, of course, these exaggerations, which would have been horrid in paint with flesh its right color instead of tapestry gray. In that medium nobody could touch him; look at those others in the Hall of Tapestries, by the *school* of Raphael, how crowded and gross in their violences; nobody else had that perfect knack of spacing for loomwork, knew that well what to take away from face and give to draperies (they come out well in the weaver's gilded reds and blues) and architectural forms. These are Raphael's dream book, through a lucky necessity in the art, of symbol and suggestion. His most beautiful Christ figure is the one standing there in the boat, in the marvelous fish haul, a tapestry — his most literal image of Christian serenity, the fish itself being so true a symbol. It is as a child would see it; he has kept that relation to truth, in all the consummate sophistication of his skill: a boat that should be sinking, apostles who should be falling out the way they are bending, the lovely variegated fish and strong reflections making the sea a tumble of brightness but no gleam effects, nothing sensational. It is all natural, beautiful, and quiet, another version of the eyes of his Madonnas or the women on the steps at Bolsena.

Dull; slick; meaningless. It was a meaningless time you might say, in Rome most of all (there was more pity and tragedy in Florence) and Raphael arriving in Rome became its perfect poet. A terribly short time, unfortunately, when love of life and tranquillity of belief and mastery of ancient physical grace (not a discovery anymore, and not yet a boredom) leave the way wide open — for intellect and design. Almost too much intellect in Raphael's case; it was Virgil's trouble too. The Transfiguration — drama! action! — was the worst possible subject for him, in this fast-changing phase anyway; perhaps he could have managed it later. It is really a little debilitating. His instinct had been not to put Apollo in a pose of exaltation either, but then the composition would have been too static; on the whole Parnassus was an embarrassing subject, although he gets around it by a tour de force of design.

But what other, comical heaven in the Farnesina, there he is in glory. Mystery of the time no. 2; real Christ, real pagan gods, myths, gaieties. These people are not serious; you don't know what to make of a mind like Benvenuto Cellini's and here is Raphael at it only not in miniature, fresh from his Madonnas and Bible stories and holy sacraments, covering a whole ceiling and a big one with these wonders of the flesh. Clever old Chigi, knowing just where to go for the greatest and funniest private ceiling in Rome. Nobody else could have done it. Perhaps he did have to relegate some of the brushwork, it is true the Three Graces have a different texture from the rest, but the forms can only be his; nobody again ever had such a touch for every trick of the ceiling trade — ceil-

ings to live with, that is. The Carracci one in the Farnese across
the river is very differently fascinating, daringly lewd for one thing
and of a terrific lushness of artificiality, with its ghostly herms em-
bracing around the corners beside the ponderous bedroom scenes
of the gods. Raphael's room is all an innocence of delight, without
double intent; if Wordsworth had had a comic sense and lived
under that sky he might have imagined such a setting for the unborn soul. A room as astonishing in its way as Room II of the
Stanze and posing every problem that did not; this is household or
really garden theatrics, and all one narrative; the room's architecture is made integral to it, by means of every kind of trick, rope
garlands, fake perspectives, painted canopies tied with little strings
as flooring for the two big Olympus scenes (banquet and council
of the gods). Except there, on the top, the characters are mostly
flying blowing rushing through the sky but with perfect grace on
all their funny errands. The love story has put all heaven in agita-
tion; Venus is hurt; Jove ponders; Mercury whizzes off to tug
Psyche back by the hand — Mercury almost steals the room, especially in one place, flying straight toward you with his arms out;
cupids tumble every which way among the clouds. There is plenty
of room for them to fly in; nothing is crowded, another unique gift
of Raphael's.

Lovely dullness, meaninglessness; wonderful lack of transport,
when life is seen whole and sensuality, tenderness, philosophic reflection are all one gift. The serious problem (Room II, the Disputà) is to make a flat wall look like an apse. — According to
Edgar Wind the Fornarina may not have existed although there
have been many scholarly black eyes over which of several houses
in Rome she lived in; according to everybody the portrait of her in
the Palazzo Corsini with Raphael's signature on the armband is
not of her and not by Raphael although it goes on being so labeled
by the gallery;* perhaps he loved Maria Bibbiena after all although he never got around to marrying her. It seems more likely
that he did not need to love anybody particularly. He was ambitious and frightfully busy and not an artist of temperament — you

---

*Now in Palazzo Barberini; still so labeled.

will never be "moved" by Raphael. He is beyond that; the mystery is never of personal expression.

Yet there is mystery — in Galathea, in the Holy Ghost; most intensely in Room II; it is why he is buried in the Pantheon.

Musco Borghese: the great Titian canvas looks out of place there; you have a tiring relation to it. Nothing in Rome has prepared you to look at paintings in this separate museum way as you would happily in other cities. You feel the suction of the city here more than anywhere, in the negative feeling of the place.

Only two artists stand in that air with any contour, because the city was so much their story: Bernini (1598–1680, from Naples) and Caravaggio (1569–1609, from Lombardy). Young Bernini; apprentice sculptures that seemed so loathsome the first time you saw them and to which eventually you bring back all the delight of his city making; you can never see them again out of that context, and should not. He would never have had such energy anywhere else. Speaking in tonnage it is a very large amount of Rome that brings you back to discover the fire and poetry and diabolical stonecutter's skill in these young extravagances, each one a moment of transition at its highest; young David about to release the sling, biting his lip; young Apollo (Apollo Belvedere thrown out of his classic stance) reaching Daphne as the branches spring from her hair and the roots from her toes and her little mouth has become an O of horror; Proserpine in horror in Pluto's arms, the god's fingers deep in marble flesh at her waist and the other hand making soft indentations in her thigh while the three horrible dog's heads bark; little galloping Louis XIV (a model) all speed, mane, hair.

"Barrocco": a Portuguese word for irregular pearls.

Baroque (Roman): death, wit, ecstasy. The ultimate in personal illumination, turned to the ultimate in stagecraft. How stale and fake and spiritless everything had become before — crushed by Raphael and Michelangelo; hopeless. It must have seemed that there would never be any freshness or new urgency of spirit in art, least of all architecture, again.

A Bernini map of Rome shapes itself for you in Daphne's vanishing toes. — The Triton, and parts of the Palazzo Barberini; Saint Theresa and the angel; down the street from there, the church of S. Andrea in Quirinale; down the street, the portone of the Quirinal; Fountain of the Rivers, and the Moor, Piazza Navona; Rome's two best sculpture angels, in S. Andrea delle Fratte, copies on the Ponte Sant'Angelo; colonnade of Saint Peter's; Scala Regia and other places in the Vatican; baldachin of Saint Peter's; out in the portico, statue of Constantine; subsequently demolished lateral tower on the facade, one of two designed; allegorical figures over arches of central nave, niches, and other works; statue of Saint Longinus under cupola; loggias above; in Chapel of Holy Sacrament, gold ciborium, modeled after Bramante's Tempietto; sunbeam cathedra, black bronze and gold, held up by four enormous doctors of the Church; monument to Urban VIII; skeleton-and-drapery tomb of Alexander VII; outworks of fortress of Castel Sant'Angelo; beginning of Montecitorio; statue of Saint Francesca Romana; elephant with obelisk, Piazza Minerva; busts of Cardinal Scipione Borghese; drawings for Fountain of Trevi; tomb with reclining statue of Ludovica Albertoni, in S. Francesco a Ripa; internal restoration of S. Maria del Popolo, with angels, altars, etc.; subsequently demolished lateral towers on Pantheon, called "the donkey's ears"; in sacristy of S. Maria in Trastevere, scene in relief of dead rising from tombs; etc., etc.

One could make similar maps for Michelangelo, Raphael, Peruzzi, Vignola, Borromini et al., not all so filled in although Michelangelo's is perhaps more so.

Caravaggio had commissions too but what he turned out for the churches was unacceptable half the time. The city is a different kind of story in this case; among all the frescoes wall and ceiling, the stuccos, the mosaics, this is the only artist of interest that Rome (although like most of them he was not Roman, and more of his work is elsewhere) offers to one's attention as an easel painter. Remains interesting even through the present excesses of rediscovery, with attendant publicizing of his luminism, homosexuality, propensity to murder, Trastevere models, flights and arrests

and sorry death of malaria on the beach at Port'Ercole. There is a
kind of somnambulism in all the paintings, round and round an
infatuation with evil, and he painted white amazingly, against his
sinister leaf greens and blood reds — white of the cloth fallen from
Christ's body in the Descent from the Cross (Vatican); white of
the saint's robe and the boy's tunic in the torture of Saint Matthew
(S. Luigi dei Francesi). The grounds are mostly green receding to
pitch or a pitch interior, with the dream or molasses light falling
on some arrested revelation or activity; there is a powerful sensuality of remorse in nearly all of them, calling for more and more
evil, which may fly in on angels' wings. He borrowed a pair of
wings from a friend in Rome for a model, but his angels are never
really held up by theirs; the one holding a palm branch toward
Saint Matthew is under great gymnastic strain to keep from falling
off the edge of a cloud; another there, over the altar, is a Roman
dead-end kid who has just broken through the wall Cocteau-
fashion to confuse the old saint. The Vocation in the same chapel,
probably the finest religious (?) painting of the time in Rome, has
the group of sinners at the table stopped in their tracks in a frozen
dreamy voluptuousness, of good looks and handsome textiles. The
naked torturer on the other wall shames his aged victim by the
vigor of his sadism.

In the Borghese there is a roomful; the most lurid, Mary, Anne,
and child Jesus with a large electrifying snake — one of those the
church rejected, probably not only because of the snake; Jesus is a
daringly handsome naked little boy; the most satisfactory, Nar-
cissus, another Trastevere youth caught up in a murky trance that
is not of self-admiration, with the canvas cut in half by the water-
line; and two other portraits that are very powerful, being outside
the contortions of religion.

Brilliant ravaged half-man, in love with the dramatics of his
states, obsessed with textures as reflections of them. He is a violent
traveler, in life and in Rome; he remains on the edge of the city's
true dynamism, a contributor, caught in the fascination of its un-
holiness. But there is a more general flaw. The strength of his perversity, which kept from anything one can feel as greatness, saved

him from a worse indecency — of all the baroque altar paintings, of the usual torture scenes.

It is the moment of the Cenci trial and the execution of Giordano Bruno. Saint Pius V had done his lurid work on the mind of Rome not long before — a face to remember, long, lean, fanatic, inquisitorial; you see it silver-plated and his hands covered with flesh-colored gloves in his coffin in Santa Maria Maggiore; put him together with Paul V Borghese in the twin chapel, who was pope when Caravaggio died, and you have quite an unbrookable pair. A time, in Rome, of the greatest stagings, the greatest fountains; there was nothing in it for painting — except what Guercino did in the palaces or Pozzo a little later for the ceiling of S. Ignazio, or along the line of violent resistances, and Caravaggio alone succeeded in that. Against the general fervor he created his own more extreme illusionism, in lights, moods, angles, the annihilation of viewing distance; reality, the limited area of it that he was able to see, is brought up against your eyeballs. Among the more hypnotic pieces of it are the snake, a horse's belly (Conversion of Saul), various pieces of cloth red or white, the precise wound in Christ's side with a man's finger on its lip. There is a deep shellac quality; these things glisten. It could all easily have been vulgar if it had not been done with such excellent craft and the real if in the end not very affecting passion there is in Caravaggio — which seems to be more than anything the curiosity of revulsion.

Pietro Cavallini
The Last Judgment, fresco, by Pietro Cavallini, who was actually Roman and had studied with Giotto; in S. Cecilia in Trastevere; ca. 1293, or a year or two before Iacomo Turriti's apse mosaic in S. Maria Maggiore. Cavallini was doing mosaics too, which must have been far greater; there is a row of them left in the tribunal of S. Maria in Trastevere. Most of his work has been hacked up, covered up, lost. Half the fresco is lost, it covered the whole back wall of the church or nearly; now there is only the upstairs half, saved somehow, in what has become the convent oratory. — Permission required. Perhaps that is why hardly anyone comes, although

surely they would anyway if it were not in Rome where there is "too much," "too much else." . . . There would be bus trips, pilgrimages, properly, Cavallini being among the greatest artists of that seething turn of the century. An aged nun takes you up through the freezing stone halls, ringing a little bell to warn the others who must not see you or be seen; you hear the faint rustle and rush of their vanishing along the way.

Christ at the center, between Mary and John the Baptist and the apostles, who are no longer the stark staring slightly crazy ones of the Byzantine mood; they are full-lipped and full-blooded, with rather fleshy faces: strong passionate men engaged in serious work. Crowds of faces, the blessed, just discernible at floor level; the damned are lost, so are the Old and New Testaments on the side walls. Below Christ, the symbols of the Passion. What is breathtaking is the angels' feathers — enormous stylized wings with jagged edges, rose red graduated to paleness, a fantasy in pink ice, with one or two in ice blue; there are heads among them at the top, and lower down bodies with crossed scarves, brightly beaded, luxurious counterpoint in texture to the pink feathers. At bottom right, below where you stand and meant to be way over your head, one angel is floating, most beautiful, sensual, serious, same stunning size of wings and an effect of the biggest airplane.

There are only two other pictures in Rome comparable in scale of achievement to this, Michelangelo's of the same subject and Raphael's Disputà.

"You would have to be always in a gay mood, or at least a healthy one . . ." There is too much. A fatigue that is like a hatred of art, or of any order in human affairs, any effort at reality, rolls down on you from some small mosaic (or suppose it were a large one, of the Tree of Life) or a badly timed glimpse of the Palatine; it is as though all the fountains had gone dry. Or the Tiber. A strange river, in many ways less like water than anything else in Rome, it does nothing for the buildings along it, not like the Seine anyway, no fishermen, no bookstalls; sometimes looking at it from a bridge you feel like a fish staring into a flowerpot, with all the mud it dumps at its mouth it has pushed the shoreline out seven or eight miles since the empire. Oh mud, father mud, to whom the Romans pray. — You go away, for six weeks, six months; anything clear and straight is better: a chalet in Switzerland, a café in Paris, a subway in New York. Or you might at this moment consider retreating from the world.

There is one place where one is likely to consider it at any time. Many places in Rome have a whisper of this, stronger for strong minds than for weak ones; many Christian works of art continue to fulfill at least half of their original function; many that are not Christian corroborate it; many accidents of time and foliage and deliberate works in water lead you to the ocean floor. They are the stroke of an angel's feather past your cheek. In all the precinct of the church of the Santi Quattro Coronati on the Esquiline, up from San Clemente on the way to the Lateran, the angel remains. If you had been there before you would have remembered this and needed to come back although not too soon, perhaps when you were seventy-five years old, and then perhaps would only walk through, not stay any longer than the first time; it would not be necessary. Everything is suitable around it, the shape of the hill, the long upward road with trees, the old brown outer wall of the tribune very big above you from the lower street. The martyrs in question were four Roman soldiers who refused to worship Aesculapius, who has now such a pretty temple in the middle of Rome's only lake, and five sculptors who would not work on his statue; the predominant centuries are fourth and thirteenth. You come in through two forgotten-looking courts, the second with ancient columns around, that having been once included in the church.

The tribune was designed for that extra length and you see right away, inside, that it is too big now, but the main thing is something else, strong and immediate. Not "indefinable" exactly. The old worn-surfaced stone columns have a darkness around them that is threatening here, and the plain surface above with little windows high up is beautiful, in the Cosmedin–Bocca della Verità style but not through being scraped back to a tourist purity as that is. At vespers there may be organ music behind the lattice upstairs in the entrance wall or the nuns singing, not loud. But it is undefinable, after all. You go around looking for objects. There are some but nothing very distinguished, except the dark sixteenth-century wood ceiling given by a king of Portugal, a thing of sobriety and repose after all the gildings and cofferings; torture frescoes in the apse, seventeenth century and as vulgar as all of them. You are alone. The stone of the columns becomes very real, an active force, of thoughtfulness, of a slow unification coming up from the depths of place, that you had been circling and being shyly touched by here or there for so many months.

In the cloister it is sharp and sudden again, a surprise as from the Roman mosaic athletes in the museum up the street. Rain; a dripping in the pool; little trees and plants well cared for; a Cosmatesque band around over the small arcade, not conspicuous. It is one of the smallest cloisters and after Michelangelo's the best, without the variety of columns of the famous ones; these are all identical. In the big squares of the porch above, more plants and some nuns' washing hung out; in a tiny round ruined chapel off the cloister, four chunks of Corinthian cornice hanging in the air, in the dark. It is a place, slowly, of extraordinary joy — temptation? cowardice? fatigue of intellect? You are aware at the same time of the material of the nuns' underwear, the cold in the halls in winter, the supreme selfishness of the abrogation of self. Yet the joy is more if you did not come from any failure and satiety; you were not tired of anything, not possessed or impressed by inadequacies in your own conduct or the world's; your senses were never less tired. Everything is vibrant, and a gladness, of which the form for that little while is the contemplation for the rest of life of one small point in the world's manifestations, to be known without distraction always, until death. You have known the release of the prisoner, from appearances. And if Christ and dogma were to serve for this, would it matter? . . . Whatever matters or happens, you have touched the quietness there is in all Rome, that has been built into it not only by monks and such, by many others too, poets and wonderers, building into the city from their solitudes this solid element, like the stone of its columns, its other permanence. They have walked there, thought, prayed, moved slowly in some small circle till they died and their faces perhaps in stone on the church floors were slowly trodden away, leaving a communal indestructible glory that informs even the marble and the gold.

The big iron key of the Saint Sylvester chapel, back off the outer court, is passed to you through a grille, one of the turning kind to keep the nun behind invisible. The frescoes, of the conversion of Constantine and his apocryphal donation, are among the most exciting Christian wall-works in Rome before Cavallini, whom they antedate by about half a century. Paintings, that is; a few, not many, of the early mosaics are as expert and affecting as this. Freshness of color, strong gestures, a quickness of feeling in every pose and in landscape too, for instance the folding fields leading up to Saint Sylvester in his hermitage, with three messengers kneeling suppliant, and the city profile later, firm and bright in its childlike seriousness, with big puppet heads of the population sticking out of the houses. In the first Constantine, a leper with specks all over his face and hands, blesses the women who are lined up with the tragic strictness of a Greek chorus; dream of Peter and Paul; messengers on hill; Saint Sylvester baptizes Constantine, who is crouched in a little tub with his specks gone; triumphal entry of the saint into the city, with the emperor humble before him. The city is jeweled, or seems so.

The angel accompanies you up the road a little way.

The singing doors of the Lateran Baptistry, bronze, silver, and gold. The custodian begins to swing one shut for you, you wait, there is a little scraping and creaking against the bronze lintel, a long moment of embarrassment, then a slow shriek beginning: oh! it is the spirit of the door, disturbed, having to come like a familiar to its witch. The groan rises, becomes the voice of whole angry generations crying forth out of their death in tremendous unison. The door is vibrating, the note is taken up all through its 750 kilos of valuable mixed metals, no shriek anymore but a loud pure musical note with a slow tremolo, then another, rising, and another, flat and passionless like a boy chorister's but as strong as Church and empire, before the fantastic instrument swings back through a last squeak to silence. Then the right-hand door; again, the slow release, the voice coming from so terribly far and on damp days hardly managing at all, a different pitch this time and an eerie note, which turns at its dying point to an eerier chord, and the old man proud afterward as if the prodigy were his own son: "Vede? Fanno una vera musica." They do indeed. Five or six notes that fill the little place with such glory as art could muster only around the triumph of Christ, painful reluctant voice of time, having to rise to it at the will of any passerby and the mere swing of a door, to sing like a ton's worth of nightingale: I CAME FROM THE BATHS OF CARACALLA!

Michelangelo: Cappella Paolina

Two frescoes: Conversion of Saul and Crucifixion of Peter — done after the Last Judgment and in the narrowing in of the themes from that great synthesis they are like a footnote to it, but they are more. The subjectivity goes further; there is no longer the need of those scatterings. This is the last breaking point of the old Renaissance world with its harmonies and truths outside of any statement. The thick golden diagonal shaft across the Saul fresco, downward from Christ's hand, is the last crack in the classic mold. — The tragic old-man's face of Saul, toppled to the ground and blinded by the revelation of Christ, is a self-portrait, ashen in color and terrible in its agony of vision. The flesh is empty; landscape is empty — a flat blocking out of blues and greens; nothing is real but the face and the shaft linking it to Christ, which the wild escaping horse along the same diagonal is there to emphasize. Some of the old heroism of anatomy remains, but it is a paleness and incidental; the terribiltà is all behind the old man's eyelids; the only limb to be considered as solid is the grotesquely thickened one above, Christ's arm, both prostrating the soul below and providing all the upward power that is the composition's whole undistracted essence.

The work has been called "mannerist," even "bad painting." Caravaggio painted the same two subjects, also on opposing walls, in S. Maria del Popolo, and put more of the surface potentialities of paint into them, along with the general emptiness; you feel the imminence and imminent need here of El Greco, to project the visionary soul with more Venetian art. In Rome the impetus of these last works of Michelangelo's will be all in the "irregular pearls" of architecture, not in painting; and there is still something of the curse of the old sculptor in the wingless angels around Christ, though not in the grouping of the many other figures, whose roughness of texture is imposed by the scale and simplicity of feeling: forms and faces as brilliant in their inner power as those of the Last Judgment but serving a still more personal urgency. Forms and faces as of the Dioscuri on the Capitol, used at their dying point for an explosion of new meanings, and for what is certainly painting and great painting although an epilogue.

An epilogue that will turn to a tidal wave. But the pictures are the end of an autobiography and it is no injustice to them to think of them also as that; there is so much else of Michelangelo that is beyond it. The self-portrait is double, although only the first face has something of the artist's own features: Saul in the anguish of his humility; and Peter the old fisherman, whose last Promethean act is to reject physical suffering. The triangular block of the second composition rests on the point of the boy's arm reaching deep into the stake hole in the ground, directly beneath Peter's head; there is no will anywhere but in the apostle's eyes; everything else moves down toward the hole in the ground, in a pattern relieved only by the spears against the sky at the left, and they are the only horror. They more than the captain ahead are the world, whose meaning the captain, like the huge corresponding figure of a leader at the right, is pointing to — the little pit, the point of the triangle. The hills a flat wash again; sky heavy; a dull mesmerized sorrow weighs on all the scene, all the world and its death, which Peter alone, by the fierce upward hold of his head, escapes. No angels. — Sangallo, first architect of the Palazzo Farnese, designed the chapel, but that is the world that Michelangelo has left, or was never really in; his mystery was always of the soul. He painted no more after this, and only sculpted Pietàs over and over, which were never finished.

A map of Rome, to speak only of Rome, shapes itself behind these two pairs of aged eyes, the Promethean, and the eyes blinded by spiritual light. A map of genius to dwarf every other there, and representing at nearly every point an equally great waste and suffering. The city used every power it had, mental and official, to ruin a great sculptor; the real tragedy seems not the tomb of Julius II but Michelangelo's being in Rome at all; it was the last place to be recalling the death of Savonarola, as the Pauline frescoes so clearly do. He is the king of misfits in art, aptly symbolized by the position of Moses in the miserable wreckage of that project. But it seems there was a deeper wisdom in this cruelty, since Rome gained so much by it, including the Dome, Michelangelo's only finished work after those two paintings.

1) S. Maria della Vittoria; 2) S. Andrea in Quirinale; 3) S. Carlo alle Quattro Fontane; 4) S. Ivo. The last two, Borromini; the first three, all in the same neighborhood. All miniatures of the baroque, among the smallest churches in Rome.

1) Beyond the leather-padded doors, the gaudiest, richest-laden little interior that will ever burst upon you at least in the Western world: silver, gold, marbles (twenty or thirty varieties), crystal, angels, allegories, corpses, Bernini's Saint Theresa amid gold beams and white cloudbanks, sunbeam or Easter-egg mystery of more gold and silver in the tribune, opera boxes filled by sculptured gentlemen observing the ecstasy of the saint, silver bas-relief of the Last Supper below; positively every inch coated with all this stuff. S. Susanna across the street has a far handsomer facade (by Carlo Maderno who did the interior here) but none of the subtlety of luxury within. A jewel-box tumble of riches, but deliberate. The question of approval or not of this Saint Theresa will no doubt continue to rage, and whether Bernini was not too Neapolitan for Rome in general; time was when the piece was considered in dreadful taste and there is certainly some amusement in one's liking it now, but it is hard not to, when its candor is so engaging, its rapture so true to the writings of the mystics, the talent so great and all Rome around to cushion the blow. The smile of the angel

as he poises his golden arrow is one of the best smiles in sculpture.

2) Bernini's purest work, done from scratch and consequently of simpler aesthetic impact than the more common baroque restoration, such as his of S. Maria del Popolo. (Borromini fell down farther than that in doing over the inside of the Lateran.) Stately little facade with semicircular portico. Inside, the oval at its most effective, giving as one comes in a startling impression of classic severity; actually there is an immense amount of ornamentation, absorbed in the forms however. The baroque here is totally unfreakish, without its frequent exaggerations and mistakes, the sculpture is a deep necessity of the architectural composition, integral to its lightness; the upward flight of cherubs in the two cupolas is easy, as of swarms of bees. — You are coming close to Saint Peter's. S. Maria della Vittoria would take you more to Gesù.

3) A very different perfection, by Borromini; one can understand the mutual dislike. Borromini goes deeper into the structure for his motion and lightnesses, making ornament more incidental, or superfluous; there is hardly any in this interior. Two-order facade, with double curve a triumph over the tiny corner space that was available. The richness inside is all of space; it is hard to see what has been done with it, the forms are so intricate; it is a solidified dance — apparently based on two crossed ovals, with a further elaboration at the corners, of twisted ovals. Soup-tureen dome, with light streaming in from the windows of the cupola. It is the building in Rome in which you most feel freed of your own weight. He used the oval in somewhat the same way in S. Agnese in Piazza Navona but not so successfully. — To be considered together with the Quattro Fontane, one of which is embodied in is outer wall.

4) S. Ivo, 1642, in the court of the old university building, the Sapienza, which Borromini had been building for some ten years before starting the chapel. Severe Bramantesque court, permitting the high fantasy of wall and tower, the famous snail tower, at the end. Concave facade, simple at base, rising through increasing complexity, to the explosion of forms (and flames, stone ones) in the six-sided tower. The key to this beautiful enclosure, court and

facade, is the hexagonal interior of the chapel, obscured by a bad later job of decoration but it can be felt just the same. Putting it together with the inside of S. Carlo one arrives at a delightful recognition. The walls are doing just what the palace wall of the Fountain of Trevi does, which is after all also an interior, with the eighty thousand cubic meters of water rushing over it.

The pillars supporting the cupola of Saint Peter's, the only part of the structure surviving from Bramante's plan, cover each the same area as the church of S. Carlo alle Quattro Fontane.

The baldachin over the high altar under the cupola is exactly the height of the Palazzo Farnese (twenty-nine meters).

The arches flanking the central nave are about six feet lower than the obelisk in the square outside.

According to Lanciani, in the 1880s some eight hundred books had been written about the Tiber, and there have probably been quite a few since. Some American archaeologists spent one whole summer paddling down it, over and over, in a collapsible rubber boat.

BESIDE THE PYRAMID

To Ebie and Peter Blume

*A*ND STILL THEY WERE THE same bright, patient stars.
. . . And plunged all noiseless into the deep night."
"Saturn, sleep on! while at thy feet I weep."

It is no small part of the beauty of the so-called Protestant
Cemetery in Rome that Keats is buried there. The word *felicity*
comes to mind around that fact, because it is of that order of experience to be brought up against all the tough intellectual rigor, the
nearly impossible demands of vision and fitness of thought, that
went into his sense of "beauty" and could make it equate with
"truth" — the very opposite of wallowing in facile landscape. Yet
of course there is another fitness in the place having remained as
beautiful as it has in the ordinary meaning, and still another in his
having some rather good company there, though mostly of later
times and on the whole of something less than the genius often
vaguely associated with it. The charm, taking that word too as
deeply as we can manage, of this piece of ground next to Rome's

one pyramid, while enhanced by thoughts of the "truly great," is both more and less than the titillation of looking at tombstones of famous people. Less because there are not so many there, far fewer than of their and other people's infant children. More because the charm is of Rome itself, in its hold on the mind of the world outside Italy.

It is a foreign enclave, of non-Catholics — Germans, Scandinavians, English, Americans, Greeks, Russians — administered by diplomatic representatives of the countries chiefly involved; an exception may have been made now and then but the rule is that Italian Protestants, or agnostics or atheists, are not allowed to be buried there unless married or related to a foreigner. So one might expect a feeling of double alienation, from life and from home, unless with Shelley one were inclined to be "half in love with death, at the thought that one should be buried in so sweet a place," which is taking the matter beyond nationality with rather a vengeance, understandably in his case. But no, although he was right about the quality of the place and would be still by some strange mercy today, it is not like any of that, or need not be. It would be too callow to call the cemetery festive, but gloomless it certainly is, and homeless its dead are not. One might even speak of it as having, as a community shared also by its lovely vegetation and the large colony of cats at the base of the adjacent pyramid, a rare sense of humor. At least it serves as sufficient comment on the outbreak of Thanatology courses and other vulgarities on the subject in our country nowadays, of the Facing the Facts and How to Be Bereaved and Like It categories, rather more horrid than the inhibitions they replace; and yes, toward those embarrassments as in other ways, surely we can imagine this little plot in Rome, unique in the world as it is, as wearing something in the nature of a smile.

Not the "infant's smile" Shelley gave it in *Adonais*, nor quite "the light of laughing flowers" he saw there over the dead. It would be a gentle and generous one, though so many battles have swirled around the spot and the names can't all be of people who were generous and peaceable in life. This quiet garden keeps the dignity of human grief. For the non-Catholic and non-Latin mind it does so far more than the enormous Campo Verano, the regular cemetery of Rome since 1837, out by San Lorenzo Fuori le Mura, quite beautiful too in its setting and planting but where pathos is crushed by the bella figura: the expense, the show, the need to outdo in pomposity of monuments, along with the sorry custom of trying to immortalize the deceased with portraits and photographs, down to the cheapest snapshots of the poor in their little boxes tier on tier in the walls. No bella figura there and there must be many who cannot afford even that. By the Pyramid, there are relatively few pretentious monuments, and probably not many of very poor people either, aside from some of the artists and students and political refugees. By and large the foreign colonies in Rome over the past two hundred years have been something short of indigent.

At the time of Keats's death, in the still sorrowful and resonant little room over Piazza di Spagna, in 1821, there were not many stones or names of any kind in the cemetery. There was no wall around any part of it, then or for another half a century, except the Pyramid and the adjoining section of the Aurelian wall at the top of the slope. It was part of what was called the Agro, the "fields of the Roman people," and looks very rural indeed in engravings of the time, with its small sprinkling of tombstones close to the Pyramid as though for protection from its age and bulk, and ox-cart tracks between the clusters. The trees around appear to be live oaks; the pines and cypresses were planted much later. Protection was needed, and Caius Cestius, he of the Pyramid, dead in 12 B.C., was not always up to the job. Monte Testaccio, down at what is now the other end of the block, the hill formed from debris of ancient potsherds, was a site of all sorts of rowdy goings-on, with drinking places in its caverns. Tombs were sometimes vandalized and funeral groups were apt to be attacked, perhaps less out of Catholic devotion than proprietary feeling about the fields. This is given as the reason for the prohibition of daytime funerals; one burial scene by torchlight, in an etching by Pinelli of 1811, looks more like a witches' Sabbat. Another prohibition may or may not have had to do with a fear of stirring up popular outrage; more likely it reflects the motto of ruling Church circles — *Extra ecclesiam nulla salus.* Until 1870 crosses were forbidden over the graves, as were the word God, quotations from Scripture, or any hint of eternal salvation.

That would have been a plus to Shelley, and no worry to Keats, who in the atrocious misery of his last months, the only months of his life in Rome, yet knew of what kind his salvation would be if any were in the cards: "I think I shall be among the English poets after my death." What pleased him was Joseph Severn's report of the wildflowers, especially violets and daisies, that grew in profusion around the ground. Severn, in his heroic efforts to soothe a mind already close to cracking, from loss and hopelessness and the particular torments of that long dying, would not have mentioned the possible violences at the cemetery, if he knew of them. No other plan was possible in any case. But in that same year an aged English aristocrat, Sir Walter Synnod, who because of his years and social station had special permission to bury his daughter by daylight, had to do it accompanied by a squadron of mounted police, and eight months later he was himself buried by torchlight. As late as 1854 the pastor officiating at the funeral of the Prussian minister's wife had to be rescued from "the rage of the people" (from a pamphlet on the cemetery by Johan Beck-Friis, published in Sweden in 1956).

One likes to think that Keats would have been pleased too to think of the sheep and goats grazing among the graves and the smattering of broken ancient columns, although he had more feeling for plants than for animals, at least large ones — he was all empathy with the cricket, the grasshopper, and the nightingale — and if the herds had been large or regular they would have finished off the daisies. Severn later mentioned them, and they are a pleasant touch in an engraving of 1820, by an English or American artist, who may have invented them for the composition. In any case there was nothing to keep them out. After years of requests and efforts by diplomats, of Prussia, Hanover, and Russia, and the more effective pleas of a Danish prince in the year of Keats's death, the papal secretary of state, Cardinal Consalvi, was still raising obstacles to any demarcation of the ground, and as the great poet he certainly never heard of lay across town in his youth, yearning for the relief of death, the cardinal was giving orders to have six cypresses around a tomb cut down because he thought they spoiled the view of the Pyramid. Keats had been buried three years since, and Shelley two, when in lieu of a fence or wall, a kind of moat was dug around the old part of the cemetery, which came to be known as "the dogs' ditch" from the corpses of dogs and cats that were thrown into it. Not that such as Consalvi were the whole story. As has often been pointed out in this connection, religious intolerance the other way around was rife in England at the time, and on the whole the bosses at the Vatican were anxious to please the English in Italy, in view of all the "gold" they began to spend there after the close of the Napoleonic Wars.

According to Beck-Friis, the records of the cemetery before World War II have been lost. There was fighting nearby when the Allies reached Rome, June 4, 1944, ending the nine months' German occupation, and one is free to imagine that some crackpot bit of looting, Neanderthal or pious, may have been responsible. An earlier memoir by H. Nelson Gay, published in 1913, states that the register of burials did exist at that time, but it must have been rather hit or miss. As far as is known now, the first was of a twenty-five-year-old Oxford student of high degree named Langton, in 1738. Before that, foreign non-Catholics in Rome seem to have been buried wherever a hidden or country spot could be found for the purpose, or else with prostitutes along the Muro Torto, then as now a center of that trade; or they could be sent, if feasible, to the Protestant cemetery in Livorno. The burial that Gay lists as the first was of another young aristocrat, also twenty-five, in 1765. He was Baron George Werpup of Hanover, killed in a fall from his carriage, who grew into something of a legend, as being responsible for the pope's official acknowledgment of the cemetery, in spite of God's exclusion from it; the story is that in his great love of Rome the young man, of enough patrician caste to have such introductions, had been determined to end his days there though no doubt not so soon, and talked the

Holy Father into that much tolerance. The age of twenty-five has a broader poignancy, or jinx, in the place. Keats is often spoken of as having died at twenty-six, perhaps because the mind boggles at the scope of his work and achievement at any such age, but actually was only four months past his twenty-fifth birthday, and the unhappy German poet Wilhelm Waiblinger was also twenty-five when he was buried there in 1830.

Back to the eighteenth century and aristocrats, who either had a monopoly on the ground or were the only ones traveling at the time, there is a Sir James McDonald, Baronet, dead at twenty-four in August 1766; July and August were the lethal months, as Shelley and his wife were to discover with the loss of their child William, through their lingering in the city into that season. But the widespread illusion of Rome as a health center could be dashed at any time, though people clung to it throughout the nineteenth century in spite of all the Daisy Millers. The first American buried in the cemetery was a victim of it — Ruth McEvers (March 1803), "a bride but 18 years of age who like so many others who lie near her, had come to Italy in search of health" (Gay). The Humboldt of the sign near the entrance is not the famous philologist and diplomat, Wilhelm, but his infant son who died in 1803, to be followed shortly by a brother. Altogether, Gay gives the figure of under thirty graves in 1818, when Shelley described the place in a letter to Peacock as the most beautiful and solemn cemetery he had ever seen; from pictures of the time one would guess closer to a hundred.

Among the adults of this company, then and up to the present, Keats is rare, though not alone, in having had next to no firsthand experience of Rome or even acquaintance with it. The voice, the air, the common language of the cemetery — and there is one, beyond all the linguistic divisions commemorated there; the flowers and rambling vines and crooked little paths have their say in it — has for one element a curious reciprocity between people and city, of a kind that occurs nowhere else. Rome knows better than even the best of its cardinals. With all its cruelties, perhaps in part because of them, it has in its depths welcome to spare for whatever fragments of humanity are drawn to it.

This is to speak of an overall charity and grace that everyone feels in the cemetery, no matter how they express it or fail to. It is true of all graveyards that visitors, sightseers, wander more slowly than they are accustomed to, "repressing haste, as too unholy there," but from this one it would be hard to find a person so stupefied as to come away without a mellower sense of life. "Lovely," "moving," "beautiful," "nice," even Shelley's now bygone "sweet" are the common adjectives — all referring to a charmed relaxation of strain around the fact of death and toward those psychologists and others, who would beat our brains out groping for ultimate answers in the absence of religion. Not that groping isn't in order, but the all-day question mark seems a little less useful than the hair shirt, or than Shelley's game of Demogorgon — now you get it, now you don't — as a guide to living. Keats in his genius of sympathy with all that makes up the flow of life, a reason among others for his being so profoundly at home with Shakespeare, said it very well in the famous letter to his brothers on "*Negative Capability*, that is when man is capable of being in uncertainties, Mysteries, doubts, without any irritable reaching after fact and reason. . . ." A sentence liable to be mistaken as crudely antiphilosophical if taken out of the whole context of his work and letters. All it means is that he had Shakespeare's generic *kind* of intelligence, as against the isolated, frameless — therefore un-Miltonic, un-Dantesque — overreaching after the Reason For It All, sure poison to poetry. The key word is *irritable*. In that sense his grave could not be more appropriate.

Yet it will not do to forget something there that he had no part of, and never would have had. A certain seediness tends to attach to foreign colonies anywhere, and more there than in Paris, since the contemporary intellectual demands are less and the tendency for many people is to sink into laziness of one kind or another, via social rounds or wistful learning or *dolce far niente*. This has been true at least throughout the relatively short age of the cemetery. The English and American artists who settled in Rome in the nineteenth century had among other good reasons for it the remarkable quality of the Roman light, also relief from the Anglo-

Saxon civic conscience; they went with a notion of and even a passion for serious work, but not one who remained to be buried
there is of interest now except to the most specialized connoisseur.
The blessings of the city were obvious; the vital drain, from lack of
responsibility except to one's art or some notion of the pleasant
life, has always been more insidious, having to do very deeply with
the matter of vocabulary. The poetic voice of the cemetery veils
more than a diversity of real languages; the pathetic gutlessness
and inaccuracy of most expatriate speech, in any language, are another part of the common bond, for many of the lives in question.
Keats would have fled, we know, long before this could happen to
his tongue or mind. Of those who stayed for good, who really
made Rome their home, the great exceptions on the side of
achievement are scholars, predominantly German or Scandinavian, whose field of interest was centered there, giving their choice
of domicile an overriding sense they couldn't have done without.

On a different level, however, for Keats as for many who were not
permanent residents, there would be a sense of belonging,
through a claim of heritage. Montaigne wrote: "Je savais le
Capitol et son plan avant que je susse le Louvre, et le Tibre avant
la Seine." Chateaubriand some two hundred and fifty years later
dreamed of ending his days, or so he professed momentarily, at
Sant'Onofrio on the Janiculum, near "la chambre où Tasse ex-
pira." And so it went over the centuries; nobody with education
was really an alien there, in one part of their being and for a while.
Young Waiblinger, body and soul at last unable to keep together
after a four-year struggle on what he could earn away from Germany, could nevertheless write in a last letter to his family, for
their or his own consolation: "I die on Roman soil."
    In his case the attachment seems to have been made up of pe-
culiarly fierce and diverse curiosities, and he might or might not
have stayed on into old age; probably not (cf. Lawrence S.
Thompson monograph, 1953). Italy was all the rage in intellectual
Germany at the time, owing in part to new windows opened on
classical and Renaissance art by Winckelmann, but Goethe, who

fanned the fad into a fever, and extended his own stay in Rome by many months until he could feel himself thoroughly reeducated — at the age of forty — could not have stayed longer than that. A striking fact of his Roman journals is that it is only in the first months that he is really open to the sights of the city; in the second half he has drawn into his own states of mind in regard to them, and a few years later we find him uninterested in being in Italy at all. All that he can acquire there has already been made part of himself, and to have that book reopened by the burial there of his only son in 1830, the same year as poor Waiblinger — a son furthermore who was neither a poet nor apparently very educable, though he was making his first visit to Rome at just the age when his father had — must have been a sad twist of irony.

In that case only a crowning one. The son, August, only survivor past infancy of five children, was seventeen before Goethe got around to marrying his mother, in gratitude, as the story goes, for her staunch behavior during the occupation of Weimar by the French troops, after the Battle of Jena. The aging young man seems to have been a fairly good secretary and accountant for his father, although heavy on the bottle, but any slim paternal hope there may have been that his mind would expand in Rome was dashed by his death, within three weeks, of smallpox. There must have been a little such hope, since Goethe *père*, then eighty, sent him off accompanied by the great Winckelmann, but the two quarreled and parted before reaching the border. The monument in this instance is more admirable than the life, with its bas-relief head by the famous sculptor Thorwaldsen looking quite imperial, although its model had been named for a mere duke and his liver was reported after the autopsy to be five times normal size, from drinking. Another version of the autopsy is that it revealed deformations of the brain, but both stories could be slander, and whoever did autopsies at the time may have been no more competent to judge a healthy brain than the best-intentioned doctors were in dealing with, or even diagnosing, Keats's TB. What is most arresting about the stone is that the person in question is identified only as Goethe's son, in Latin, with no first name. A further

Goethe connection nearby is August Kestner (1854), diplomat and son of the Lotte of *Werther* renown.

Rome was a home of the mind to all these people, probably even to August Goethe, as it was to the world — at least the world of the more or less privileged, and of the West, say from Jerusalem to Boston and Philadelphia and eventually San Francisco. Classical education had given it to them, as an extension of their living quarters, and a very real one; the experience of being there would be fifty-fifty discovery and recognition.

For actual living, insofar as he had any gift for that, Shelley was more comfortable in other parts of Italy. One can't imagine him settled in Rome, or anywhere else for that matter, yet one feels his memory far from *dépaysé* up against the old wall where his ashes — not his heart as many have been led to think by the words Cor Cordium on the stone — ended up after the cremation on the beach near Viareggio. He is rightfully there, and Rome had the right to receive him, more specifically than by the somewhat abstract justice of all the earth belonging to all people. *Prometheus Unbound*, high authorities to the contrary notwithstanding, is very far from his best poetry but was certainly one of his greatest efforts, in collaboration with — that is not stretching much — what were then the very lonely and overgrown ruins of the Baths of Caracalla. The "vastness" that so worked on him, and on Goethe, was of the time; the French Revolution and Napoleon have their part in the underlying craving and image, meat and drink to Shelley and which Keats had the sense to resist. Nowadays we don't think of using the word *vast* for the ocean, still less, to put it mildly, for the Colosseum; only the universe qualifies now, or a new variety of canned olives. Another Shelley word no longer with us and never much with Keats is *sublime*. But all the vocabulary of his letter to Peacock on those baths tells the nature of his inspiration there, and something of the nature of his failure in it: steep mountains, immense labyrinth, pinnacles and masses, immensity, immense, chasm, enormous, lofty crags, peaks, vast desolation; ending with: "Come to Rome. It is a scene by which expression is overpowered; which words cannot convey." They couldn't and didn't, for him,

but it was at least true that for his time, and his world-weary youth
and bent of mind in his time, Rome and only Rome did provide
the vastness in works in stone and excesses of history that might
serve as stimulus and setting for the farthest flaunting of the
human spirit, in scorn of every fetter and pettiness.

Not a bad idea; it only made for poor poetry and worse, or no,
politics of a kind needed to implement any such ideal. Nobody
has expressed any opinion of Shelley since his death without getting into a hornet's nest; it can't be helped. The champions of
Prometheus Unbound would have it that failure to admire has got
to be a sign of our own inadequacies. That is asking for it; they
have got to be secret messiah-bugs, or never have breathed outside
a library, to so mistake the intention for the deed. The deed as poetry. Those endless pages are one of the great white elephants of
English literature, to be read, if they ever are outside the classroom or the addict's den, only because their author did far better
on other occasions, not many but a few. Keats was terribly right, if
courteous in his censure. But hush, this is a cemetery. He did do
far better and that is why Severn's painting of him hard at work,
that is gazing easel-ward, among the ruins, without a thought for
vipers or malaria or any human vulnerability in spite of all the personal disasters already in his wake, can after all affect us, as his
grave does. An extra fact about that, far from the key but still an
important one for these days of "vast" willful ignorance — yes,
here the word is all right — is that he was hard at work and had
been all his life, with time out for one other sublimity but not
much for food; his classical education was of the best, and his
reading and reading habits seem to have been prodigious, perhaps
more than Keats's. This tends to be forgotten by some of his
would-be emulators on the Love and Liberty fronts.

Those peaks and chasms were not Browning's Rome or what
he made of it all, and would never have been Keats's. But they too
knew their way around there, from long back. It is hard to take in,
given Keats's age and the grueling years he put in on medical
studies, how it was possible for him to have read as much and as
deeply as he had. His powers of absorption, which would have

been of little use without equally strong habits of work, were clearly abnormal if the word means anything. The autopsy report in his case refers to lungs, not deformations of the brain, but that organ must have had something unusual about it, of a beneficent if not blessed kind. Evidently, in the short time he had had, he had exposed himself much less to history than to literature including classical mythology, but that would do for a start and a very good start in Rome. Among the various *ifs* of his career that it is futile to speculate on is what he would have made of a healthy experience of the city, long enough for him to readjust the literary connotations and grow under that influence as he had under every other. It would have been nothing like the same exposure for Goethe, or Shelley either, that's certain, but then Keats was not like anyone else in anything; the charm and goodness of his nature alone would have set him apart, even without poetry, but for him there could be no such without. He had defined his life and it was that, though he would say of Fanny Brawne toward the end, "O that I could be buried near where she lives."

There was no time; he had really only the Rome in his head to be buried in. Few artists have been as lucky as he in their eventual biographers, notably for our period, in English, Bate, Gittings, and Ward. After their unusually heartfelt as well as thorough works, nothing remains to be said about the ghastly sea voyage with Severn to Naples, the further wretched days of quarantine there when he tried to divert the company with talk of the "classic Scenes he knew so well," the slow carriage journey, and the room in Rome. Somehow he lasted there, unwillingly since all hope was gone, just over three months. So was fulfilled his "languishment / For skies Italian" of three years earlier. The sad travelers passed the Colosseum on their way into the city, but that seems to have been Keats's only sight of it, and all he could know of Saint Peter's was the view of the dome from the top of the Spanish Steps. In the beginning some walks, in the near vicinity of Piazza di Spagna, and even a few slow horseback rides, were still possible, but although he would not let his engaging humor die and remained good company as long as he could, he was yearning for laudanum, not education. What he did see of the city that was big compared to some periods in the Middle Ages but tiny in the present-day scale — with a population of about 130,000 — was a compound of beauty and decay that to many visitors was more depressing than uplifting. Oppression lay heavy on this Rome of Pius VII, though it is strange to find the word *monotonous* used by foreign observers for the life of the Roman people; but the large foreign colonies knew those people only as servants. Their own great poet, Belli, was to give a very different view of them. He was there, going on thirty, and could have regaled Keats with a most un-English kind of wit and class antagonism if he had ever heard of him, and if they had had any language to converse in.

The Caffé Greco on Via Condotti, scarcely two hundred yards from the door on Piazza di Spagna, is about the same age as the cemetery and has had many of the same clientele. Indeed it had and still has in one or two respects something of the same atmosphere — of a pleasantly relaxed welcome transcending generations, without strain, and of privacy without loneliness. Accounts of the café's history have it that "Keats and Shelley" were often there. The coupling of the names, source of schoolroom gags of the Brian-and-Kelley-and-Sheets type as long as such poetry was taught, is by now too ingrained to be stopped — as if one should try to separate Sodom and Gomorrha or Scylla and Charybdis; nobody says Shakespeare, Spenser, Milton, Dante, *and* anybody, so the meaning must be that it takes two of these, three with Byron, to make a whole poet. But forgetting that, the statement cannot be accurate with regard to Keats. He was far too ill, though he may have gone once or twice in the early weeks. The café was a favorite place of foreign artists and Shelley probably went there occasionally, as Browning no doubt did more often, with his friends the W. W. Storys and others; later the roster of celebrities came to include Buffalo Bill, who was graciously amazed to see the riders he had brought with him equaled at their own tricks by cowboys on the estate of Prince Gaetani.

The only princely family, a then upstart one, that appears in the Keats story is as unpleasant as their name has remained ever since. To be sure their action in that case was only in what they considered the normal run of business, not a special and deliberate wickedness, but they cannot have failed to know that the young man involved was a poet, and dying. They were the Torlonias, immortalized over a century later by Ignazio Silone, in *Fontamara*, as the vicious landowners of his native countryside. Closer to Keats's time they were noted by Stendhal as bankers, making huge profits through extortionate rates of exchange from the English in Rome. Their dealings with poor Severn, at his wits' ends for money and trying to keep the fact from his friend, are told in the biographies; the Torlonias did nothing either technically wrong or humanly right in the affair, and on that latter score would seem to have been true to their history ever since.

The house on Piazza di Spagna, of the eighteenth century and probably of the same date as the adjacent stairs built by the French, was bought early in this century by public subscription, through the efforts of Lord Rennell of Rodd and others including a number of English and American writers. Its third floor, second by European counting, where Keats died, was officially opened as the Keats-Shelley Memorial in 1909. It is really a little library and museum of the English Romantic movement in general, but not many people stay to read, and an occasional American tourist will wander up who has never heard the two names; when the *guardiano* patiently explains that they were two young English poets who were buried in Rome a long time ago, they say "Oh" and go away. The bare little corner room, of the rosetted ceiling, is the one, for those who do know; it is a little Gettysburg of the history of poetry, and a conspicuous fact, as on the world's practical battlefields, is the number of people who have been moved to tears by it, however rarely they may have been anywhere else. Sinclair Lewis confessed to being one of those; one would not have expected it from the author of *Babbitt*, but he was a disturbed and complicated character, and "Bright star, would I were steadfast as thou art," or almost any line from the three great odes, do in that place put a person's frailties up for sale. The legend on Keats's gravestone, beginning "Here lies all that was mortal of a young

English poet," seems there more than ever a travesty, intended though it was, in the first disarray of sorrow, as an act of friendship. The key words of that inscription — "in the bitterness of his heart / at the malicious power of his enemies" — reflect the disease, not the man, still less anything at all of the poet. There are no such words among those that crowd on the mind in the small room, as they do, from one of the most radiantly simple vocabularies ever put together in English. ". . . keen, fitful gusts . . ." "while thy hook / spares the next swath . . ." "with patient look, / Thou watchest the last oozings hours by hours . . ." "the small gnats mourn / Among the river-sallows . . ." Those *hours* in the plural — who else would have done it? And the line Robert Frost would borrow from: "And I have many miles on foot to fare." One of the words is not Keats's own but from his young English doctor there, kind if incompetent, who spoke of him repeatedly as "noble."

In some respects his memory is better off in the cemetery than in the apartment now. The Barcaccia fountain that it pleased him to hear under his window cannot be heard for the traffic or often seen for the crowd of idle or just weary young, spillover from the steps, packed around it eating lunch or cooling their feet. Horses and carriages must have made other pleasant sounds outside the window, though muted by mud; the piazza is such a tourist center now, and the stairs up to Trinità dei Monti had been such an elegance for quite a while then, it is odd to think of its having been left uncobbled, whether to spite the French or just because it was out of the way — not to the English though; it was their central hangout. A more practical question is how the apartment was heated. There seem to have been sunny days, while Keats was still ambulatory, to justify the great English dream of sunny Italy as the cure for all that ailed their bodies or minds, but the thought of a Roman winter as TB treatment is bound to appall anyone who has shivered through one in good health. Of course it was too late anyway; he could as well have died in Happy England among many friends instead of in a foreign place with a single one, and only Rome would have been the loser. No, Severn would have been that too, though he was half dead himself from the strain by the end.

The museum had to take down its plaque and go secretive, like much of the city, during the nine months of German occupation in 1943–44. At night people would run for safety over the rooftops and many were hidden in houses in the neighborhood. Signora Vera Cacciatore, curator for several decades, has written about those vicissitudes in a pamphlet on the house, but not about her own and her husband's courage in protecting the valuable collection of manuscripts, letters, prints, etc. that could never have been brought together again, nor about one of the more ironic episodes of the period. The main treasures of the place were sent in two or three boxes for safekeeping, along with objects from other museums, to, of all places, the abbey of Monte Cassino, shortly to be one of the most totally pulverized buildings in Italy. A friendly priest, broad-minded or who had not read much Shelley, rescued the boxes at the eleventh hour and brought them back, riding on a cart attached to the retreating Hermann Goering division. Immediately after the Allied entry the night of June 4–5, the identity of the building was restored and literary-minded English and Americans in uniform, and perhaps some who had never read much but felt drawn to a reminder of civilization at that juncture, began turning up. One who touched Signora Cacciatore particularly was an American who described himself as a student, who was assigned with another soldier to guard the house the first night. "He asked whether he might be allowed to go alone for one moment into the room where Keats died. He handed his rifle to his companion and, with a candle, went up the dark stairways and made his way round the dark rooms once occupied by Keats and Severn. . . ." Tears showed behind his glasses afterward, understandably, whether he had come via Naples or Anzio.

They were among the lucky. Across the busy modern street from the newer end of the Cemetery of the Pyramid as it is sometimes called — the negative non-Catholic makes a feeble and somehow disgruntling name for it — there is a much newer and more orderly one, agreeably planted too but with stones all alike and in rows in the fashion of military cemeteries. It is the English one, including Australians, New Zealanders, and others, for the area around Rome, part of the price of that Liberation; the Americans killed in the same push were transported to a much bigger general graveyard elsewhere. But there are stones and names of a few other soldiers nearby, in the old place; they were the foreign Garibaldini, dead in the defense of the Roman Republic in 1849 or the late expeditions trying to recapture Rome in the '60s.

Now people sometimes scurry for refuge for a different reason to the downstairs hall of the house on Piazza di Spagna. There are police roundups on the steps now and then, aimed at drug business or any selling without a license, so a good many run till it blows over. Some will be Italian, but more are young foreigners, from the self-appointed Lower Depths of our society. The signora takes a charitable and motherly view of them on the whole; they have caused her no trouble; and it rather pleases her, perhaps because any literary recognition is better than none, that so many of the other young people who actually go up the stairs are above all entranced by mementoes of William Godwin (*Political Justice*, free love; "Godwin-perfectability" as Keats put it), his daughter Mary Shelley (*Frankenstein*) and her mother, Mary Wollstonecraft (*Vindication of the Rights of Woman*). For sex mores, Shelley's "Epipsychidion" would be timely too, leaving out the brainy side of bed-hopping, but that would require opening a book — inadvisable: it might reveal what a disagreeable hypocrite and money-grubber Godwin was, for instance. For sweet illusion's sake it is better for all this stuff, along with Byron's and Shelley's revolutionary and libertarian outpourings, to be more heard about than read, though it would be interesting to see what tags and scraps of the political notions of those well-heeled rebels would fit into the lowest-level current bombast of our maniacs of social protest, the kidnappers et al., if they were only larded with scatology and obscenity every few words. True, tyranny for a Greece under the Turks or Venice and Lombardy under the Austrians, like social injustice in the England of the idiot George III, had forms with only the shakiest parallels in industrial countries today, though the crimes of rulers may be as bad. The ancient Greeks those

liberty-lovers loved would not have thought their innocence ex-
cusable, but some of it was; nobody in 1820, least of all poets, was
foreseeing the ghastly turnabout of Liberty and Social Justice, to
use the Romantic capitals, brought on by the Russian Revolution;
what does amaze is that the poets in question had learned nothing
from the French Revolution.

Byron saved himself from insipidity by turning to satire, and
being quite good at it. Shelley, as Santayana wrote, was inedu-
cable, "impervious to experience . . . Being incapable of understanding reality, he revelled in creating world after world in idea"
and if met by opposition was outraged and "cried aloud for liberty
and justice." Santayana grants him genius, even sees this strange
imperviousness as a condition of its particular kind, and so perhaps would have included the rest of the same syndrome, an identical procedure in love, of which Montaigne long before had
written differently — it was not an invention of Shelley's: "Between ourselves I have constantly observed that there are two
things which, strange to say, always go together: super-celestial
feeling and subterranean morals. Such as dwell on the soul apart
from the body design to get beyond themselves and escape from
humanity. It is folly; instead of transforming themselves into angels they transform themselves into beasts."

One comes to feel there are two worlds up there in the Keats-
Severn rooms, among the prints and framed letters and leather
bindings — "O world! o life! o time!" versus ". . . if a sparrow
comes before my window I take part in its existence and pick
about the gravel." But that is a bombastic thought, something less
than half true. One unifying element, whatever the term Romantic for that period in poetry really means, is a common and
peculiar intimacy with death. Something aside from all biographical facts; not Homeric; not that of people acquainted with plague
or Hitler's camps or massive assaults on life; not chivalric; not
quite like any other period in literature. In Shelley's case the
nearest to it is the kind of remark heard sometimes now from
among the more desperate and degraded young. "Death might be
a good trip." But Keats too, though so differently, seems to have

been born into a loneliness somehow without antecedents, all
sorts of good times and better didn't keep death from being half a
friend, as against "the immortal sickness which kills not." Precisely
in time for them, the mold had cracked, and they were the ones
endowed enough to know it. Of course it is always cracking in one
way or another, but more often in ways that produce, instead of
poets, "mock lyrists, large self-worshippers . . . and careless Hec-
torers in proud, bad verse." It must have been some such background upheaval that gave both Keats and Shelley such ecstatic
youthfulness in joy, as though they were the first ever to have seen
sunlight on the sea, and in melancholy so prematurely old a view
of "darkness, death and darkness," "where black gates were shut
against the sunrise evermore."

The funeral, on February 26, was held at or sometime around dawn;
that was sometimes permitted. The little group and the minister
were all English. It is rather a long way from the house; the carriages
would have started out in the dark, through many dismal streets,
and probably nobody was in a mood to care that Saint Paul passed
by the Pyramid when it was brand-new, on the way to his be-
heading, as Paul that day can hardly have cared what sort of vulgar
new shape of vanity it was. He wouldn't have seen the Aurelian wall,
with the gate the coffin vehicle and the others went through that
morning in 1821; that didn't appear until the third century, when
there began to be a menace from northern people the Romans
called barbarians; and the outer facade of the gate that we see now
was put on still later, under Honorius in the fifth century. But it was
all old and fine enough to provide the best kind of custody, and pos-
terity, whatever its platitudes, would take care of the book reviewers.
It has only not cared or dared to have Keats's inscription changed,
the stone replaced if necessary, and there is no conceivable reason
for that not to be done. The distortion of his image has been made a
sacred cow by nothing but duration, and we have to trust there will
be at least as much of that in store to sanctify the correction.
    Severn and Charles Brown who collaborated in the extra words
came to have bitter compunction about it and wished to have

them removed. Keats wanted to be past the need or confinement of a name and that at least was respected; his name is not on his stone, only on Severn's put beside it so many years later, as his friend, with the painter's adored two-year-old son, dead from an absurd accident in his crib, between them. The lyre Severn designed for Keats's tomb, with half its strings missing as a sign of the unfinished life — as the Humboldts had set up broken stubs of columns by their small children's graves — is not intrusive. But for words there should obviously be none but the strangely simple ones he requested, which are only as modest as a person of great gift and soul and knowing his worth, unless nothing has any, should be: *Here lies one whose name was writ in water.*

Shelley is generally said to have been a charmer, in friendship and society as in his aberrant love affairs, and he was indeed gracious toward the poet with whom he shares the chief glory of the cemetery. In a letter referring to his invitation to Keats to be his guest in Pisa, when he knew how ill he was and that everyone thought the only hope was Italy, he had written his well-known comment: "I am aware, indeed, in part that I am nourishing a rival who will far surpass me; and this is an additional motive and will be an added pleasure." It was generous. He liked being that, not counting tradesmen in the human picture, mainly doing evil through obtuseness about some obvious facts of life, sexual and other; one such fact was that Keats was never at ease in his company. To that precise mind and rigorous heart, the verbalizings must have seemed as sloppy as the life, the charm finally wearisome. It would have been the perfection of agony in his dying to be beholden to that tormented household.

The discomfort would be far more than intellectual, but strong that way too. Keats was himself, as far as might be compatible with poetry, of those to whom "the miseries of the world / Are misery, and will not let them rest," a tribe never to be confused with "fanatics," who "weave a paradise for a sect." "Only the dreamer evenoms all his days" — and the days of those closest to him. Yet his new volume *Lamia*, the pages turned back to "The Eve of St. Agnes," was one of two books found in Shelley's pockets when the body washed up on shore the next year — the other was a volume of Sophocles — and *Adonais* is perhaps Shelley at his best, though interminable and with few single lines as good as those leading up to the "pestilence-stricken multitudes" of the "Ode to the West Wind." It more than atones for his skylark, but then Keats had poems to live down too and succeeded even less, if less pretentiously, in any long one, though he was coming close to mastery of the form in the second *Hyperion*: a nearly insuperable business, without the dramatist's or storyteller's art and with traditional stuff of the epic gone, to be replaced from scratch or Greek mythology.

As tribute to Keats, *Adonais* is more skittish, even without Shelley's letter to Byron apologizing for having perhaps overrated the dead poet's talents and explaining on what grounds, of sympathy in his mistreatment by the press, he had been so carried away. On that score he had reason to feel a passionate fraternity, but it was with far deeper reference that he had written, as his widow Mary mourned, "his very own elegy." The chronic obtuseness is there, about Keats's true nature and strength, and the Doric variant of the spelling of Adonis gives a remove from common associations with that beautiful youth more needed for a self-image than an objective one. The Adonis associations per se are, except for the Death and Resurrection theme, much more in line with his own character, of the two: being fought over by two goddesses, one of them Aphrodite; death wish versus voluptuous amour; the ritual of the young man's image being thrown into the sea, and so on. A skillful elegy it is nonetheless, though far from comparable to *Lycidas* in its form in English, and although this is a triviality as against its impact, it speaks well for certain basic decencies, along with the lasting attainments, of the Romantic movement. Even Byron, vile about Keats, was up to some decent fits of loyal rage concerning Shelley — "hooted from his country like a mad dog for questioning a dogma"; which was a fashionable stance and not quite the whole story, but was close enough to do them both credit.

The irony of Shelley's dying so soon after seems slight; death at sea was suitable for him, and surely the time of it suited him. He too has a stone to one of his children, the little boy William, beside his, and the year-old Clara had died in Italy; so had Byron's and Claire's beautiful five-year-old daughter Allegra to whom Shelley had been attached, victim of a father's self-infatuation, as those other children were not. That was not Shelley's vice; self-indulgence and self-deception were and they figure in his own children's deaths. However, there are many children of conventional parents in the cemetery and if one can speak of murder, especially in regard to Clara and Allegra, it is only in the sense of lethal conflict of interest. Before that for Shelley there had been the suicide of his first wife, "poor Harriet" as we have come to think of her, who would have Mark Twain among the knights of her memory eventually, and the other suicide, of Fanny Imlay, and God knows what and what deaths in Naples, behind the so-called Hoppner scandal. Beyond the general Romantic familiarity with death, at the age of nearly thirty he was terribly familiar with the real thing, as Keats was from a quite different process — of nursing his dying brother Tom — and ready for it in soul, as Keats was only because his lungs were destroyed. One was beginning, the other burned out. But they are companions in one extraordinary fact, of other companionship. Edward Trelawny, who was to survive Shelley by fifty-nine years, as Severn survived Keats by fifty-eight, and who burned his hand in connection with the funeral pyre though perhaps not quite as the legend has it, has the neighboring stone.

Already in 1822 what is called the "antique" part of the cemetery, where Keats was interred, was closed for any more graves except by very special permission, so Shelley's ashes were placed, five months after the burning of the beach, in the new part; a consular official, Mr. Freeborn, had had to keep them quite a while in a cellar at his office, while he waited to come across an English minister kind enough to officiate for an atheist. Trelawny arrived in Rome soon after, disliked the spot as being in a crowd of the nondescript, and had them moved to where they are now, in an embrasure of the old wall at the top of the hill. He first meant to have inscribed on the stone an epitaph in Latin by Leigh Hunt but changed his mind in favor of the not much more appropriate lines from *The Tempest*, "Nothing of him that doth fade . . ." etc., which are not exactly *sub specie aeternitatis* since everybody knows Ariel is speaking there of a pretended, not a real death; but perhaps Shelley would have liked that. In larger letters, under the poet's name, is the baffling COR CORDIUM, endlessly referred to but that seems unidentified as to source, unless Hunt made it up. Trelawny paid for the plot, later a cause of dispute between heirs of both, and installed his own blank stone, mystification of tourists until nearly the end of the century. An odd aspect of both these sets of associated graves is that neither Severn nor Trelawny was among the older or closer friends of the poet they chose a long lifetime later to be buried beside. Severn was hardly more than an acquaintance of Keats's when they set out for Italy, though as a serious artist himself he was worthy of the intensities of the ensuing months — some of the friends back in England didn't think so — and must have come to feel them as the crux of his own life; whatever Mrs. Severn thought of it, she was buried earlier in Marseilles. Trelawny, the outgoing cheerful buccaneer, adventurer, no artist but sensitive to Shelley's mental stimulation and perhaps more as they say now lifestyle, had known him only about six months, but for him too it was a high point of life that no number of amorous and other affairs would ever beat.

A tangle of legend and conflicting stories soon grew up around the events preceding Shelley's burial, and persists; not that it matters except as a sample of the waywardness of human records and memory, especially under the seduction of big names. It is often heard that Byron burned the body on the beach, and it is true that he was there, and at the same rite for Shelley's friend and comariner Williams the day before, along with Leigh Hunt who had just arrived in Italy and various Italian officials and policemen to keep back curious onlookers, but it was Trelawny who arranged everything; evidently about that he can be believed. The third corpse from the boat, of the hired eighteen-year-old English boy, was not burned but buried in quicklime on the beach, as the others were too for five weeks before the burning; this was according to sanitary regulations, based on extraordinary dread of contamination from ships, very properly, as Severn's account among others of the plague in Rome in 1837 makes horribly clear. So far the stories jibe, except as to the exact places involved. The onlookers are described either as "villagers" or as "well-dressed." In the legend that stuck, Trelawny burned his hand snatching Shelley's heart from the flames; in his first account, he and others, using metal poles since they were not allowed to touch anything and it was too hot anyway, carried the metal grille holding the fire into the sea to cool it; he then in curiosity about one part not having been consumed, burned himself pulling out an oily organ that modern speculation suggests may have been the liver but that in the guise of heart was to cause some strange jealousies and acrimonies as it changed hands; whatever it was went to Mary and eventually to Boscomobe, England. Byron wanted the skull but Trelawny, knowing he had used another as a drinking cup, did not want it so profaned; besides in the digging up of the body it had been struck by a mattock and later fell into two pieces.

The whole appearance of the body as dug up was described as nauseating, with details; the official Italian records, brought to light by Dr. Biagi at the end of the century, give it as nothing but bones, though it would seem that the heart story must have had something more than that to go on. That Shelley, who couldn't swim, was a nincompoop as a sailor and in general inept physically seems agreed, more than why his and Williams's boat got to be named the "Don Juan," as a bit of enforced loyalty to Byron, instead of the "Ariel" as Shelley had wanted, and the two reports of how it was brought up from the bottom, and how far out, differ totally. As to digging up the child William's remains in the cemetery so they could be by his father's, Severn, who was involved in the matter before Trelawny's arrival, wrote that in the grave marked as the boy's they found bones of someone five and a half feet tall, so covered them back up; in another version, no trace of William's grave could be found. In any case that third stone marks a memory, not a grave, and Mary, who first spoke of wanting to be buried there — Trelawny jauntily wrote her, "You may lie on the other side if you like" — eked out a fairly long, churchgoing widowhood in England and was buried in Bournemouth, having written a good deal without ever recapturing the flash of *Frankenstein*. Her main occupation seems to have been building up an image of Shelley as the moral and conventional character he would have shuddered even to meet at a party — he couldn't stand being "bored by idle ladies and gentlemen" — with attendant defamation of Harriet; a job taken over for the next generation by their only, and commonplace, surviving child, Sir Percy, and even more by his strenuous and propriety-bugged wife, Lady Shelley.

In 1910 the director of the cemetery, Signor Trucchi, gave an account of the Shelley plot, beginning with a reference to 1823. "At that time the administration of the affairs of the cemetery was very irregular and the name of the purchaser of the ground remained unregistered, but my father remembered having been told of the purchase. Many years passed and as I had never heard from the owner of the ground I supposed that he had died. To my great surprise, however, in the latter part of 1880 I received from England a letter signed Trelawny, in which the writer stated that, as he was the owner of the plot of ground near the grave of Shelley and that, as he was an old man and could not expect to live much longer, he thought it was time for him to prepare his grave. He gave me an idea of the measurement of the box that would contain his ashes. . . ." Trelawny was then eighty-eight. In October of the next year, 1881, an English lady turned up unannounced, with the box, "about four o'clock in the afternoon," but as she had known nothing about needing certain official documents she had to take it home with her, presumably to a hotel room. Everyone was very kind, and within a fortnight Trelawny was "moored at last on the stormless shore," as Swinburne had already expressed it immediately after the old man's death in August ("Lines on the Death of Edward John Trelawny"). "Heart of hearts, art thou moved not, hearing / Surely, if hearts of the dead may hear, / Whose true heart it is now draws near? / Surely the sense of it thrills thee, cheering / Darkness and death with the news now nearing — ? / Shelley, Trelawny joins thee here."

The Swinburne pathos is of course only one of several varieties of Shelley-worship that have gone on ever since his death. One form, somewhat in line with the efforts of the widow and her daughter-in-law, shows up in the contortions of an otherwise sober biographer, in the 1940s, to dispel any thought that having once eloped with Mary, Shelley could possibly have been such a cad as to sleep with anybody else. The disease seems to be most acute among pedants and the near-illiterate, whether on metaphysical or some vague version of political grounds; the poetry as poetry gets rather lost in the swoon. George Bernard Shaw, no swooner in general, in his Fabian youth took part in some Shelleyite gatherings, while knowing that *The Cenci* was an abominable play. By and large it appears to be neither ideas nor work but the life, with its peculiar brand of nonconformism, that gets people, under Victorian restraints or the contrary, though of course the idea of the work, and the idea of the ideas, have to be there to ennoble it all. For cult purposes, below the Demogorgon orbit, Shelley's own statement about his "passion to reform the world" is really all that is needed. Such is sainthood, and there is always somebody to make money from it. There has been over some generations a lucrative market in Shelley forgeries, also in such relics as locks of hair, presumably false, not to mention the portrait of the poet as Christ, after a model by Leonardo. Of course the Shelley-haters have had their innings too, though never again as in his lifetime; the Rossettis and Co. put them in left field. But it is far less the witless detractors than the idolaters who drive the best of the poetry, and the best that must have been there in the man, out of sight, and it has to be for the best that one grieves.

One Shelley biographer, John Addington Symonds, came to be buried beside the Pyramid (1893), not from idolatry but because he was often in Rome and happened to die there. One among later biographers was not so lucky in where he ended up, and may be taken as a small footnote to the story, for which the principal can't be held responsible; yet his spirit hovers over it, and on the Swinburne theory, would no doubt be shaking its head. The book, two heavy volumes published in 1927, avoids the more blatant sexual exculpations of its successor, partly because it was the "Epipsychidion" side of the matter, with or without Intellectual Beauty, that made the scholar in the case feel more equipped than most to deal with that particular poetic soul. He found sanction there, as others have, for his own worst failings, and it brought him no end of grief. His name was Walter E. Peck. He was a tall gangly man, of rather noble brow and flaccid lips, quick gregarious humor, and impetuous energy. He was a professor at Hunter College, New York, then for women only, and he made the most of the fact, until after various scandals including a charge of bigamy, he was fired. By 1938 he had run through handouts from friends and was down to begging from acquaintances; he would bring the plea by phone down from a dollar to a quarter and if the person called could no longer bear to see him would wait outside for the coin to be thrown to him in the street. Then he disappeared, to turn up some years later as a hopeless but cheerful and still learned alcoholic on skid row, otherwise known as "one mile of hell." In that neighborhood he was liked and respected, was known as the Professor, hung out with a coterie of kindred fallen intellectuals at a place called the Pitcher Joint and when in condition sometimes wrote or lectured for the *Bowery News*. A sociology class at N.Y.U. went to interview a group of Bowery bums, who returned the visit in the classroom a few weeks later, because they were paid for it, not out of any wish to mend their ways, according to the *New York Times* account. Walter Peck, Oxford D. Phil., was one of them, and was described as *claiming* to have written a life of Shelley. But that was cleared up for the obituary, in January 1954, when he had been found unconscious in a Bowery doorway. His *Shelley* was in all big libraries, and still is. He was buried in whatever we use for a potter's field.

Caius Cestius wasn't exactly a nobody. He was a praetor, tribune of the people, and member of the college of the Septemviri epulones, the group in charge of providing the sacrificial feast of the gods, and he must have fancied himself extremely and been very rich. Thomas Hardy in 1887 hit on a way of thinking about him, which might not go down too well with the Germans, Swedes, Scandinavians, and other citizens of the world through love of Rome, in fact to an unkind view it might seem chauvinistic.

But it does express a phenomenon very pertinent to that piece of ground and that is going to be with us for at least another few thousand years if we are going to get that much: that is, being buried on what is called foreign soil can as well be a cheerful thought as not and has many special attractions in this case, but native language is a home hard to do without. Keats knew it well: "Since every man whose soul is not a clod / Hath visions, and would speak, if he had loved, / And been well nurtured in his mother tongue." Hardy's poem on the Pyramid is not one of his best, but then one scarcely thinks of him as comfortable on the continent at all, or in any metropolis. "Who, then, was Cestius, / And what is he to me? / I can recall no word / Of anything he did; / For me he is a man who died and was interred / To leave a pyramid // Whose purpose was exprest / Not with its first design, / Nor till, far down in Time, beside it found their rest / Two countrymen of mine." He calls the two "those matchless singers" and "two immortal shades," and sees the Pyramid as beckoning pilgrims to their tombs "with marble finger high." Shelley in *Adonais* saw it a little differently: "And one keen pyramid with wedge sublime . . . doth stand / Like flame transformed to marble." Both descriptions are bizarre, and the monument would not look like much in Egypt. Still, its geometry is beautiful, more so in contrast to all other shapes in Rome, and with acquired beauty far beyond that. We do have reason to be grateful to Cestius, who "in life, maybe, / Slew, breathed out threatening."

One further and touching bit of Romantic association in the cemetery reads: "William Wordsworth C.I.E. Grandson of Wordsworth, 1835–1917. Late Principal of Elphinstone College. Pioneer of Indian Education. Wise, magnanimous, tender-hearted."

Cemeteries are a dying institution. Long before we are all talking Urthspk or whatever our one world language is to be, we will all have to be writ in water, for lack of ground, or strewn in wonder-working ashes on whatever soil is left. Considering the present population of Rome this seems rather imminent at Campo Verano although it only dates from the plague year 1837, but not beside the Pyramid, where there is still a good deal of room and no such pressure; for one thing the directors are quite choosey about whom they let in. You don't feel pressed for time there, and again as at the Caffé Greco can enjoy the company with some feeling of leisure, especially as it is all more or less contemporary. As against the Pyramid and even the Aurelian wall of two hundred years later, which can be lumped together as representing about two-fifths of recorded human history — not speaking of artifacts — the others we are concerned with can be thought of as only having a different number on the same short street; they are our very close neighbors in time. But then cemeteries, unlike individual tombs of the mighty, have never kept their identities more than a few hundred years. It has been a distinction of man in most of his habitats to make such gestures against oblivion, but it is only a slight postponement, requiring some version of Divine Will to be much help.

There are about four thousand now in this particular group of neighbors, and as such things go, the achievers among them do make up quite an eminent group. Alexandria may never have had such a university; the rude forefathers of the hamlet, or the slums either, were never less represented.

The Augustus Hare (1834) of one of the few graves permitted in the Keats section after 1822 is not the Augustus J. C. Hare of the still indispensable *Walks in Rome*, who was born in that year, but his uncle, a churchman and theological author, one of the misguided many who went to Rome for their health and died within a year. Richard Henry Dana (1882), of *Two Years Before the Mast*, but who preferred to be known for his work in jurisprudence, had been in Rome working on a book on international law. He and his wife had been charmed by a visit to the cemetery, as Henry James had been a few years earlier, and agreed that it was the one place in the world where they would wish to be buried. James didn't go that far, and was curiously blind to any but English graves, but the brief piece he wrote on the subject is both tender and penetrating. The place, he wrote, "gives us the impression of our looking back at death from the brighter side of the grave"; and about "the pagan shadow" cast on it by the Pyramid: "It is a wonderful confusion of mortality and a grim enough admonition of our helpless promiscuity in the crucible of time."

There is the Norwegian historian Peter Andreas Munch (1865); the Swedish diplomat and Egyptologist named Nils Gustaf Palin, murdered in his house on the Aventine in 1842 by a burglar who was an ex-convict — one of the more contemporary notes in the place; still another Swedish diplomat, Carl Bildt (1931), minister in Rome for twenty-eight years, who retired there to write studies of his famous compatriots associated with the city, such as Saint Bridget and Queen Christina (Hardy was not the only chauvinist); and many more of that intellectual slant, archaeologists, classicists, art historians, and such rather oddball scholar-writers as the aforementioned J. A. Symonds, the Shelley biographer, early admirer of Whitman, translator and exegete of classical and Italian Renaissance literature, and more or less secret pioneer in the study of homosexuality. Among diplomats of less divided interest are Otto von Bülow (1901), minister plenipotentiary of Prussia; George Perkins Marsh (1882), first United States minister in Rome; and among several American representatives, one who died of malaria three weeks after reaching Rome in August 1848. His name was Jacob L. Martin, and he is interesting in having combined an admiration for Pius IX with a great enthusiasm for the Roman Republic, shortly to be crushed by the French troops, the pope having meanwhile forfeited his reputation as a liberal and fled to Gaeta in the kingdom of Naples.

There are quite a few churchmen, including the founder of the Anglican Church in Rome, and probably a number of foreign librarians; in general a smell not of hay, as for Gray in his "Elegy," but of tons of book dust is the haunting one beyond the flowers along many of these little paths, far more than perfumes of great ladies though there are some of those. Composers, actors, singers of note, apparently none; crooks, thieves, scoundrels if any, no longer to be so identified — "their import gone, their wisdom long since fled." Novelists none, at least to be recognized outside their own countries; Rome was never any good for that; it was natural for James Joyce to prefer Trieste; and to one unable to judge the

Scandinavian poets it appears that Keats and Shelley are rather lonely in the higher ranks of their art. In creative work, as we say of kindergarten, the visual arts are by a long way at the top numerically, and when one thinks of the mainstream of art elsewhere, of such names as Cézanne and Rodin, these suggest the gracefully academic at best; but then Rome is a city of foreign academies, part classical, part of art and architecture, and a number of directors of same are in this roll call. The artists include Elihu Vedder, American (1925) to whom Melville dedicated a poem; a painter from Schleswig who antedates Keats, Asmus Jacob Carstens (1798); the two Swedish sculptors Johan Byström (1848) and Ruth Milles (1941); and the English sculptor John Gibson who had lived forty-eight years in Rome (1866). A good many other sculptors of renown in their time have works there, statues and bas-reliefs commissioned or for tombs of relatives and friends, and one particularly prominent angel, called "The Angel of Grief," surmounts the gravestone of the artist himself, William Wetmore Story, and his wife (both 1895). He was a good friend and companion, author of the engaging *Roba di Roma*, less systematic than Hare's *Walks* but one of the century's better chitchat and travelogue books on the city he knew and loved so well; Henry James wrote his biography, and a copy of the same angel was put up at Stanford University as a memorial to the victims of the California earthquake of 1906.

There was a steady Russian colony in Rome long before 1917 but of course the big influx was then, as in other European capitals. There is a Prince Yusupov (1920), father of one of the assassins of Rasputin; and commemorated in French, not Russian, a Senator Paul Jordanow, dead in 1920 and joined by his wife, evidently of French aristocratic origin, forty-two years later. They are by the path at the lowest edge of the ground, and what arouses one's sense of story, that is, of the personal ingredients of history, is the plaque on the wall across from their graves: "Nicholas Jordanow, son of the Senator, shot in Moscow 3 July 1925." Either they had left Russia without him, or he went back on his own, to rescue belongings or in a flush of revolutionary zeal and contempt for the family traditions. Tolstoy is linked to the unique community, as

Goethe is, through one of his children, Tatiana Tolstoy Sukho-
tine, who had settled in Rome and died there in 1950. For the most
part the Russian stones recall not books or jewels so much as the
convivial samovar and one ikon for hoarded treasure in dismal
lodgings lifted above the cracked and threadbare by infectious
humor and song and indefinable dignity, with rent paid by oafish
boarders and the Vatican newspaper, *l'Osservatore Romano*, cut
into neat squares for toilet paper.

Other stories, as in any graveyard, are simply that, with no particular bearing on public events, but the inscriptions here add up
to a social study on a certain theme: Attitudes and Social Standing
of Foreigners in Rome in the Nineteenth Century and After, with
side glances at the precariousness of human fate. "She devoted
her life to her children." "The worthy woman is the crown of her
husband. . . . Her sons grow and call her blessed" (Proverbs XII
and XXXI). That one is in Italian and pertains to an Italian military
family named Carnevali, with a tomb almost showy enough not to
be infra dig in the Catholic cemetery; there may have been an
American heiress in the picture, that having been a chief resource
of Roman upper society in the late nineteenth century. But one
blue-blooded Newport girl, Olivia Cushing, married a Norwegian
instead, Hendrik Christian Anderson, evidently no relation to fairy
tales, and although sticking to the accepted pattern by at least
living in Rome, entertained notions that would not have gone well
in Newport, or as Henry James said of Margaret Fuller in Italy,
"discovered ways that were not as the ways of Boston." The
couple's legend reads: "Our dream of a city of all nations dedicated to the creative spirit of God in man was our hope and prayer
in life. Here the dreamers sleep." One hopes they sleep well, and
they may, not being in hearing of Keats: "The poet and the
dreamer are distinct, / Diverse, sheer opposites, antipodes."

The sleep idea gets heavy handling from a Mr. Forbes of
Portsmouth, England, who on a monument to his two young
wives together says they both "fell asleep" on the given dates, aged
respectively twenty-eight and twenty-two, having been twenty-six
and sixty years his junior. He survived the second loss only six

years, dying in 1933 at the age of eighty-eight, "after living in Rome sixty-two years." The "Glory, Glory, Glory!" under the second wife's name sounds rather overexultant, but it is probably unfair to wonder if they had help falling asleep, or if he picked his own epitaph, "This was the noblest Roman of them all." He could have lent some of his scriptural tags, to their benefit, to the unhappy Brown family, Mr. Brown being "of the city of London, Merchant," whose son Robert "lost his life at Tivoli by his foot slipping on coming out of Neptune's Grotto" — they meant the young man was coming out, not just his foot — "on the 6th of July 1823. Aged 21 years." There follows under "Reader Beware" one of those long sad efforts to express the inexpressible, common to bereaved Anglo-Saxons of limited vocabulary at the time: virtuous and amiable youth, bloom of health, pride of life, disconsolate parents, irreparable loss — which must have been all too heartbreakingly true, and is a reminder that one of the chief consolations of religion has always been to spare people in extremity the urge to fall back on their own prose. In opposite style is a mysterious little stone that looks recent and has no dates or quotes, only two names not engraved but painted in black: Betty Muller, Henry Sonneman. Double suicide? car accident? principles that would prevent their going under the same name? It is curious.

So in still different and most ornate vein in the Bathurst story, probably the most famous in the cemetery outside intellectual history, because it is written at length on the tomb, in English on one side and Italian on the other, and because of its large bas-relief, by a sculptor named Richard Westmacott Jr., of angel receiving the young girl in the case. The sculpture is of the pseudoclassical school that adorned so many gardens of the rich throughout the century, in the general vein of Story's cultivated work too; it is a question whether such art serves its purpose, of easing grief and defying what later thinkers have called the absurdity of life, any better than the Brown family's prose, but it may have, for the minds most urgently in need. One of the two incidents related by the widowed mother calls up an image of the Tiber in the center of Rome looking as it does now on the outskirts, which is running between sloping fields and gardens; the embankments were not built until after 1870, and this is 1824. Rosa Bathurst, sixteen, high-born and known for her beauty, was killed in a fall from her horse while riding with friends beside the Tiber; the river was in flood, the ground slippery, the horse excitable; all this is told, along with her virtues and the mother's desolation, which was double; her husband some years before had disappeared on a diplomatic mission in Central Europe, at the age of twenty-six, and was never heard of again. The inscription is the one above all others there that affected James "irresistibly as a case for tears on the spot. . . . The whole record has an old-fashioned gentility that makes its frankness tragic. You seem to hear the garrulity of passionate grief." That tomb however is second in conspicuousness to that of one of the period's most glamourous beauties, Lady Temple (1809), née Watson of Massachusetts, wife of Sir Grenville Temple; there are seven grieving figures in ancient Roman costume on her bas-relief, by the Swedish sculptor Göthe. Charles A. Mills (1846) has a modest flat stone but owned one of the most conspicuous houses in Rome, on the most "scenic" edge of the Palatine; what remains of it, now a museum, is still called Villa Mills. The notorious arrogance of the upper-class English in Italy, only now beginning to be somewhat subdued, may not have been characteristic of all these people; if not they would have been highly unusual. But even the unusual Shelley shared his compatriots' contempt for the mass of the population there and made his own little England for company. Aside from sights and climate the country was little more than a fish tank to nearly all of them, only you had to watch out not to get swindled.

The Browns were evidently just unfortunate tourists, so less representative of the lives in question than Mr. Hooker of Vermont, who was so enamored by Rome on a visit that he returned and "established himself as a banker," remaining forty-seven years until his death in 1894. Many other Americans probably of varying degrees of means, and who may or may not have been weekend intellectuals, made the same choice; they are from all over the eastern United States, one from Alabama; and many who at last went home to die recorded that other place-love in stones or plaques in the walls. One would have to be able to read quite a few languages to know how many like-minded ones of no ultimate distinction, business people or what the English call "gentlemen," took the same step from the rest of Europe. There are bound to have been quite a few, of Edith Wharton cut or some other, who positively loathed their own country, especially if it was the United States, and so were happy to pay the price, if they were even aware of it, of living where nothing happening around them would be really any of their business, ever again. The aunt and uncle of Edith Wharton who died and were buried there, Margaret and Joshua Jones, were among the casualties of the tuberculosis-cure illusion and may not have shared her passionate distaste for her native land. It was for such transients, caught by disease or accident, that Henry James felt the most sympathy in the cemetery; he speaks of their "trouble within trouble," from "misfortune in a foreign land," which comes oddly from one of our most renowned expatriates.

The prize, for all categories below that of Keats, goes to Isabel Brown, no relation to the London merchants; not rich; not beautiful, or if she was it would not have been the talk of the town; no sculptor of salon fame or of any sort ornamented her grave, and it is doubtful that she ever saw the inside of the Caffé Greco. Under the name we read: "The Faithful Lizzie. For forty-two years devoted maid of the Marchesa Malaspina"; with the vital data, born in Buenos Aires 1863, died in Rome 1942, and "Rest in Peace." It was good of the marchesa to put in her real name, and for all we know they may have had a lovely relationship. One forgets how many Lizzies there have been and still are, maids or governesses teaching their languages to children of the aristocracy and upper bourgeoisie of Rome. One still alive, German, in her eighties, some fifty years with a titled family rare in their rank for brains and goodness of heart, has put together over the years a long compendium of everything ever written about August Goethe and may know more about him than anyone alive, with only the possible failing of refusing to think ill of him, but in that she may be as near the truth as some of Goethe's biographers. She is a Faithful

Lizzie of higher degree, eating at the family table; she seems content; marriage could have been worse, and Mary Wollstonecraft is not for everyone.

There is another compatriot about whom that same lady knows more than most people do nowadays — bearing out the Hardy syndrome, noticeable among living expatriates and wanderers, whereby people from the same country tend to stick together. There are of course pockets, in world society, of fairly real cosmopolitanism, jet-setters, hippies, scholars, artists especially in Paris, and perhaps the Catholic clergy in Rome constitute a kind of melting pot; at the cemetery Keats and Shelley have an aspect of world property, but by and large visitors tend to linger over their own conationals. However, the German-born Malwida von Meysenbug, dead in 1903 at the age of eighty-seven, does recall the very different kind of internationalism that swept Europe in the middle to late nineteenth century. Not of marxist stripe, for this picture; Rome was not harboring any of that for a long time to come. There are no such rebels in the cemetery, nor apparently, though this is subject to correction, any of what have come to be called the Romantic Revolutionaries except Malwida von Meysenbug herself. By the time she moved to Rome late in life she seems to have given up on all that and gone into mysticism and such. The English version of her memoirs closes with her friendship with, and adulation of, Wagner in Paris, before that move. But her earlier life had been in the thick of that political upsurge, insofar as it had a thick, notably through the Russian intellectual and socialist forerunner Alexander Herzen, in whose household she lived for a time in London, as a kind of amanuensis, or super-Lizzie, to his children after his wife's death.

Actually, though impoverished, she was the contrary of a Lizzie, less through being of high birth herself than through her staunch if not always brilliant efforts to spell out women's rights and social justice in general. Armed with a formidable lack of humor along with more endearing qualities, she was something more than a hanger-on among the great of social ferment, short of class struggle. Daughter of a prime minister of the little duchy of

Hesse, she was a political exile in her own right, in a time when the unification of Germany as a cause went with concern for the poor and heterodoxy in religion as a mark of sedition. She worked, contributed, tried to think straight in the roiling confusions of a nationalist and antimarxist libertarianism that had been rocked by the defeats of 1848 but was nevertheless a prime mover, ideologically, in 1860–70; and Herzen in his emphasis on "young" Russia and the idea of the Russian peasant commune was influential as well as prophetic beyond that. The internationalism was in befriending each other's patriotisms, and just being friends, though not much with people of the host countries, England or France, in spite of those being the two where the exiles could publish their journals. Polish and Hungarian democrats were among Malwida's friends. So was Mazzini, no dreamer in the sense of the Anderson tomb but strangely close to it in the vocabulary that the German lady found enrapturing, about "his almost mystic belief in the importance of Rome" and how Rome would "rule the world a third time, but this time by the power of love, of true brotherhood, which will go forth from there and with the strength of a shining example draw the other nations after it." Herzen, also a friend of Mazzini, can't have gone for that, if only as a Russian; neither could have imagined the gorilla caricature that Mussolini would make of it.

The word Romantic hardly suits either of them; having to deal pragmatically with real social forces and possibilities, whether in words or committees, and with whatever short-term successes and setbacks, they were both far beyond such unworldly rhapsodizings as Shelley's, though Herzen was very close to him on the matter of personal, meaning mainly sexual, freedom. In any case their thoughts, hopes, struggles, and depressions, and their writings, were big in the mental baggage that the always genteel von Meysenbug eventually brought to Rome, and they make her an odd little link, on the politico-philosophical side, between Shelley, beacon or windbag of dissent as one cares to see it, and the tragic victim of Mussolini buried near him a century and a quarter later, the marxist leader Antonio Gramsci.

The chain is just the regular one, history, that children find so astonishing when it is put to them in the form of real people, this one touching fingers with that one and so on along in time, with themselves of course the end of the line; nobody can imagine a real person beyond that or their own progeny, which is part of the fallacy of Romantic rhetoric, but that was of the time; even Keats could speak of "the general and gregarious advance of intellect," a notion replaced in our era by dread of a general and gregarious abandonment of that faculty. The chain is there just the same, and what it consists of beyond the merely biographical is to be touched and felt in this cemetery more than in most. The Fräulein from Hesse was born two years after Waterloo, six before Shelley's death, and when Garibaldi whom she came to know was a boy of nine in Nice. The young Romain Rolland, whose correspondence with her has been published, was a friend of her old age in Rome, where he used to play the piano for her, and his was one of the prominent names in the international outcry in the early 1930s against the atrocious conditions of imprisonment of Gramsci, already many years in prison and then close to death.

The mounting protests from abroad had some effect, too late. Gramsci, a hunchback whose health had never been good, was transferred from the prison near Bari to a prison clinic farther north, and later to one in Rome. There, though still under guard, he had relative freedom, since any one of several diseases tormenting him was enough to finish him off soon and prevent his being dangerous to the fascist regime meanwhile. He had been so weak for a year and a half that nobody had dared tell him about his mother's death, at home in their village in Sardinia. He had gone on writing and sending messages to her and was perplexed at her not answering — in dictation, as she herself had never learned to read and write. His term was to expire on April 21, 1937, and those left at home, including his aged father, were wild with joy and plans to receive him because for once in his embattled life he was going there to rest instead of back into the struggle. It was too late for him to go anywhere. He died on the 27th, at the age of forty-six.

His father, who had never tried to follow the politics of that one and another of his seven children, tore his hair and beard and struck himself like a madman on hearing the news, shouting: "Assassins! they've killed my son! they've killed him!" He survived only two weeks. Antonio, as anticlerical as he was critical of the zealots of opposition to the Catholic Church — "anticlerical pornography" was a phrase he used — could be buried beside the Pyramid because his wife, Giulia, then and for years back in Moscow with their two young children, was considered a Russian, though her family was of Swedish origin and had lived for long periods in Rome. Her letters to him had become impersonal and far between a long time before and he had never seen their younger son. In the one carriage that followed the hearse in the rain there were only one of his brothers and his devoted sister-in-law Tatania, human mainstay, with no reward beyond brotherly affection, of his ten and a half years in prison.

Now that Gramsci is published and studied around the world, the look in history of the tyrant and bully who killed him, as he did so many others who couldn't toe or sideslip the cynical line of the time, is of course no more ironic than that of Gramsci's own cause. At his death he was still in some vague sense a leader of the Communist Party, a party that could scarcely be said to exist under the circumstances; he was appointed to the top leadership by the Comintern in Moscow, which he was visiting as a delegate, in 1923, after the arrest of all the executive committee in Italy, less than a year after Mussolini's March on Rome. A warrant was out for his arrest too, but the next year he was elected a communist deputy, one of nineteen, and took the risk of returning to Italy with "parliamentary immunity" — a safeguard blown up within a few weeks by the murder of the socialist deputy Matteotti. In the ensuing government and national crisis, Gramsci seriously misjudged the strength of fascism and its chances of riding out the storm; on the question of tactics for what was left of their own party, he seems to have been right in his disagreement with his old coworker and future successor Palmiro Togliatti, who would twist and turn with the rest of the world's pro-Soviet leaders later on but just then was holding out against all political alliances, maintaining that fascism must be succeeded at once by the Proletarian Workers' State — a comic-opera script for that place and time, if the tragedies were overlooked. Gramsci had disagreed with Lenin earlier in a similar conflict, and although he went along with the upshot, he called the "schism of Livorno," whereby the Italian Communist Party was formed in a break from the socialists in 1921, "the greatest triumph of reaction." His own hopes had centered around that time in the factory occupations by workers in Turin, where he had spent his university years and all his early political life, but that movement had been easily squashed. Later he would comment on the lack of "jacobinism" in the Risorgimento, something Mazzini would have been proud to agree with; dealing with the complications of that legacy would be a job done among the further, and for that time nearly overpowering, complications arising from the mystique of the Russian Revolution.

That Gramsci would have parted company with those who clung to that mystique through its nightmare convulsions there seems little reason to doubt, though the Italian CP continues to claim him as an exclusive intellectual property and heir to Lenin's thought, as though his writings had been of ten, twenty, or thirty years later than they were. Silone, of very different temperament, who broke with the party in 1928, has lately said that Gramsci was a man who had "improved, intellectually and spiritually, in prison." That could only mean growth in independence of mind, with the further implication that such growth might, the mind being willing and able, be easier to come by in the stark ultimacies of prison solitude than in the vanity-feeding hurly-burly of everyday politics. Gramsci's mind was willing, and that it remained able to the end, in a body so nearly destroyed, subject to periodic blankouts along with chronic fever and other more painful symptoms, is a mark of a heroism not often within human capacity.

By 1933, having refused to bow to the regime by requesting a pardon, he began to be haunted by a dread of becoming so worn down by disease that he would no longer be the same person, and would give in. "You hear it said, 'He's held out five years, why not six?' . . . The truth is that a man in the 5th year is not the one he was in the 4th, the 3rd, the 2nd, etc. He is a new personality . . . in whom precisely the years passed have destroyed the moral restraints, the strength of resistance that characterize the man of the 1st year. A typical example is that of cannibalism" (letter from prison). Stalin's monstrous purges, which would give such thoughts a reference beyond anything dreamed of in Italy, were just getting into full swing at the time of Gramsci's death. It seems inconceivable that once exposed again to news, books, conversation, he would not have made the extrapolation from his own sufferings, or would have needed them, for a true judgment, in spite of the most intense paternal feelings about his two sons who were being brought up as Young Pioneers. No orator, he had always been more the intellectual than the organizer, and the kind of mind he brought to bear on such subjects as the French Revolution, the Risorgimento, the relation of social forces in the Italian south, could hardly have been washed indefinitely by the great marxist deception and murder train. Or if it could have, that would be sadder than his death.

Scholars will judge what his writings amount to, as a contribution to marxist theory, and as critiques of Croce and other philosophical mentors of Gramsci's various stages of development. His literary comments, as on Tolstoy, Chekhov, Dante, are certainly not free of the gross social-purpose criteria of Soviet-oriented circles in the '20s and '30s; and the stock political phrases, "dictatorship of the proletariat," "withering away of the state," etc., like the view of trade unions as a revolutionary force, are sadly outdated now. Yet his curiosities had always been wide-ranging, and on subjects not crusted over with Moscow-line orthodoxy both his thinking and his style can be very pungent.

One such subject, a minor one but big biographically, was the upsurge of banditry in his native Sardinia toward the end of the nineteenth century, when pressure from northern Italian industrialists had brought tariff regulations that cut off the island's agricultural exports, especially to France. In the suddenly ruined

economy, miserable enough before, both crime and Sardinian na-
tionalism were bound to boom, and they give to Gramsci's childhood background a striking similarity to the Sicily that would
produce the most legendary of modern bandits, Salvatore Giuliano, half a century later. "Elementary terrorism," the grown man
would call the highway holdups, kidnappings, cattle rustling: an
anarchic and futile misconception of "the class struggle," but he
would vividly recall the romantic hold of the big bandit names of
the time for such schoolboys as himself. Peasant and village families, not his own but like them in their grinding poverty, sheltered
and protected those assassin "heroes," as they would Giuliano in
Sicily for a number of years, and quite a few intellectuals joined in
the adulation (G. Fiori, *Vita di Antonio Gramsci*, 1966).

Not foreign intellectuals; nor would most of them have condemned the bandits with much understanding either; that was not
their Italy. The nearly incredible conditions of life of Sardinian
miners and their first efforts to revolt were also basic to Gramsci's
youth, and like the rest of his upbringing pertain to an aspect of
the country to which Byron and Shelley in their time were as
oblivious as any Bathurst or dreamer Anderson. But then so does
the whole life of this man, deformed in body, who spent his early
years close to starvation in order to feed his mind, becoming at
one stage the white hope of philology at least for the professors in
Turin, and the last ten and a half no less determined to keep that
mind intact, while his liver was as good as pecked out by a vulture.
Shelley's Prometheus does have that much reference after all; it
applies — so does Byron's properly forgotten "Prisoner of Chillon"
— even while giving for our time, somewhat less clear-cut than either his or Gramsci's, an oversimplified idea of who Jupiter is.

In Keats's section of the cemetery there are still some of the violets
and daisies he loved, though even before Severn's death the
flowers were being stolen in quantity from around that grave.
Where Gramsci's simple stone is, in the new part, there is no room
for turf, but iris and azaleas and oleanders bloom in every sort of
patch and crevice, in a tumble of ivy, among the stones with

names and the ones without, which serve to hold up the narrow terraces. The body of George Santayana, who in his last years was cared for by nuns on the Aventine and who had called Catholicism a "vista" for his imagination, was on the grounds for one night in 1952, in the mortuary chapel; apparently he had wished to be buried in unconsecrated ground, which caused some confusion or resistance by the authorities, and it took a day of finagling by the Spanish consul to arrange for burial in the communal Tomb of Spaniards at Campo Verano. Beside the Pyramid, one of the additions of the past decade is the grave of an American painter of talent who committed suicide, and if there is a loneliness to be felt, a sense of all this being, as Henry James put it, in a foreign land, it is that grave and Gramsci's that seem to qualify as well as any. Gramsci is one of the very few there buried in his own country, but he is not among his own people, either by nationality or conviction. But then if he had stayed in the land of his convictions he would probably have died sooner and more violently and had no grave at all.

There is no great carousing anymore at the foot of Monte Testaccio, only a few gypsy wagons halted there from time to time as a base for begging operations, and the district around and far beyond the Pyramid is a screeching turmoil of traffic. A mystery, among so many, is the quiet that strikes as soon as you turn the last corner before the cemetery gate; there did come to be a gate, because donors gave a wall and by that time it was permitted. Stones of a different association have come to light in this century, to add to whatever solace may derive from the others, of a lovely shade of gray and rounded by innumerable rubbings of feet and hoofs and wheels; they make up a section of the ancient Via Ostiensis, the street Saint Paul walked over on his last day, to the place where the three fountains would spring up in his memory. Those stones, of the old thoroughfare, are fenced off now way below the level of the cemetery and next to the base of the Pyramid, so the cats that manage to make their way in there from their main habitat on the noisy piazza side can prowl over them without being able to get up among the graves. They do it in slow gingerly steps, because it is not the kind of footing they are used to. They have to explore, and wonder, and try not to do anything foolish, and in time return to the food supply on the unquiet side.

They couldn't care less what part they play in our reconciliation. But some of those whose names are on the ground above knew once, in their time, what it was to be on the receiving end in that charmed precinct: "Free from all pain, if wonder pain thee not," "Rich in the simple worship of a day."

June 1974

G. G. BELLI

Roman Poet

*G*IUSEPPE GIOACCHINO BELLI, 1791–1863; member of
various academies and author of some mediocre verse in literary Italian; known for a series of over two thousand sonnets in
popular Roman speech, misleadingly referred to as dialect. These
were not published in his lifetime. There is a monument to him,
which is also a double fountain and a bench for people to sit on, at
the end of the Garibaldi bridge in Trastevere. The inscription
reads: TO THEIR POET / G. G. BELLI / THE PEOPLE OF ROME. From
the Roman sonnets:

Once there was a king who sent out an edict to his people,
saying, "I am I and you're s—, so shut up. I make straight crooked
and crooked straight; I can sell you all at so much a bunch"; and
so on. The executioner took this edict around among the people
and they all replied, "It's true, it's true." — Pope Gregory XVI (Papa
Grigorio): "If anybody else knows how to govern, let them." —
"And when your children are hungry what are you supposed to

feed them? indulgences?" — A woman, after a splendid defense against a charge of prostitution: "Well, Your Honor, let's leave it like this: you come around some afternoon and we'll see what we can do for you." — Two women fight over the use of a tenement fountain; two coachmen commiserate on the lack of business; a street vendor outside the Pantheon with horrible threats chases away a prospective rival; priests and aristocrats refuse to pay their bills to various tradesmen.

On crimes: "Pe' grazzia de Dio sempre se fanno. By God's grace they're never lacking." On tips (*pourboires*): "If Rome lasts it'll have to last like this." Religion: "You're not supposed to understand, just believe." "In the beginning was a word; now it's a chatter without end." Birth: All this fuss "because yesterday your wife gave birth to a new servant of the pope and his monks?!" Death: "The Lord regulates certain things." Idleness: "I'm not myself when I exert myself." Theater: "You go to laugh, not to cry." Public executions: "I'm a fan, I know the executioner as well as I do the pope." Coronation of Napoleon by himself: "What manners! what modesty!" SPQR: Soli Preti Qui Regnono (Only Priests Rule Here). Priests: ". . . and dress their salads at home with oil from the lamps of Christ." The Madonna: she rolls up her sleeves for her friends. Pins: it destroys friendship to make a present of one. Dome of Saint Peter's: has any other nation got a cupola like that? Mother's advice: keep yourself on show "and who breaks, pays." Twenty-mile trip, to Castel Gandolfo: "Oh travel is a great thing; you haven't lived if you haven't seen those parts of the world."

In the statue in Trastevere the poet is grave, almost sorrowful, with nothing plebeian in pose, wears a top hat and frock coat and seen from a little distance might be Henry James. He leans on a column with two human faces — replica of a column of the Temple of Janus Quadrifons, near which he used to stand half the night, taking in the life and language of the quarter. The reliefs below show Romulus and Remus suckling and Father Tiber, and at the back a group of Romans gathered at Pasquin's corner, laughing at some story or pasquinade, There are pines behind, and during the long gay neighborhood Festa di Noialtri (Us

Others, Us the People) the trees along with all the streets around are hung with colored lights, so that the poet stands in a circle of Christmas trees, in July, and seems the monarch and presiding spirit of the festival.

It is proper. The critic Luigi Morandi, who some twenty years after Belli's death was able to bring out the first fairly complete edition of the sonnets, described them as "one of the most notable literary monuments of all times and all places." The language may be unfortunate but the judgment is true. Belli's name belongs among the greatest in nineteenth-century literature in Europe. Yet he is just barely mentioned in the most voluminous Italian textbooks; he is not taught in the schools nor included in any standard anthology. Except in Germany he has had no foreign critical attention, and even in Rome only a small group of intellectuals bothers to know his real genius; by the general public, insofar as there is one, he is apt to be put down as a kind of comedian in verse and the forerunner of an immeasurably less brilliant although likable poet, Trilussa, of this century. It has been a strange conspiracy — as if the world knew nothing of Gogol, the best-known of his admirers in his lifetime and the European writer of his century whom he most resembles. The most striking subsequent resemblance, of another kind, is with James Joyce, who also greatly admired his work.

During his life what fame the sonnets had was in the cafés, where they would be quoted and misquoted. Gogol evidently heard Belli recite them himself, which he is said to have done marvelously well, and spoke of him at length to Sainte-Beuve, who in 1839 reported their conversation on "this Belli, so utterly unknown to all travelers. . . . He writes sonnets in the dialect of Trastevere, but sonnets in sequence and forming a poem. He is original, witty in everything but best of all in his artist's eye; it seems really that he is a great poet, penetrated with Roman life. . . . In his forties, basically melancholy, rather withdrawn."

The affinity with Gogol is in many ways remarkable, and could lead to interesting speculations on the nature of czarist as compared to papal despotism. The two are even in nearly the same degree poet-novelists, allowing for obvious differences in their media. The storyteller in Belli is subject always to the spacing and the intensity of language required by the strictest of poetic forms; the sonnets are never loose; on the contrary the sonnet form, for the use he made of it, led him more and more into a heightening and compacting of language values enough to account for Joyce's enthusiasm and with no parallel in the novel before *Finnegan's Wake*. But the sonnets, although self-contained, do form one tremendous sequence, and his purpose in it was at least on one level consciously panoramic. He hoped that they might form "a monument of what the plebs of Rome is today"; that he would have depicted "all the moral, civil, and religious life of our people of Rome." Even on the narrative or "depicting" level it turned out to be more than that. The portrait is not only of the plebs, *noialtri*, but of a whole society, always from the mouth of the people it is true, but no less vivid for the rest of the structure, from the pope down. It is a record, in sweep and intimacy comparable to the great European novels of the century, of the tormented period of 1830–48 in the Rome of the Papal State, also known at the time as the city of the six Ps: papa, preti, principi, puttane, pulci, e poveri — pope, priests, princes, whores, fleas, and the poor.

For a project of such scope he might seem to have chosen the least apt of literary forms, but there were reasons for it, one of them indicated on his monument and it is one of the more extraordinary facts of Rome: "To Their Poet . . ." In fact there had been no other, not only of the people but of Rome in general, nor any other literature; in modern times the city had produced no writers whatever. Its genius had all been plastic and decorative, for the eye; it expressed itself in stones, furnishing, water, spaces of every kind; in words it could inspire all manner of appreciations from outsiders but to itself, literally speaking. Rome was a blank. Its soul was a mass soul; it was too busy being Rome; besides there was no independent middle class. No novelists, no playwrights — the city famed for satire had no possibility of producing a Molière or Goldoni or even so much as a new Plautus; the poets of Italy too were coming from everywhere else, and being venerated by Rome, along with other foreign writers, because they came and venerated Rome. There are mementoes of them all over the city and they are the most touching sign of its own wordlessness; a chunk of purified wood is still propped up because Tasso used to meditate under it when it was an oak; the Goethe monument and the Keats-Shelley Museum are landmarks. No Romans, that anybody ever heard of; except Belli. His subject matter was a society of tremendous and conflicting vitalities of which the absolutely only verbal expressions of any vitality at all were the obscene ballad and the political epigram: Pasquin. The mental materials were lacking for anything else, even if papal tyranny had offered any prospect of publishing.

That it did not was of course a point. It would have been writing for oblivion to portray a Julien Sorel rising to influence in the Papacy, and Belli's poems were at least good for a laugh in the café. But the deeper point was that nobody would have cared much about such a hero. Rome's specialty, beyond the special connection of its rulers with God, was the absence of psychological interest, of any overriding concern with personal continuity as against tradition, on which the novel depends. On the philosophic side, since the Counter-Reformation it had been a society describable in a few commonplaces of superstition and skepticism, hardly conducive to major literature. What remained was the barb, the episode, the flash — related to an uncanny native gift of observation and the habit of mind for which the Romans had been known long before: *Moritur et ridet.* Belli's poems are all of people and his skill in characterization is superb, for all five human Ps of the six, but none of his characters is that in the usual sense. They are never in the making. There is none of the novelist's concern with development of situation or consciousness, only with the finished product, so that it makes little difference in what order the poems are read. Development there certainly is and of a high order, but it is from accumulation; personality is only a detail in the one vast still camera shot of the city's peculiar, subtle, and unprivate humanity. Or one might say there is one main character: the people; the two others it has dealings with are the Vatican and the aristocracy.

Such a simplification, or what might be taken for that, would probably not be true or interesting anywhere but in Rome. There it was, and is, the true form of the Comédie and the Condition Humaines, and the true form of its expression is also what Belli made it: not private reflection and effort but one long publicity — speech: monologue or dialogue. The Roman knows his experiences only in telling about them. He had to be known out of his own mouth, and so inevitably, in conflict with every prevalent notion of what constituted serious writing and written language, not in proper Italian but in Romanesco. But it took a poet of genius to hit on the idea, and no common ear to be able to carry it out. A lucky if unhappy set of biographical circumstances were needed too, for the two-thousand-year spell to be broken.

Belli was not himself of the people, but of a bourgeois family dependent on government service, tossed about in the papal troubles with Napoleon and in his childhood made penniless by his father's death. Of the great political forces of those years the sonnets, written in the '30s and '40s, are a document as vivid as of the later struggles between papists and liberal revolutionaries, or "jacobins." "Napujone" still stalked Rome as he did the rest of Europe, and one of Belli's keenest dramatic sketches is of the invader's mother. "Madama Lettizzia," eking out her life of souvenir in her palace on the Corso — with references to Madame's notorious stinginess and latter-day habit of looking at herself in the mirror:

> Che fa la madre de quer gan colosso
> che potava li Re co la serécchia?
> Campa de consumè, non butta un grosso,
> dice uì e nepà, sputa e se specchia.*

"What is happening to the mother of that great colossus / who lopped kings off with a sickle? / She lives on consommé, won't spend a cent, / says *oui* and *n'est-pas*, spits and looks at herself in

---

*Text from Vighi-Caffarelli; edition, 1944. The fuller Vigolo edition, 1952, uses Belli's spelling, with many double consonants, more difficult for foreign readers.

the mirror." In the fifth line, typically, she is spoken of as "poor old woman — *povera vecchia*." Another sonnet conveys the ominous feeling of emptiness in the city during the second French occupation, 1809–14; if Napoleon had lasted a little longer Rome would have become "Frascati, Schifanoia or Castel-Formicolone" (small villages nearby).

> Er Papa a Fontebbrò, Montecavallo
> vòto; San Pietro vòto; e un cardinale
> nun lo trovàvio più manco a pagallo.

"The Pope in Fontainebleau; Montecavallo / empty; Saint Peter's empty; and you couldn't have found / a cardinal anywhere for love nor money" (Montecavallo — the Quirinal).

Belli's mother took in needlework and died when he was sixteen. A time of wretched dependence on relatives, during which he had some Jesuit education, was interrupted by short periods of white-collar work in princely houses, but he seems to have been of too strong and touchy a nature to stand the humiliations of such employment in Rome's rigid caste structure. At the age of twenty-five he married a rich widow some years older than he, to whom he remained loyal if not faithful, but whether to save his domestic dignity or hers he took on a new job in the Stamps and Registry Office and held it for ten years; he had perhaps expected a little more relief from the marriage. He attended meetings at the literary academies and turned out various writings in the respected vein of the time — stilted and pseudoclassical. Then on a trip to Milan he was shown the poems of Carlo Porta, in Milanese dialect. They gave him the needed push toward a fresher resource of language, and he began at once the new process of creation that would bring his real gift so torrentially forth during the next few years, and at a lesser pace for a few more after that, until its sudden and rather terrible stop in 1848.

Meantime he was helped by being retired from his job on a full pension, presumably through pull. It was the technique of all favor and progress in the bureaucratized and venal capital, dominated since 1831 by the figure of Gregory XVI. "Here there's a vicar of Almighty God; then there's a vicar, the vicar's vicar. Keep these distinctions in mind, so as not to confuse one vicar with another; because a plain vicar is one thing, and a vicar's vicar is something else." The use of bribes enters into dozens of the sonnets, in moods from rage to gentle slapstick. As a mild instance of the psychology of influence, one narrator tells proudly how through pull with a Swiss guard he was able to get into the Vatican Museums, although it becomes clear that it was on a day when the museums were open to the public. Another gives the recipe for the whole process of bribing — never start at the top or "you'll get a kick in the rear"; the cardinal secretary of state has his middleman, that one has his, and so on, "and you have to push the wad up from one hand to another. The top guy, of course, always wants to stay under cover so he can say he didn't get anything."

All his life Belli would have to be up and down these sordid stairs. After his wife's death he was again in financial need, and having to support his son, Ciro, to whom he was passionately devoted, he professed loyalty to the target of his fiercest satire, "Papa Grigorio," in order to have a new job in the bureaucracy that he still continued to lampoon without mercy in his verse. The crimes of corrupt government, which in this case was synonymous with the clergy, against humanity and "the law of Christ," have never been pictured with greater wit and rage or more thoroughly. But the "monument" was to a great deal more than that. It "denies, mocks and destroys," as the poet Carducci observed, but in a spirit that Carducci evidently failed to grasp. Not that anything Roman would be called "spiritual"; the Madonna rolls up her sleeves for her friends; so does God, who is so powerful "he can piss in bed and call it sweat." The spirit is there nevertheless, and its lineage is plain — from Juvenal, and even more closely from the figures of the Sistine Chapel, seen however in one picture with the guts and the bawdy flesh in the tenements below.

Belli's debt to the Milanese, Porta, seems not to have gone beyond an eye-opening in the matter of language. According to those able to read the difficult Milanese dialect, aside from drawing on popular speech the two poets had little in common. Very different material was waiting to engage a Roman talent. The language problem too was of another kind, the plebeian speech of Rome not being in any proper sense a dialect, which gives Belli's work quite a different scope than if it had only a local range of intelligibility. The sonnets could not be translated without too much loss but can be understood by anyone with a reading knowledge of Italian. The peculiarities are for the most part not of vocabulary but only of pronunciation. Certain vowels and consonants are transposed (Ital. "altro," Roman "antro"; "ultimo," "urtimo"; "il," "er"; "Napoleone," "Napujone"); or there will be a thickening of sound ("niente," "gnente"). Infinitive verbs lose their last syllable ("andare," "andà"; "potere," "potè") and all tenses and persons of verbs undergo some change, confusing to the eye but not to the ear and the ear is crucial in reading Belli in any case. S before a word may be a matter of Roman coloring and dispense with a string of adjectives: from French *papier* comes *pappiè* and for a real jeer *spappiè*, used of the documents carried by government functionaries. The only frequent Roman word that has no relation to Italian is *mo* from the Latin, for "adesso," "now." For words making up a special local vocabulary Belli himself left notes, since amplified by his editors, who have also written copious notes on local references, not always needed.

In spite of the slightness of such difficulties, less than for most regional dialogue in America, the prejudice against written dialect has undoubtedly counted largely against Belli, having served too often only for quaintness or local color. In this case it was strictly necessary. You are always hearing. The settings of the sonnets, along with the basic technical fact that they are all conversation, are derived entirely from the theater — reflecting the deep theatrical sense of the Romans themselves, also indicated by the large number of sonnets dealing with popular theaters of the time, and the many images drawn from puppet shows. In the poems the work of staging and actors is all done by the ear, that is, by the extraordinary illusion of speech that could not have been achieved except by such orthography, and the point is hardly a quaintness.

It is the full drama of "a city of always solemn remembrance," as Belli called it in speaking of his project and the unique character of the Roman common man. "Nor is Rome such that her people do not form part of a great thing, *non faccia parte di gran cosa . . .*"

An emphasis as misleading has been put on Belli's obscenity, largely as the result of the Morandi arrangement in the first edition; the more salacious sonnets were all published in the last volume, the sixth, and consequently the poet became known chiefly as the author of Volume Six. It was an injustice both to that volume and to the other five. Bawdiness is part of the general vigor of Rome, and Belli presented it as truly as anything else. His obscenity is tremendously funny, being entirely without strain. There is nothing suggestive about it; there is nothing left to suggest. The defense of the prostitute before the judge, referred to earlier, is strictly biological; all the common English four-letter words would be needed to translate it, and there are many others as uninhibited, including scenes in the confessional. Sexual candor is simply there, like God or beauty, and may reach a truly Roman immensity, as in Belli's great figure of a prostitute, the Santaccia, or be only incidental, as in the delightfully comical pair of sonnets entitled "Li Posti," about a fat man who has bought a seat at the theater and is engaged at not being able to fit into it.

Most of all, however, sexual allusion is in the actual stuff of the language, which could no more be stripped of it than of its huge stock of proverbs or of its anarchy and rage. The words sometimes have their literal meanings and more often do not; they can appear in connection with the most exalted themes, and may contribute a sardonic flavor or not, being often only the natural expression of wonder or vitality. For the strength and flowing spoken quality of Belli's language the proverbs, sometimes only alluded to, are equally if not more important, for example: "Better alone than in bad company"; "Trouble shared is half a joy"; "Every knot comes to the comb" (every action brings what it deserves); "Who pisses clear can s— at the doctor" (be honest and you won't get into trouble); "You know where you're born, not where you die"; "Seventy-two thieves run the world" (the College of Cardinals); "Every lamb to its butcher"; "All the flies go on the thin horse"; "You can't make sawdust without a saw"; "It's better to be the head of an anchovy than the tail of a sturgeon."

Not that such sayings weigh in the sonnets. They are part of the raw material of language that Belli drew from and added to, together with traditional imagery of other kinds. In Rome this included a particularly vivid fund from classical-Christian culture, which gives the language a scope, dignity, and stability altogether vanished from any modern slang in English, and partly accounts for the rather mysterious majesty that pervades Belli's work as a whole. A judge is "that Nero," "that Pharisee"; of a bully, "Alo! and out come the arrows and thunderbolts!"; shoemakers are all Mastro Crespino, after their saint, and executioners Mastro Titta, after a famous one named Gianbattista. The neighborhood, in this case, happens to coincide and be in a relation of mutual nourishment with the roots of a civilization — a *gran cosa*. A period of the past will be "the time of Nero" or "the time of the Cenci" as a New Yorker would speak of the time of Mayor LaGuardia; and sometimes the humor of a poem will lie in historical pretention and grotesques of history in the popular mind, as in the café lecture on Romulus and Remus building the Vatican. It is a language also of enduring metaphors, rather than the temporary ones of most modern city slang; hen's milk is a synonym for the greatest delicacy; "to mend with a golden thread"; "he unbuttoned my patience"; one of the poorest of the poor is a "black-stomach," "panzanera"; cottoning to bad characters is "scratching backs with one's hump."

Aside from its vitality, as against the cultivated speech of the time, this language offered a dramatic compression and quickness impossible in literary Italian. It is full of shortcuts, and so makes possible in fourteen lines a spaciousness and ease of pace that reach a kind of illusionism: the presentation is so full, yet with no stinting in the flavor of actual speech — pauses, repetitions, exclamations — that one seems to have heard a story or discourse of ten or fifteen minutes. Not that Belli did not bring to it superlative skill as well, notably in keeping his eye on the dramatic core. If verbosity is part of that he gives it: the whole irony of one speaker's defense of the pope is in his repeating "Nun dico bene?? — Am I right?" nine times in fourteen lines; but there are no superfluities, no rhetoric; few adjectives. Furthermore the given language was only a point of departure. He brought an electricity of his own to it, to make it read like common talk and tell what common talk cannot.

There is no aspect of it that he does not in some way extend and transform. Its natural onomatopoeia and wealth of metaphor stimulate him to extreme inventions of sound and imagery, its brevity to still more terse combinations from which meanings explode forth from one another like fireworks, its punning humor to gargantuan puns that can impact the scabrous with the sublime in a word. From the familiarity in it of the broadest generalities — "love," "death," "god," like "broom," "foot" — he can keep the trivial in focus while extending its backdrop to infinity. Its peculiar grammar becomes another vehicle for wit. He creates marvels of nonsense, which remain pebbles at the bottom of the pool. The whole game becomes at times a great surrealism of words, more astonishing in that nobody before him had even attempted to write Roman speech and nobody has done so since without falling into some degree of violation, of which Belli was never guilty. If "andare" is given for "andà" or "di" for "de" it is in satire, on the speaker or his subject. The game, of which the end product is marked above all by range and naturalness, was played within the appalling confines, first of the sonnet form, and second, of his subject's linguistic and mental equipment. The inventions are never captious; however improbable, they keep the common human touch.

Not to distinguish categories: A sonnet entitled "One Better Than the Other" is a satire on defenders of the pope, consisting of nothing but their last names. Another is made up of about sixty synonyms for the male organ. On a more ordinary level there is the Bishop of Eau de Cologne, and (from Trent, Trenta, thirty) the Council of Thirty-odd People — which might be called the Roman view of the Counter-Reformation. On the French occupation, the names of villages joined to Frascati to convey the absurdity of Rome's condition include the meanings "to eschew boredom" and "anthill." Rote calls of children's games with a slight twist are a frequent Bellian device. Garbling of church Latin is more frequent and gives him his most crucial pun: "magnà" (*mangiare*, to eat) blends with the liturgical "magnus" and "magnificat," taking on accretions from many moods and themes, the mumblings of priests and hunger of the poor interpenetrating more with every renewal, and it is only as the climax of this wordplay that one can feel the irony of one of the most moving of the sonnets, the "Miserere for Holy Week." From many Roman paintings, as well as from the familiar tinklings around the necks of horses, comes the "bell-collar of angels" of "Judgment Day." Truth cannot be kept back; it is like diarrhea, "la cacarella," which carries to a rhyme with an invented and most liquid word, "sbrodolarella," an adjective from the verb form "to slobber" from the noun "broth" — combined here with "holy": "la santa verità sbrodolarella."

The suffix -*accio*, "bad," very frequent in Roman speech, becomes a delicate and various instrument. A repetition of it serves to give the viciousness of the cholera epidemic, subject of a number of sonnets: "sto serra-serra de porcaccia infamaccia ammalatia" — "serra-serra," from the verb "to constrain, lock up," is usually applied to a crush, as in a bus: "this squeeze of a dirty pig of an infamous disease." A more absurd pair of repetitions conveys a servant's befuddlement over the mysteries of printing: "Ma inventà l'usi / de potesse poté stampà la stampa / su le facciate de li foji chius! — But to invent ways to enable you to be able to print the print on the face of closed pages!" A rigmarole of rhyme says enough on the prevalence of the honorary title Cavaliere ("yesterday, today, tomorrow, always") — "cavajeri jeri, cavajer oggi, e cavajer domani! / e sempre cavajeri . . ." Phrases from the ghetto that had become general currency give some fast double entendres. In the story of Susanna and the Elders an already satiric expression on the price of an object, "Scimme scimme cosi tonni," from Hebrew *scemin*, a tiny coin, plus "round things," or money, takes a clever sexual turn, applied to the old men; "round things" become "soft things" and "scimme" is not far from "scimmie," "monkeys." Most of Belli's malapropisms are invented but some were already fixed in Roman speech, to be newly applied. "Persica durace," from Italian "pesca duràcina," a clingstone peach, used as an epethet for the pope means both "die-hard" and "ruddy-complexioned," or that he drinks.

And so on. A particularly striking subtlety comes into expressions of quantity, size, and degree, little or much; the words un po, "a little," are magical for Belli, he can make them do almost anything. In one untranslatable case, referring to Popes Clement XIV and Pius VI, they can really be called magnificent: "They say that under Pope Ganganelli, and also under *un po' de Papa Braschi* . . ."

But Belli's greater gift was in keeping verbal skill subservient to his great range of thought and mood and matter, and it is this that gives the work its general drive and pace and explains one's being able to read hundreds of poems of the same length and meter with no sense of monotony. The lines snap and crackle ("Presto, a te, tira via, giù, un antro piede") or pull out to a long suspense and the slowest sonorities ("Eppuro, o bene o male, o a galla o a fonno") or slip casually by ("La piu mejo de Roma che se trova"). A more impressive variety is in the taking hold of the material. Every unit is a new experience, held in the larger continuity however by the one very complex character, "the people," and their scene, Rome. The greater number of the sonnets are monologues but one is hardly aware of it, the second speaker or the group is so present; or the talk will be of a kind not assuming a response. You are brought in at the thick of the scene, or at some time interval from it; or the matter may be general and the only scene the one implied by the speaking — a Shakespearean soliloquy. The sonnets may be short stories, of the most episodic focus or of such range they have the effect of whole novels, or broad character sketches, or expressions of basic attitudes, or simple descriptions of places and scenes in Rome. Political satire, the element with which Belli will probably always be chiefly associated, may be overt, or altogether absent, or a matter of one sly twist, as in a woman's telling about her two canaries, ending with the female sitting on her eggs "like the pope on his throne." It is clear that it is a woman there, another achievement; it is nearly always clear from the first line, as much as if one were in fact at the theater, whether the speaker is a man or a woman.

Except as it is bound up with political and spiritual outrage there is very little that is cruel in Belli; there is also a nearly total lack of sentimentality; and many of the finest sonnets are nonpolitical. Read aloud, as they should be, there are few that do not get some form of laughter out of you — the roar, the pensive whinny, the sidesplit. You laugh at the most tragic reflections, which is not to say they are being ridiculed: they are not, any more than Hamlet's; you laugh even at the beautiful "Miserere," although the poem is the opposite of irreverent. It is a rare form of wit, not relying on the shocking, revenge, or the grotesque, one might call it more than anything generous, since it arises from human sympathy rather than any self-superiority; and quite often it is only of accuracy: you laugh at the suddenness of your own transition from not seeing to seeing.

Story sonnets. Of the domestic dramas one of the finest is "La Nottata de Spavento," The Night of Terror, remarkable for the woman's progression through shock, pleading, resolution, to the great Roman ace, the appeal to paternity.

> Come! Aritorni via?! Cusi infuriato?!
> Tu quarche cosa te va p'er cervello.
> Oh dio! che ciài lì sotto? ch'edè quello?
> Vergine santa mia! tu te se'armato.
>
> Ah Pippo, nun lassamme in questo stato;
> Pippo, pe'carità, Pippo mio bello,
> posa quell'arma, damme quer cortello
> pe'l'amor de Gesù Sagramentato.
>
> Tu non eschi de qua; no, nun so' Tuta,
> s'eschi. Ammazzame puro, famme in tocchi,
> ma nun te fo annà via: so' arisoluta.
>
> Nun volé che sto povero angeletto,
> che dorme accusi caro, a l'upri l'occi
> nun ritrovi più er padre accant'ar letto.

"What! You're going back?! / In such a rage?! / Something's going through your head. / Oh God! what are you holding under there? what's that? / Holy Virgin! You're armed. // Ah Pippo, don't leave me in this state; / Pippo, for pity's sake, Pippo my love, / put down that weapon, give me that knife / for the love of Jesus Sanctified. // You're not going out of here; no, my name's not Tuta / if you go out. Kill me if you like, cut me in pieces, / but I'm not letting you go: I'm determined. // You wouldn't want that poor little angel, / sleeping so sweetly there, when he opens his eyes / not to find his father anymore beside his bed."

Many of the stories are not of emotional crisis but only a moment lifted out of the normal repetitive run of things, at home, at work, in the neighborhood; a woman goes on vacation and comes back; a lazy girl is scolded by her mother. A little classic of storytelling with the imposing title "Se More" (French, On *Meurt*) is about the death of a donkey: "Poor darling . . . I was bringing him back from the miller's with a ton of grain on his back and he'd already fallen ten times because he was stumble-footed, the dirty pig. . . . So I beat him over the head. . . ." "La Bona Famija," The Good Family, maintains a breathless delicacy in describing a poor family's usual evening meal, in a mood never quite of gaiety nor of resignation, nor of complaint. There are little street dramas, and charming anecdotes of the wonders of the world, in one of which a man tells of having heard about beavers for the first time, touching also on a basic matter of Roman pride: "If he'd called them masons, all right, but *architects*! . . ."

Places in Rome. The artist's eye that enamored Gogol is most evident in these. "Piazza Navona," which gets in a thrust at the government as well, is one of many that in clarity and romantic feeling offer an analogy to Piranesi's etchings of the same subjects. The names are of streets around; the lake refers to the old custom of flooding the piazza for horse races through water; the "cavalletto" was an apparatus still in use in Belli's time for public whippings and it was a current gag that the last five or ten strokes were given for charity, or the Bonificenza. The transition to that from the four lyrical metaphors that close the first quatrain is typical.

The spire is the obelisk over Bernini's Fountain of the Rivers.

> Se pò fregà Piazza Navona mia
> e de San Pietro e de Piazza di Spagna.
> Questa nun è una piazza, è una campagna,
> un treàto, una fiera, un'allegria.

> Va' da la Pulinara a la Corsia,
> curri da la Corsia a la Cuccagna:
> pe tutto trovi robba che se magna,
> pe tutto gente che la porta via.

> Qua ce so' tre fontane inarberate;
> qua una guja che pare una sentenza;
> qua se fa er lago quanno torna istate.

> Qua s'arza er cavalletto, che dispenza
> sur culo a chi le vò trenta nerbate,
> e cinque poi pe la Bonificenza.

"Our Piazza Navona can thumb its nose / at both Saint Peter's and Piazza di Spagna. / This is not a piazza, it's a countryside, / a theater, a fair, a joyousness. // Go from the Pulinara to the Corsia, / run from the Corsia to the Cuccagna: / everywhere you'll find food for sale, / everywhere people carrying it away. // Here there are three rearing fountains; / here there's a spire like a judgment; / here they make the lake when summer comes back. / / Here they put up the sawhorse, that dispenses / on the backside of whoever wants them thirty lashes, / and five extra for the Bonificenza."

The ruins too are those of Piranesi's Rome, not propped up and classified as they are now but still awesome and slumbering, the Basilica of Maxentius for instance, known then as the Temple of Peace, "er Temp' in Pace," which in Roman also means "the life of Riley"; "What a grandeur of God! what a construction! . . . Even if it were only for the clay, not to mention the bricks! Think of the furnaces! . . . What a monster palace; there's no end to it. Who lived there? A whole lot of people; all rich." A more fearful awe and spaciousness, this too an etching and also an intimation of

death, lie around the desolation of the Roman campagna, called
The Desert: "Silence everywhere . . . ten miles without seeing a
tree! . . . The only thing I saw on the whole trip was an oxcart with
the driver murdered beside it."

The same steel-point quality applies to customs of the time,
many of them now obsolete. Of the famous high-powered gaieties
of the Roman carnival there is no record as full and delightful as
Belli's; one charming sonnet in this vein describes the cheeses and
sausages in delicatessen windows carved into sculptures of biblical
characters for Easter; another, particularly sharp in line, more a
Hogarth, shows a group of dandies making ribald comments on the
audience in a theater lobby. A rollicking amusement, the real
tough Roman slam-bang of life is in many of these sonnets as no
foreigner has ever captured it — the truth of it is too secretive. In
foreign travel writing of the time Roman lustiness always appeared
in some degree childish, senseless, and cruel; its main admixtures
here are mental alertness and a subtle and moving affection for the
city and the life it offers: one thing that never occurs to any character in Belli is wanting to live anywhere else, except in heaven.
But there is one quality that can only be known in the reading, not
of a few sonnets but many, because it grows slowly; that is their
power of evocation. As you work your way through the strangeness
and difficulty it becomes hallucinating. Not this scene or that but
the whole deluge and enigma of the city's life are there, to be seen,
touched, smelled, heard, participated in; it is more Rome than
Dickens's London is London; you are in over your head.

Legends and history. There are the famous legends, as of
Marcus Aurelius's horse and the Bocca della Verità; and anecdotes
that had become quasi-legend and are quite often a jibe at English
tourists, as on the Englishman who could not resist the beauty of a
marble angel on a pope's tomb in Saint Peter's. Of the tales from
history one of the funniest is of the inauguration of the apocryphal
Pope Joan, La Papessa Giuvanna, always a Roman favorite; in this
version she is exposed by giving birth "right there on the chair."
The local sense of historical time leads to some quaint turns of
phrase, for example, "since antiquity was antiquity," and the

French occupation is given as the reason "why they can't make any more of these antiquities."

Popular philosophy. There are too many of the sonnets that one thinks of as "the best" but some substitute praise is in order for "La Bellezza."

Che gran dono de Dio ch'è la bellezza!
Sopra de li quadrini hai da tenella:
pe via che la ricchezza nun dà quella,
e co quella s'acquista la ricchezza.

Una chiesa, una vacca, una zitella,
si è brutta, nun se guarda e se disprezza:
e Dio stesso, ch'è un pozzo de saviezza,
la madre che pijò la vorse bella.

La bellezza nun trova porte chiuse:
tutti je fanno l'occhi dorci, e tutti
vedono er torto in lei doppo le scuse.

Guardamo li gattini, amico caro.
Li più belli s'alleveno: e li brutti?
E li poveri brutti ar monnezzaro.

"What a great gift of God beauty is! / You have to put it higher than money: / because riches won't give you that, / and with that you get rich. // A church, a cow, a girl, / if they're ugly, you despise them and don't look at them: / and God himself, who's a well of wisdom, / the mother he took he wanted beautiful. // No doors are closed to beauty: / everybody makes sweet eyes at it, and everybody / sees the blame in it after the excuse. // Look at kittens, my dear friend. / The prettiest are raised: and the ugly ones? / The poor ugly ones to the garbage heap."

Another with the same title is fiercely realistic, like a cry of rage at the nature of human illusion. "Take a look at the beauties of my grandmother. . . ." The eye here is Leonardo's for every hideous detail: the skin under the goiter, the eyes lost in a round hole, the nose "conversing with her chin," the legs and arms like sticks of a

fan. "Well, my grandmother was beautiful once. Let time have its
way and if I'm not mistaken you'll look worse than that." But this
tone is not quite natural to Belli, and seems more a deliberate exercise in the tradition of François Villon.

"La Morte co la Coda," Death with a Coda — the final image,
of the ocean, loses everything without the extraordinary movement of the vowels in the next to last line.

Qua nun se n'esce: o sémo giacubbini,
o credémo a la legge der Signore.
Si ce credémo, o minenti o paini,
la morte è un passo che ve gela er core.

Se curre a le commedie, a li festini,
se va pe l'ostarie, se fa l'amore,
se trafica, s'imp(o)zzeno quadrini,
se fa d'ogn'erba un fascio . . . eppoi se more!

E doppo? doppo viengheno li guai.
Doppo c'è l'antra vita, un antro monno,
che dura sempre e nun finisce mai!

È un pensiere quer mai, che te squinterna!
Eppuro, o bene o male, o a galla o a fonno,
sta cana eternita dev'èsse eterna!

"There's no getting out of this: either we're jacobins, / or we
believe in the law of the Lord. / If we believe, plain guys or
dandies, / death is a step that freezes your heart. // You run to
shows, to parties, / you go to the taverns, you make love, / you do
business, you pile up cash, / you take what you can get . . . and
then you die! // And after that? after that the troubles begin. /
After that there's the other life, another world, / that keeps on
lasting and never ends! // It's a thought, that never, that balls you
all up! / And yet good or bad, afloat or on the bottom, / that
bitching eternity has to be eternal!"

The trade of another speaker gives to a reflection on the life of
man the image of coffee beans in a coffee grinder, "stirred around

and around and around," the big ones sometimes displacing the little ones but all moving inexorably and without understanding to the bottom, "to fall at last into the throat of death."

On weather. For a Roman poet it was appropriately a subject in itself. The relation of atmospheric conditions to psychic states inspired many of the sonnets and Belli's farthest excursions into abnormal psychology, starting from some point of popular credence but infused both with scientific awareness and the poet's own distrust of the civilized mind. The "lupo mannaro," or victim of lycanthropy, associated here with a certain kind of heavy rain, appears in several images and most dramatically in a poem of that title, in which the victim, feeling his humanity failing, shrieks warnings to his wife whom he returns shortly to devour. But there are gentler weather themes. Of the clarity of the Roman sky, and Italian good weather in general, there have been many expressions in paint but none in words to compare with "Er Tempo Bono," with its innocence of language to suit the Mediterranean air, in praise of the glory of God. — "Cantina" is "cellar," standing for the darkness of all Roman tenement indoors.

Una giornata come stammatina,
senti, è un gran pezzo che nun s'è più data.
Ah bene-mio! te senti arifiatata;
te s'òpre er core a nun stà più in cantina!

Tutta la vorta der celo turchina;
l'aria odora che pare imbarsimata;
che dilizzia! che bella matinata!
Propio te dice: cammina-cammina.

N'avem'avute de giornate tetre,
ma oggi se pò di una primavera.
Vaida che sole, va'. spacca le pietre.

Ammalappena ch'ho cacciato er viso
da la finestra, ho fatto stammatina:
hâh! che tempo! è un cristallo; è un paradiso.

"A day like this morning, / listen, we haven't had in ages. / Ah, what a great feeling! you begin to breathe again; / your heart opens so you can't stay indoors. // All the vault of the sky so blue; / the air smelling like balm; / what a delight! what a beautiful morning! / It really tells you to get going. // We've had plenty of gloomy days, / but today you can call a springtime. / Look what sunshine, look: it's splitting the stones. // As soon as I stuck my face / out the window this morning, I said: / hah! what weather! it's a crystal, it's a paradise."

Stories from the Bible. Of the sacrifice of Abraham: "Then he called Isaac and said to him: 'Make a bundle, get the hatchet, load the donkey, call the boy, put on your sweater, say good-bye to your mother, find my hat; and come on, because God Almighty wants a sacrifice that you can't know about.'" He is a bad father, a *padraccio*. When Isaac asks him at last where the victim is he says, "A little farther on," but a little farther on he turns and shrieks at him, "Isaac, to your knees! the victim is you." "Pacenza," said Isaac to his *padraccio*, and knelt down but an angel appeared in time. "*Baah, baah* . . . and what's that? It's a sheep." The prophet Samuel is another cold character. But for that matter God is not blameless either; "at that time the Hebrews were friends of his and had the true religion," and one gathers he might have been a little quicker to avenge them against the Malachites, instead of waiting "four hundred years." In any case they are all Romans; the Red Sea is much closer than Castel Gandolfo. Lot and his wife are sent away down the Lungara, along the Tiber, and the workers on the Tower of Babel are Roman masons who know the trade if anyone does. "'I'm boss, you're foreman. . . . Come on, my boys, let's work with a will!'" But when they got level with the cross on Saint Peter's suddenly "nobody understood Italian anymore; and when one said 'Give me the sieve' the other handed him a bucket of water." But the stark ultimate majesty of the stories remains through all local contributions and puts these versions very high in the world's retelling of them. God transcends his own wayward-ness, most beautifully in his dialogue with Cain, and he too is Roman but he is also as grandly and reverently God as on the ceiling of the Sistine Chapel; so Cain the bully, the *cristianaccio*, ends up "crying in the moon."

Similar judgments, skepticism, concreteness, the same innate sense of the dramatic crux apply to stories from the New Testament. Obscenity can enter even here and be no more shocking than anywhere else. The Madonna herself, being beautiful, is no more immune than Susanna before the Elders to some all-round considerations of her womanhood; what she does appear immune to, for the Roman mind, is the fleshless fingers of theology, which only makes her more plainly the whole show, and by the same token Jesus does not come out very well. At least he is baffling as a character. The sacred is something else. The story closest to burlesque is of the Wedding of Cana (here, of the Dog, *cane*) in which Jesus and his mother enter on different sides in a question of the wine supply for the feast, exactly in the manner of pagan deities; with the difference that for the "vice" of speaking badly to her on that occasion God lets him come to a terrible end. He is at his least attractive in answering Martha's complaints of Mary Magdalen, "she with her rosary, with her masses, with her novena, with her *via crucis* . . . that saint painted on paper, who only turns up at mealtime" while Martha slaves all day in the house. This is of course a woman speaking. The stories, like the historical ones, are strewn with such anachronisms as the *via crucis* in this context.

Characters. Although sometimes based on specific scenes or narratives of whole lives many sonnets are primarily delineations: a meek husband, a cagey shoe salesman, a braggart, a duchess who gambles; it is a huge gallery of portraits, for vitality and shrewdness not surpassed by Dickens. There is no obvious nonrealism in them, yet in some the tremendous beat of life in Rome, the actual corpuscles of the city's exorbitance, seem to have concentrated, giving them a stature as of Michelangelo's prophets although the subject may be, is in one case, a fish vendor. Another vendor, the one who chases away a rival from in front of the Pantheon, Ricciotto de la Ritonna, is of this nature; his rage has dimensions to rival the Pantheon itself; the masterliness of his procedures is worthy of the name of Agrippa that is carved on it.

But the character who emerges as most colossal, together with the pope who however is the subject of many sonnets, is the great prostitute, the Santaccia, who appears in only two. That is enough; you could hardly cope with any more of her. The first sonnet tells of her stupendous prowess; in the second she becomes one of Belli's most explicit figures of Christian holiness, symbolized in the charity of the poor to one another. It involves a shy country boy with no money to pay her, whom she takes on "in soffraggio de quell' anime sante e benedette." "Suffrage" of course in its ecclesiastical meaning, and the blessed souls those in purgatory; the rest of her sentence, which gives the turn and splendor to this, is not printable in English.

It is indicative of the Roman lack of interest in stages of personal development that Belli's enormous cast of characters includes no children or adolescents, except as appended to their parents. His people are always the mature product, who will always be as you see them and seem to have been born that way. It took the middle class of Rome until the twentieth century to squeeze out from between the upper and lower millstones the interest in personal possibility, if not responsibility, that appears in the novels of Alberto Moravia.

"Viva la faccia de chi cia quadrini! — God bless the rich!" Roman history synthesized: "All women are whores and men a pack of thieves." A zealot is newly appointed to head the office in charge of public morals, of whose predecessor Stendhal had written: "M. le cardinal Zuria, un peu savant, très méchant, très gros, encore plus libertin . . ." In Belli's version they had gone from the frying pan to the fire: "At least with that other one who kicked the bucket, if there was some complaint to smooth over you sent your wife or sister and wrote off one sin with another."

Although clearly formed by the tyranny of the Papal State and the absolute class distinctions of its society, Belli is no Swift. The good humor in his subject was too pervasive, his own misanthropy — or so one feels it: the basic melancholy that Gogol noted in him — too deep for the social point to be the whole abyss. The flicks of the whip can fall anywhere; he has many moods, even for the injustices and corruption that appalled him. He can make fun at the same time of the government and the congenital Roman objection to any government, in which he was certainly not lacking himself; he touches as subtly on the wiles and cynicism of the poor as on the brutal selfishness of the rich, and at times the scourge more often reserved for the ruling powers turns on the people as well, for their fickleness and treachery. There is also a great deal of amiable comedy in his political and social picture. The melancholy relaxes — it was after all only his version of a general trait in Rome, the other side of the quick joy in life that he also shared, and at least in verse he could slam-bang with the best of them; he is quite often being hilarious for the fun of it, and having a wonderful time. Nevertheless his love is all for the poor. It is hard to think of a single portrait of an aristocrat or functionary in his pages that is not essentially damning, which is far from true of the others; and occasionally the real grinding grievances of the poor do drive him to poems of straightforward tragic pity or atrocious heights of irony. They even take him in a few cases, as nothing else in life does, rather close to sentimentality. After the clergy, the two themes in this sphere to which he returns most obsessively are hunger and the law courts.

"Er Ferraro," The Ironworker, is a vehement statement of poverty, with no laughter at all. "Er Luogotenente," The Lieutenant, in which an officer of justice makes his advances the price of freeing a woman's husband, is equally bitter; so are others on papal justice, sardonic mockery giving way to a rage of denunciation: "Pe' quer Cristo, è una gran legge tiranna! — It's a tyrant's law!" The courts, and hunger: they begin to emerge as a city's twin nightmare. There is humor, or rather sarcasm, only in the last line of "La Viggija de Natale," on the food one can see being carried into the houses of the rich on Christmas Eve, and this sonnet was written on the same day (November 30, 1832) as a group of three entitled "La Povera Madre," a passionate narrative of a starving mother whose husband has been jailed in the Castel Sant'Angelo for having taken part in the revolts of '31. One of the most sweepingly bitter poems in the series, if not in all literature, is "Li Du Generi Umani," The Two Human Species.

Noi, se sa, ar monno sémo usciti fòri
impastati de merda e de monnezza.
Er merito, er decoro e la grannezza
so' tutta marcanzia de li signori.

A su' Eccellenza, a su' Maestà, a su' Artezza
fumi, patacche, titoli e sprennori;
e a noàntri artiggiai e servitori
er bastone, l'imbasto e la capezza.

Cristo creò le case e li palazzi
p'er préncipe, er marchese, e 'r cavajere,
e la terra pe noi facce de c. . . .

E quanno mòrse in croce, ebbe er pensiere
de sparge, bontà sua, fra tanti strazzi,
pe quelli er sangue e pe noàntri er siere.

"We, you know, were brought into the world / kneaded in shit and garbage. / Merit, manners, and stature / are all stuff of the gentry. // To His Excellency, to His Majesty, to His Highness / vanities, phoney medals, titles, and luxuries; / and for us craftsmen and servants / the stick, the load, and the halter. // Christ made houses and palaces / for the prince, the marquis, and the knight, / and the earth for us ass-faces. // And when he died on the cross, he thought / to spill, in his goodness, among such tortures, / for them his blood and for us the whey."

"Li Padroni de Roma," The Bosses of Rome, is more matter of fact — Margutte, a character in *Orlando Furiosso*, is used satirically for "crusader."

Èccheve li padroni ch'a noi giutti
ce cucineno mejo di li cochi,
ché spesso ce trovamo tra du' fochi
e da tutte le parte sémo fritti.

Prima viè er Pape a consolà l'affritti;
doppo, li Cardinali, e nun so' pochi;
poi viè quell'antra fila de bizzòcchi
de li Prelati, e mette fòra editti.

Dietro a li Cardinali e a li Prelati,
vièngheno a fà le carte sti Margutti
de capi de le regole de frati.

Poi vièngheno a tajà la testa ar toro
l'Immasciatori, e poi, prima de tutti,
le donne belle e li mariti lòro.

"Here are the bosses who cook / us scum better than any cook, / because we're often between two fires / and get fried on all sides. // First comes the pope to console the afflicted; / then, the cardinals, and they're not few; / then comes that other bunch of bigots / the prelates, putting out edicts. // After the cardinals and the prelates, / there come along to finish the job those marguttes, / heads of the orders of monks. // Then to cut off the bull's head come / the ambassadors, and then, first and foremost, / the beautiful women and their husbands." — The word *educts* is always satirical; they are part of the "spappié" under which the population was smothered, and several sonnets were written to ridicule specific edicts, as on the hours when cafés could open on holidays.

For the savagery of "Li Du Generi Umani" only the image of Christ was sufficient; his name, as an exclamation, was the only one that could convey the horror of the courts. This is no longer Jesus the child and man of the Bible stories, to be scrutinized in his human behavior; this is where the Roman mind splits, as Belli alone has shown, being himself not free of the split. Sacredness enters, and Christ is its incarnation. In one of the stories the Gospel is referred to as "a good story"; in connection with the Vatican state it is the symbol and object of ultimate violation; the ferocity of Belli's anticlericalism is the measure of its sacredness. It remains sacred through any amount of sacrilege. Many of the sonnets are funny at its expense; many more hold dogma, Holy

Trinity, transubstantiation and all, up to ridicule; the welter of Roman ritual is an invariably comic theme, when it is not something sharper, and excessive gestures of devotion are another. How far the poet shares the feelings of his characters in these matters is not always apparent; the chief mark of theirs is inconsistency, and he is surely portraying at least something of himself in making it so funny. The native of the Holy City, in his only native representation, goes around armed with a rosary in one hand and a knife in the other; he considers that to stay in the Madonna's favor you should "say an Ave Maria in the morning and tip your hat now and then," and that if indulgences are to be had a good Christian will step up and grab for them; he is above all practical, strongly disapproves of the fanaticism of the Spaniards, and does not expect religion to interfere with either pleasure or business; the literal meaning to him of the Passion does not prevent the end of carnival from seeming like the end of life itself. In short, he is something of an intellectual hooligan.

What keeps him from having to face the fact is the Gospel. According to "The Religion of Our Times," "the Gospel can be given to the pork-butcher" — it has been forgotten. This follows a murderous enumeration, in twenty-three articles, of what has taken its place: genuflexions, fasts, ashes on the head, ex votos, Madonnas at every corner, etc. Jesus is compared to the "civetta," the screech owl, a common metaphor in Italy because of its partiality for the heart, usually meaning a coquette; Jesus loves the heart. He is forgiveness, but it seems that he is not going to forgive everyone. He is also Michelangelo's mighty avenging Christ of the Last Judgment, and in this role he speaks the toughest of Romanaccio; he speaks with the rage and in the language of the vendor Ricciotto outside the Pantheon, but this is no street scene. When the "cavajeri" of this earth, "yesterday, today, tomorrow, always," come before him he will call them a terrible name, say "Drop those crosses!" and send them to "l'infernaccio." There is hardly a priest from Belli's collection who would not go the same way; the picture is unmitigated; clergy versus religion.

The saying in Rome is, "Do what the priest says, not what the priest does." There is not much omitted here of what he could possibly do, and all the gamut of the moods of wit is in play. The chief vices depicted are venality, gluttony, and lust. Priests are seen: robbing poor-boxes; making assignations in the confessional; playing practical jokes on each other with the host, out of jealousy over "a cute little nun"; dodging their bills to tradesmen; accepting a bribe of a piece of chocolate; having homosexual orgies in a church at night; being gigolos to noble ladies; winking at the failings of a "pasqualino" (a man who goes to church only on Easter) out of mercenary interest; calling on a lottery winner to "brotherly love" to relieve him of his winnings; refusing to call on a dying man at night. They are "a den of thieves," a "canaille without end." The only thing they say that you can believe is "Dommino nun so' digno."

Monks are no better. On the antiquity of the Franciscan and Dominican orders:

> Secent'anni! Oh vedete quant'è antica,
> oh immagginate quant'è parsa ar monno
> la voja de campà senza fatica.

"Six hundred years! Oh look how old, / just imagine how it's spread over the world / to want to get on without working." During the cholera epidemic when the government threatens to call up more soldiers for a precautionary guard around the city, a Roman proposes that monks be made to serve instead of the people, since they have nothing useful to do: "Just so they leave the Franciscans so all the women won't rebel." A natural rumor during the cholera was that monks had been poisoning the water; the speaker is not much concerned however, since he "acts like the pope" (the verb is "papeggiare"), or in other words would only mind if they poisoned the wine.

Another target is some of the more suspect holy relics in which the city abounds, recalling another Roman saying: "Qui si fa la feder, e altrove ci si crede. — Faith is made here, and believed elsewhere." A whimsical and charming sonnet concerns a certain

Saint Philomena, actually an unidentified pile of bones found in a catacomb a little before Belli's time, out of which a saint was fabricated, to the disgust even of some higher prelates. One of several much hoarier relics that come in for the same treatment is the stump of column in the church of Santa Prassede at which Christ is supposed to have been scourged. The speaker doubts that all of the Redeemer's body could have been beaten at anything that height; perhaps one part or another, but not all: "I tell you I measured myself against the column this morning, and even my backside was just barely under cover." The word for backside here is the Roman for Colosseum, "culiseo," from the shorter word for that piece of anatomy and the shape of the monument. One of the wittiest sonnets in this line was inspired by the pope's gift of one of his bedroom slippers to a missionary leaving for India.

Over all the rest — all the vicars and the vicars' vicars — huge and grotesque like some comic balloon counterpart to Michelangelo's Dome, is Pope Gregory XVI, Papa Grigorio. The times were difficult and the portrait may be unfair. It is true enough to contemporary feelings on the subject, and one of the world's great works of anticlericalism; and some of the pope's personal qualities that are held up to ridicule were well known: his avarice, timidity, opposition to any progress. "Il n'est pas méchant," Stendhal wrote, "mais il a toujours peur." In any case the spirit goes beyond personal vindictiveness, and even beyond social outrage. The betrayal of Christ is the true subject of this savage caricature, and it is here that you feel Belli himself as most tragic: the misanthrope cursed with speech and pity, the yearner after God. Even the symbol of the betrayal, "poor friar," "poor old man," so afraid "if a swallow comes twittering by he takes it for a cannonball," comes through the deluge of scorn and derision less hateful than pitiable. "Il n'est pas méchant"; not good either; he seems in his foolishness a huge prank played by evil, against Christ. One hideously vicious poem entitled "Recreation," more terrible from his being called, as in others, Our Lord, accuses him of quite imaginary cruelty: nobody really thought this of Gregory; he is amusing himself in his garden feeding turtledoves to a hawk, "and all Our Lord's fun is seeing that horrible beast crushing the breast and gnawing at the heart." It is the poet's nightmare image of God's vicar on earth; the portrayal of the actual pope is something else, and essentially no more than Pasquin had done for the Barberini and many others. The difference, and this was perhaps Belli's realest curse, was that he brought literary genius to it.

The pope is Nasone, Big Nose — in fact he had an enormous nose and Mediterranean humor loves a physical deformity although there is no other instance of it in Belli. The people called him that, also a scatological nickname referring to his pusillanimity, a word that became extended to coins bearing his image. The "magno" pun brings him another nickname; Gregory the Great (Magno) being in Roman Gregory Eat, this one is called Grigorio Bevo, Gregory Drink. The theme of his drinking is a big one in the sonnets. "Mango" and "mangiare" in one form or another are more integral; the hunger of the poor remains obsessive in this part of Belli's work; in nearly every twist and turn of the subject it is some way recalled; it was not necessary to mention Jesus. "If he eats, why should we?" — or pray for rain, so that we can eat: "Rain or no rain, he's eating." But the nose gives the dimensions of the picture. "Quer brutto pidicozzo de naso a peperone" — "pidicozzo" is a fruit pit; the face is a little hidden thing under the huge appendage of the "pepper nose." He has a cancer of the nose; His Majesty the Emperor sends him a doctor from Vienna, who prescribes "air, rest, and fresh wine"; a malicious lie, Belli calls this in a footnote, "as His Holiness was already familiar with these expedients." Startled by a sound of bugles at night, he is at the window in his nightshirt "with his nose half in and half out; that far he would risk it." He thought it was the liberals again: and what did he see? — "er Prencipale," the owner, the Boss, a fearful synonym for the Sacrament, being carried across the piazza. It rhymes with the "urinale" he has thrown away in his terror.

He had reason to be frightened of the liberals, those "dogs of jacobins." There had been riots after his accession in '31 and again in '37; the people were shouting for "Bread and work!" He is determined not to appear in public, even for Corpus Domini, until it blows over. "God will see my terror and make it rain another month, to give me an excuse to stay in." In an epigrammatic sonnet, "The Crimes of Today," he excuses a priest named Don Marco for adultery, theft, assault, and other crimes, but when someone whispers to him that Don Marco is a jacobin he convicts him on the spot without a trial. The sonnets defending him are among the most ironic, but one written in '46 shows perhaps a little more pity for his folly and weakness, "poveretto," among such political agitations; the thrust is all in the speaker's absurd change of metaphor from one of a rider on a spavined horse: "Between the whippers-on and the pullers-in, I'd like to see which of us could tune the pennywhistle to the guitar."

There is a series of sonnets on Gregory's luxurious holiday trips to the summer palace at Castel Gandolfo and other country places, and the shrewd opening words of one are: "Già, un antro viaggio. — That's right, another excursion"; it has become the habitual news. "After all I've done to get to the Papacy I want to enjoy it in peace. I want to eat and drink and sleep as I please; if anybody else knows how to govern, let them." One report of a holiday comes from "la santissima puttana in persona — the holy whore herself," who was the wife of the pope's barber Gaetanino and appears as the reason for the latter's spectacular rise to favor, which is another point of attack. A boat trip inspires a regret: "Couldn't some whale, like Jonah's, have made a bite of supper of him, without being so kind as to throw him back on the beach?" The prophet is well mentioned. The scale and energy of this grotesque take you, once more, to the Sistine Chapel; like Jonah there, Papa Grigorio overlaps his frame, and it could be those images of God, creating the sun and moon, touching Adam's finger, God as Belli had heard him speaking to Cain, that haunt every sordid or paltry image here. There is a revolting scene of the pope's drunkenness on one trip; a graphic and insinuating description of the pavilion in his garden and its connection with the barber's wife; even more insinuation goes into reports of the childish games he plays in his garden, especially with a certain "sly, winsome prelate." And how could you say he was stingy? —

look at the silver and gold he willed to his nephews, and to his creditors a fortune in empty bottles.

More savagely forthright is a sonnet containing an image of the wrinkles on the papal stomach that in the old days used to play at sixes and sevens and now from the fruits of his holy office are stretched tight.

> Cusì ce neghi eh, pallonaccio a vento,
> insino er mollicume che t'avanza
> de quer pane che magni a tradimento.

"So you deny us, eh, you ugly balloon, / even the crumbs left over / from that traitor's bread you eat." *Mangiare: tradimento.* In the great chorale of the "Miserere" there is no longer room for the sorry figure of this particular traitor. He comes in however for his own magnificent climax in terms of that equation — in a pair of sonnets on the papal kitchen and wine cellar. The sense of the gargantuan comes to its fullest here, the image in the fourth line of the kitchen poem and the awe in the list after it reducing to a pinpoint the solitary figure at the end, beautifully introduced by the one extra vowel that gives the cook's sudden embarrassment. "La Cucina der Papa":

> Co la cosa ch'er coco m'è compare,
> m'ha vorsuto fà vedè stammatina
> la cucina santissima. Cucina?
> che cucina! Hai da di *porto de mare.*

> Pile, marmitte, padelle, callare,
> cosciotti de vitella e de vaccina,
> polli, ova, latte, pesce, erbe, porcina,
> caccia, e 'gni sorte de vivanne rare.

> Dico: "Pròsite a lei, sor Padre Santo."
> Dice: "Eppoi nun hai visto la dispenza,
> che de grazzia de Dio ce n'è antrettanto."

> Dico: "Eh, scusate, povero fijolo!
> Ma cià a pranzo co lui quarch'Eminenza?"
> "Nòo — dice — er Papa magna sempre solo."

"The cook being a buddy of mine, / he wanted to show me this morning / the holy kitchen. Kitchen? / some kitchen! you'd have to call it a seaport. // Oil presses, pots, pans, kettles, / sides of veal and tenderloin, / chickens, eggs, milk, fish, vegetables, hams, / game, and every kind of rare food. // I said: 'Here's how, Mr. Holy Father.' / He said: 'And then you haven't seen the pantry, / there's as much of God's grace again in there.' // I said: 'Well that's tough, poor thing. / But does some cardinal keep him company at dinner?' / 'No-o — he said — the pope always eats alone.'"

The same visitor is driven to more open sarcasm in the wine cellar. "What a splendid archive of stamps and edicts! What an oratory / What a fine sacristy!" With no Germans and Russians to help him, can the pope possibly drain so many cruets? "Between dinner and mass? And then some!"

There are two unforgettable pictures in another vein. In "Lassateli Cantà," Let Them Talk, a poor man who is a fervent devotee of the pope tells how he prostrated himself before him and how the pontiff deigned to let his foot be kissed and even to lift a hand in blessing, then withdrew, since the man was "like a rag" at his feet and unable to move. The cruel Mediterranean glare of light that Belli plays on this simple everyday episode takes it into his own brand of superrealism, creating out of the discrepancy between the rag and the swollen sovereign, the "sovranone," a little fantasy of horror. The same light, and although more secretively, somewhat the same point, appear in the grandiose picture of "E Ciò Li Tistimoni," And I Have Witnesses, in plastic vision perhaps the greatest of the sonnets. To be read very slowly. The sonorities are reminiscent of some of Shakespeare's speeches reporting similar scenes in the *Histories*, but this is weirdly static; it is papal Rome seen by a Daumier, just barely touched with life and motion, half human, half that of big rubber puppets bobbing along in their pretentious solemnity over the passions of the crowd. On the nature of the "chiacchierata" nobody would be deceived, and to Belli's audience the cardinals' "agreeing" would be supererogatory. Yet by a mysterious delicacy, and although the scene is deliberately set at

Pasquin's corner, the poem goes beyond satire, conveying along with the failings of its representatives the centuries of solemnity of the papal office — or more: of the whole *gran cosa*, of all Rome. — The Nunziata (Annunciata) is the church from which the cortege was returning to the Vatican. The effect of the repetitions of "zitto," "seri," and "lesta" is obvious and not reproduceable; the suffix -*accio* is perhaps nowhere in Belli more effective than here after the word *blessing*.

Quanno ch'er Santo Padre passò jeri
pe Pasquino ar tornà da la Nunziata
stava cor una ciurma indiavolata,
peggo d'un caporal de granattieri.

E faceva una certa chiacchierata
ar cardinal Orioli e a Farcogneri,
che je stàveno a séde de facciata
tutt'e dua zitti zitti e seri seri.

La gente intanto strillava a tempesta;
e lui de qua e de là dar carrozzone
'na benedizzionaccia lesta lesta.

Poi ritornava co le su' manone
a gistì a quelli; e quelli co la testa
pareva che je dàssino raggione.

"Yesterday when the Holy Father passed / Pasquin coming back from the Nunziata / he had the devil's own frown on his face, / worse than a corporal of grenadiers. // And he was saying something or other / to the Cardinals Orioli and Falconieri, / who were sitting facing him, / both of them silent and long-faced as could be. // The people in the meantime were raising a storm of shouting; / and he to this side and that from the big carriage / tossing off a lousy blessing. // Then with his big hands he went back / to gesturing to those two; and they with their heads / seemed to be agreeing with him."

At his death in 1863 Belli left an order that the manuscripts of the sonnets should be burned; however he could have burned them himself. He had been silent then for fifteen years. The excesses of the republicans in '48 had horrified him; he called them "red Jesuits," and in an Italian sonnet addressed to Giuseppe Mazzini, written on the day of Pope Pius IX's reentry into Rome, in April 1850, he pilloried the liberals as fiercely as he ever had their enemy though without the genius; they were assassins and Mazzini a colleague of Beelzebub. From then on he gave himself to orthodoxy and all the proprieties, supporting the new pope in his most reactionary measures. The sonnets, he wrote, were opposed to his "true, intimate feelings" and had been written "out of mere perversity, and in times of mental derangement." But they were saved just the same, through the wisdom of his friend and confessor, Monsignor Tizzani.

The degree of change of heart, or tragic failure of heart, in this last phase of his life has naturally been a leading topic in all discussions of Belli. Some have called his final state madness and compared him to Gogol in that too; the wish to keep his son, Ciro, from any association with the liberals became an obsession, but a juster parallel to his turn of mind at this stage would appear to be with Dostoevski. Only for Belli it was his death as a poet. In any case it eludes present-day terms of the theme of Revolt and Disillusion; he was always closer to Death and Transfiguration. "Either we're jacobins or we believe in the law of the Lord . . ." The *Roman Sonnets* are undoubtedly to be reckoned among the forces that before long did overthrow the Papal State, but to their author that would have been the worst irony of all. He was never a jacobin, a man of party or program; his anticlericalism was too deeply Roman for any cure but in the image of another world, "che non finisce mai." It would be impossible in this one not to hope for a little more of the law of the Lord, but he had called the liberals assassins before — they would be another government to object to — and it must have been not so much disillusion as exhaustion that set in when they proved the point. He was played out; he was through.

He might well have been long before, for other reasons. His great poem, in labor as in other respects in the company of the best in his century, had been in every practical way utterly thankless. None of it was published; it had not earned him so much as a grosso; by the arbiters of literary taste it was not even taken seriously. The laughter of friends was the one recompense for a creation of twenty years. But all that cannot have been nearly so hard as to give words to a city that had had none since the old gods, of beauty and heroes, like ugly kittens had been thrown out to die.

One of Belli's titles is: "Give Caesar to Caesar and God to God." In Rome the two images were always nearly one, always struggling to be one; the beauty and failures of Christianity would never be extricable there, and there could be no great Roman poetry that was not dominated by them. They helped in their squeeze on the mind, that "serra-serra" of an ideological impossibility, to make tragedy impossible, but only helped: there could be no tragedy anyway where life at every instant is a meeting point of all time past and future. Belli walked the edge of these awful contradictions as long as he could stand it. The poor could not have been loved as he loved them if he had not been so poor and there had not been so many of them, but it was in sharing their own hooligan hopelessness, which was inseparable from both their God and their godlessness, that he was able to write so truly of the Roman triumph of life on earth. He gave majesty to farce, because no other words could carry such a burden — of memory and neighborhood with God. He joined Pasquin's voice to the religious vocabulary of Michelangelo and Palestrina, to give the blasphemous town, the *caput mundi*, along with its first in literature, what seems destined to have been its last great work of explicitly Christian meaning in any art; he brought to the excoriation of its rulers and the craving for its God all the city's strength and beauty, its charity and mysterious community; then fell into the consistency of despair, and left Rome again to the voices of its stones and fountains.

It was not the God of the saints. As Jesus speaks in Romanesco, sending the "cavajeri" to "l'infernaccio," God speaks here in the

Roman flesh, and it is through the very exorbitance of the flesh
that the poet has reached for him. The flesh of the poor; and it is
their voices that one hears, with Palestrina, in the deep exalted
strains that close the "Miserere for Holy Week." From the flesh of
all the poor, in its appetites and sufferings, its liberal hunger —
magna, magna — rises the great music of the redemption, the
recognition of all human guilt, which loses none of its glory in an
obscenity or the funny, desperate splintering of the words of the
psalm: *Miserere mei, Deus, secundum magnam misericordiam
tuam* — Have pity on me, God, according to your great mercy. In
"Judgment Day" they are all visibly there, together with everyone
else — another poem that is half a painting, with its baroque angels taken from almost any church in Rome, but given life, going
about their business in the only law court that Belli could respect.
"Er Miserere de la Sittimana Santa":

> Tutti l'Ingresi de Piazza di Spagna
> nun hanno antro che dì si che piacere
> è de sentì a San Pietro er miserere
> che gnisun istrumento l'accompagna.
>
> Defatti, c . . . !, in ne la gran Bertagna
> e in nell'antre cappelle furistiere,
> chi sa dì com'a Roma in ste tre sere
> *Miserere mei Deo sicunnum magna?*
>
> Oggi sur *magna* ce si' stati un'ora;
> e cantata accusì, sangue dell'ua!,
> quer *magna* è una parola che innamora.
>
> Prima l'ha detta un musico, poi dua,
> poi tre, poi quattro; e tutt'er coro allora
> j'ha dato giù: *misericordiam tua.*

"All the English in Piazza di Spagna / can't talk about anything
but what a pleasure it is / to hear the miserere in St. Peter's / with
not a single instrument accompanying it. // In fact, holy nuts!, in
Great Britain / and in all the other foreign churches, / who can say

like in Rome on those three nights / *Miserere mei Deo sicunnum magna.* // Today they stayed on that magna an hour; / and sung like that, blood of the grape!, / that *magna* is a word to fall in love with. / / First one musician said it, then two, / then three, then four: and all the choir finally / came out with it: *misericordiam tua.*"

"Er Giorno der Giudizzio":

> Quattro angioloni co le tromme in bocca
> se metteranno uno pe cantone
> a sonà: poi co tanto de vocione
> cominceranno a dì: "Fora a chi tocca."
>
> Allora vierà su una filastrocca
> de schertri da la terra a pecorone,
> pe ripijà de persone,
> come purcini attorno de la biòcca.
>
> E sta biòcca sarà Dio benedetto,
> che ne farà du' parte, bianca e nera;
> una pe annà in cantina, una sur tetto.
>
> All'urtino uscirà 'na sonajera
> d'angioli, e, come si s'annassi a letto,
> smorzeranno li lumi, e bona sera.

"Four huge angels with trumpets in their mouths / will stand each in his corner / and blow: then in an awful voice / they'll begin to say: 'Step up.' // Then a jumble of skeletons from the earth / will come up on all fours, / and take on the shape of people again, / like chicks around the mother hen. // And this mother he will be the blessed God, / who'll divide them in two parts, white and black: / one to go to the cellar, one to the roof. // At the end there'll come out a bell-collar / of angels, and as if everybody were going to bed, / they'll put out the lights and goodnight"

INDEX

Other Steerforth Italia Books